COUNTERPOINT
IN COMPOSITION

McGRAW-HILL SERIES IN MUSIC

William J. Mitchell, *Consulting Editor*

ATKISSON: *Basic Counterpoint*
CHASE: *America's Music*
CROCKER: *A History of Musical Style*
LERNER: *Study Scores of Musical Styles*
RATNER: *Harmony: Structure and Style*
RATNER: *Music: The Listener's Art*
SALZER and SCHACHTER: *Counterpoint in Composition*
WAGNER: *Band Scoring*
WAGNER: *Orchestration: A Practical Handbook*

COUNTERPOINT IN COMPOSITION

THE STUDY OF VOICE LEADING

FELIX SALZER

*Department of Music, Queens College
of The City University of New York*

CARL SCHACHTER

The Mannes College of Music

McGRAW-HILL BOOK COMPANY, *New York, St. Louis, San Francisco, London, Sydney, Toronto, Mexico, Panama*

COUNTERPOINT IN COMPOSITION

Library of Congress Catalog Card Number 68-30981
54497

1 2 3 4 5 6 7 8 9 0   HDMB   7 6 5 4 3 2 1 0 6 9

To the Memory of Leopold Mannes

PREFACE

In offering this book at the present time, the authors feel that a few words of explanation are called for. Why should it be necessary to devote time and effort to learning the principles of a musical language no longer employed by most composers? Indeed, much of the music written today has little or no connection with any phase of earlier music.

Although our current term "new music" had its equivalents at various times in the past (*ars nova, nuove musiche, Zukunftsmusik*), these were hardly used with as much justification as at present. For, although no one would deny the marked differences between, for example, Machaut and Dunstable, Palestrina and Monteverdi, or Mendelssohn and Wagner, they fade into relative insignificance compared with the differences between Bartok, Schönberg, or even Webern, on the one hand, and John Cage or Stockhausen on the other. From this point of view the tonal language of the past might be termed dead in somewhat the sense that the Latin language is dead. Many may understand it, some may use it for specialized purposes, but no one speaks it, or writes a poem, a play, or a scientific treatise in Latin.

In another sense, however, the music of the past is far from dead. It lives, first of all, in the interplay between the performer and the sensitive listener. There still exists a considerable number of young performing musicians who are anxious to deepen their understanding of the music that, after all, constitutes the bulk of their repertory.

In addition, that music continues to have meaning for those composers who recognize that an understanding of its inner workings can be an invaluable help in attaining craftsmanship regardless of their particular mode of expression. Some of them attempt to forge their own connections with the past and believe that some aspects of earlier music might emerge transformed in a still unknown musical language of the future.

These points of view are in accord with our own; we believe that musicians must maintain contact with the music of the past, and have written this book for teachers and students who share this outlook. For the teacher to maintain and strengthen this contact with the past, however, is not so simple a matter as it might at first seem. Several obstacles immediately confront us. One of these is the composition of the student body in all too many music departments. First of all, there is the growing number of students admitted as music majors who cannot express anything musical on an instrument or with their voice, who have defective musical hearing, and who lack, as paradoxical as it may seem, a real interest in music. Even with the better students, however, one observes a noticeable weakening of what one might term the musical instinct. In analysis, and in performance as well, many of these more gifted young musicians seem to miss the most fundamental and obvious relationships in a musical score and try to impose upon the music an overly personal and consequently a contrived interpretation. They no longer have the music in their blood, so to speak, and it becomes for them a kind of intellectual game.

The issue is confounded by teaching methods that seem to lack a workable relation between theoretical abstraction and concrete musical experience. If one deals only with abstractions, the result is a dry and unproductive theory for the sake of theory. If one excludes abstractions altogether, the student lacks the means to organize and articulate his musical experiences, and is led to the aimless verbalizing about music so prevalent nowadays. Every successful teaching method must strike a balance between these perspectives. All too often, however, we find an overemphasis on one to the detriment of the other.

The consequences of this situation are all too evident. On the one hand there is the student who is unable to write a decent chorale phrase or improvise a simple folk tune accompaniment. Nevertheless he has been taught to spout confidently about the characteristics of the "classical" style or the musical language of the late Beethoven without knowing more than a handful of his works. Not only has he been left unaware of compositional techniques as such, but in all probability, he has been led to believe that by skimming superficially through some works of a composer one is entitled to make generalizations about the composer's style. In the last analysis this student is the result of a general neglect of musical techniques, for all too long now condescendingly called "skills."

On the other hand there is the student taught to write endless harmony exercises, perhaps in four clefs, following complicated and arbitrary rules, or able to manufacture on paper something called a fugue; but at the end he has gained no insight into the harmonic or contrapuntal organization of a Bach Invention or a Schubert Waltz. He is the product of academic harmony and counterpoint courses taught with a minimum of relevance to the music with which they are supposed to deal.

The authors hope that the present book, with whatever faults it has, may contribute to counteracting these trends and that it will help point the way for other teachers to devise their own solutions to what has become a very real problem.

Counterpoint in Composition is designed to be used in a comprehensive theory program embracing the study of harmony, counterpoint, and analysis. It treats counterpoint not only as a self-contained discipline but also in its relation to other aspects of musical design. Since it presupposes some previous study (see below), work will normally begin in the second year; however, unusually well prepared classes might start in the second semester of the first year.

The student should have had enough work in basic ear training to be able to hear simple musical relationships in two- and three-part texture. He should know the fundamentals of musical notation and nomenclature, including clefs, scales, key signatures, intervals, and elementary chord grammar (construction of triads and seventh chords, figured bass symbols, chords built on scale degrees). Concerning more advanced chord grammar we should like to make the following observation: Many students, because of teaching methods still prevalent today, feel uncomfortable if they cannot assign a name or symbol to every vertical combination of tones. We hope to show that for musical understanding the architectonic function of a sonority far outweighs in importance its grammatical label. Therefore we have not hesitated to include at a relatively early stage examples containing chords that the student might not be able to name. By studying these examples, however, he may gain an insight into the voice-leading origin of such chords, an insight far more significant for musical understanding than the mere labeling.

Chapters 1 through 5 deal with elementary counterpoint, that is, with exercises in the five species in two- and three-part texture. The reader will notice that we have departed from the usual method in that we present each species both in two and in three parts before proceeding to the next. This will necessarily make the first chapter rather heavy going, for a large number of fundamental concepts are introduced. We believe, however, that the student will gain a quicker and more secure grasp of the materials from this approach than from the traditional procedure of working through all five species in two parts before going on to three-part writing. We have not included species exercises in four and more parts since they offer no fundamentally new problems except those concerned with doubling, spacing, and the crossing of voices. These problems, in our opinion, can be more profitably studied in connection with chorale writing (Chapter 8) and exercises in imitation (Chapter 9).

A strictly logical presentation would require us to proceed directly from elementary counterpoint to combined species. We feel that this procedure, however, is pedagogically unsound. By postponing work in combined species until Chapter 9, we have been able to present this difficult material in its relation to composition. Exercises in combined species form an essential part of theoretical training, for they systematically present important procedures of voice leading. If they are undertaken before the student has learned to relate theoretical abstractions to the fabric of composition, their proper musical significance is all too often lost in a tangle of unrelated and quite complex detail.

We have therefore followed elementary counterpoint with two chapters (Chapters 6 and 7) that show the all-important connection between basic contrapuntal procedures and living music. The moment one begins to deal with the counterpoint of composition it becomes essential to take harmonic organization into account, for compositional texture shows the mutual influence of harmony and counterpoint. We have done this in both Chapters 6 and 7.

Chapter 8 deals with the voice leading of the chorale. Here the student himself learns to apply his knowledge of voice leading to a musical context in which harmonic and contrapuntal elements function in close combination.[1] This chapter contains an investigation of the voice leading of Bach's chorales. In our opinion the Bach chorales present a microcosm of musical structure. The same techniques that in other styles require a long span of time for their unfolding present themselves in the chorale in the space of only a few measures. Furthermore, the chorales embody techniques characteristic of earlier as well as later music. Both their concentration and the wide applicability of their procedures make Bach's chorales of central importance in the study of voice leading. It is conceivable, of course, that the teacher may wish to begin work on this chapter concurrently with Chapter 7. This would be a perfectly valid approach. Similarly, Chapter 6 can be begun while the study of elementary counterpoint is still in progress. We recommend, however, that Chapter 6 be taken up only after the completion of third species. The reader will note a small amount of duplication between Chapters 7 and 8. This results from our wish to make these chapters as self-contained as possible, so that the teacher may present them in the order he deems best.

---

[1] This is the reason why, to the possible surprise of some readers, we have included a chapter on chorale writing in a counterpoint text.

Chapter 10 is mainly analytic. In this final section of the book we attempt to awaken the student's awareness of the historical evolution of fundamental techniques of counterpoint.

In ideal circumstances a period of three years would be devoted to the study of this book (together, of course, with work in other aspects of music theory). Such ideal circumstances very seldom exist in our colleges and universities. However, if some of the exercises and some analytical illustrations are omitted, a period of two years will suffice.

In the course of the book frequent references are made to other works whose contents supplement those of the present volume. Most notably we refer to William J. Mitchell's *Elementary Harmony*, 3d edition (Prentice Hall, Englewood Cliffs, N.J., 1965), and to Felix Salzer's *Structural Hearing*, 2d edition (Dover Publications, New York, 1962).[2]

The teacher will note the absence of exercises specifically devoted to canon, invertible counterpoint, and fugue. This omission reflects our desire to counteract the usual belief that such exercises represent the final goal of studies in counterpoint. The so-called contrapuntal forms are not forms at all, but procedures; furthermore, they are more often than not harmonic as well as contrapuntal. And contrapuntal skill can be just as evident in a sonata, a set of variations, or a mazurka, as in a fugue. Of course the polyphonic techniques associated with canon and fugue form a highly important and fascinating study. In this connection

---

[2] Among our examples of species counterpoint we have included a few from the following works of other authors:

J. J. Fux, *Gradus ad Parnassum* translated by Alfred Mann, W. W. Norton, New York, 1943. Paperback edition, 1965.

Heinrich Bellermann, *Der Contrapunkt*, Julius Springer, Berlin, 1862.

Heinrich Schenker, *Kontrapunkt*, 2 vols., Universal Edition, Vienna, 1910 and 1922.

Herman Roth, *Elemente der Stimmführung*, vol. 1, Carl Grueninger Nachf. Ernst Klett, Stuttgart, 1926.

Erich Hertzmann and Cecil B. Oldman, editors, *Thomas Attwood's Theorie und Kompositionsstudien bei Mozart* in Mozart *Neue Ausgabe sämtlicher Werke*, X:30–31, Bärenreiter, Kassel, 1965.

Concerning two examples by Mozart taken from the Attwood papers we should like to make the following observations. Example 5-21g would seem to be a variation of Fux, Fig. 82 (see Alfred Mann, *The Study of Counterpoint*, p. 64). The figures denoting vertical intervals in Examples 5-21g and h seem to contain errors. In m. 8 of Example 5-21g we have corrected an obviously wrong 3 to a 7. In our opinion m. 9 should also be figured 7-6, as it was Mozart's practice to figure dissonant suspensions rather than embellishments. In Example 5-21h, m. 8, we believe that the last figure should read 5(dim.) to show the passing tone.

we refer the reader to Alfred Mann's excellent *The Study of Fugue* (Rutgers University Press, New Brunswick, N.J., 1958).

The analytic approach evident throughout this book is based upon the work of Heinrich Schenker. Analytic insights are projected in the form of voice-leading graphs. These graphs employ symbols derived from musical notation to reveal the function of tones and groups of tones in relation to their immediate context, to larger contexts, and ultimately to the composition as a whole. These different levels of context—or structural levels—are referred to in several ways. Sometimes we use Schenker's terms *foreground, middleground,* and *background;* at other times we use the equivalent terms, *immediate, intermediate,* and *remote levels of structure.* Sometimes a single graph suffices to explain the voice leading; for more complex passages several progressive reductions are offered. Usually these will lead from the foreground, the immediate level, to the background.

To clarify the symbols used, we offer the following *glossary:*[3]

The indication of pitch is the same as in normal musical notation. Sometimes registers are simplified.

Note values, for the most part, indicate structural level rather than rhythmic relationship. The following note shapes are employed: half notes, quarter notes with stems of varying length, note heads without stems, and occasionally, eighth notes.

Half notes indicate the structural background.

Quarter notes indicate intermediate levels; distinctions between these levels are indicated by stem length; the higher the level, the longer the stem.

Stemless notes represent foreground events.

In analyzing fragmentary sections, half notes are often omitted and quarter notes serve to indicate the structural background of the context under view.

[3] For a more complete glossary, see William J. Mitchell and Felix Salzer, editors, *The Music Forum,* vol. I, Columbia University Press, New York, 1967, pp. 260–268.

Eighth notes can be used to represent appoggiaturas, neighboring tones, and embellishments.

Notes in parentheses indicate tones of the underlying voice leading bypassed or substituted for in the actual composition.

Structural connections between different tones can be indicated by solid beams and slurs. These indications are used for all levels of structure.

Dotted slurs and beams indicate the structural retention of a single tone.

⤸ Short, curved arrows indicate applied dominant relationships.

⟶ Straight, solid arrows under the bass indicate a passing motion.

× Crossed lines indicate interchanged tones.

CS A contrapuntally derived chord on a high level of structure (contrapuntal-structural chord).

DF A chord of double or overlapping function: structural as well as prolonging; harmonic as well as contrapuntal.

EM An embellishing tone or chord.

N A neighboring tone or chord.

P A passing tone or chord.

$\frac{N}{P}$ A neighbor-passing chord.

VL A tone or chord used for voice-leading purposes, for example, to break up parallel fifths or octaves.

$\hat{3}\ \hat{2}\ \hat{1}$ Capped Arabic numerals denote the scale steps comprising the fundamental melodic structure of a composition.

Other symbols will be explained as they appear in the text.

ACKNOWLEDGMENTS

The authors gratefully acknowledge the helpful interest and the generous assistance of Professor William J. Mitchell, who read the manuscript and offered valuable suggestions. We also wish to thank Thames Hickman for his skillful and artistic autography of the musical illustrations. Hedi Siegel was most helpful in the final stages of preparing the manuscript, and we wish to express our thanks to her.

We would like to thank the following publishers who kindly granted us copyright releases: Harvard University Press, Cambridge, Mass. (Examples 6–46, 6–53, and 7–28); Prentice-Hall, Inc., Englewood Cliffs, N.J. (Examples 1–20a and 1–21f); G. Schirmer, Inc., New York (Examples 6–29 and 7–42); Boosey and Hawkes, New York, American agents for M. P. Belaieff, Leipzig (Example 10–20); Smith College Music Archives, Northampton, Mass. (Example 6–26); Bärenreiter, Kassel (Examples 1–84d, 2–26g, 3–41g, 5–21g, and h); Theodore Presser, Bryn Mawr, American agents for Universal Edition, Vienna (Examples 1, 2, 1–21a, 2–26f, 2–31e, 3–45e, 4–16g and h, 4–47e, 9–60b, and f).

Felix Salzer
Carl Schachter

CONTENTS

INTRODUCTION

THE STUDY OF COUNTERPOINT, ITS MEANING AND PURPOSE

During a vast period of time, approximately a thousand years, Western composers learned to shape and control simultaneous as well as successive combinations of tones; to understand this music we must be able to grasp the coherence, order, and beauty embodied in complex tonal structures. In the course of its history Western music has undergone many profound changes; a glance at any good historical anthology will reveal a multitude of divergent styles. It would be incorrect, however, to regard this history as merely an accumulation of ever-changing modes of expression. In this regard music is comparable to a language. The English of Chaucer's time, for example, differs greatly from that of the present day. Yet close acquaintance reveals an underlying relationship; despite the changes in usage it is fundamentally the same language. Until recently the same has held true of music. As we deepen our knowledge of the music of the past, we begin to realize that the same principles of musical organization—principles, of course, of a high degree of generality—can be found at work in music of markedly divergent styles. Beneath the surface of stylistic change we can perceive the sometimes halting, sometimes swift development of a musical language.

Because that language, as was mentioned in the Preface, is increasingly becoming a thing of the past, one might at first think that its study has become easier. For one can more easily examine a completed product than an ongoing process. The past, however, is not a kind of storehouse from which we can draw ready-made experiences. On the contrary, it must be constantly re-created and replenished in the light of present-day knowledge and outlook. We shall succeed in maintaining a living tradition only through constant efforts to broaden and deepen our knowledge. As yet much remains unknown or misunderstood.

Counterpoint offers a case in point. For many teachers, *instruction in counterpoint* continues to pose a troublesome problem; there exists at present a bewildering diversity of approaches with respect both to content and to method. Courses labeled "Counterpoint" at three or four different schools may well contain nothing in common except the name. Counterpoint is often—perhaps usually—given a peripheral rather than a central role in our music curricula. Either it is isolated stylistically to music of the sixteenth century—and to a single phase of sixteenth-century music at that—or it is conceived of as leading to or comprising studies in invention, canon, fugue, etc. In musical analysis—at least as frequently practiced—the role of counterpoint is disregarded in music lacking such procedures as imitation or part interchange. Such music is called "harmonic." The narrowness of this approach is revealed by the reluctance of some scholars even today to recognize the importance of contrapuntal organization in the works of Chopin or Schubert. It is hardly surprising, therefore, that to many teachers and students of music theory counterpoint seems to occupy a position of secondary importance.

We hope that the present book will contribute to the solution of such problems. It is our aim to present counterpoint in a way that emphasizes its central role in Western art music; in particular, we have attempted to introduce fundamental concepts of broad applicability rather than to begin with the specific details of a single musical style—details that may or may not prove relevant to other styles as well. In other words, we are trying to introduce the language rather than a dialect.

How is this to be accomplished? We believe that the *species approach* to counterpoint, codified by J. J. Fux, remains the best introduction to the language of music. For through this approach the basic elements and processes of voice leading can be revealed. However, the species approach must constitute a point of departure rather than an end in itself. The relation of species counterpoint to compositions of varying styles must be shown and—most importantly—the teaching of counterpoint must reveal the almost limitless possibilities for the imaginative transformation of the elements of voice leading into the fabric of living music, be it by Josquin or by Wagner.

Fux's *Gradus ad Parnassum*, first published in 1725, enjoyed a virtually unparalleled success. As is well known, Fux systematized the teaching of counterpoint by organizing the materials in terms of five categories or "species." His method was a model of pedagogical ingenuity. Difficulties are introduced gradually; each new section is built upon materials already mastered. Hailed as an extraordinary work by musicians of the eighteenth century, the *Gradus* was used and highly praised by Haydn, Mozart, and Beethoven. Indeed, it was accepted deep into the nineteenth century as the basic text in counterpoint; most late–eighteenth- and nineteenth-century treatises (such as those of Cherubini, Albrechtsberger, and Bellermann) are based upon Fux. When Beethoven's studies with Albrechtsberger were translated into French by Fétis in 1833, the following names appeared on the list of subscribers: Cherubini, Berlioz, Meyerbeer, Chopin, Rossini, Auber, Paganini, Moscheles, Hummel, and Liszt.[1] Furthermore, Mendelssohn, Brahms, and many other eminent musicians of the nineteenth and twentieth centuries were trained in the Fux system.

After this period of unquestioned acceptance the Fux method began to lose its general appeal; its value was increasingly often questioned. Toward the end of the nineteenth century some musical scholars began to express doubts, pointing to seemingly great contradictions between the species exercises and composition, among these the "artificial" rhythmic rigidity of the exercises. Many teachers no longer completely believed in what they were teaching but continued it for want of a "better" method. Students must have experienced a feeling of futility in their work. When they pointed to discrepancies between Fux's rules and the progressions of composition, they were pacified with meaningless explanations about the need for mental discipline before embarking upon free composition.

In fact, a complete estrangement had developed between theory and practice—between "strict" and "free" counterpoint. Strict, or species, counterpoint was increasingly often accepted as an academic ritual only; it seemed that no connection whatever existed between Fux's rules and limitations on the one hand and a work by Beethoven or Chopin on the other. And Hugo Riemann undoubtedly spoke for a large number of theorists and musicologists when he proclaimed that Fux's method was already out of date at the time of its publication.[2] By Riemann's time the teaching of Fux's approach had largely degenerated into the dreary and meaningless ritual of "academic counterpoint."

Another consequence of Fux's work, the so-called *"sixteenth-century counterpoint,"* arose out of an attempt to return to his original purpose. It is well known that Fux designed his method as a means of expounding what he and indeed many Baroque musicians believed to be the ideal form of counterpoint—the counterpoint of Palestrina. Fux's exercises, however, show some elements characteristic of eighteenth- rather than sixteenth-century style. From a stylistic point of view, therefore, the *Gradus* does not present a purely Palestrinian idiom. This latter goal

[1] See Alfred Mann, *The Study of Counterpoint*, rev. ed., New York; 1965, p. xiv.
[2] Hugo Riemann, *Geschichte der Musiktheorie*, Leipzig, 1898, p. 415. See also Ernst Kurth, *Grundlagen des linearen Kontrapunkts*, Max Hesse, Berlin, 1922, pp. 128–133. These and similar criticisms of Fux have led some twentieth-century authors and teachers to dispense with the species altogether.

was aimed at by Heinrich Bellermann (1862), but attained by Knud Jeppesen's *Counterpoint, the Polyphonic Vocal Style of the Sixteenth Century* (1931). Jeppesen has devised exercises in species counterpoint that are quite Palestrinian in appearance. The surface similarities between these modal exercises and Palestrina's music have convinced many teachers that the answer to old and vexing problems had been found. Jeppesen's presentation of the species approach seems to have elevated the "academic ritual" into a theory of composition. To many of the teachers and students who had become confused about the method to follow, a book such as Jeppesen's must have come as a profound relief.

Jeppesen's outlook—and that of his followers—can be summarized as follows: Counterpoint must be studied in connection with a specific musical style in which contrapuntal problems have been successfully solved; there must be the greatest possible correspondence between written exercise and composition. Only two such styles are to be taken as models, those of Palestrina and of Bach. For various reasons Jeppesen chooses Palestrina. Fux's approach should be used only if it is so modified that details of vocabulary (dissonance treatment, relation between melodic contour and rhythm, etc.) closely approximate the music of Palestrina.

We are convinced that this opinion results from several basic misunderstandings which have developed and hardened since the times when great composers studied and praised Fux's treatise.

Whatever Fux's aims may have been, species counterpoint or indeed any approach to counterpoint cannot serve as a method of composition in any style whatever. The failure to make this distinction is, in our opinion, the principal shortcoming of Jeppesen's otherwise admirable work. He virtually identifies "sixteenth-century counterpoint" with sixteenth-century composition, whereas counterpoint is only one of the elements of composition. To make counterpoint serve its true purpose, it must first be separated, so to speak, from composition. This thought found its first expression in Heinrich Schenker's *Kontrapunkt*, I.[3] Out of Schenker's ideas and our own teaching experience we developed the approach to counterpoint that we shall expound in the following chapters. This approach is based on several fundamental considerations:

[3] Heinrich Schenker, *Kontrapunkt*, 2 vols., Vienna; 1910, 1922. Vol. I, pp. 15*ff.*

1. *The study of counterpoint is above all the study of voice leading.* Wherever there is voice leading, wherever there exists motion and direction of voices, in any style or period whatever, there is counterpoint. The view that contrapuntal studies lead solely to the understanding and writing of sixteenth-century vocal polyphony, or of inventions, canons, and fugues, is narrow and misleading. It completely ignores the **pervasive influence of the contrapuntal concept,** so characteristic of Western tonal, as well as modal, music.

2. Within the development of the tonal language three major subdivisions can be discerned, although of course, considerable overlapping exists. The first period shows a musical fabric growing out of the perfect consonances and based largely on the $\frac{8}{5}$ sonority (circa twelfth to fourteenth century). The second develops gradually out of the first, increasingly, however, using the triad as the matrix. This period embraces a span of time stretching from the fifteenth through the nineteenth century. In the tonal music of the late nineteenth and, especially, the twentieth century (third subdivision), dissonant sonorities no longer show an ultimate dependence on the triad; as a consequence, dissonant chords can assume the structural functions held by the $\frac{8}{5}$ chord of medieval tonality and the triad of later times. In this book we are dealing with the music of the central period, the period of triadic tonality (circa 1450–1900). Once a solid foundation has been established in this repertory, many of the principles demonstrated here can be applied to earlier and later music.[4]

3. The present book draws a *distinction between the contrapuntal and the harmonic concepts;* it presents them as contrasting, but by no means as mutually exclusive. In distinguishing between contrapuntal and harmonic progressions, we include among the former much that

[4] Counterpoint in medieval and in twentieth-century tonal music has been dealt with in Felix Salzer, *Structural Hearing,* 2nd ed., New York, 1962. A more comprehensive study of early medieval counterpoint will be found in Felix Salzer, "Tonality in Early Medieval Polyphony," *The Music Forum,* vol. I, New York, 1967, pp. 35–98. This article contains an attempt to deal pedagogically with thirteenth-century counterpoint (see pp. 71–81).

is usually considered harmonic. Of the two great organizing forces, counterpoint is the older and the more inclusive. Medieval polyphony is dominated by contrapuntal thinking. Progressions of a definitely harmonic nature make their appearance in the fourteenth century, but attain real importance only in the second half of the fifteenth century. The growth of harmonic organization influences but does not diminish the role of counterpoint; most works show the cooperation and mutual influence of the two organizing forces.

4. Species counterpoint—far beyond its narrow application to any limited period in the history of music—can be so formulated as to present an ideal introduction to the basic voice-leading principles underlying the works of many stylistic periods and composers.

5. Specifically, species counterpoint makes two distinct contributions; its study, therefore, has two purposes. The first purpose is to teach the student—preferably at an early stage of his training—how to create examples of purely contrapuntal writing. These will take the form of simple and limited, but nonetheless meaningful and coherent, exercises. Such exercises are, of course, not to be considered as compositions; if they are the result of imaginative teaching, however, they will include the basic principles of directed motion so fundamental to Western music. Thus they will strengthen the student's ability to hear musical relationships. By teaching him how to think and plan ahead, the species exercises will help the young musician to organize and control his musical ideas. As a result, they provide an invaluable foundation for later work in theory and composition.

The second purpose of the study of species counterpoint can be summarized as follows: A significant—if indirect—connection exists between the progressions of each species and the voice leading of composition. Counterpoint, as manifested in composition, is the elaboration of basic progressions presented in Fux's method. This connection was first pointed out by Heinrich Schenker. In his *Kontrapunkt*, vol. 1, p. 268, we read the following:

> Thus the following contents (see Example 1) are to be traced back to a determining two-voice setting (see Example 2).

To this Schenker adds a statement pregnant with implications:

> . . . the real connection between strict and free setting can be found in similar derivations.

The above example and Schenker's words strongly indicate that the relevance of species counterpoint to composition does not depend upon similarities of the surface. This, in our opinion, is a compelling reason why instruction in species counterpoint should not be restricted to the explanation of a single phase of sixteenth-century music.

The relation of species counterpoint to the voice leading of composition resembles the connection between a fundamental scientific or philosophical concept and its manifold elaborations and developments. Therefore the usual distinction between "strict" and "free" counterpoint—unless understood in Schenker's sense, the one leading organically to the other—is misleading and has created serious misunderstandings. For there is nothing "strict" about a fundamental idea, and the developments and transformations of such an idea are in no way

EXAMPLE 1   Brahms, Variations on a Theme of Handel, Op. 24

EXAMPLE 2

characterized by calling them "free." *Elementary counterpoint* versus elaborated or *prolonged counterpoint* will serve as more meaningful terms. The term *prolonged counterpoint* and the more general term *prolongation* are to be understood as a broadening of concept, and not necessarily as a lengthening in time. These are inclusive terms conveying such ideas as the elaboration, development, manipulation, and transformation of underlying principles.

If the counterpoint of composition, or prolonged counterpoint, is presented as the development and expansion of fundamental principles, it will not appear as the expression of a supposed liberation from the confinement of an academic method. It will be revealed instead as the significant and fascinating artistic elaboration of basic ideas of musical continuity and coherence. The second purpose of the study of species counterpoint, therefore, is to understand the connection between the fundamental principles of voice leading and the complex and subtle manipulation and individualization of these principles in the compositions of divergent stylistic periods. The awareness of this connection leads to an understanding of the rich and fascinating life underlying the sensuous surface of music. This understanding offers far more to the performer, composer, theorist, or historian than can be achieved through superficial style imitations.

We believe, therefore, that a book on counterpoint should first cover the essential principles of voice leading based on a slight modification of the Fux method.[5] After this secure foundation has been established, the textbook must then demonstrate the extraordinarily varied application of these principles in the musical masterworks of many different styles. It is for this overriding reason that analysis cannot be divorced from the study of counterpoint. How can the purpose of contrapuntal studies be achieved if their application to living music is not made an integral part of the approach? The separation of analysis from counterpoint—a separation all too frequent nowadays—can lead only to a deadening isolation; the method becomes estranged from the art itself. Emphasis, therefore, must be given to the specific techniques of prolonged counterpoint. The insight thus achieved will enable the student not only to understand the manifestations of prolonged counterpoint in composition but also to express these techniques in his own written work.

Fux's method touches on the sources of musical continuity. We are here confronted with a remarkable event in the history of music theory and analysis. Fux—far beyond his immediate aims—has created an approach basic to the counterpoint of an entire era, embracing several centuries. This must be the reason why the great masters of the eighteenth and nineteenth centuries so admired the *Gradus*. They must have felt intuitively that Fux discussed basic principles of voice leading and voice direction which, transcending the confines of specific stylistic expression, had bearing on their own work. How else can we explain that a book written in 1725 with a limited grasp of the Palestrina style was consulted for their own studies or teaching by composers of the most contrasting stylistic outlook?

---

[5] The reader is urged to compare this modification with the original treatise as translated by Alfred Mann, *op. cit.*

PART ONE
THE TECHNIQUES OF
ELEMENTARY
COUNTERPOINT

CANTUS FIRMUS AND FIRST SPECIES

1. CANTUS FIRMUS

GENERAL CONSIDERATIONS

The study of counterpoint is the study of voice leading. Its aim is to develop the ability to hear, to understand, and to control the fundamental relationships that arise when two or more melodic lines combine into a meaningful whole. Voice leading has two main aspects: the organization of each of the component lines, and their combination into an intelligible musical fabric. Once he has mastered the first aspect, the writing of single lines, the student will be prepared for the more difficult task of writing in several parts. We shall begin, therefore, with the construction of the *cantus firmus,* the given line to which a counterpoint will later be set. The principles governing the writing of cantus firmi are fundamental to the study of counterpoint; in all five species the same basic considerations of melodic organization prevail.

In the cantus firmus we find melodic organization in its simplest form. The meaning of a tone depends entirely upon its contextual relationships in the horizontal dimension. Harmonic implication, rhythmic profile, and motivic design are all eliminated in order to allow the utmost concentration upon purely linear factors. The cantus firmus, therefore, is not a melody—at least not in the usual sense—but an abstraction from melody in which the linear element is separated from the other aspects of melodic design.

For all their simplicity, cantus firmi need not lack esthetic quality.

Indeed, a well-constructed cantus reveals in embryo many of the characteristics of more highly developed musical organisms. Among these are direction, continuity, variety, balance, and completeness; these esthetic factors will come into discussion in later sections of this chapter.

RHYTHM AND LENGTH

If it is to combine with counterpoints in the various species, the cantus firmus must consist of tones of equal time value. The consequent absence of rhythmic differentiation—indeed of rhythmic organization—has an important pedagogic value, for it brings into sharp focus purely linear factors. The effect of the line must arise out of melodic contour alone without the help of rhythmic variety. In the cantus firmus all tones receive equal stress; there is no grouping into strong and weak beats. It is best, therefore, to write the cantus in whole notes; smaller values would almost inevitably suggest metrical organization, the periodic alternation of strong and weak pulses.

The cantus must not be so lengthy that the sameness of time values becomes irritating. At the same time it must be long enough for a beginning, a climax, and an end. The length can vary; as a rule the cantus will not contain fewer than eight or more than sixteen tones.

TONAL MATERIALS; MELODIC RANGE

Simplicity also prevails in the choice of melodic materials. This simplicity results in part from the vocal character of elementary counterpoint. The cantus firmus and, indeed, all the melodic lines of the species exercises are to be conceived in terms of the human voice. Vocal expression constitutes, historically as well as logically, a basis, a point of departure for the more specialized and differentiated techniques of instrumental writing. Some intervals, easy enough to strike on an instrument, are difficult to sing. In general terms, small intervals are easier to sing than large ones, consonant intervals are easier than dissonant, and diatonic easier than chromatic.

Specifically the cantus firmus should not contain intervals larger than an octave, dissonant leaps, or chromatic half steps. The dissonant leaps include all sevenths and all augmented and diminished disjunct intervals; we include the augmented second in this group for, although it results from the alteration of stepwise motion, the augmented second sounds more disjunct than conjunct. By chromatic half step we mean the augmented prime, such as F natural–F sharp or B natural–B flat. This chromatic interval does not occur in any diatonic scale. By contrast, the diatonic half step or minor second (e.g., D natural–E flat) occurs in every scale and need not result from chromatic inflection; the minor second, therefore, can occur freely.

The usable intervals, therefore, are the following: **major and minor seconds, major and minor thirds, perfect fourths, perfect fifths, major and minor sixths, and perfect octaves.** In general, the larger intervals must be treated more cautiously than the smaller ones. In the horizontal dimension the stability of an interval depends upon size as well as upon consonance or dissonance; a melodic tenth has much more tension than a melodic third. (In the vertical dimension, on the other hand, the distance spanned by an interval affects its stability only under special circumstances. Normally a vertical tenth is no less stable than a third.)

Vocal considerations also influence the melodic range of the cantus firmus. The range of the voice, of course, is more limited than that of most instruments. The cantus, therefore, should lie within a rather small compass. A tenth between the lowest and the highest tone is the maximum range. Actually, most cantus firmi move within narrower limits, many falling within the compass of a fifth or sixth.

DIRECTION

When we hear a melodic line we experience more than a mere succession of tones; we hear a tonal motion. That music is a kinetic art, that it embodies motion, forms part of the experience of every musically sensitive person; the analogy between music and motion occurs in writings from the earliest times to the present. A musical motion has direction if it shows a clearly defined beginning and goal. In composition, with its intricate network of relationships, the quality of direction results from a number of factors—melodic, contrapuntal, harmonic, and rhythmic. In the limited world of species counterpoint there is but one factor, melodic climax in its relation to the beginning and end of the exercise.

Let us compare the three lines in Example 1-1. In the first example, the initial tone C dominates the entire line; D and B are ornamental tones. There is no climax, no goal of motion other than the point of origin. (Of course, ornamental motions can play an important role as parts of a larger whole. In third species we shall explore this possibility.)

Example 1-1*b* already shows a rudimentary kind of direction. The first three tones carry the line up to F; the last four bring it down to a

EXAMPLE 1-1

restatement of C. However, the repetition of the high point F and the consequent immobilizing of the line in the middle of the exercise prevent this example from establishing a satisfactory sense of direction as a whole.

The last example is, of course, the best constructed of the three. The fifth tone, A, forms a clearly defined climax; the line moves in two large curves from C to A and from A down to C. The high point is at once the goal of the first motion and the initial point of the second. The student will note the deviations from the main direction in both the ascending and the descending segments. These deviations, though they form subsidiary goals, do not diminish the sense of direction or rob the high point of its effect. As we shall see, they fulfill a necessary function in the shaping of the cantus.

To summarize: Each cantus firmus must contain a climax or high point. This tone will serve as the goal of a motion from the first tone of the cantus; it will simultaneously function as the beginning of a second melodic curve down to the final tone. The climax tone should not be repeated.

It is possible to construct a line in which the climax is the lowest rather than the highest tone. Such lines are generally most effective in a bass register. In a bass line, a descent moves away from the neutral middle range; it is consequently experienced as an increase in tension. A good cantus firmus must function well in all registers. Therefore we shall not employ the low point until we begin two-part counterpoint.

CONTINUITY

A cantus may contain a beginning, climax, and end, and yet prove unsatisfactory. This will inevitably occur if there is no clear and logical *connection* between beginnings and goals of motion. Let us consider Example 1-2. The line contains a high point and is not altogether lacking in direction. Nonetheless, it is unusable for our purposes. The tones between beginning and high point in the first part, and between high point and end in the second, do not carry the line forward in a convincing manner. Each tone seems to function as an independent point rather than as part of a larger whole.

If we compare Example 1-2 with Example 1-1c, we see at once that the latter is composed primarily of stepwise or conjunct motion; the former, on the other hand, moves mostly by leap (disjunct motion). Of course it is unsafe to generalize from one observation. But the musical practice of many centuries bears out the conclusion that melodic continuity is connected with predominantly stepwise motion. In Chapters 6 and 7 we shall observe that even large leaps can constitute expansions or inversions of underlying stepwise progressions.

Indeed, the very terms *conjunct* and *disjunct* mean joined together and separated. The expressions "motion by step" and "motion by leap" convey the same idea in more graphically metaphoric terms.

To summarize: For the sake of continuity, the cantus firmus will contain predominantly stepwise motion.

VARIETY

Once again, let us consider an example (see Example 1-3). The line does not lack direction or continuity. But it is too homogeneous, too undifferentiated. It fails to satisfy a fundamental esthetic need—variety. Let us compare Examples 1-3 and 1-1c. Undeniably 1-1c shows greater variety, and, consequently, a more distinct melodic profile. Two factors are responsible: the use of leaps and the momentary changes in the direction of the line. In Example 1-3 we find no leaps; melodic direction changes only once, after the high point. In Example 1-1c we find three leaps; the line changes direction five times.

In the interest of variety, then, we must employ some disjunct mo-

EXAMPLE 1-2

EXAMPLE 1-3

tion. Most cantus firmi contain two or three leaps. In the next section we shall discuss in detail how to employ leaps so as not to destroy the continuity of the line.

All cantus firmi change direction several times. These changes between ascending and descending motion result in the deflections in the main direction of the line mentioned above.

To summarize: Each cantus firmus will contain two to four leaps. The direction of the line will change several times in the course of the exercise.

USE OF LEAPS

In the last section we saw that a cantus firmus must contain leaps for the sake of variety. Earlier, however, we learned that leaps can prevent melodic continuity. How may we employ them so that their effect will be beneficial? First of all we must not use too many in close succession. Although it is impossible to set a precise limit, we may say in general that three (or possibly four) leaps are a reasonable maximum for a cantus of normal length. Of course large leaps interrupt continuity more than do small ones. As a rule, a cantus will not contain more than two leaps larger than a fourth.

The number of leaps is by no means the only consideration; the manner in which they occur is of greater significance. Let us consider Example 1-4. In Example 1-4a the leaps are followed by motion in the same direction; the leaps in 1-4b are followed by a change in direction.

The first procedure causes a segmented, discontinuous line; the ear groups together the tones on either side of the leap and separates the tones of the disjunct intervals. In the second example, however, the continuation in the opposite direction "fills in" the leap and helps integrate it into the line as a whole. The result is a far greater degree of continuity. As a general rule, therefore, leaps should be followed by a change of direction.

For obvious reasons the larger leaps require more careful treatment than do the smaller ones. Skips of a third can be continued in the same direction. The cantus firmus of Example 1-5 (by Schenker) offers an illustration. A stepwise descent from the high point A to the final tonic would offer little melodic variety; after so much stepwise motion, the line needs the relief of disjunct motion. The reader will note that the "omitted" tone is F, a tone that has already occurred twice in the course of the line. A third statement of F might unbalance the melodic line (see below).

When the leap is larger than a third, a change of direction should follow. In most cases this change of direction should be stepwise; conjunct motion, with its minimal tension, counteracts the disruptive force of the leap better than disjunct motion (see Example 1-4b). In addition, non-stepwise motion following a leap tends to isolate the second tone of the leap. If the prevailing context is stepwise, it is sometimes possible to follow one leap with another in the opposite direction without breaking the continuity (see Example 1-6, a cantus by J. J. Fux). The student should avoid the use of two leaps in the same direction or more than two consecutive leaps even with a change of direction.

EXAMPLE 1-4

a)

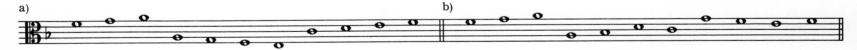

EXAMPLE 1-5

EXAMPLE 1-6

To summarize: Leaps larger than a third should be followed by a change of direction preferably in stepwise motion. Avoid two consecutive leaps in the same direction. Avoid more than two consecutive leaps.

BALANCE

A cantus firmus is in a state of balance when no single element predominates to such an extent that the stability of the whole is impaired. Imbalance can result from a number of causes. Among these are: excessive motion in a single direction, unresolved melodic tensions, repetition of single tones, repetition of groups of tones.

We have already noted that changing direction helps to create variety. We have also seen that a reverse of melodic direction is required after a large leap. To these observations we can now add a third. The student should take care not to continue a stepwise motion too long in the same direction. The vagueness of the preceding statement is intentional; a long cantus firmus can better assimilate an extended scalewise progression than a short cantus; it is therefore not possible to establish a universally valid limitation. In most cases, five tones seems to be the limit. Compare the three lines of Example 1-7. The first two examples are satisfactory lines. The third, which extends the scale one degree further, seems awkward. The descending scale takes up too great a portion of the total line; as a result, the end sounds rather abrupt.

Excessive motion in one direction can also result from a combination of conjunct and disjunct intervals. Compare the melodic fragments in Example 1-8. In Example 1-8a the ascending octave continues the direction of the preceding tones; in 1-8b, the octave changes direction. Example 1-8b seems more in proportion. In general, a leap of a fifth or larger should change direction. Indeed, even smaller leaps seem to function with maximum effectiveness when they reverse the preceding direction.

Example 1-9 shows yet another aspect of the problem. The first excerpt shows a combination of several small leaps and stepwise motion outlining an octave. As a whole, the line makes a rather haphazard impression. It seems to represent a stepwise ascent with a few tones arbitrarily omitted. Example 1-9b is much better. Here the change of direction effected by the initial leap of a fifth and the subsequent bending back of the line creates a far more balanced melody.

To summarize: Avoid excessive motion in one direction, whether caused by stepwise progression alone, stepwise progression followed by a large leap, or stepwise progression interlaced with several small leaps.

UNRESOLVED MELODIC TENSION

Let us study Example 1-10. In a, b, and c the brackets indicate that dissonant intervals are formed by the first and last tones of a motion in a single direction. Tones which begin and end motions are more prominent than the tones in between. Therefore, dissonances outlined

EXAMPLE 1-7

EXAMPLE 1-8

EXAMPLE 1-9

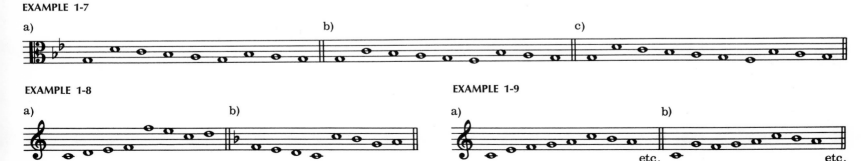

by such tones produce a melodic tension for which elementary counterpoint cannot provide a meaningful context.[1] In Example 1-10*d* the line reaches its climax on the leading tone. The listener expects a continuation to the tonic and does not accept the seventh step as a satisfactory high point; linear balance, therefore, is disturbed. The same holds true of the raised seventh step in minor.

REPETITION OF A SINGLE TONE

The requirements of the cantus firmus exclude the immediate repetition of a tone (see Example 1-11). In the first place, such repetition extends the value of the tone and consequently interferes with the necessary rhythmic equality of the cantus. At the same time the repeated tone receives an undue emphasis. This emphasis on a single tone creates a static point which sets the line as a whole out of balance.

Example 1-12 presents a somewhat different problem. Here, there is no immediate repetition. However, the frequent recurrence of C creates a condition of extreme imbalance. No single tone should sound so often that it dominates the entire exercise. The high point of a line

[1] The larger the number of intervening tones, the less the impression of outlining a dissonant interval arises.

should never be repeated. The lowest tone is somewhat less sensitive; it can sometimes recur. (If the initial tonic is the lowest tone, it *must* recur at the close of the exercise. See below.) Tones preceded by large leaps receive a certain emphasis; their repetition is more problematic than that of tones preceded by stepwise motion.

REPETITION OF GROUPS OF TONES

An impression of redundancy results from the repetition of a distinctive group of tones. In the sphere of composition with its wide frame of reference, motivic repetition constitutes a valuable—indeed, an essential—resource. But the limited world of the species exercise cannot offer sufficient scope for the effective use of repetition. Let us consider Example 1-13. Where the entire line is so short, the repetition of even three tones is disturbing.

In addition, the repetition creates the impression of a break in the continuity of the line. It is as though the cantus interrupts its course after the fifth tone, begins again at the sixth tone, and finally arrives at a conclusion. Now such breaks in the surface continuity are highly appropriate in composition. For there, as we shall see, it is possible to establish underlying motions which unify the articulated surface patterns. These means are lacking in the simple species exercises. (See,

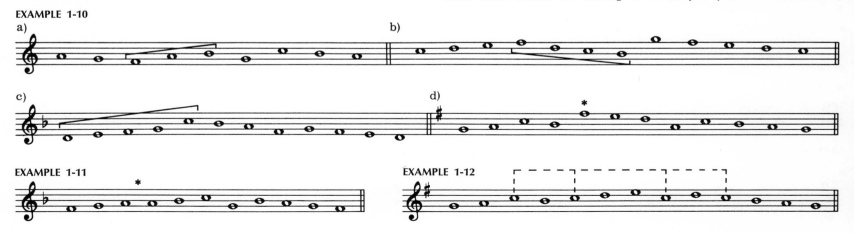

EXAMPLE 1-10
a)   b)

c)   d)

EXAMPLE 1-11   **EXAMPLE 1-12**

however, Chapter 7, Section 4, Repetition and Articulation.)

For similar reasons, the student should avoid the use of so-called *sequences*. A line such as Example 1-14 is not in keeping with the purposes of species counterpoint. From our present point of view, the line breaks up into a number of quasi-independent units; within the narrow framework of the exercise, we cannot create a broader context that might give meaning to these details.

BEGINNING AND END

If the cantus firmus is to form a self-contained whole—if, in other words, it is to possess the quality of completeness—it must begin and end on the tonic. After the initial tone, the line can continue by step or leap; the approach to the final tone, however, must be by step.

The reason for this is obvious. After a leap the ear expects a compensating motion in the opposite direction. Consider Example 1-15. The line stops abruptly. We cannot accept the final E as a satisfactory conclusion because we expect a continuation that will fill in the leap. In Example 1-16 we find such a continuation; the two E's (marked with asterisks) occupy the same pitch, but each has a different function. The first is a temporary detour within the descent from A to E. The second is the clearly established goal.

In ending the cantus firmus it is usually best to approach the final tonic from above. As a general rule, upward motion produces increased tension, while downward motion decreases tension. Therefore a descent to the final tonic, other things being equal, creates the most stable

ending. Most counterpoint texts, though they may vary widely in other respects, recommend cantus firmi that end with the descending progression 2-1. However, for reasons of variety or balance, it may sometimes be best to approach the tonic from below. In this case the final note must be approached by a half step. Only this smallest diatonic interval can produce a conclusive effect in ascending direction. In the minor mode, therefore, the seventh degree must be raised.

The next-to-last tone will generally enter by step. It must never follow a leap larger than a third; otherwise, the ending will be disconnected from the rest of the cantus. In minor the progression 6-7-1 (8) requires the raising of the sixth degree in accordance with the melodic form of the scale. This alteration forestalls an augmented second (Example 1-17).

MODAL CANTUS FIRMI

Many authors, following sixteenth-century practice, present counterpoint on a modal basis. Such is not the approach of the present book. We conceive the purpose of instruction in elementary counterpoint to be the study of fundamental problems of voice leading, not the imitation of a specific musical style. Since we diverge from sixteenth-century —or at least from Palestrinian—practice in certain details of dissonance treatment and of melodic progression, we find it appropriate to demonstrate the elements of voice leading in a tonal, not a modal, framework. Most of the exercises and examples, therefore, reflect the system of major-minor tonality.

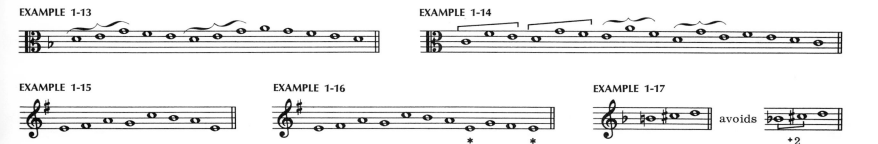

EXAMPLE 1-13

EXAMPLE 1-14

EXAMPLE 1-15

EXAMPLE 1-16

EXAMPLE 1-17

Although they are not central to our purpose, we do not exclude modal exercises. It will be perfectly feasible to apply to a modal context the principles developed in this book. By so doing the student will open his ear and mind to melodic-contrapuntal possibilities that might otherwise escape him; he will consequently find himself in a better position to understand and appreciate the great musical treasures of the Renaissance. In later sections of this book—especially in Chapter 10—the reader will find a number of musical citations from the modal polyphony of the Renaissance.

In writing modal cantus firmi, the student should bear the following in mind:

1. In relation to voice leading the Ionian and Aeolian modes (on C and A) can be considered equivalent to major and minor.

2. The distinction between authentic and plagal modes becomes problematic in polyphonic music; the student, therefore, can disregard this distinction.

3. In polyphonic textures the Lydian mode (on F) regularly employs B flat; this mode, therefore, becomes equivalent to transposed Ionian.

The elimination, for our purposes, of the plagal modes and of Ionian, Aeolian, and Lydian as distinct from major and minor leaves us with three modes: Dorian, Phrygian, and Mixolydian.

The Dorian mode, untransposed, centers on D. When functioning as a leading tone, the seventh step is raised to C sharp. The sixth step occurs in variable form, sometimes as B natural, sometimes as B flat. In general, the natural is used in ascending lines and the flat is used in descent. Example 1-18 shows a few possibilities.

The Phrygian mode is built on E. The half step between the first and second degrees produces an equivalent in descending direction to the ascending leading tone in Ionian (major). In Phrygian melodic lines, therefore, the second step functions as the leading tone; the seventh step, D, is rarely raised to D sharp. In polyphonic music the Phrygian mode seldom uses B flat; this alteration would produce a diminished fifth or augmented fourth with respect to E, the central tone. Example 1-19 shows some Phrygian cantus firmi.

G is the central tone of the Mixolydian mode. As in Dorian, the seventh step is raised when a leading tone is desired. B flat frequently occurs in descending progressions in this mode (Example 1-20).

The reader desiring more information about the modes should

EXAMPLE 1-18

a) (with B flat)　　　　　　　　　　　　　　　b) (with B natural)

EXAMPLE 1-19

a) (J. J. Fux)　　　　　　　　　　　　　　　b)

EXAMPLE 1-20

a) (Jeppesen)　　　　　　　　　　　　　b) (B flat optional)

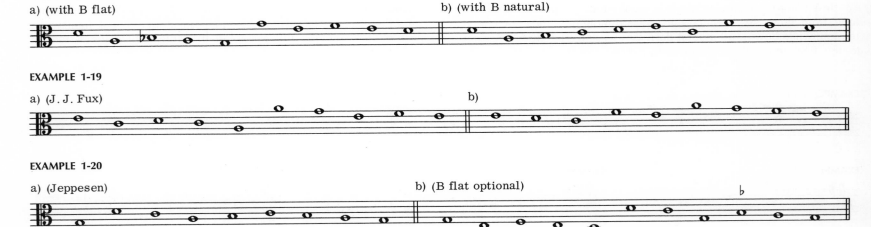

consult standard reference works and histories of music. Jeppesen's *Counterpoint* contains much valuable information presented in clear and concise form. The compositional application of the modes to polyphonic music poses a number of problems, however; for modal theory mainly developed in terms of single-line music. In recent years musical scholars have significantly increased our understanding of modal polyphony, but a good deal remains incompletely understood.

EXAMPLES

Example 1-21 presents a number of cantus firmi in different major and minor keys. Some of these have been drawn from earlier counterpoint texts; others have been written by the authors. The reader can use these examples as models for his own cantus firmi; in addition, they can be used for the later exercises in two- and three-part counterpoint.

EXAMPLE 1-21

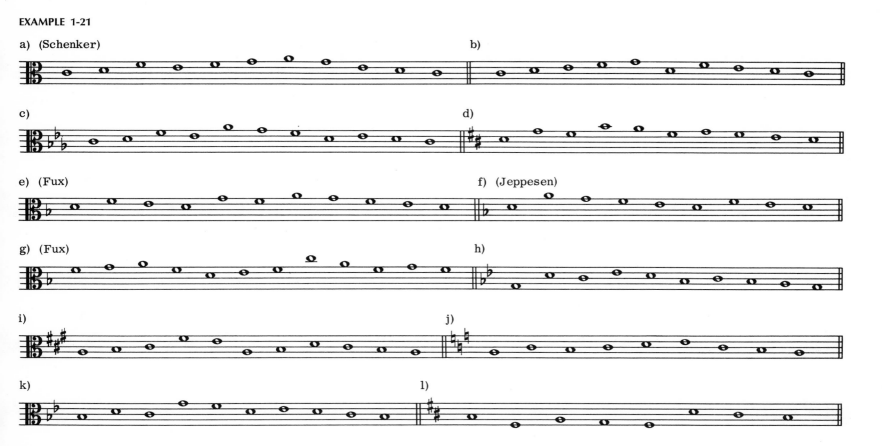

a) (Schenker)

b)

c)

d)

e) (Fux)

f) (Jeppesen)

g) (Fux)

h)

i)

j)

k)

l)

EXERCISES

1. Criticize and correct the cantus firmi of Example 1-22.

2. Write at least twelve cantus firmi in different major and minor keys. Vary the length from eight to sixteen tones. Place the high point in various positions within the line.

2. TWO-PART COUNTERPOINT, FIRST SPECIES

GENERAL CONSIDERATIONS

Writing cantus firmi has given us practice in shaping and organizing single lines. We are now ready to begin the study of counterpoint in two and three parts. In two-part counterpoint we add a second line, called the *counterpoint,* to the cantus firmus. In each of the five species the counterpoint shows a specific rhythmic relationship to the cantus; the different rhythmic relationships, in turn, create various possibilities of voice leading. In first species, the added voice, like the cantus firmus, moves in whole notes; the contrapuntal texture, therefore, is note-against-note.

The melodic character of the added line or counterpoint resembles that of the cantus firmus. In writing a two-part counterpoint, therefore, we shall make use of the same general principles of melodic construction that we learned in the section on cantus firmus. As we shall see, the presence of another voice adds a few considerations.

THE TWO DIMENSIONS: HORIZONTAL AND VERTICAL

When we write single lines we are concerned only with the horizontal dimension of music, with the unfolding in time of a succession of tones. In two-part counterpoint a second dimension is added: the vertical.

EXAMPLE 1-22

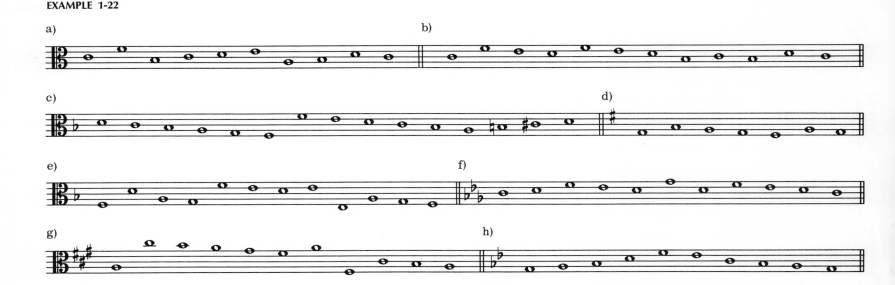

We must learn to organize simultaneous as well as successive combinations of tones. The horizontal dimension is the primary one; it is the motion of the two lines that produces the vertical intervals of two-part counterpoint. At the same time, vertical relationships play a vital, if secondary, role. Good counterpoint is not the mere addition of one part to another; the two must fuse into a meaningful whole. We cannot achieve such a whole without control of the vertical dimension; a logical contrapuntal fabric can never result from the haphazard collision of the component parts. Writing counterpoint involves the constant mutual adjustment of the two dimensions. We must strive to make the added voice as perfect and logical a line as possible; for in a contrapuntal texture, each line must preserve its integrity. But we cannot shape the new voice in a musical vacuum; we must at all times consider its relation to the cantus firmus.

VERTICAL CONSONANCE AND DISSONANCE

The ability to combine two or more voices into a logical whole depends in large measure upon the control of vertical consonance and dissonance. This control represents one of the chief goals of the study of elementary counterpoint; in each species we shall come to grips with a new aspect of this important problem. First species will teach us how to deploy the vertical consonances. In the later species various types of dissonance treatment will be introduced.

In a consonant interval the tones blend into a stable sonority, a sonority that tends to remain in a state of repose. In a dissonant interval, on the other hand, the combination of tones gives rise to a tension that demands continuation; dissonances, therefore, serve to intensify musical motion. In tonal music, until the twentieth century, consonances provide the stable framework within which dissonances move. The meaning of a dissonance, however prominent or strikingly used, depends upon its immediate or ultimate relationship to a context determined by consonances; consonances represent the primary sonorities that can create large contexts while dissonances are the transitory and dependent—but vital—elements that activate and enliven these contexts.

Consonance and dissonance are not absolute qualities; the different consonant intervals possess varying degrees of stability, and the dis-

sonances possess varying degrees of tension. And, of course, context can exert a modifying influence upon an interval. Furthermore, conceptions of dissonance and consonance have undergone historical development. In early medieval polyphony the combination of octave and fifth, $\frac{8}{5}$, dominated musical texture; the fourth was a favored consonance, too, whereas thirds and sixths were considered dissonances. Later the fourth became an equivocal interval, sometimes consonant, sometimes dissonant. And thirds and sixths acquired consonant status.

These changes took place before the fifteenth century. For a period of some five hundred years thereafter—through the nineteenth century—composers remained in agreement about the identity of the consonant intervals. During this long period of time the musical language experienced many profound stylistic changes, but the consonant framework—the foundation of counterpoint—remained constant. The practice of composers reveals the following to be the consonant intervals: perfect unisons, fifths and octaves, major and minor thirds, major and minor sixths. The perfect fourth, as was mentioned, is an equivocal interval. It functions as a dissonance in a two-part texture, but becomes consonant in some configurations of three or more parts. All consonant intervals arise from, or can be combined into, major and minor triads. Since the fifteenth century the triad has been the matrix for the vertical combinations of Western polyphony; we refer to this repertory, therefore, as *triadic* music. (Students of the history of music will remember that the triad was used by composers long before it was recognized as a functional unit by theorists.)

The above-mentioned consonances—excluding the ambiguous perfect fourth—constitute the vertical intervals available to us in two-part first-species counterpoint. After we learn how to use these materials in a simple context, we shall be prepared for working with the more complex textures that arise out of the various uses of dissonance. First species provides us with a frame of reference for all our later and more advanced work in counterpoint.

To summarize: First-species counterpoint uses only consonant intervals. These are: perfect unisons, major and minor thirds, perfect fifths, major and minor sixths, and perfect octaves. Dissonances will not occur; the dissonant intervals are: all seconds, all sevenths, all augmented and diminished intervals, and, in two-part writing, the perfect fourth.

THE CONSONANT INTERVALS: VARYING DEGREES OF STABILITY

As was mentioned earlier, the various consonant intervals possess different degrees of stability; dissonances show varying degrees of tension. We shall learn in the later species that the differences among the dissonant intervals have little bearing upon contrapuntal treatment; a passing tone, for instance, fulfills the same function whether it forms a fourth, tritone, second, or seventh. The treatment of the consonances, however, varies considerably depending upon the degree of stability of the different intervals.

In general we must treat with the greatest care those consonances that show a high degree of stability. For such intervals maintain a strong vertical equilibrium; they awaken, consequently, little desire for continued motion. Excessive use of these intervals can impede the flow of the melodic lines. Of all the intervals the unison is the most stable, the most absolutely consonant. As we shall see, the very stability of the unison restricts its use, in first species, to the beginning and end of the exercise, where the quality of complete stability is most appropriate.

The octave is second only to the unison in degree of consonance. Contrast of register, however, creates some differentiation between the otherwise equivalent tones. The octave, therefore, can be used more freely than the unison; however, too many octaves will produce a hollow texture, and will tend to hold back the forward motion of the lines.

Next in our scale comes the perfect fifth. The fifth contains two different tones; it is the most stable interval possessing a contrast between the component tones. The fifth plays a crucial role in triadic music; it is the definitive interval of the triad. C–G, for example, defines a triad with C as fundamental tone. And because tonality, in triadic music, is grounded in the triad, the fifth is a strong key-defining interval. C–G, therefore, suggests not merely a triad on C but, by extension, the key of C. Of course, the fifth alone cannot suggest major or minor quality; for this a third is required as well. The vertical strength of the fifth is such that, as in the case of the octave, excessive use can impede melodic flow. However, the contrast between the two tones makes the fifth somewhat less sensitive than the octave.

The remaining consonances, the major and minor thirds and sixths, are less stable than the perfect consonances listed above. All of these intervals (including, of course, the tenths which are registrally expanded thirds) reveal a greater tendency toward motion than do the unisons, octaves, and fifths. Because their vertical stability is less, thirds and sixths are better able to promote horizontal, linear flow. Therefore, these intervals will predominate in a two-part contrapuntal texture except at the beginning and end, where maximum stability is desired. Within this group of imperfect consonances the thirds are more stable than are the sixths; and major thirds are more stable than minor. Both thirds occur in relation to the fundamental tone of a triad; the major third in the major triad, and the minor third in the somewhat less consonant minor triad. The sixths, on the other hand, result from the inversion of thirds; they are derived, rather than fundamental, intervals. The major sixth, of course, results from the inversion of the minor third and the minor sixth from the inversion of the major third. The major sixth is slightly more unstable than the minor; both sixths are considerably more active intervals than are the thirds. Of all the consonances the sixths most closely approach the quality of dissonance; and, indeed, in the late Middle Ages they were the last of the intervals to be accepted by composers as consonant. Unlike the other consonances the sixths have never been commonly used to end a triadic composition.

THE PERFECT FOURTH

We stated above that the perfect fourth functions as a dissonance in two-part counterpoint; it will therefore not occur in first species. The fourth is the most ambiguous, the most problematic of the intervals. In some contexts it demonstrates the stability characteristic of consonance; in others it generates sufficient tension to make it dissonant. It is dissonant when it occurs in a two-part setting or between the bass and an upper part in a texture of three or more parts. The fourth is consonant in a setting of more than two parts when it occurs between two of the upper parts of a triad, an $\frac{8}{5}$, or a $\frac{6}{3}$ chord (Example 1-23).

The fourth, of course, is the inversion of the fifth; as an inversion it is a derived interval, far less stable than the fifth which it represents. The contrast between the stable fifth and the less stable fourth is greater than the contrast between the sixths and their fundamenal forms, the major and minor thirds. It is easier, therefore, to hear the sixths as representatives of the thirds than it is to hear the perfect fourth as surrogate for the fifth. Unless context suggests the contrary, we are much more inclined to hear the fourth as a tone of melodic figuration tending to resolve down to a third. (This explanation is in keeping with historical evidence. In the pre-triadic polyphony of the early Middle Ages the fourth was an unequivocal consonance. In that music the third is not treated as consonant; the fourth, therefore, cannot tend to resolve to it. Since there is no pull toward the third, the fourth has no ambiguity; it can only be heard in relation to the fifth. When the third acquired consonant status, the fourth began to function as an interval with dissonant tendencies; this reversal of roles is already clearly in evidence in the music of fourteenth-century Italy.)

The fourth, then, will be consonant only when context clarifies its relationship to the fifth; in all other cases it will be heard as an unstable interval with a marked tendency to resolve to the third, the upper voice descending a step. When the fourth occurs in two-part texture or with respect to the crucial bass part in counterpoint of three or more parts, it is dissonant. As an upper-voice interval of a triad, $\frac{8}{5}$, or $\frac{6}{3}$ chord, the relation to the fifth is evident; the interval is consonant. (In the prolonged counterpoint of composition it is possible to create contexts in which the fourth—even alone, or with respect to the bass—is consonant. When the bass arpeggiates a triad, for example, a fourth that arises is heard in relation to the unfolded chord and is consonant. Such possibilities do not occur in elementary counterpoint.)

RELATIVE MOTION

The simultaneous presence of two voices creates four types of relative motion:

1. Similar motion, in which the voices proceed in the same direction without maintaining a constant distance from each other (Example 1-24).
2. Parallel motion, in which the voices proceed in the same direction at a constant or virtually constant distance. (Consecutive thirds, sixths, and tenths are considered parallel, even if the quality of the intervals changes. See Example 1-25.)
3. Contrary motion, in which the two voices proceed in opposite directions (Example 1-26).
4. Oblique motion, in which one voice moves and the other remains stationary (Example 1-27).

As we shall see, first species offers little opportunity for the use of oblique motion.

INDEPENDENCE OF PARTS

In a good exercise, each voice must maintain its own integrity; no part should function as a mere duplication or accompaniment of the other. It goes without saying that the word "independence" must not be interpreted in an absolute sense, as though each voice could go its own way without any regard for the other. Control over the vertical

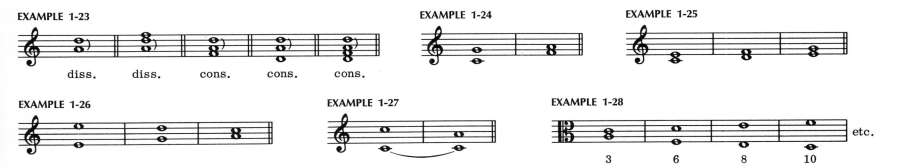

EXAMPLE 1-23

diss.   diss.   cons.   cons.   cons.

EXAMPLE 1-24

EXAMPLE 1-25

EXAMPLE 1-26

EXAMPLE 1-27

EXAMPLE 1-28

3   6   8   10   etc.

relationships is necessary for the clarity and intelligibility of the contrapuntal setting. Such control is perfectly compatible with the maintenance of a distinct and individual contour for the single lines.

Of the various types of relative movement, contrary motion best promotes the independence of parts. The voices move in opposite directions; the interval between them constantly changes. (See Example 1-28.)

Oblique motion, also quite productive of independence, is available in first species only on those few occasions where the counterpoint ties a whole note from one measure to the next. The other species of counterpoint—not based on note-against-note texture—make significant use of oblique motion.

In similar motion the voices demonstrate less independence, both moving in the same direction (Example 1-29).

In parallel motion, not only is the general direction the same, but also the specific contour (Example 1-30). When properly used, parallel motion is a valuable technique of voice leading. However, parallel motion involving certain vertical intervals is problematic and, consequently, excluded from the contrapuntal exercises.

PARALLEL UNISONS, OCTAVES, AND FIFTHS

Parallel motion in unisons and octaves results in the duplication of a single voice rather than two independent parts. With unisons the duplication is complete; octaves, at least, offer contrast of register. However,

registral difference is not sufficient to offset the impression of doubling rather than independent voice leading. (See Example 1-31.)

Octave doubling occurs quite frequently in concerted and keyboard music as a means of emphasizing a given voice. These doublings do not represent a contradiction of the rule prohibiting parallel octaves; they concern the instrumental (or vocal) setting rather than the basic voice leading.

Parallel fifths present a somewhat different problem from that of unisons or octaves. The fifth, after all, contains two different tones; there is no longer a question of real duplication. The fifth, however, is unique among the consonances in its ability to define a triad and, by extension, to suggest a key. The tones C–G can only belong to a C triad (major or minor); the interval suggests C as a key. A third, on the other hand, can belong to one of two triads: C–E forms part of the C major and the A minor chords. Example 1-32 gives an illustration.

In a succession of thirds (or sixths), therefore, the individual intervals do not possess the strong key-defining implications of the fifth. In the absence of strong vertical stability the ear can easily perceive the horizontal flow of the two voices (see Example 1-33).

A succession of fifths in parallel motion, however, is much more difficult to hear in terms of horizontal motion. The vertical stability of each fifth is so great that the forward motion ceases, as it were, at each interval. And, where the key-defining quality of each vertical sonority is quite explicit, the tonality of the whole is thrown into doubt (Example 1-34).

The rule prohibiting parallel fifths and octaves remains a funda-

EXAMPLE 1-29

EXAMPLE 1-30

EXAMPLE 1-31

EXAMPLE 1-32

mental principle of voice leading from the Renaissance through most of the nineteenth century. Many important compositional techniques evolved as a result of this principle. In the sections on prolonged counterpoint the student will learn that seeming violations of this principle in music of the period are not in fundamental contradiction to it. Rather, they represent the extension and manipulation of the principle through the influence of compositional factors other than those of pure voice leading. Fifths and octaves occur frequently in Medieval and post-Romantic music. It lies beyond the scope of the present chapter to explore the voice-leading principles of these periods.

To summarize: Parallel motion in fifths, octaves, and unisons must be avoided.

PERFECT INTERVALS APPROACHED IN SIMILAR MOTION

The vertical stability of the perfect intervals can interrupt the forward impulse of the voice leading even where parallel motion is not present. If the intervals of the perfect fifth, octave, and unison are introduced in similar motion, the effect illustrated in Example 1-35 is produced The voice leading of Example 1-35 is often called "hidden" fifths and octaves. The origin of this term lies in the assumption that the listener mentally fills in the melodic skip, thus creating the prohibited parallel succession (Example 1-36). In style periods when improvisational additions to the printed score were common, such "fillings" were, in fact, at times provided by the performer.

The approach to the perfect intervals in similar motion is not nearly as problematic as parallel motion involving these intervals. As we shall see, textures of more than two voices can employ this voice leading under certain conditions. However, the clarity and sensitivity of two-part texture demand great care in the use of fifths and octaves. In our two-part exercises, therefore, we shall avoid the approach by similar motion to the perfect intervals.

PARALLEL THIRDS, SIXTHS, AND TENTHS: VARIETY OF VERTICAL RELATIONSHIPS

The principle of variety, so important in the horizontal dimension, obtains with equal force in the realm of the vertical. One application of this principle requires a reasonably equal distribution of the various consonant intervals. Therefore we must somewhat restrict the use of parallel thirds, sixths, and tenths. In general, no more than three such intervals should appear in succession. In the case of an unusually long cantus firmus four might prove acceptable. The student will remember that most cantus firmi contain from nine to twelve tones. It is easy to see that a series of four or five similar intervals will fill half or more of the exercise and rob the contrapuntal texture of a possible source of variety.

For the sake of variety the student should try to make use of all the available types of relative motion. Contrary motion should predominate slightly because of its ability to promote independence. A con-

EXAMPLE 1-33

a)   b)

EXAMPLE 1-34

F?   G?   A?

EXAMPLE 1-35

EXAMPLE 1-36

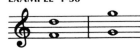 =  =

stant and unrelieved use of contrary motion, however, would result in monotony and would not be desirable even if it were possible.

UNISONS IN FIRST SPECIES

In the note-against-note texture of first species the use of unisons creates certain difficulties. The interval is highly appropriate to the beginning and end of the exercise where its extreme stability is in place. (Because of the construction of most cantus firmi the unison occurs more frequently at the beginning and end of the lower than the upper counterpoint.) In the middle of the exercise the unison can create the impression that one of the voices has suddenly dropped out. And, particularly if it involves the tonic, the unison can sound like an ending (see Example 1-37). The unison, therefore, will occur only at the beginning and end of the first-species exercise.

FURTHER RESTRICTIONS ON THE PERFECT INTERVALS

The use of compound intervals (intervals greater than the octave) makes possible a succession of fifths or octaves by contrary motion (Example 1-38). These so-called antiparallel fifths and octaves are to be avoided in two-part writing; because of the dependency of the voices, the simultaneous occurrence of two leaps is problematic in itself. The leaps, in this case, also emphasize the perfect intervals in a way that brings out their vertical, key-defining quality. For the same reason a progression from unison to octave (or the reverse) should be avoided, over and above the general restriction on unisons (Example 1-39).

The alternation of fifth and octave, however, can prove a perfectly logical and useful voice leading (Example 1-40).

The first and last tones of the cantus firmus will always be counterpointed by perfect consonances; their vertical stability helps to establish the key and strengthens points of structural definition. In the

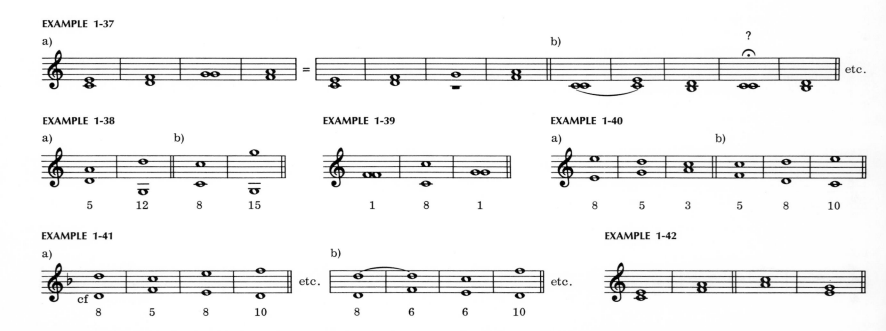

EXAMPLE 1-37

EXAMPLE 1-38

EXAMPLE 1-39

EXAMPLE 1-40

EXAMPLE 1-41

EXAMPLE 1-42

middle of the exercise thirds, sixths, and tenths should predominate. Fifths and octaves, though by no means excluded, will not occur as frequently as the imperfect consonances. Comparison of Examples 1-41a and b will reveal the smoother horizontal progression effected by the use of the imperfect intervals.

SIMULTANEOUS LEAPS

The emphasis created by disjunct motion can prove disruptive when it occurs in both voices at the same time (see Example 1-38). In addition, the presence of simultaneous leaps impairs the independence of the parts. Leaps in similar motion are worse than those in opposite directions for reasons of independence. Large leaps are more problematic than small ones for reasons of continuity. Whenever possible avoid simultaneous leaps, especially leaps in the same direction involving melodic intervals larger than a fourth.

OVERLAPPING OF PARTS

If, without crossing parts, the lower voice moves to a tone higher than the preceding tone of the upper voice, or if the upper voice descends to a tone lower than the previous one of the lower voice, the parts are said to overlap. Example 1-42 is an illustration. In voice leadings of this type it is difficult to follow the progression of the individual parts. In the interest of clarity, therefore, avoid the use of overlap.

VOICE CROSSING

The crossing of parts, i.e., temporarily shifting the lower voice above the upper or the upper voice below the lower, is a legitimate and valuable compositional technique. The pedagogical purposes of the species exercises, however, are better served by avoiding the more complex types of voice leading until the simpler ones have been mastered. For this reason it is best at this stage to exclude crossings and leave the relative positions of the voices constant throughout the exercise.

SPACING

The most natural spacing for two-part vocal writing is between adjacent voices—i.e., soprano-alto, alto-tenor, and tenor-bass. In general, the distance between the parts should not exceed a tenth. Only for the sake of an important melodic event should wider spacing occur—and then, only temporarily. If, for example, the upper voice ascends to its climax in contrary motion to the cantus firmus, the limit of the tenth might justifiably be exceeded. After the high point, however, normal spacing should reappear. The student will find that overly wide spacing —particularly in the spare texture of the species exercises—sounds rather empty and bare.

USE OF TIED NOTES

In the cantus firmus tied (or repeated) notes do not occur. In first species the occasional use of ties is possible. The difficulties of writing an exclusively consonant counterpoint are greater than those of constructing a single line. In a number of instances the student will find that the use of tied notes represents the best expedient for avoiding dissonant intervals, parallels, etc. The tied notes are always an expedient rather than desirable in themselves. For they produce a static area in the line. The student should not tie more than two consecutive whole notes. And he should endeavor to use the ties not more than twice in the course of an exercise of average length. The use of ties automatically produces oblique motion.

BEGINNING THE EXERCISE

Let us consider Examples 1-43 and 1-44. The first tone of the counterpoint must confirm the tonality of the cantus firmus and serve as the point of departure for the melodic development of the added line. In the upper counterpoint the first tone may be an octave or fifth above the cantus. Both intervals will confirm and establish the key. (Most cantus firmi begin with an ascent. Therefore, it is usually difficult to begin the upper counterpoint with a unison—see Example 1-43d. Unless the cantus descends, the unison will bring about either an overlap or a crossing of parts. The unison in itself is a perfectly good beginning interval.)

The lower counterpoint will begin with a unison or octave. The fifth below the tonic will throw the exercise out of the key; therefore it may not occur. The unison and octave are equally good; the choice will depend upon the contour of the line and the placement of the climax.

CLIMAX

The upper counterpoint, like the cantus, should move to a high point for the climax. The lower counterpoint, on the other hand, may employ either a high point or a low point. (See section on *cantus firmus,* pages 4 and 5.) It is conducive to independence when the climax of the counterpoint does not coincide with that of the cantus.

ENDING THE EXERCISE

The end of the exercise requires the stability of the tonic in the counterpoint as well as the cantus. The final interval, therefore, will be an octave or unison. Most cantus firmi descend to the final tonic. In the majority of cases, therefore, the upper counterpoint will end with an octave

rather than a unison; the lower counterpoint, for reasons of spacing, will most often end with the unison.

The next-to-last measure must contain both the leading tone and the second degree of the scale. The cantus will contain one of these tones; the counterpoint must bring the other. Since most cantus firmi approach the final tonic from above, the leading tone will usually occur in the counterpoint. The minor mode requires the raising of the leading tone at the cadence; if the leading tone is preceded by the sixth degree of the scale, that tone must also be raised to avoid the melodic interval of an augmented second. (Except for the end, exercises in minor will mostly use the natural form of the scale. In the middle of the exercise the presence of the raised sixth and seventh steps might tend to produce a cadential effect.)

NOTATION OF COUNTERPOINT EXERCISES

The cantus and counterpoint should appear on separate lines. When the student writes several counterpoints to a single cantus, he can write the cantus halfway down the page and place the counterpoints above and below it. It will then be necessary to write the cantus only once. (In this case it is helpful to write the cantus with red pencil for ease in reading.) Many counterpoint texts require the use of the C clefs. Students already familiar with these clefs will gain valuable additional practice from their use in counterpoint exercises. All students should

EXAMPLE 1-43

EXAMPLE 1-44

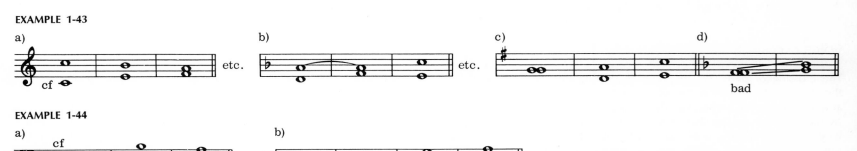

use at least the alto clef, together with the treble and bass. It is much easier to maintain good spacing with a combination of alto-treble or alto-bass than with treble-bass.

PROCEDURES OF WRITING

The exercises of species counterpoint provide remarkably effective training in mental hearing. The student's ability to hear and mentally grasp melodic continuity and voice-leading relationships will grow steadily if he proceeds in the proper manner. The following suggestions will be helpful.

1. If the cantus is unfamiliar, sing it through several times. If possible, learn the cantus by heart before attempting to set it. Study the contour of the cantus with respect to high point, the placement of leaps, etc.

2. Never work out the exercises at the piano. Try to hear mentally the contrapuntal texture; test the melodic quality of the counterpoint by singing it. You may check the accuracy of your mental hearing by playing the exercise after you have completed it. It will help your hearing if instead of playing both parts you play one and sing the other. (Of course you may have to transpose the exercise into a register suitable to your voice.)

3. When writing, think primarily in terms of horizontal continuity and direction. Never write one tone at a time; always plan at least three or four measures before writing. After sufficient practice you should be able to work out an entire two-part exercise mentally before writing it out. Even at the beginning stages of study it is important to keep this somewhat distant goal in mind. You must begin immediately to strengthen your capacity for the hearing and musical planning of contrapuntal relationships.

4. After writing the exercise (or a substantial part of it), *but before playing it at the piano,* check it carefully for errors. Writing the vertical intervals underneath the exercise will prove helpful. Listen for diminished fifths and (horizontally) augmented fourths. These intervals look like their perfect counterparts. Frequent occurrences of the tritone dis-

sonances indicate that the student is proceeding in a mechanical fashion without hearing what he writes.

5. If you find a mistake, make your corrections carefully. It is sometimes necessary to make extensive changes in order to remedy even one problematic measure. Occasionally one has to begin the entire exercise over again. The beginning student may be bewildered by the seemingly inexhaustible number of rules and restrictions. Especially in first species —by far the most limited of the five—it may at times seem difficult to write an exercise without violating some of these regulations. The student must assume that a perfect solution is possible and bend every effort to find that solution. This effort will be worthwhile for it will stretch his capacity for musical hearing and thinking. It is important to realize that some of the rules are absolutely binding—those concerning dissonance treatment, parallel fifths and octaves, etc. Others— those dealing with too many statements of a given tone, too much stepwise motion, etc.—express tendencies. Read the text with care in order to discriminate among these varying degrees of stringency.

6. In order to develop the capacity for planning ahead and mentally hearing a large part of the exercise, it is helpful to establish the focal points of the counterpoint at the outset. This means that you should sketch in the beginning, climax, and end before working out the details. Often it will become necessary to revise your original plan. In the course of writing it may become clear that a different placement of the high point will yield a better result or that the first tone will prove a better point of departure if it is a fifth rather than an octave above the cantus. You must not feel obliged to retain your original plan in all cases; use it flexibly as a means of giving shape and direction to your thoughts.

Example 1-45 illustrates a preliminary sketch. The counterpoint is below the cantus; we shall begin with the lower octave and aim for a high point in bar 6.

Our first solution (Example 1-46) relates correctly to the cantus firmus but forms an unsatisfactory line. The high point, isolated by leaps preceding and following, does not form an integral part of the line. In particular, the continuation of the high point presents an awkward descending sixth without a compensating upward motion following it.

Example 1-47 is better. In changing bar 7, however, we have inadvertently produced a sequential, two-note pattern (see brackets).

Example 1-48 eliminates the repeated pattern. In order to do so, we must accept a larger number of perfect consonances than were in Example 1-47. There are not so many, however, as to spoil the exercise; all things considered, Example 1-48 is the better solution.

Example 1-49 contains further illustrations of first species.

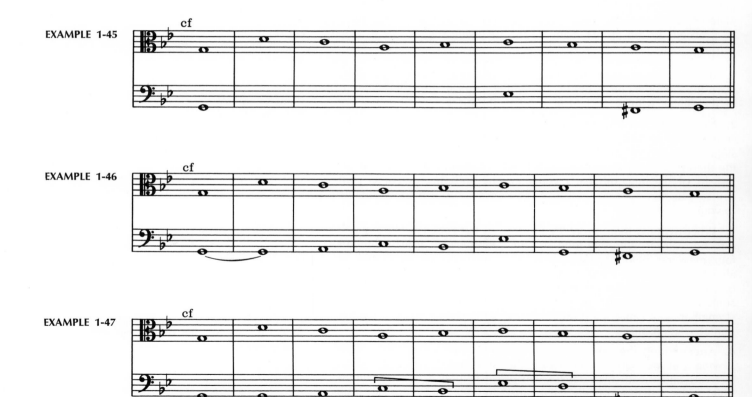

EXAMPLE 1-48

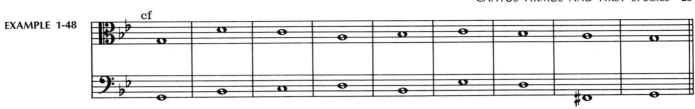

a)

EXAMPLE 1-49

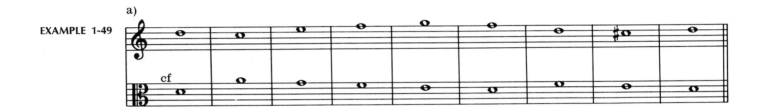

b)

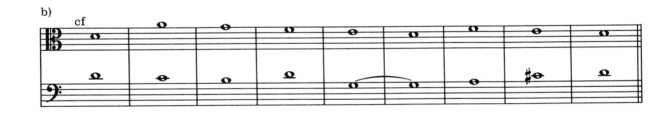

c)

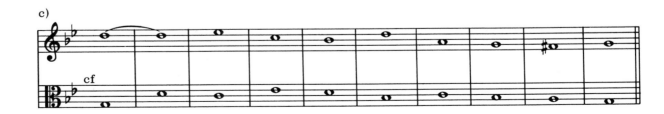

EXAMPLE 1-49 (continued)

d)

e)

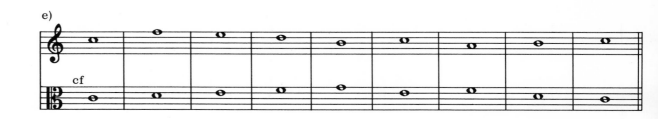

f)

g)

Roth

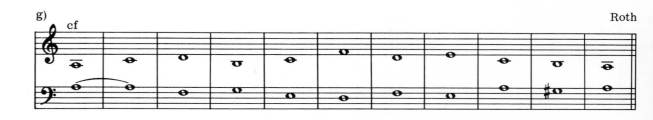

EXERCISES

1. Before proceeding to the writing of exercises in first species the student should practice Examples 1-48 and 1-49 in the following manner:

First sing the cantus and play the counterpoint at the piano. Then reverse the procedure, playing the cantus and singing the counterpoint. (Select the most favorable register for your voice.)

2. Select four cantus firmi—two major and two minor. Write two first-species lines above and below each cantus.

3. THREE-PART COUNTERPOINT, FIRST SPECIES

GENERAL OBSERVATIONS

In proceeding to the addition of two voices in first species to a cantus firmus, we begin to explore the basic procedures of three-part writing. Even within the restricted framework of first species the combination of three voices results in a musical fabric of some complexity. First of all, we now have the contrast between outer voices and middle voice. In two-part writing the upper and lower part are more or less equally prominent. In three-part writing, however, the highest and lowest voices, by virtue of their position within the texture, stand out more distinctly than the middle voice. This primacy of the outer voices by no means requires that the middle voice be reduced to a mere filler; the relationship between the outer parts, however, is usually more crucial than that between an outer part and the middle voice.

In addition, we can now combine simultaneously two types of relative motion. For example, the outer parts can move in similar or parallel fashion, while the motion of the inner voice is contrary to both (Example 1-50).

Furthermore, we have available a greater number of vertical sonorities than in two parts; these sonorities, moreover, can occur in a wide variety of spacings. The three voices can move close together, they can be spread more or less evenly, or two voices close together can contrast with a third voice removed in register from both (Example 1-51).

It is more difficult to write a good exercise in three parts than in two, because the more complex texture makes greater demands on our ability to hear and to plan. In addition, the presence of two other parts throws obstacles in the course of the unfolding of the single line; each voice must now regulate its motion with respect to a second counterpoint as well as to the cantus. It is best to assume, while writing an exercise, that a correct and musically valid solution exists, and that careful, intelligent work will reveal it. And it is important that the student hear, think, and plan ahead with the focus of attention on horizontal continuity. A mechanical filling-in of one note at a time will never develop the student's musical capacity.

In three-part counterpoint the cantus firmus can appear in any of three positions, as top voice, middle voice, or lowest voice; the following three permutations are therefore possible:

CF	1	1
1	CF	1
1	1	CF

(CF stands for cantus firmus, 1 for first species.)

HORIZONTAL AND VERTICAL DIMENSIONS

In three-part counterpoint, as in two-part writing, the horizontal dimension is primary. The propulsive energy, the shaping impulse belong to the melodic, linear flow; vertical considerations can limit and control but cannot altogether determine the course of the melodic lines. If in this section we seem to focus more upon the vertical dimension, it is only because the principles of melodic construction learned in connec-

EXAMPLE 1-50

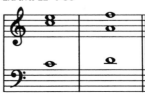

EXAMPLE 1-51

tion with cantus firmus and two-part counterpoint apply, with very little modification, to three-part writing as well. It is in the vertical dimension that the most drastic departures from two-part writing occur.

The combination of two voices gives rise to vertical intervals; when three voices sound together, chords result. In a purely contrapuntal setting the succession of chords arises from the motion of voices regulated by the laws concerning consonance and dissonance, forbidden parallels, etc. Counterpoint organizes chord successions but not on the basis of harmonic function; such organization, of course, belongs to the discipline of harmony. The presence or absence of functional relationships among the chords is irrelevant to the purpose of the species exercise. Consequently, statements like "the II chord often proceeds to the V" do not belong to the sphere of counterpoint.

In writing his exercises, therefore, the student must not concern himself with chord relationships or harmonic direction. This setting aside, this "bracketing" of the harmonic concept can awaken the student's ear to the realization that "chord" and "harmony" are not synonymous terms, and that successions of chords can result from purely contrapuntal impulses. Such contrapuntal chord progressions can occur in music of all styles—even those styles where the harmonic element is strongest. Only an awareness of their contrapuntal origin can lead to an understanding of such progressions and of the musical contexts in which they occur.

The absence of harmonic organization makes it possible to shape each voice on the basis of melodic, linear considerations. In a musical fabric conditioned by harmonic relationships the lowest voice contains more skips and has less melodic continuity than the upper parts; it is, of course, the function of the bass line in composition to clarify the harmonic organization of the musical texture. In our purely contrapuntal exercises, however, there will be no need to differentiate the lowest part in this fashion. The bass line can and should be as melodic in character as the upper parts.

By the same token, the middle voice of the exercise must constitute a logical and coherent line. We have already mentioned the relatively greater prominence of the outer parts compared with the inner voice. The middle part, however, is not so covered that it can be allowed to lose its melodic profile. The student must aim to create a balanced texture in which each voice maintains its integrity. Indeed,

the ability to hear and to shape an active middle voice represents an important aspect of musical technique. Even in the so-called melody and accompaniment texture where the top voice claims the focus of attention and the middle voice (or voices) must recede somewhat into the background, there is often more contrapuntal activity in the inner parts than is apparent at first hearing. How often do we hear Chopin Mazurkas or Schubert Impromptus performed without any awareness of their contrapuntal design?

VERTICAL CONSONANCES

As we know, first-species counterpoint employs only consonant sonorities. In two-part writing only consonant intervals occur; in three-part writing all chords must be consonant. Like consonant intervals, consonant chords possess enough inherent stability to stand on their own, to serve as goals of motion, to determine contexts in which dissonances can function. Again like the intervals, the consonant chords contain varying degrees of stability. All consonant chords have in common the fact that they are triads (complete or incomplete) or are related to triads through the changing of position ($\frac{5}{3}$ $\frac{6}{3}$).

The student can easily discover for himself the fact that among chords of three tones (excluding doubling) only triads can be consonant, for all other sonorities of three tones contain a dissonant second, seventh, or ninth. Furthermore, all chords of four or more tones (not counting octave doublings) are dissonant for the same reason. All consonant chords, therefore, are triadic; however, the converse is not true. Not all triads or triad derivatives are consonant. Let us examine the various possibilities:

EXAMPLE 1-52   **EXAMPLE 1-53**   **EXAMPLE 1-54**

The combination of perfect fifth and major third (or their compound forms, perfect twelfth and major tenth) produces a major triad (Example 1-52).

The combination of perfect fifth and minor third results in the minor triad (Example 1-53).

The combination of diminished fifth and minor third gives us the diminished triad (Example 1-54). Here the crucial fifth of the triad forms a dissonance; this triad, at least in root position, is dissonant, and may not occur in first-species writing.

Unlike the diminished triad, the augmented triad (consisting of augmented fifth and major third) does not occur in the major or natural minor modes. It might arise through the raising of the leading tone in minor; however, it contains a dissonant augmented fifth and should therefore be excluded (see Example 1-55).

If we combine a minor third and minor sixth we produce a $\frac{6}{3}$ or sixth chord. This sonority corresponds to the first inversion of a major triad; note, however, that both intervals above the bass are minor (Example 1-56). In the first chord of Example 1-56 the student will note a perfect fourth between the upper parts. This fourth always occurs when the sixth of the chord appears in the top voice. Between the upper voices of a $\frac{6}{3}$, the fourth becomes a consonant interval. The bass gives it support and clarifies beyond doubt the relationship of the fourth to the fifth. Without changing the fundamental character of the chord (i.e., the intervals between upper voices and bass), one can produce the form seen in the second chord of Example 1-56; consequently the fourth does not sound like an appoggiatura. To be sure, the sixth chord is less stable than either major or minor triads in $\frac{5}{3}$ position. As we shall see, the

$\frac{6}{3}$ cannot function as the first or last chord of an exercise where maximum consonance is required. Because it lacks complete stability without being dissonant, the sixth chord possesses a fluid, mobile character highly appropriate to the main body of the exercise.

The same fluid character belongs to the $\frac{6}{3}$ that corresponds to the first inversion of a minor triad. It is formed by combining a major third with a major sixth. Here too the perfect fourth occurs when the sixth appears in the top voice; the fourth is made consonant by the bass (see Example 1-57).

The first inversion of the diminished triad contains a minor third and major sixth. This chord contains a dissonant interval, an augmented fourth or diminished fifth (see Example 1-58). In this chord, unlike the root-position diminished triad, the dissonance is between upper parts; the lowest tone is not involved in any dissonant relationship. Consequently, the diminished $\frac{6}{3}$ is considerably more stable than the root-position chord, and is indeed only slightly less stable than the major or minor sixth chords. Often the diminished $\frac{6}{3}$ is listed among the consonant chords. Strictly speaking this is not true since it contains an unequivocally dissonant interval. However, the fact that the dissonance does not involve the lowest part and the similarity in degree of tension between this chord and the other $\frac{6}{3}$ chords allows us to employ the diminished $\frac{6}{3}$ as if it were a consonance.

The student must remember that the *only* situation in which he may use the tritone dissonance—augmented fourth or diminished fifth—is between the upper voices of a diminished $\frac{6}{3}$ chord. Any other verti-

EXAMPLE 1-55

EXAMPLE 1-56

EXAMPLE 1-57

EXAMPLE 1-58

EXAMPLE 1-59

cal tritone or any melodic tritone whatever remains incorrect. In addition, we should like to call attention to the erroneous but rather prevalent idea that any dissonance is permissible in three-part texture if it occurs between upper voices. Only in a triad or $\frac{6}{3}$ chord is this the case. In the chord of Example 1-59 there exists no dissonance with respect to the lowest voice. Nevertheless the chord is a dissonance and must be excluded. The dissonances of the second and seventh are too strong to be canceled out by the presence of a supporting tone in the lowest part; furthermore, the resulting sonority is non-triadic.

The combination of major third and minor sixth produces the $\frac{6}{3}$ position of the augmented triad. Here, too, the dissonance occurs only between the upper parts. However, the augmented triad and $\frac{6}{3}$ chord almost always result from chromatic alteration; they do not constitute sonorities basic to the diatonic system. Therefore they are not appropriate to exercises in elementary counterpoint designed to introduce the student to procedures of voice leading of the most fundamental and general character (see Example 1-60).

The combination of a sixth and fourth above a given tone results in the $\frac{6}{4}$ chord, a sonority corresponding to the second inversion of the triad. In this chord the fourth occurs between the lowest tone and one of the upper parts; since it involves the bass, the fourth is dissonant, and gives a dissonant quality to the chord as a whole. Therefore, the $\frac{6}{4}$ chord may not occur in first-species counterpoint, which restricts itself to consonant sonorities (Example 1-61).

In summary, we present Example 1-62 listing all the complete consonant chords available for first-species writing.

VERTICAL CONSONANCES: INCOMPLETE CHORDS

In a texture of three or more parts, a sonority composed of a tripled tone or two different tones plus octave or unison doublings is termed an *incomplete chord*. This term is valid only with reference to triadic music, in which the three-tone triad constitutes the vertical norm. In pre-triadic music—for example, early medieval polyphony—chords such as the $\frac{8}{5}$ or $\frac{8}{4}$ are in no sense incomplete. Since we are here concerned with the counterpoint of triadic music, we can employ the term.

Compared with the full triad, $\frac{5}{3}$ or $\frac{6}{3}$, incomplete chords give a rather thin, empty impression. Therefore it is generally preferable to make use of complete chords whenever possible. However, the complete exclusion of incomplete chords is neither necessary nor desirable. For the melodic integrity of the voice parts must remain the primary consideration; and, in order to accomplish a specific melodic purpose in one of the parts, it might well be necessary to sacrifice fullness of sound. The student must make sure that he does not employ incomplete chords without reason or excessively (no more than two such chords in immediate succession is a good rule of thumb). And he should take care to use those incomplete sonorities that are most appropriate to the place in the exercise in which they occur.

Apart from differences in doubling or in the major or minor quality of intervals, there are four incomplete sonorities: the single tone tripled, and the fifth, third, and sixth with one tone doubled. The single tone tripled is the most problematic of these combinations. The tripled tone becomes so emphasized that it tends to interrupt and check the preceding contrapuntal flow. Therefore it is suitable only at points of articulation and must *never* be used in an exercise except in the first or

EXAMPLE 1-60

EXAMPLE 1-61

EXAMPLE 1-62

etc.

the last measure. There, of course, an emphatic tonic is appropriate. Example 1-63a shows an incorrect use of this combination; 1-63*b* is correct.

The fifth with doubling contains only perfect consonances (the fourth between upper parts, as in Example 1-64, is consonant here, just as in the $\frac{6}{3}$). Consequently this sonority possesses great stability but little fullness of sound or tendency to move forward; like the tripled tone, though to a lesser degree, it tends to impede the course of a previously sounding motion. The fifth with doubling, therefore, functions best as an initial or closing chord, and should not occur in the middle of an exercise. Very occasionally, for the sake of a good voice leading, we may employ this chord outside of the first or the last measure.

The third with doubling is the most versatile of the incomplete group (see Example 1-65). With doubled tonic it can appear at the beginning or end of the exercise. Although the third lacks the key-defining power of the fifth, it is stable enough to provide a solid beginning or

end when combined with the doubled tonic. It functions smoothly in the middle of the exercise; the imperfect consonance gives both fullness of sound and a tendency to move forward.

The sixth with doubling is much less stable and cannot begin or end an exercise (Example 1-66). In the middle, however, it is perfectly admissible.

UNISONS AND DOUBLING

In three-part writing unisons are slightly less disturbing than in two parts. However, the difference is not sufficiently great to warrant their use except in the opening or the final measure. (In four-voice texture the presence of two additional tones offsets the unison sufficiently to allow its occasional use.) Example 1-67 shows possible uses of the unison at the beginning or end of the exercise; note that the unison occurs only as a doubling of the tonic.

Doubling, of course, will occur only in connection with incomplete

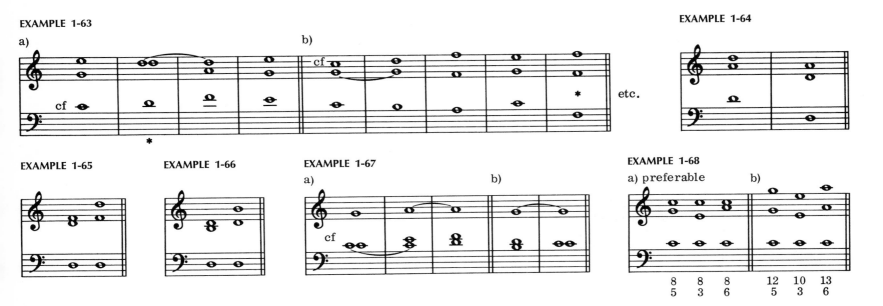

EXAMPLE 1-63

a)   b)

EXAMPLE 1-64

EXAMPLE 1-65   EXAMPLE 1-66   EXAMPLE 1-67   EXAMPLE 1-68

a)   b)   a) preferable   b)

chords. Therefore only two possibilities exist: doubling the lowest tone of the parent interval, or doubling the upper tone. The latter possibility will produce an octave between the upper parts; the reader will remember that unisons can occur only at the very beginning or end. The octave between upper parts represents rather extreme spacing and will seldom occur. As a matter of course, therefore, doubling of the lower tone of the interval makes good sense. By reinforcing the bass part we produce a better-balanced sonority than the somewhat top-heavy result of duplication between the upper voices. In chords containing a fifth and third, moreover, the lowest tone is also the more stable component of the interval. In the sixth with doubling the situation is more problematic. Here, the lower tone is no longer the most stable element; nevertheless, the importance of the bass part and considerations of spacing remain the same. Since the sixth and its derivative chords form the least stable of the consonant combinations, duplicating the less stable tone does not effect any fundamental change or throw the chord out of balance. Therefore we may double the lowest tone in the incomplete sixth chord as well as in the two other types. Example 1-68 illustrates various possible doublings; note that the recommended forms are preferences rather than ironclad rules. The less desirable doublings can be justified if they result from convincing voice leading.

Two rules of doubling, however, must be regarded as absolute. The leading tone must not be doubled under any circumstances. (This, of course, refers to the leading tone in major and the raised seventh step in minor. The seventh step of the natural minor does not function as a leading tone and may be doubled.) Also, the tonic is the tone to double in the first or last measure if an incomplete chord is employed.

SPACING; OPEN AND CLOSE POSITION

An increase in the number of voices generally produces a wider space between highest and lowest parts. Therefore the top and bottom voices in three-part texture will usually lie farther apart than the voices of two-part counterpoint but not so far apart as the soprano and bass of four-part writing. Except for the first and last measures, where unisons can occur, the fifth is the smallest interval possible between the *outer* voices. (In two-part counterpoint the third is the smallest interval be-

tween parts; in three voices the third remains the smallest distance between *adjacent* voices.)

In general, the outer voices should not lie farther apart than two octaves. Three tones are not sufficient to fill in a wider distance; the fabric of sound will become stretched and thin. Indeed, for the most part the outer voices will be considerably closer together. For the most part the distance between them will range from a minimal fifth or sixth to a twelfth or thirteenth; the tenth would constitute the average or normal space between the highest and lowest parts. Only when the top voice ascends or the bottom voice descends to a climax will wider spacing be justified.

When the outer voices lie an octave or more apart, the middle voice should generally lie closer to the top than to the bottom of the texture. Closely adjacent voices in low register tend to produce an opaque, unclear sonority. Listen to the chords of Example 1-69 with attention to clarity of sound.

As a general rule, the upper parts should lie within the compass of an octave; the lowest and middle parts can exceed this limit. On occasion the top and middle voice may move in contrary direction, the top voice up and the middle voice down. This voice leading may well produce abnormally wide spacing between the upper parts. Since voice leading takes precedence over vertical sonority, good and logical linear progression will justify temporarily poor spacing. As soon as possible, however, normal spacing should be restored (consider Example 1-70).

The student has probably encountered the terms *close* and *open position*. When the upper voices of a chord are so close together that no other tone of the chord can be inserted between them, the chord is in close position. Otherwise it is in open position. (In three-part writing close position produces a third or fourth between the upper parts, while open position produces a fifth or larger interval.) Example 1-71 illustrates close and open position.

Both open and close position should occur; mixing the two types of spacing will give variety of sound. Close position produces a more compact and intense sonority than open, particularly if the middle voice (as is often the case) lies near the top of its range. Open position creates a more evenly balanced sound and consequently can be sustained for a somewhat longer time. Open position, therefore, should predominate.

OUTER-VOICE RELATIONSHIPS

The outer voices of three-part counterpoint, except for wider spacing, should form a perfect two-part counterpoint. The need for variety of intervals in two-part texture has particular relevance to the outer voices of three-part writing. In Example 1-72 a considerable variety of chords cannot mitigate the excessive use of tenths between the outer parts.

In Example 1-73 there is a variety of intervals, but most of these are perfect consonances. As in two-part writing, the outer voices should balance perfect and imperfect intervals, with the latter predominating. Too many perfect intervals in the outer voices will impede smooth forward motion. In Example 1-73 the student will also note the excessive number of incomplete chords produced, in large measure, by the numerous octaves between outer voices.

EXAMPLE 1-69

EXAMPLE 1-70

EXAMPLE 1-71

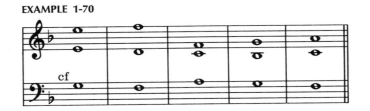

EXAMPLE 1-72

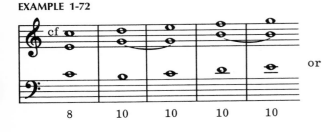

or

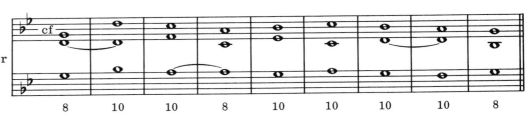

EXAMPLE 1-73

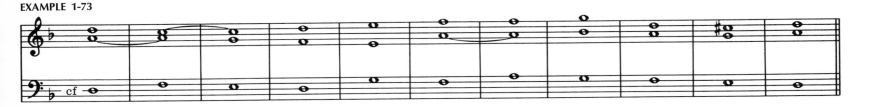

RELATIVE MOTION

In general, the rules of two-part counterpoint continue in force. Parallel (and antiparallel) fifths, octaves, and unisons remain as incorrect in three voices as in two and for the same reasons. In addition, the prohibition of more than three consecutive intervals of the same kind between any two parts must also be maintained.

However, the addition of a middle voice modifies to some degree the rule concerning the approach in similar motion to a fifth or octave. Between outer voices the rule of two-part writing continues to prevail (see page 17). Between an inner voice and one of the outer parts, however, we can approach a perfect consonance in similar motion if the following two conditions obtain:

1. The remaining outer voice must move in contrary direction to offset the similar motion (Example 1-74).
2. If the similar motion occurs between the top and middle voices, the top voice must not move by skip. A skip in the highest voice is so prominent an event that it will emphasize and underline the interval approached in similar motion (Example 1-75).

Parallel motion of all three parts will occur only in a series of $\frac{6}{3}$ chords. The sixth of the chord must lie in the top voice; otherwise, parallel fifths will result (Example 1-76).

BEGINNING THE EXERCISE

The first measure must contain the tonic in the lowest part if the key is to be defined. The upper parts may double the tonic at unison or octave; or they may contain the third or fifth above the tonic. No tone should be doubled but the tonic.

If the cantus lies in the lowest part, the first measure can contain a complete tonic chord. If the cantus lies in one of the upper voices, the opening chord will necessarily be incomplete. For it will then be necessary to double the tonic of the cantus in the lowest voice. In the first measure an incomplete sonority can be one of the following three types: tonic tripled, tonic doubled with fifth, tonic doubled with third. The top voice, incidentally, need not restrict itself to fifth and octave; the third can appear there, too. This represents a slight deviation from

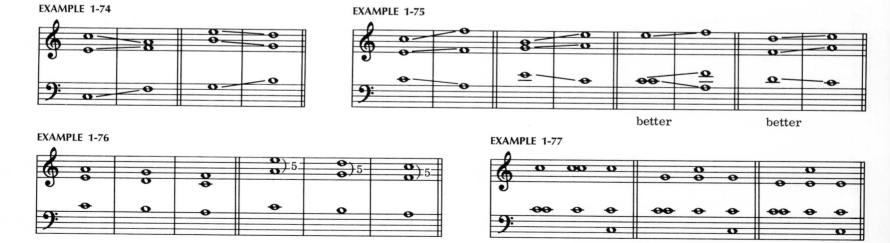

EXAMPLE 1-74

EXAMPLE 1-75

better   better

EXAMPLE 1-76

EXAMPLE 1-77

the procedures of two-part counterpoint that normally govern outer-voice relationships. See Example 1-77.

ENDING THE EXERCISE

As in two-part counterpoint, the next-to-last measure must contain the two tones adjacent to the tonic: the leading tone (raised in minor) and the second step of the scale. These two tones are involved in the most binding melodic relationships to the tonic and form an indispensable part of any strong contrapuntal cadence. Our new task will be to embody these tones in a chord that will support and intensify their melodic drive to the tonic. Such a chord must fulfill the following requirements:

1. It must be a complete sonority of three tones. Doubling might well lead to parallel octaves; in any case, the thin effect of an incomplete chord would weaken the cadence.

2. The chord must be consonant. If the vertical sonority is to support the melodic tendencies of the second and seventh steps, these tones must be integral parts of the chord. (As will be remembered, we count the diminished $\frac{6}{3}$ as consonant.) Of course, first species requires consonance in any case. However, the leading-tone chord remains consonant in the remaining species where dissonances are introduced.

Several chords meet these conditions. Example 1-78 shows the diminished $\frac{6}{3}$; this is the only possible chord for cases where the second step is in the lowest voice. Consequently this chord will generally occur when the lowest part contains the cantus.

Example 1-78 illustrates the proper continuation of the diminished $\frac{6}{3}$ into the final measure. Both the second and the seventh steps move to the tonic. The added tone has a tendency (stronger in major than in minor) to descend to the third step of the scale. If this tone occurs in the soprano it must descend, as in Example 1-78a. If it appears in the middle voice it can descend as in 1-78b. However, in this less exposed position, it can also ascend to the fifth of the scale, as in 1-78c.

If the leading tone is in the lowest part, the only possible chord is a $\frac{6}{3}$; a $\frac{5}{3}$ will contain a diminished fifth and will not fulfill the requirement of consonance. Example 1-79 demonstrates the continuation into the last measure. Again, the two tones adjacent to the tonic move to it in contrary direction. The added tone can be tied into the last measure (or repeated); this will produce a fifth with doubling. Or the tone can descend a third; this will create a third with doubling. The fifth gives more vertical stability; however, the third might be preferred for melodic reasons. The leap of a third is usually better in the middle than in the top voice. However, its use in the top voice might well be justified if it prevents the excessive repetition of the fifth degree of the scale.

If both the second and the seventh step occur in the upper parts, the only possible solution is to let them form the third and fifth of a triad. In this case the lowest voice will necessarily approach the final measure with the leap of a fourth or a fifth. From a purely contrapuntal standpoint this melodic progression is less satisfactory than the conjunct motions of Examples 1-78 and 1-79. Nevertheless, it is sometimes

EXAMPLE 1-78

a)   b)   c)

EXAMPLE 1-79

a)   b)   c)   d)

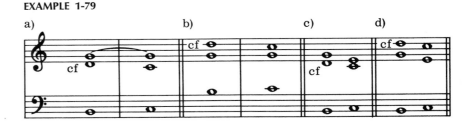

impossible to avoid this cadential form without impairing the design of one of the upper parts. The reader will have noticed that this ending corresponds to the harmonic V–I cadence. In contrapuntal exercises there is no reason to aim specifically for such a harmonic progression. On the other hand, it should not be excluded if it grows naturally out of the voice leading and represents the result of logical melodic motions. Indeed, the historical origin of this progression must have been similar. At first it arose out of the interplay of melodic lines before musicians had developed any awareness of the dominant-tonic relationship as such. Later composers used it for its own sake and directed the contrapuntal flow accordingly. Example 1-80 illustrates its use. Again, the tones adjacent to the tonic both move to that tone by step, the dominant by the leap of a fourth or fifth. The similar motion into the octave is acceptable here even between outer parts. The emphasis on the vertical sonority of the octave is appropriate here as it underlines the final tonic.

CROSS RELATION

When using the leading tone at the end of an exercise in minor the student should take care to avoid the natural seventh step in the preceding measure. A direct chromatic progression in the same voice is, of course, excluded. If the chromatic succession is distributed between two voices—if in G minor, for example, F natural in the top voice is followed by F sharp in the bass of the next measure—the result is called a *cross relation*. This voice leading can be logical and beautiful. Because, however, it implies chromaticism, it is not appropriate to species exercises.

PROCEDURES OF WORK

Some students may encounter difficulty in hearing and following three voices without the aid of a piano. And indeed this represents no easy task. In three-part counterpoint even more than in two-part it is very helpful to memorize the entire cantus before writing the exercise. This will greatly simplify the hearing problem; attention can now focus on the added voices without the distraction of continually verifying the cantus.

Proper study of the examples in this book will help develop the ability to hear three parts. These examples can serve as exercises in hearing without the help of the piano. Furthermore, the student should make similar use of his own written work. If necessary he can gradually construct a mental sound picture of three-part texture by combining the lines, two at a time at first. Let us assume, for example, that the cantus is placed in the lowest part. The student should first form a mental image of the cantus and the top voice. Then he can mentally hear the cantus and the middle voice, and finally put all three voices together. (Focusing on the two top voices without the lowest part is less useful; for one thing, fourths require the support of the bottom voice if they are to function as consonances. Trying to hear the upper parts alone, therefore, will sometimes produce a distorted picture of the counterpoint.)

Playing two voices and singing a third is also extremely useful. The student should sing each voice in turn, playing the two others at the piano. Again, if necessary, the student can begin with two parts and gradually build up the three-voice fabric. It may be necessary for the student to change the register of the exercise by one octave (or to transpose it) in order to accommodate it to his vocal range.

EXAMPLE 1-80

To write the exercise at the piano is to lose most of its benefit. The piano should be employed only to help check the exercise after it has been written and to verify the mental impression of the student. At first it might seem quicker and easier to write at the keyboard, but the foundation of contrapuntal technique lies in the development of mental hearing. To hear the exercise as a whole before committing it to paper should be the ultimate goal. To be sure few if any can accomplish this at the beginning of their studies in counterpoint. It must be the student's aim, however, to increase constantly his mental grasp, and to be able to conceive larger and larger segments of the texture as he gains experience in writing.

In writing the exercise the student should plan ahead just as in two-part work. It is advisable to begin with an approximate idea of the general contour of both added voices; planning in advance the location of the climaxes will also prove helpful. To an even greater extent than in two-part writing these preliminary plans will often undergo modification in the course of writing; their main purpose is to focus the mind and ear, not to provide an unnecessarily rigid framework.

After the initial planning, the actual writing can begin. The student must *never* proceed one measure at a time, but must always conceive and write a continuity of at least three or four measures. Ideally he should plan both added voices for the group of measures before putting them on paper. Should this prove too difficult at first, he can write down one voice for the three or four measures and then add the second. To write one voice in its entirety before dealing with the other is a poor procedure. The first voice will probably be satisfactory, but the quality of the second is likely to prove inadequate.

The easiest combination arises when the cantus lies in the lowest part. Few students find it difficult to perceive relationships above a given bass. In addition, the added voices consist of one outer and one inner part. Should the student have to write the two voices alternately, he will usually find it most convenient to deal with the top voice first and then add the middle part. When the cantus lies in the highest part, the procedure is similar. In other words, the student will attend to the lowest voice for a group of measures and then add the middle voice. This second permutation is slightly more difficult, since now the relationships must be calculated below the given voice.

By far the most difficult arrangement places the cantus in the middle. Here the student must add two outer voices. It is a virtual necessity to think of both added voices at once. However, the focus of attention should first be given to the bass, and the top voice conceived on the basis of a previously thought-out or lightly sketched-in bass. This difficult arrangement is perhaps the most beneficial of all and must not be neglected. Indeed, the student should work out all three permutations with every cantus firmus; it is a good idea, in fact, to write several exercises in each of the permutations.

The student will find it helpful to follow the summary below:

1. Memorize the cantus firmus. Sing it several times.

2. Sketch the basic contour. Fill in the first measure, the planned climaxes, and the final cadence. (Bear in mind that these preliminary plans may have to be altered or even abandoned.) Example 1-81 shows such a preliminary sketch.

3. On the basis of the plan, write the exercise. Never write less than three measures at a time, if possible in both parts. Should it be necessary to write one part at a time, sketch the outer voice before the inner; if both outer voices are to be added, sketch the bass before the soprano.

EXAMPLE 1-81

Do not write one voice as a whole before adding the second part. After sketching three or four measures of the first part, add the second voice for these measures. Check all three voices for errors before proceeding.

Let us continue the sketch as a sample exercise. The cantus is in the middle part and we must add the two outer voices.

The student will notice that the high point in the top voice and the low point in the bass are close in range to the initial and final tones. Moving in whole notes against a short cantus firmus, we cannot hope to achieve lines of much sweep or amplitude. We shall try, how-

ever, to prevent them from becoming really constricted. Example 1-82 completes the exercise on the basis of our plan.

The result is by no means completely satisfactory. Neither the top nor the lowest voice contains a leap larger than a third. The top voice suffers from a static beginning caused by the consecutive pairs of tied notes. If we substitute E for the initial G, we greatly improve the contour. The total range of the line becomes greater, and we eliminate one of the ties. (The use of E in the final measure is not recommended; it would produce two leaps of a descending third, C–A, G–E, in unnecessarily close proximity.)

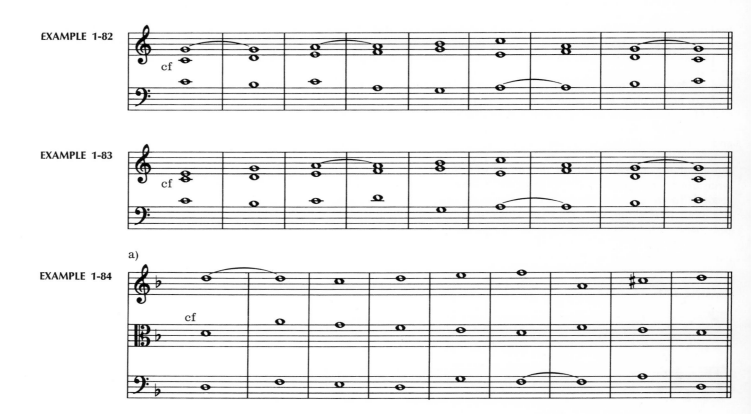

EXAMPLE 1-82

EXAMPLE 1-83

a)

EXAMPLE 1-84

We can also improve the bass by substituting D for A in bar 4. We gain a leap of a fifth, adding impetus to the coming line. We eliminate a tone repeated again in bars 6 and 7; thereby we achieve a more varied and balanced bass part. In addition the D allows a complete chord. Example 1-83 shows the revised and corrected version.

Example 1-84 will serve to illustrate first species in three parts.

b)

EXAMPLE 1-84 (continued)

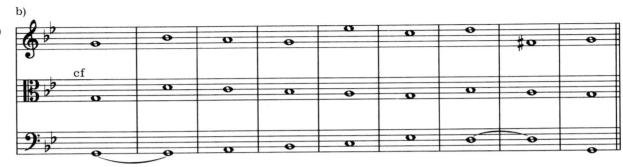

c)

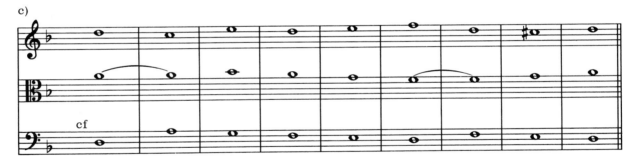

d)

Fux – Mozart

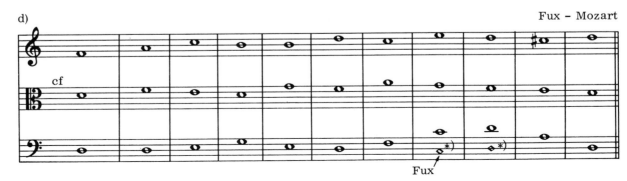

Fux

EXERCISES

1. Before proceeding to the writing of three-part exercises the student should practice Examples 1-83 and 1-84 in the following manner:

Sing one part while playing the two others at the piano. Begin by singing the lowest part, then the highest, finally the middle. (Select the most comfortable register for your voice; if transposition at sight poses a problem, write out the exercise in the new key.)

2. Select two cantus firmi, one in major, the other in minor. To each cantus write exercises in each of the three permutations.

SECOND SPECIES

1. TWO-PART COUNTERPOINT

RHYTHMIC ORGANIZATION

In second species, two half notes are set against each whole note of the cantus firmus. Despite the uniformity of note values within each voice, this species contains two elements of rhythmic differentiation: the contrast of whole and half notes between the two parts, and the consequent impression of strong and weak beats. From one measure to the next, both voices move; the ear receives two impacts. In the second half of the measure, the counterpoint moves against the sustained tone of the cantus; the ear receives only one impact. The strong beat, therefore, falls on the first half of the measure, and the weak beat on the second.

The counterpoint may begin either with two half notes or with a half rest and one half note. The latter possibility is preferred as it produces greater independence between the two voices.

The final tonic will sound inconclusive if it falls on the weak beat. Therefore, the last measure of the counterpoint will always contain a whole note. The penultimate measure will usually consist of two half notes. Quite often, however, the construction of the cantus firmus or considerations of voice leading will require the use of a whole note in the next-to-last measure. The remainder of the counterpoint will always consist of two half notes per measure.

DISSONANT PASSING TONE

First species deals only with consonant relationships; in second species, the use of dissonance is introduced. All the dissonances of tonal music arise out of three fundamental types: the dissonance created by motion (passing tone), the dissonance caused by the ornamentation of a stationary tone (neighboring note), and the dissonance produced by rhythmic displacement (suspension). In third and fourth species we shall concentrate upon the two latter types; in second, we focus our attention upon the dissonant passing tone.

Example 2-1 compares a possible first-species progression with a second-species fragment using dissonant passing tones. In both excerpts, the lower counterpoint is entirely stepwise and progresses in contrary motion to the cantus. Despite their similarities, however, the two examples produce very different impressions. In the second-species example, the contrast of note values creates a considerably greater degree of independence between the parts. In addition, the dissonant passing tones materially further the sense of directed motion. Measures 2 and 3 begin with stable intervals. The tension of the dissonant passing tones creates the expectation of continued motion to a new stable point. At the beginning of the next measure, this expectation is fulfilled.

The dissonance, then, creates a point of tension between two points of stability. Since the second half note is rhythmically less stable than the first, it constitutes the logical place for the dissonance. The passing tone, moreover, does not merely occur between the consonances; *it connects them.* The second consonant tone serves as the goal of the preceding motion; at the same time, it becomes the point of departure for the continuation of the line. To ensure the closest possible connection between the dissonance and the two consonances, the passing tone must be approached and continued by step.

In Western music (until about the turn of the twentieth century) the dissonance serves as a dependent element in a context ultimately determined by consonant tones. In second species, the dissonance functions as a passing tone—as a stepwise connection between two consonant tones a third apart. Since directed motion is a fundamental characteristic of Western music, the passing tone—created by motion—is a basic type of dissonance.

CONSONANCE IN SECOND SPECIES

The dissonant passing tone occurs only on the second beat; it follows as a logical consequence that the first beat of every measure will be consonant. Often it is impossible (for reasons of voice leading) or undesirable (for reasons of melodic design) to employ the dissonant passing tone. In these cases, the second half of the measure will also be consonant.

Unlike dissonant tones, consonances may be approached by leap as well as by step. Example 2-2 shows the available consonant tones above and below middle C. Note that the only adjacent consonances sharing a common tone are the fifth and sixth. Within the measure, therefore, a stepwise motion from one consonance to another is possi-

EXAMPLE 2-1

EXAMPLE 2-2

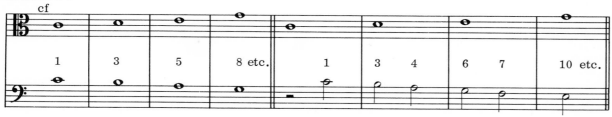

EXAMPLE 2-3

ble only when the intervals are the fifth and sixth. From one measure to the next, all the interval progressions of first species remain available. (See Example 2-3.) For variety, no more than three consecutive measures should start with the same interval; this also applies to later species.

PERFECT INTERVALS

In first species, unisons occur only at the beginning and end of an exercise. In a note-against-note texture, the sudden appearance of a unison can sound like an ending or can create the impression that one voice has suddenly and arbitrarily dropped out. In a texture of two notes against one, these effects will not occur if the unison falls on the second half note and is left by stepwise motion in the opposite direction to that by which it was approached. (See Example 2-4.)

Unisons on the first half note will produce the same result as in first species. Except for the beginning and end of the exercise, they must be excluded.

The division of the measure into strong and weak beats adds certain considerations to the problem of parallel fifths, octaves, and unisons already discussed in the chapter on first species. Let us examine three possibilities: perfect intervals on directly adjacent beats, on consecutive first beats, and on consecutive second beats.

Example 2-5 demonstrates parallel fifths and octaves on directly adjacent beats. These are exactly analogous to the forbidden fifths and octaves of first species and must be excluded.

Example 2-6 shows fifths and octaves on successive first beats. Since only a single tone separates the two perfect intervals (and that tone falls on the weak beat), the impression of parallel motion is still present. As a rule, these progressions—sometimes called accented fifths and octaves—should be avoided. Occasionally, however, their use is justified (Example 2-7).

In Example 2-7a, the immediate approach to the second fifth is by

EXAMPLE 2-4

3   1   3   4   5 etc.   8   1   3   4   5 etc.

EXAMPLE 2-5

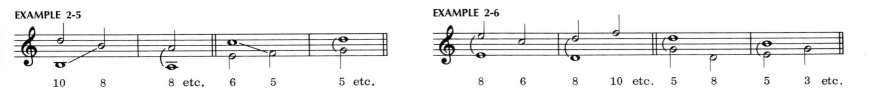

10   8   8 etc.   6   5   5 etc.

EXAMPLE 2-6

8   6   8   10 etc.   5   8   5   3 etc.

EXAMPLE 2-7

a)

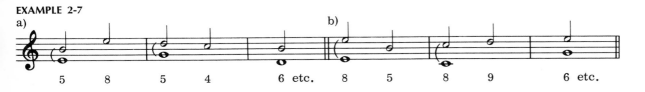

5   8   5   4   6 etc.   8   5   8   9   6 etc.

b)

contrary motion. The second fifth is introduced and continued by a stepwise progression all in the same direction. The second of the two fifths is so little emphasized that the impression of parallel fifths is weakened. The accented octaves of Example 2-7b occur in precisely the same manner. However, the nature of the octave makes this progression more difficult to use convincingly than one consisting of fifths. The student should employ accented octaves only in an exercise containing few other instances of this interval on strong beats. Their use should produce broader linear benefits not attainable by other means.

Example 2-8 presents perfect intervals on successive second beats. Since the function of the second half note is to connect the two adjacent first beats, no strong relationship exists between consecutive second beats. These afterbeat octaves and fifths may be used freely so long as they do not form sequences.

Example 2-9 shows several situations in which the octave is approached in contrary motion. In the last progression (2-9e), a combination of factors makes the octave considerably more obtrusive than in the four preceding instances. The octave is emphasized by the leap in the upper, more exposed voice, by the contrast between the disjunct soprano and the stepwise lower part, and by the rhythmic progression from a weak to a strong beat. Such an octave is called an *ottava battuta* (beaten octave) and should be avoided.

A similar treatment of the fifth (*quinta battuta*) is forbidden by some theorists. However the fifth is a less sensitive interval than the octave, and the occasional use of this voice leading might be justified by melodic considerations.

The approach to the octave and fifth in similar motion presents no new problems in this species.

MELODIC ORGANIZATION

For the most part, the principles of melodic organization studied in the chapters on cantus firmus and first species prevail in second species as well.

Whether or not the exercise begins with a rest, the initial tone remains an octave or fifth from the cantus in the upper counterpoint, a unison or octave in the lower.

Second species provides many more possibilities for melodic progression than does first species. Consequently, the expedient of repeating or tying a tone is no longer necessary.

As in first species, the tone immediately preceding the final tonic will be the leading tone. If the penultimate measure contains a whole note, that note will be the leading tone; if it contains two half notes,

EXAMPLE 2-8

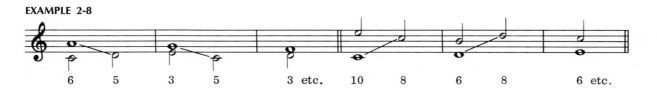

EXAMPLE 2-9

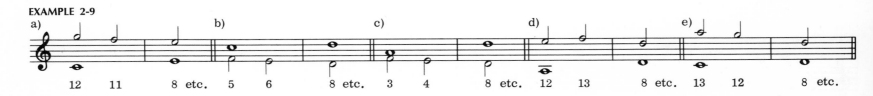

the leading tone will fall on the second of these half notes. The minor mode requires the raising of the seventh step if the final tonic is to sound conclusive. If the leading tone follows the submediant, that tone must also be raised (see Example 2-10).

The greater number of tones in the exercise, compared with first species, makes it now even more desirable to plan at least one subsidiary high point before or after the main climax. Just as in first species, however, the climax itself should not be repeated.

VARIOUS FUNCTIONS OF THE SECOND HALF NOTE

Writing exercises in second species gives us the opportunity to learn many important and basic types of melodic progression, and to begin to understand how a detail of motion can function within a larger context. We can best sharpen this understanding by becoming consciously aware of the various ways in which the second half note of the measure can carry the line forward from one downbeat to the next. These possibilities of motion represent, in miniature, prototypes of important techniques of composition.

We have already discussed the most typical role of the second half note, the dissonant passing tone. The passing tone can also appear in consonant form when the adjacent consonances, the sixth and the fifth, appear consecutively (see Example 2-3). Of course it is not always possible to employ passing tones. Even where it is possible, it is not always desirable to do so, for too much unrelieved stepwise motion can result in a line lacking in variety and differentiation. Let us, therefore, examine some other possibilities.

Sometimes a melodic fourth between first beats is connected by a single intermediary tone. Such a motion cannot, of course, be completely stepwise; it must contain the leap of a third. Although the third does not provide the absolute continuity of stepwise progression, it is so small a leap that the impression of a manipulated passing motion is produced. Example 2-11 shows how the motion of a third stands for a stepwise progression using smaller note values. (This stepwise progression will become a possibility when we employ mixed note values in fifth species.) In Example 2-11a the leap occurs between the first and second beats; in Example 2-11b it occurs after the second beat. As a general rule the first possibility is better. A leap "across the bar line," that is, from weak to strong beat, carries with it the danger of leaving the weak beat without continuation, dangling in mid-air, as it were. However, a small leap such as a third can occur without ill effect if it is followed by a change of direction, preferably stepwise. This technique of the *skipped passing tone* occurs frequently in composition, where

EXAMPLE 2-10

EXAMPLE 2-11
a)   b)

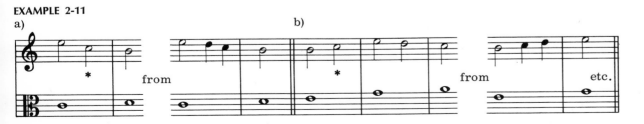

the intermediary tone may be dissonant or consonant. In our counterpoint exercises, of course, the tone on the weak beat must be consonant if, as here, it is approached or followed by a leap.

For reasons of variety and balance (e.g., to provide relief from excessive stepwise motion) it is sometimes advisable to span a melodic interval larger than a fourth on consecutive downbeats. These larger intervals can be subdivided into two small leaps as in Example 2-12. In these progressions, the *subdividing tone* effects a smoother, more gradual change of register than is possible with a single large leap. The subdivided interval must not be dissonant, or larger than an octave. And the goal tone should be followed by contrary motion, stepwise if possible. Otherwise, a series of aimless, arbitrary leaps will result.

A large leap from first to second beat produces a change of register within the measure. Such leaps should be used sparingly; too many will produce a broken, discontinuous line. In its proper place, however, a change of register can add variety and profile to the line. We know from Chapter 1 that a large leap should change the immediately preceding direction; that is, a descending line will be followed by an ascending leap and vice versa. Avoid too many consecutive leaps, even with changes of direction. A change of register functions most effectively when it is followed by—and thus appears to motivate—a continuous line of several tones in stepwise contrary motion. A change of register can be produced by the intervals of the fifth, sixth, and octave. Of course, the larger the interval, the greater is the registral contrast. However, the largest of these intervals—the octave—contains a strong element of continuity, for the two pitches are heard as registral variants of the same tone. In this case we can speak of a *transfer of register,* for a single tone appears to move from one register to another. This technique of transfer of register assumes great importance in the prolonged counterpoint of composition. See Example 2-13.

We have seen that leaps of a third often represent a passing motion with one tone omitted; the larger leaps of the fifth, sixth, and octave, on the other hand, effect a change of register and therefore do not stand for an abbreviated stepwise progression. What about the leap of a fourth? When followed by stepwise motion in the same direction, the fourth also summarizes a stepwise passing motion. When the fourth is used as in Example 2-14, it should change the previous direction; if it appears within a motion all in one direction, the fourth will cause an arbitrary and unmotivated gap in the line (Example 2-15).

Another typical use of the fourth brings us to an important new technique. For reasons of variety (e.g., to avoid the excessive repetition of a given tone) a leap of a fourth can *substitute* for direct stepwise progression. Substitution, like the other functions of the second half note, becomes an important compositional technique with a variety of applications. Example 2-16 shows how the leap of a fourth can bypass —but still relate to—underlying stepwise progression.

In addition to providing melodic variety, the device of substitution can fulfill another function. In Example 2-17 we see that the skip of a fourth prevents the parallel fifths that would arise if direct stepwise progression were employed. Substitution, therefore, can improve voice leading.

Stepwise motion, instead of occurring from one half note to the next, may be retarded so that the rate of movement will be a full measure rather than half a measure. In these cases, the function of the second half note will be to help delay the melodic progression in a logical manner. Example 2-18 shows two possibilities, both involving

EXAMPLE 2-12

a)   b)

EXAMPLE 2-13

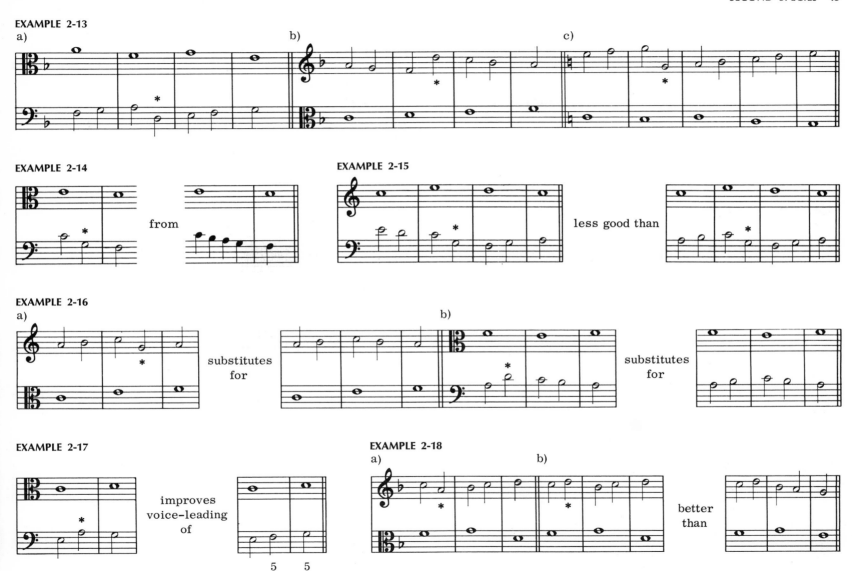

EXAMPLE 2-19

a)   b)

leaps of a third. The first, in which the leap occurs after the strong beat, will prove to be the most generally useful. In the second, the leap occurs across the bar line. Here, the melody should preferably continue in a direction contrary to that of the leap. In general, leaps from weak to strong beats should effect a change of melodic direction.

Melodic progression is retarded to a still greater degree when we employ the consonant neighboring note. (The reader will remember, of course, that the *dissonant* neighbor is reserved for third species and

EXAMPLE 2-20

a) Dissonant passing tone   b) Consonant passing tone   c) Skipped passing tone

d) Interval subdivision   e) Change of register   f) Substitution (to achieve melodic variety)

g) Substitution (to improve voice leading)   h) Delay of melodic progression   i) Consonant neighbor

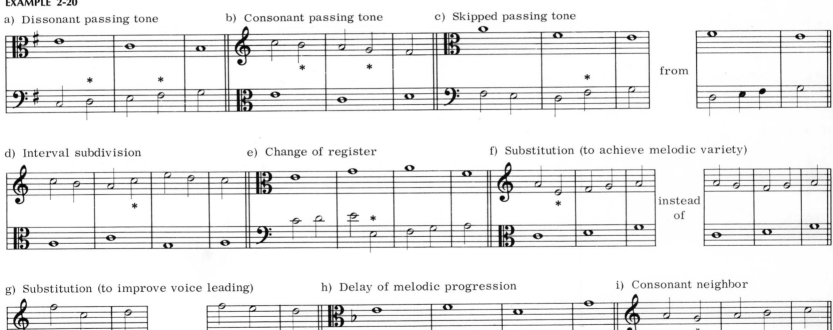

does not occur in second.) The use of the consonant neighbor is not in itself incorrect. However, if used too often, it carries with it the danger of producing a static line. Neighboring and embellishing progressions are more appropriate to the quicker-moving quarter notes of third species; the general nature of second species is direct motion from one point to another. Like the consonant passing tone, the consonant neighbor makes use of the adjacent consonances, the fifth and sixth (Example 2-19). Use the consonant neighbor to achieve melodic variety and to forestall the impression of an overly active, restless melodic line. Beware of monotonous repetitions like those of Example 2-19*b*.

Example 2-20 presents in summary the various functions fulfilled by the second half note of the measure. In evaluating his work, the student will find it helpful to analyze his exercises in terms of this list of functions. We stress that these examples are intended to help the student understand specific details of melodic progression. They are not to be employed as formulas out of which the student can artificially assemble a melodic line.

PROCEDURES OF WORK

Let us now work out an exercise in second species, starting with a preliminary sketch (Example 2-21). Second species is more flexible than first; it offers many more alternative possibilities. In sketching the leading-tone measure, therefore, we have provided for two solutions: two half notes or a whole note. Only later will we be able to choose between them.

Example 2-22 fills in the rise to the melodic peak. Notice the accented fifths on the first beats of the second and third measures. Because of the stepwise, non-sequential continuation of the second fifth, these are admissible.

Example 2-23 completes the exercise. Two weaknesses call for correction. From measure 3 to measure 8, we have only stepwise motion; the line lacks variety. The brackets in bars 7-10 point up a repeated pattern of three tones. The foreshadowing of the cadence in bars 7 and 8 makes the ending redundant.

EXAMPLE 2-21

EXAMPLE 2-22

Both of these faults are eliminated in Example 2-24a, which presents a satisfactory line. In measure 5, we substitute A for C; through the substitution, we gain a leap and a change of melodic direction. The end requires more extensive adjustment. By stating F at the beginning of bar 8, we can move to a whole-note leading tone in bar 9, thereby eliminating the repetition. This change requires a modification of bar 7. We can no longer use a dissonance; we must find a consonant tone that will retard the melodic progress by allowing a stepwise descent from the first beat of bar 7 to the first beat of bar 8 (tone of melodic delay). We have chosen C as the best of the various alternatives (see Examples 2-24b, c, and d).

In the course of working out Example 2-24, we hit upon yet another solution. If we alter our original plan, we can carry the line up to a high point on F in bar 6 (Example 2-25). This version is interesting. In second species, it is seldom advisable to move by step up or down an entire octave. In Example 2-25, however, the octave ascent is by no means bad. Its first few tones compensate for the downward leap of measure 2. And the downward leap of an octave in measure 6 balances the stepwise ascent. Notice that we have used B flat rather than C as the second tone in bar 7. So soon after the octave leap of bar 6, it is best to use as small an interval as possible. Stepwise motion would produce melodic redundancy even worse than that of Example 2-23. The leap of a third is the best solution here. Example 2-26 contains additional illustrations.

EXAMPLE 2-23

cf

EXAMPLE 2-24

a)

cf

b)   c)   d)

+4

EXAMPLE 2-25

EXAMPLE 2-26

a)

b)

c)

EXAMPLE 2-26 (continued)

d)

e)

Fux

f)

Schenker

g)

Mozart

EXERCISES

1. Before proceeding to the writing of exercises in second species, the student should practice the preceding examples in the following manner:

First sing the cantus and play the counterpoint at the piano. Then reverse the procedure, playing the cantus and singing the counterpoint. (Select the most favorable register for your voice.)

2. Select four cantus firmi—two major and two minor. Write two second-species lines above and below each cantus.

2. THREE-PART COUNTERPOINT

GENERAL CONSIDERATIONS; BEGINNING OF EXERCISE

The addition of a third part in whole notes adds few problems for the student already familiar with second species in two voices and with the basic principles of three-part writing. However several important considerations must be discussed.

The combination of a cantus firmus, a first-species part, and a second-species part can result in the following six permutations:

CF	CF	1	2	1	2
2	1	CF	CF	2	1
1	2	2	1	CF	CF

(CF stands for cantus firmus, 1 and 2 for first and second species respectively.)

Should the second-species part begin with a rest, the first half of the initial measure will contain only two voices. In this case (as in two-part counterpoint), the intervals of the octave, unison, and upper fifth provide the most stable beginning. If it helps to achieve good voice leading, the use of the upper third or tenth is also acceptable. (See Example 2-27.)

The lower sixth, however, lacks sufficient stability to serve as the initial interval. The lower fourth is a dissonance; it must, of course, be excluded (Example 2-28).

CADENCES

The leading tone can occur in the following three positions:

1. as the second half note in the next-to-last measure of the second-species part

2. as a whole note in the next-to-last measure of the second species part

3. as a whole note in the next-to-last measure of the first-species part

In all cases, the leading tone must form part of a complete and consonant chord. This automatically excludes the use of the cadential lead-

EXAMPLE 2-27

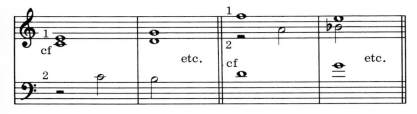

EXAMPLE 2-28

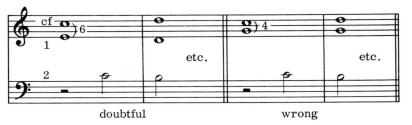

doubtful   wrong

EXAMPLE 2-29

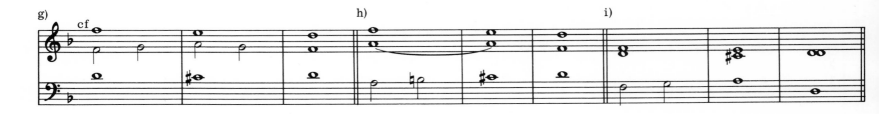

EXAMPLE 2-30

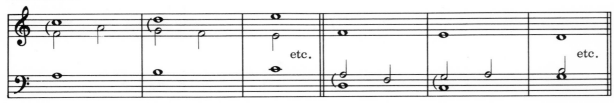

ing tone as a dissonant passing tone in the second-species line. Example 2-29 demonstrates some of the possibilities:

PERFECT INTERVALS

When the second-species part lies in the middle voice, accented fifths and octaves between that voice and one of the outer parts are more tolerable than in two-part writing. (It will be remembered that accented fifths and octaves are those that occur between successive first beats.) See Example 2-30.

IMPERFECT CONSONANCES

In the interest of variety, the student must take care to avoid an abundance of parallel thirds, sixths, or tenths between the cantus and the first-species line. As in two-part counterpoint, no more than three such intervals should occur in succession.

EXAMPLE 2-31

a)

b)

EXAMPLE 2-31 (continued)

c)

d)

Schenker

e)

FUNCTION OF THE SECOND HALF NOTE

If the first half of the measure contains an incomplete chord, the second half note of the second-species part can complete the chord. By this procedure, the somewhat thin effect of the incomplete chord is mitigated. In addition, however, the second half note must always perform a clear and logical melodic function.

The melodic activity of the second half note in three-part counterpoint naturally results in chords rather than in intervals as in two-part writing. These chords demonstrate contrapuntal functions equivalent to those found in the intervals of two-part counterpoint. The student will easily discover for himself the various passing chords, chords improving voice leading, etc. occurring in Example 2-31.

EXERCISES

1. Before proceeding to the writing of three-part second-species exercises, the student should practice the above examples in the following manner:

> Sing one part while playing the two others at the piano. Begin by singing the lowest part, then the highest, finally the middle. (Select the most comfortable register for your voice.)

2. Select two cantus firmi, one in major, the other in minor. To each cantus, write exercises in each of the six permutations.

3

THIRD SPECIES

1. TWO-PART COUNTERPOINT

RHYTHMIC ORGANIZATION

In third species, we employ a rhythmic texture of four notes against one; the species part sets four quarter notes against each whole note of the cantus firmus. In this species, the rhythmic contrast between the cantus and the counterpoint is far more marked than in second species.

The student should conceive the quarter notes of third species at a rate of speed twice as fast as the half notes of second species. In other words, the cantus firmus moves at more or less the same speed in both species. Too slow a tempo is unsuitable to the ornamental melodic motions characteristic of third species.

The presence of four quarter notes creates two levels of rhythmic differentiation in the species voice. The first quarter is the strong beat of the measure; the second and fourth quarters are weak. The third quarter holds an intermediate position; it is less strong than the first quarter but stronger than the others. We shall call the third quarter relatively strong or relatively accented.

As in second species, the final tone of the counterpoint will be a whole note. The next-to-last measure will consist of four quarter notes. The counterpoint may begin with four quarter notes or a quarter rest and three quarter notes. As in second species, beginning with the rest is preferable.

DISSONANCE IN THIRD SPECIES: GENERAL CONSIDERATIONS

As in second species, the first tone of each measure must be consonant with the cantus. The remaining tones may be dissonant. Unlike second species, which restricts itself to a single type of dissonance, third species allows us to combine several types. We retain the passing tone; however, we may now use the neighboring note or auxiliary as well. The relatively quick rate of speed makes possible the use of ornamental idioms such as the upper-lower or double neighbor and the nota cambiata. We shall discuss each type of dissonance separately.

DISSONANT PASSING TONE IN THIRD SPECIES

When it appears on the fourth quarter, the passing tone differs only in duration from the dissonance of second species (Example 3-1).

When the passing tone occurs on the second quarter, the consonance to which it moves contains the same tone in the cantus rather than a new one. The fact that the cantus tone does not change creates a number of new and important interval progressions (see Example 3-2).

The passing tone can also occur on the relatively accented third quarter. This configuration presents us with species counterpoint's closest approximation to the accented passing tone of prolonged counterpoint. Since the cantus does not move to a new tone against the passing tone, the third-quarter dissonance is much less strong than would be a dissonance on the first quarter. The latter—a true accented passing tone—cannot be incorporated into the species exercises as it would receive undue prominence. Example 3-3 shows various pos-

sibilities for the use of the passing tone on the third quarter.

Almost always, the dissonant passing tone occurs between two consonances. The diatonic system, however, necessarily requires one diminished fifth in every key. In C major, for example, all fifths are perfect with the exception of B–F, which is diminished. Situations occasionally arise in which the diminished fifth must precede or follow the perfect fourth; here, of course, there is a second dissonance rather than a consonance following the dissonant tone. In Example 3-4, the dis-

EXAMPLE 3-1

EXAMPLE 3-2

etc.

EXAMPLE 3-3

EXAMPLE 3-4

sonances both represent passing tones; the two passing tones fill the space of a fourth. The function of the dissonant tones is quite clear; hence we can employ this somewhat extended form of the passing dissonance.

DISSONANT NEIGHBORING NOTE

Third species adds to the passing tone the second fundamental type of dissonance—the neighboring note. This new type of dissonance arises out of a melodic impulse very different from that which produces the passing tone. The passing tone forms a stepwise connection between two *different* tones; the neighboring note represents the stepwise decoration of a *single* tone. Example 3-5 provides comparative illustrations of both types of dissonance.

Like the passing tone, the neighbor occurs in compositions of the most divergent styles. Both types of dissonance can occur in expanded form as well as in the elementary progressions of the species exercises, as will be discussed in Chapter 6. Our experience with second species has shown us that it is possible to construct musical lines (albeit very

simple ones) using only the passing dissonance. It would be impossible to construct equally good lines using the neighboring note alone. Such lines would lack continuity and direction; without stepwise connection between different tones, the melodies would become discontinuous series of static points and leaps.

The student must not infer that the neighboring note lacks genuine importance. In third species as well as in composition it performs an essential function: it delays or retards ultimate melodic progression without halting local melodic activity. In Example 3-6, use of the neighboring dissonance allows us to traverse the melodic space of a third rather than the fifth necessitated by use of passing dissonances only.

A neighbor on the second quarter returns not merely to the same tone but also to the same vertical interval as that presented on the first quarter. Example 3-7 presents some typical progressions.

When it occurs on the fourth quarter, the neighbor returns to the same melodic tone but to a different vertical interval (Example 3-8).

On the third quarter, the neighboring note creates the same interval progressions as on the second; the rhythmic context, however, is very different. Here, the neighbor appears on a stronger pulse than the two statements of the fundamental tone it decorates. The relatively

EXAMPLE 3-5

EXAMPLE 3-6

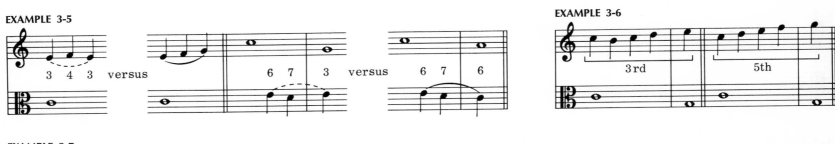

EXAMPLE 3-7

accented neighbor must be used sparingly. The passing tone—a dissonance that moves the line forward—occurs more appropriately in relatively accented positions than the essentially decorative neighboring note. For the sake of variety, however, we may occasionally employ the dissonant neighbor on the third quarter (see Example 3-9).

CONSONANT NEIGHBORING NOTE

Alternation of the two adjacent consonances—the fifth and sixth—can produce consonant neighboring notes as well as consonant passing tones. The consonant neighbor, because of its vertical stability with respect to the cantus, can occur freely on any of the three last quarters of the measure (Example 3-10).

EMBELLISHING TONE

We use the term *embellishing tone* to indicate the non-stepwise decoration of a single tone. This melodic function, therefore, represents a kind of disjunct analog to the stepwise neighboring tone. Because it is preceded or followed by a leap, the embellishing tone in species counterpoint must be consonant. Too large a leap will isolate the decorative tone from the main body of the line. The third is best; in any case, the interval of the fourth should not be exceeded; in progressions *d* and *e*, Example 3-11, the embellishing tone is followed by stepwise motion to the main tone.

COMBINATION OF UPPER AND LOWER NEIGHBORS (DOUBLE NEIGHBOR)

The fundamental purpose of the species approach is to acquaint the student with basic voice-leading techniques—techniques that occur in expanded form in compositions of a variety of styles. For the most part, the species exercises do not themselves include the expansions or prolongations of basic contrapuntal principles. To a limited degree, however, it is possible to introduce certain aspects of prolonged counterpoint within the context of species writing. Let us consider the progression in Example 3-12.

EXAMPLE 3-8

EXAMPLE 3-9

EXAMPLE 3-10

Here, the second and third beats both present dissonances; the interval of a third separates the two dissonances. We seem to violate a fundamental principle of counterpoint: stepwise introduction and continuation of dissonance. Actually, the violation is more apparent than real. Both dissonances are neighboring notes of the first tone of the measure; the melodic line moves from one neighbor to the other before returning to the main tone. The ear easily grasps the relation of both neighboring dissonances to the consonant tone they decorate. Because that tone frames the two neighbors, the impression of a leap out of and into a dissonance does not arise. In other words, stepwise connection occurs but not between immediately consecutive tones. Example 3-13 explains the voice leading of this important melodic progression.

The combination of upper and lower neighbors represents an ornamental idiom found in compositions from the Middle Ages on. Examples 3-14 to 3-16 show its direct use in works from the fourteenth, sixteenth, and nineteenth centuries.[1]

The combination of upper and lower neighbors can occur with either the upper or the lower neighbor as the first dissonance (Example 3-17).

As a rule, the idiom sounds smoothest if the upper neighbor precedes the lower. In this configuration, the higher, more obtrusive tone comes on the weaker beat.

It is best if one of the neighbors is a half step (minor second) from the main tone. If both lie a whole step from the main tone, the melodic connection may become somewhat weakened (Example 3-18).

The idiom carries with it a danger of becoming a static area, detached from the line as a whole. That danger is minimized if we follow the last tone by a stepwise progression continuing the preceding

---

[1] Because it was avoided in a segment of the sixteenth-century repertory (most notably in Palestrina's music), the double neighbor has been excluded from most textbooks in "sixteenth-century counterpoint." This exclusion begins with Fux who, however, bases his treatise on Palestrina's music alone and thus does not characterize it as representing the output of an entire century. As Example 3-15 shows (and this is but one of many possible illustrations), the idiom was known to and used by sixteenth-century composers. It is interesting to note that Mozart, who followed Fux rather closely in his counterpoint teaching, departs from him in introducing the double neighbor in third species. See Mozart *Attwood Papers*, pp. 53 and 56.

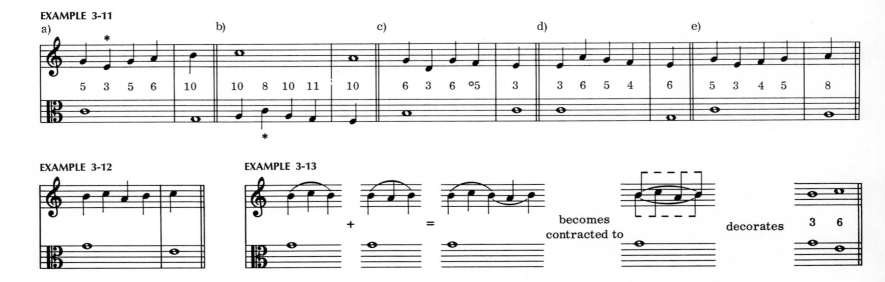

EXAMPLE 3-11

a) b) c) d) e)

| 5 | 3 | 5 | 6 | 10 | | 10 | 8 | 10 | 11 | 10 | | 6 | 3 | 6 | °5 | 3 | | 3 | 6 | 5 | 4 | 6 | | 5 | 3 | 4 | 5 | 8 |

EXAMPLE 3-12   **EXAMPLE 3-13**

+ = becomes contracted to decorates 3 6

EXAMPLE 3-14   Landini, Per servar umiltà

EXAMPLE 3-15   Tallis, Heare the voyce and prayer

EXAMPLE 3-16   Chopin, Etude, Op. 10, No. 4

EXAMPLE 3-17

EXAMPLE 3-18

melodic direction. Example 3-19 compares the proper continuation (*a* and *b*) with illustrations of disjunct motion (*c*) and change of melodic direction (*d*).

Our last progression (*d*) points up an important and interesting fact. The first, third, and fifth tones form a stepwise motion filling in a descending third. This melodic pattern is very prominent, so much so that the ear tends to register it as the basic motion impulse of the progression. Consequently, we hear a descending stepwise motion embellished by échappées (or incomplete neighboring notes) rather than a stationary tone prolonged by upper and lower neighbors. This represents a simple illustration of the importance of context in determining musical meaning. The same four tones acquire a new meaning when their continuation is altered (Example 3-20).

This idiom must begin on the first beat of the measure. Otherwise, it will cease to sound like the decoration of a single tone. It is not necessary that both the second and third quarters contain dissonances. Often, one of these tones is consonant with the cantus firmus (see Example 3-21).

THE NOTA CAMBIATA

Like the combination of upper and lower neighbors, the *nota cambiata* (exchanged note) is a compositional idiom that has found its way into the species exercises. This figure has formed a traditional part of third species since the time of Fux's *Gradus,* in which it received its first theoretical description. The nota cambiata does not occur in as wide a variety of literature as does the upper-lower neighbor idiom. It is, however, a favorite progression of the masters of the fifteenth and sixteenth centuries, and it has been used as an archaism by later composers as well.

Example 3-22 demonstrates (*a*) and explains (*b*) the nota cambiata. The idiom arises from the decoration of a two-note figure formed by the first and last tones, in this case D and C. The decoration is composed of two interlocking motions, D–C–B and A–B–C; the two motions converge upon the fifth and final tone of the idiom.

In the above example the second tone is dissonant. The stepwise continuation of this dissonance is not eliminated by the leap following;

EXAMPLE 3-19

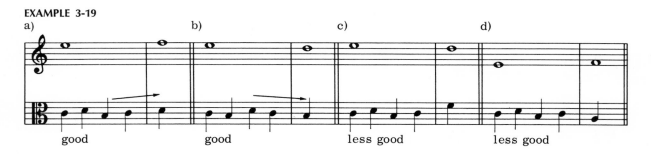

good   good   less good   less good

EXAMPLE 3-20

EXAMPLE 3-21

it is postponed until the fourth quarter. The third tone of this figure must be consonant since it forms the beginning of the second, subsidiary melodic progression. The fifth tone, the goal of the two motions, will naturally be consonant. The leap following the dissonance must be a third.

Some books based on sixteenth-century practice allow the nota cambiata only in the downward direction shown in Example 3-22. Ascending motion, however, in no way alters the fundamental meaning of the progression. The upward direction of Example 3-23, therefore, can be used.

The cambiata idiom must begin on an accented beat. In general, the first quarter of the measure forms a better beginning than does the third. When the progression begins on the third quarter, the tone following the leap occurs on the first beat of the next measure. The consequent emphasis on this tone makes it sound like a goal rather than an interpolation. The ear therefore tends to register the first three tones as representing a stepwise motion within a fourth with one passing tone omitted (see Example 3-24).

We now cite three excerpts from Renaissance polyphony, Examples 3-25 to 3-27, illustrating the difference between the nota cambiata and

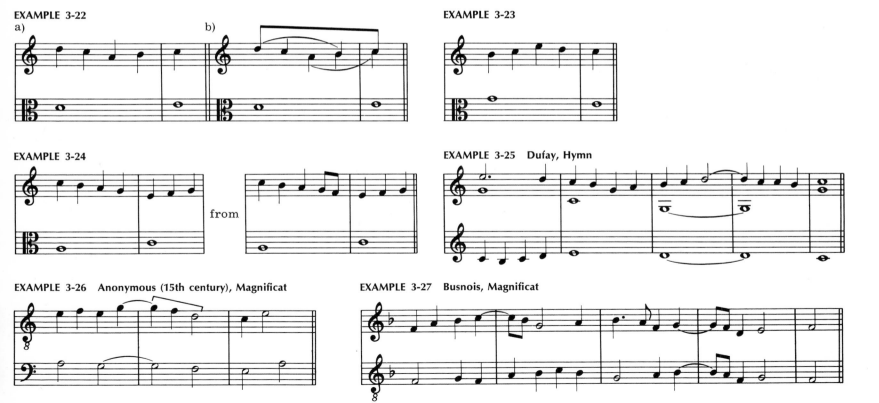

EXAMPLE 3-22

EXAMPLE 3-23

EXAMPLE 3-24

EXAMPLE 3-25 Dufay, Hymn

EXAMPLE 3-26 Anonymous (15th century), Magnificat

EXAMPLE 3-27 Busnois, Magnificat

the outwardly similar idiom of the skipped passing tone. The first, by Dufay, contains a nota cambiata. The second, from an anonymous *Magnificat* of the fifteenth century, shows the skipped passing tone; the tone following the leap does not initiate a subsidiary melodic progression. The third, from a *Magnificat* by Antoine Busnois, contains both figures. Note the differentiated rhythmic profile; in composition, the nota cambiata is not restricted to even values. The use of imitation produces a striking dissonance in the fourth quarter of the second measure. At the end of the example the lower voice accompanies the upper at the interval of the sixth. Only the final tone shifts to the lower octave in order to produce a stable cadence. Because it parallels the cambiata figure of the upper part, we read the lower voice as a modified nota cambiata. Such progressions, intermediate between the cambiata and the skipped passing-tone figure, are by no means uncommon.

THE UNISON

As in second species, the unison should not appear at the beginning of the measure except at the very beginning or end of the exercise. The

unison, however, can occur on the second, third, or fourth quarter. When it arises on the second or third quarter, it will be continued as well as approached in oblique motion. This represents a detail of voice leading not possible in second species (see Example 3-28).

FIFTHS, OCTAVES, AND UNISONS

Immediately consecutive fifths, octaves, and unisons—that is those from fourth to first quarter—must, of course, be excluded (Example 3-29).

Fifths and octaves with one intervening tone (from third to first quarter) are also incorrect. The presence of only a single tone between the perfect intervals is not sufficient to offset the impression of parallel fifths or octaves. With two intervening tones (second to first beat) take care not to emphasize the intervals through a leap (Example 3-30).

Octaves and fifths with three intervening tones (from first to first quarter) are permissible. The presence of three tones between the two perfect intervals removes to a considerable degree the impression of parallel octaves and fifths. The student, however, is cautioned against excessive use of these accented fifths and octaves. No more than two

EXAMPLE 3-28

EXAMPLE 3-29

EXAMPLE 3-30

poor   good

consecutive downbeats should contain the same perfect interval. It is also problematic to emphasize one or both of the perfect intervals through large leaps, sequential progression, etc. (see Example 3-31).

Afterbeat fifths and octaves—that is, progressions where neither of the two perfect intervals falls on the first beat—can occur even if fewer than three quarter notes intervene (Example 3-32).

MELODIC LEAPS

For the most part, third species follows the same melodic procedures as second. The quicker rate of motion, however, imposes some changes in orientation. These changes, in general, involve disjunct rather than stepwise motion.

In the first place, large leaps—those of a fifth or greater—should be employed rather more sparingly in this species. In a vocally conceived line, such leaps occur more often in long than in short values. Sudden changes of register are easier in and more appropriate to instrumental than vocal writing. It is neither necessary nor desirable to lay down precise rules as to the number of large leaps that can safely occur

within an exercise. If he sings his exercises, the student will quickly discover where he has trespassed the boundaries of vocal style.

In third species, it is best to avoid the technique of subdivision— that is, the use of two small leaps in the same direction to replace a single large leap. This type of progression is more appropriate to the slower-moving second species. Let us consider Example 3-33. In quarter notes, the melodic line traverses too much space in too short a time; the effect can be somewhat jerky (a). Two small leaps may occur in immediate succession only when the direction changes. The change of direction reduces the amplitude of the total motion and creates a far smoother melodic line (b).

Finally, the student must be careful of melodic leaps that continue the direction of immediately preceding stepwise motion. In general, leaps should coincide with a change of direction, even following stepwise motion. After two or three conjunct tones, it is possible to leap in the same direction without bad effect. After a group of more than three stepwise tones, however, a leap in the same direction will produce the same unbalanced effect as two consecutive leaps. The lack of balance is increased if the leap is emphasized by a metrical position from fourth quarter to first. Example 3-34 illustrates this.

EXAMPLE 3-31

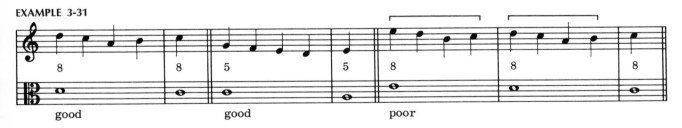

good   good   poor

EXAMPLE 3-32

BALANCE OF MELODIC LINE

A good third-species line will show balanced use of the various types of melodic motion. In particular, ornamental progressions must occur in such a manner as to retard but not to arrest the forward propulsion of the line. In Example 3-35, excessive use of melodic embellishment produces a static, sluggish line.

Example 3-36 demonstrates another type of defect. Here we find motions from one point to another; the motions, however, are small. Instead of a broad melodic arch, we find a succession of melodic fragments; no overall direction emerges.

We have already called attention to the unbalanced effect caused by excessive motion in the same direction in a short period of time.

CLIMAX

The high or low point will produce maximum effect if it falls on a strong part of the measure. Either the first or the third quarter will serve. In third species, it is essential to organize the total line by planning one or two subsidiary climaxes before or after the main one. In view of the great number of tones in a third-species exercise, any other procedure will almost inevitably result in a formless, undirected row of quarter notes. The subsidiary high or low points, of course, must not repeat (or anticipate) the actual tone of the main climax. Decorating the climax tone with a neighboring note does not produce a forbidden repetition of the climax, for the ear registers two statements of a single prolonged tone rather than two distinct tones. See Example 3-37.

IMPLICATIONS FOR ANALYSIS

A third-species melody represents a contrapuntal organism more complex than an example of first or second species. Indeed, many characteristic progressions of third species are best understood as elaborations or prolongations of underlying first- or second-species progressions. In general, the instances of ornamental motion reduce to first species, while

EXAMPLE 3-33

EXAMPLE 3-34

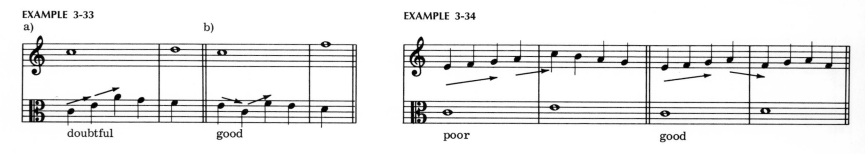

EXAMPLE 3-35

the progressions between two different tones derive from second species. It will be most beneficial to the student if he carefully analyzes his own exercises as well as illustrations in this chapter. He will gain insights that will help him in the more difficult tasks of melodic analysis from the literature. Example 3-38 presents some characteristic illustrations. The underlying first or second species is placed underneath the

prolongations of third species; the student should compare the progressions.

Not every extended third-species progression can be reduced to a satisfactory setting of first or second species. In Example 3-39 we see the beginning of an exercise whose reduction results in a poor second-species line.

EXAMPLE 3-36

EXAMPLE 3-37

EXAMPLE 3-38

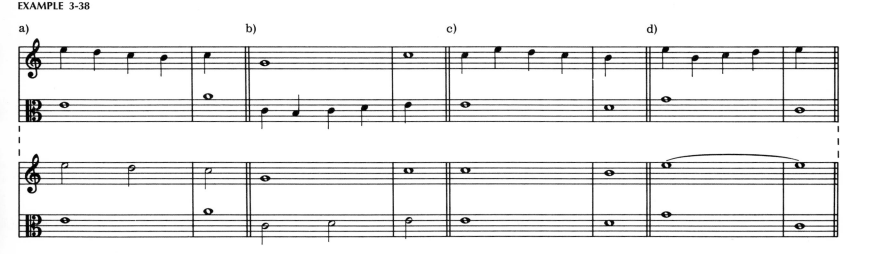

ENDING THE EXERCISE

Example 3-40 presents a number of cadential formulas. The student should note that the leading tone must occupy the fourth quarter of the next-to-last measure. If it appears earlier in the measure, it must recur on the last quarter.

Example 3-41 illustrates third-species writing.

EXERCISES

1. Play and sing Example 3-41 in the manner suggested in Chapters 1 and 2.
2. Select four cantus firmi, two in major and two in minor. Write two third-species lines above and below each cantus.
3. As a supplementary exercise, write a whole-note part corresponding to a cantus firmus and set a third-species line against it. As far as possible try to form a mental sound image of both voices before committing them to paper.

EXAMPLE 3-39

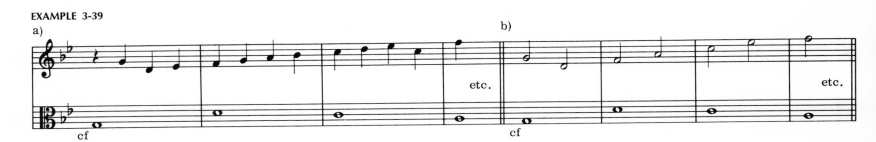

EXAMPLE 3-40

EXAMPLE 3-41

a)

b)

c)

d)

EXAMPLE 3-41 (continued)

e)

f)

g)

Mozart

h)

n.c.   n.c.   Roth

2. THREE-PART COUNTERPOINT

GENERAL OBSERVATIONS: CROSSING OF VOICES

As in second-species three-part counterpoint, there are six possible permutations of cantus, first-species part, and third-species part. The student must gain experience in all of these combinations. When the third species occurs in the middle part, it is sometimes difficult to shape it in a freely flowing manner. Because of its comparatively large number of tones, third species generally traverses a wider range of pitches than the other species. Often, considerations of spacing prevent the middle voice from having enough room to encompass this wider range. Therefore, the technique of voice crossing might be appropriately introduced at this point. Of course, if the middle part crosses the lowest voice, the former must take over the function of bass; failure to observe this fact can result in errors of voice leading. Example 3-42 demonstrates the crossing of voices.

BEGINNING THE EXERCISE

Third species follows exactly the same procedure as does second in regard to beginning the exercise. If the species part begins with a quarter rest, the first quarter will generally contain the intervals of the octave, unison, or upper fifth; upper third and tenth are also possible (Example 3-43).

ENDING THE EXERCISE

The leading tone can appear in the following two positions:

1. as the fourth quarter in the next-to-last measure of the third-species part. If the leading tone appears earlier in the measure, it will be repeated on the fourth quarter.

2. as a whole note in the next-to-last measure of the first-species part.

EXAMPLE 3-42

EXAMPLE 3-43

EXAMPLE 3-44

poor spacing

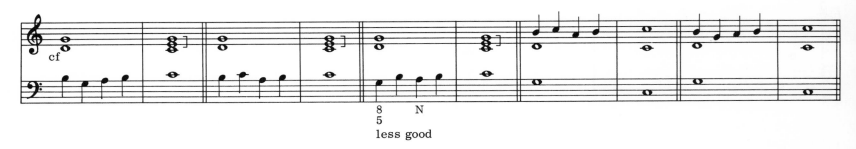

better

8
5

less good

As in the preceding two species, the leading tone must form part of a complete and consonant chord. Example 3-44 demonstrates some possibilities.

Example 3-45 will serve to illustrate complete exercises.

EXERCISES

1. Play and sing Example 3-45 in the manner suggested in Chapters 1 and 2.
2. Select two cantus firmi, one major and the other minor. To each cantus write exercises in each of the six permutations.
3. As a supplementary exercise write two original whole-note parts against a third-species line, thus dispensing with the cantus firmus.

3. THREE NOTES AGAINST ONE

GENERAL OBSERVATIONS

The exercises of species counterpoint are not designed to give experience in the treatment of different rhythms per se. Except for fifth species, they consist of uniform note values; the rhythmic element is deliberately kept as simple and undifferentiated as possible to permit concentration on questions of line and voice leading. Other branches of his theory studies will give the student opportunity to gain insight into the manifold rhythmic combinations possible in the various meters.

A texture of three notes against one does not form an essential part of elementary counterpoint study, for it leads to no new concepts of voice leading. However, counterpoint in triple meter can be introduced simply for the sake of variety. If it is undertaken after second species, dissonances will be restricted to passing tones. If it is taken up in connection with third species, the dissonant neighbor can also occur.

A meter of $\frac{3}{2}$ or $\frac{3}{4}$ can be chosen; in the former, the cantus will consist of dotted whole notes; in the latter, of dotted halves.

DISSONANCE TREATMENT; FIFTHS AND OCTAVES

As mentioned above, the dissonant neighbor can occur together with the passing tone. Dissonances cannot occur on the first beat of the

EXAMPLE 3-44 (continued)

less good   cf

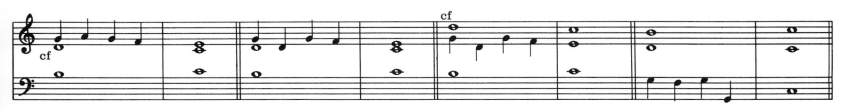

cf   cf

EXAMPLE 3-45

a)

b)

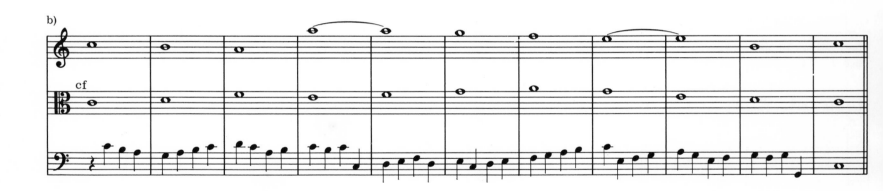

EXAMPLE 3-45 (continued)

c)

d)

e)

Schenker

EXAMPLE 3-46

EXAMPLE 3-47

EXAMPLE 3-48

measure, but may appear on either the second or the third beat. (In triple meter, both the second and the third beats are weak.) Example 3-46 shows some typical possibilities.

The ornamental idioms of third species—the cambiata and combined upper and lower neighbor—require four tones per measure and consequently cannot be used. Rules governing octaves and fifths will follow the procedures of second species. Accented fifths and octaves (on successive first beats) may occasionally occur but by no means as freely as in third species, where three tones—one of them relatively stressed—intervene.

BEGINNING AND ENDING THE EXERCISE

The exercise may begin with a rest of one beat and two tones in the first measure. Example 3-47 demonstrates various possibilities in two and three parts.

The next-to-last measure in two-part counterpoint will contain three tones, of which the third will be the leading tone. If the leading tone appears on the first beat of the measure, it must recur in the last. In three-part writing, the leading tone can also appear in the first-species part. Example 3-48 illustrates some typical cadential formulas.

Example 3-49 serves as illustration.

EXAMPLE 3-49

a)

b)

Roth

FOURTH SPECIES

1. TWO-PART COUNTERPOINT

GENERAL OBSERVATIONS

In fourth species the added voice consists of tied half notes. Against the whole note of the cantus firmus, the counterpoint contains two half notes; the first of these halves is tied over *from* the preceding measure and the second is tied over *into* the following measure. A rest always occupies the first half of the opening measure. In the next-to-last measure, the second half note (the leading tone) is *never* tied over; the last measure contains a whole note. Example 4-1 demonstrates this rhythmic organization by suspension.

Obviously the species part diverges from the normal rhythmic division of the preceding species. Now activity occurs only on the second pulse; the first beat serves merely to extend the already present tone. Rhythmic and melodic activity, therefore, is shifted or displaced from the first half of the measure where it normally occurs. Indeed, if we compare Example 4-1 with a first-species line, we see that the tied half notes correspond to the whole notes of first species displaced by half a measure.

Displacement of part (or more seldom all) of the texture so that rhythmic emphasis conflicts with the prevailing meter is called *syncopation*. Fourth-species counterpoint, then, is characterized by syncopated rhythm. (As we shall see, it occasionally becomes necessary to abandon the syncopated rhythm in the course of an exercise. This procedure will characterize only a small part of the exercise and will not nullify the essentially syncopated nature of the species.)

DISSONANT SUSPENSION

The suspension, the third basic type of dissonance, differs markedly from the passing and neighboring tones. To be sure, passing and neighboring dissonances differ from each other; the passing tone moves between two different points, the neighbor decorates a stationary point. Both, however, result from melodic activity. The origin of the suspension, on the other hand, is not melodic but rhythmic. If a tone is lengthened or displaced its latter part forms a suspension; a dissonance may result. (A suspension can also arise through the repetition of a tone; repetition is so closely related to lengthening that it need not be considered a special case.) Example 4-2a shows a consonant interval progression; on the basis of this progression, suspension dissonance is produced through: (b) displacement, (c) lengthening, and (d) repetition.

In fourth species, of course, suspensions will arise only through the first of these procedures, through displacement or syncopation. Example 4-3 illustrates the process whereby syncopation produces dissonant suspensions. Example 4-3a shows a typical first-species progression; *b* shifts the upper voice by half a measure to produce the dissonant suspensions of fourth species. Not every first-species progression can be so transformed into fourth species. Only those that fulfill the requirements for resolution can serve as the basis of syncopated, fourth-species counterpoint.

Undoubtedly the suspension produces the strongest impact of the three basic types of dissonance. Passing and neighboring dissonances arise through melodic motion; the melodic activity draws the listener's attention, and the dissonance is clearly a by-product of this activity. In the case of the suspension, there is no melodic motion in the voice that produces the dissonance. The focus of attention, therefore, is drawn to

EXAMPLE 4-1

EXAMPLE 4-2

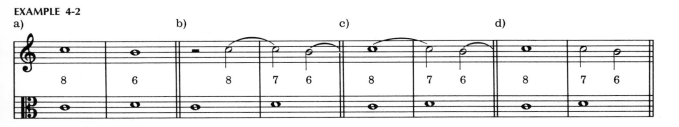

EXAMPLE 4-3

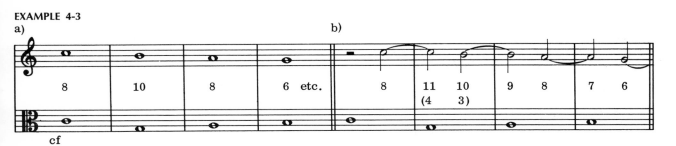

the interplay of the two voices alternating dissonant stress and consonant resolution. The dissonance's falling on the strong part of the measure undoubtedly adds to its impact.

The reader may well have thought about the possibility of displacement in the reverse direction: that is, through advance rather than delay.

Here, in Example 4-4, the dissonance falls on the second, weak half of the measure and anticipates the forthcoming consonance. The anticipating dissonance does *not* occur in fourth species. Indeed, it is a less fundamental type of dissonance than the suspension. It generally occurs in composition as surface figuration and properly belongs to prolonged rather than elementary counterpoint.

Example 4-3*b* illustrates the basic principles governing the use of dissonant suspensions in fourth-species counterpoint:

1. The dissonance results from the tying over of a consonant tone. This

consonant tone is called the *preparation* of the suspension.

2. The dissonance occurs *only* on the first half note of the measure; the second half is always consonant.

3. The resolution of the dissonance is *stepwise* and *downward*.

The stepwise continuation of the dissonant suspension requires no explanation; it represents a fundamental principle shared with passing and neighboring dissonances. But the stipulation of downward motion is unique to fourth species and the suspension dissonance. What reasons justify this restriction?

In general, upward motion is associated with an increase, downward motion with a decrease in melodic tension. Since the suspension has the most powerful effect of the basic types of dissonance, it generally requires the strongest possible resolution. When we follow a

EXAMPLE 4-4

incorrect in 4th species

EXAMPLE 4-5

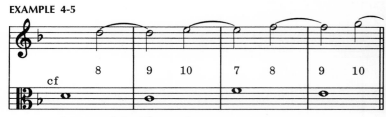

incorrect in 4th species

EXAMPLE 4-6

dissonant suspension with upward motion to a consonance, we of course resolve the dissonance; but a residue of tension remains in the melodic motion. As a result, the horizontal dimension and the vertical work at cross purposes; they contradict one another, for the resolution of the dissonance coincides with an increase in melodic tension (Example 4-5).

If the suspension resolves downward, the two dimensions are brought into correlation. Resolution of the dissonance coincides with a relaxing of melodic tension (Example 4-6).

Of course, upward-resolving suspensions occur in compositions of a variety of styles. Even where they are most frequent—in nineteenth-century music, for example—they appear far less often than suspensions that resolve down. Downward resolution characterizes the great majority of suspensions and indeed of appoggiaturas, accented passing tones, and metrically emphasized dissonances in general. Within the framework of elementary studies in counterpoint, therefore, the restriction to downward resolution is logical and appropriate. The suspension patterns of fourth species form a highly important part of the vocabulary of tonal music. They occur in compositions from the beginning of the Renaissance through the nineteenth century in virtually unaltered form as well as transformed by various types of prolongation.

Before turning to a more detailed discussion of specific problems, let us summarize what we have learned about dissonance treatment in fourth species:

1. The second half note in each measure must form a consonance with the cantus firmus.

2. The first half note may form a dissonance or a consonance. If it is dissonant, the first half note must be a suspension; it must be tied over from a consonance in the preceding measure.

3. The dissonant suspension must resolve by step and down to a consonant tone. A consonance on the first beat will be free to move by leap or step, up or down to another consonant tone.

DISSONANT SUSPENSIONS IN THE UPPER COUNTERPOINT

In the upper part four dissonant suspensions are theoretical possibilities: a seventh resolving to a sixth (7-6), a fourth resolving to a third (4-3), a ninth resolving to an octave (9-8), and a second resolving to a unison (2-1). (Example 4-7 illustrates.)

These four possibilities are by no means equally good. The 7-6 and 4-3 suspensions are by far the most useful. Resolution to an imperfect consonance creates a texture at once fluid and sonorous. By contrast, the 9-8 suspension, resolving to an octave, produces less momentum and a thinner vertical sonority. As we shall see, a series of 9-8 suspensions leads to forbidden octaves. Even an isolated 9-8 should occur only when justified by melodic requirements. The 2-1 progression is even more unsatisfactory, for the unison lacks the contrast of register that gives vertical substance to the octave. The 2-1 should be excluded or at best reserved for emergencies.

Example 4-8a shows a special type of 4-3; here the fourth is augmented. There is no reason to exclude this suspension (as some authors do); when it occurs in connection with a convincing melodic progres-

EXAMPLE 4-7

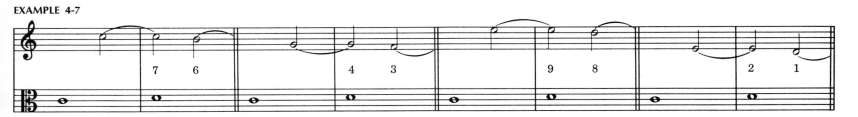

sion in the species voice, it is perfectly satisfactory. The same holds true for the diminished fifth of Example 4-8*b*.

DISSONANT SUSPENSIONS IN THE LOWER COUNTERPOINT

The theoretical possibilities are 2-3, 4-5, 7-8, and 9-10 (see Example 4-9).

By far the best of the lower suspensions are 2-3 and 9-10; they alone resolve to imperfect consonances. These two suspension forms are very much alike, differing essentially in register only. The 2-3 suspension, because the voices lie so close together, contains a more palpable friction, as it were, than the 9-10. The 2-3 suspension, therefore, is one of the most vivid and effective elements of the contrapuntal vocabulary.

The 4-5 suspension is incorrect in a series as it gives rise to consecu-

tive fifths. Even a single 4-5 is less than completely satisfactory because of the perfect quality of the consonant interval. As with the 9-8 in the upper counterpoint, occasional use can be justified by melodic considerations.

The 7-8, however, should be altogether excluded from two-part exercises. The tone of resolution is already present in the upper voice; the effect of the resolution, therefore, becomes greatly diminished. It is generally a risky procedure to anticipate the tone of resolution by having it sound in another voice. Only when the lowest voice anticipates the tone of resolution (as in the 9-8 upper suspension) is the danger minimized.

The reader will note that fewer possibilities for dissonant suspensions exist in the lower counterpoint than in the upper. The two preferred types of dissonant syncopation are essentially similar; in the upper counterpoint, the 7-6 and 4-3 differ markedly. For this reason, the

EXAMPLE 4-8

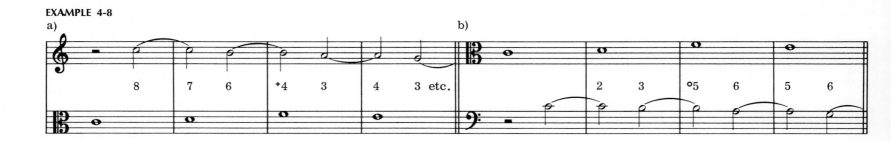

EXAMPLE 4-9

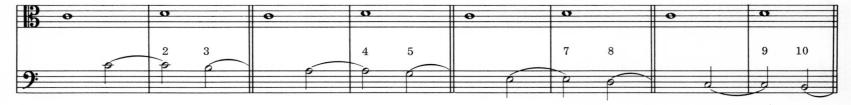

lower counterpoint—to a greater extent than the upper—will have to rely upon consonant syncopations for variety of vertical intervals.

CONSONANT SUSPENSION

Consonant suspensions fall under no restrictions regarding stepwise or downward continuation. Therefore, the only possibilities for upward or disjunct motion will arise when consonances begin the measure. Consonant syncopations should not occur too frequently; they should by no means form the predominating element of the contrapuntal fabric. Indeed, the principal role of the consonant syncopations will be to provide variety of melodic movement; without them, there can be no relief from the stepwise downward progression required by the dissonant suspensions.

Perhaps the most significant of these consonant syncopations are those involving the alternation of fifth and sixth. We have already learned from our work in second and third species that the fifth and sixth form the only adjacent consonances; we have seen how this creates the possibility for consonant passing and neighboring tones. In exactly the same fashion, these intervals can produce consonant syncopations capable of stepwise continuation. Four possibilities exist; the successions 5-6 ascending and 6-5 descending in the upper counterpoint; and the successions 5-6 descending and 6-5 ascending in the lower counterpoint (see Example 4-10).

If these progressions occur for a single measure only, they are completely unproblematic. However, as soon as they extend in series over two or three measures, the question of consecutive fifths arises. In playing the progressions of Example 4-10, the student will probably notice that the fifths are slightly stronger in the 6-5 than in the 5-6

EXAMPLE 4-10

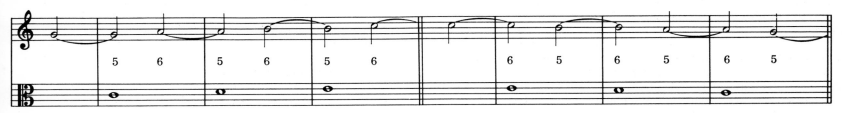

progressions. The syncopated rhythm emphasizes the second half note of the measure. This emphasis decreases if both intervals are consonant but it exists nonetheless. The 5-6 successions, therefore, may be freely used. The 6-5 progressions require more caution. Because of the slight emphasis on the fifth, they should not appear, for example, in contexts where this perfect interval is otherwise stressed. But there is no need to banish the 6-5 series altogether.

SUSPENSIONS IN SERIES

The 5-6 and 6-5 progressions are by no means the only syncopations that can appear in an uninterrupted series. The remaining consonant syncopations will seldom do so—they all produce leaps, and on melodic grounds we must avoid more than two leaps in the same direction. However, the 4-3 and 7-6 suspensions in the upper counterpoint and the 2-3 or 9-10 in the lower will very often occur in series. For the sake of variety, it is best not to allow more than three statements in a row of the same suspension form. This, of course, corresponds to the rule that we should avoid more than three parallel intervals in first species, or three consecutive first-beat intervals of the same size in second or third species.

A series or chain of suspensions forms the closest permissible approximation to the sequence in species counterpoint. Indeed, it is an important but little-known fact that many of the sequential progressions of composition ultimately derive from consonant or dissonant syncopation series (see page 448ff). In the literature the most frequently used series are the 5-6 and 7-6 with suspensions in an upper part and the 2-3 and 9-10 with suspensions in the bass. Curiously enough, the 4-3 upper suspension occurs comparatively seldom in series, though it appears very often as a single suspension. Even in the species exercise, the 4-3 series, though perfectly correct, has not quite the fluid character of the 7-6 or 2-3. The 7-6 series flows more smoothly than the 4-3 because of the less stable quality of the sixth compared with the third. The 2-3 derives its fluency from the fact that the fundamental lower tone appears in the syncopated voice; the resolution, therefore, is less final than where the third results from motion in the upper part.

FIFTHS AND OCTAVES

Earlier we touched briefly upon the problem of fifths and octaves; we dealt with it in connection with the consonant syncopations 5-6 and 6-5. Now let us discuss this question in greater detail. Obviously, the process of syncopation prevents the occurrence of immediately consecutive octaves and fifths. There will always be at least one interval between any two statements of the fifth or octave. Furthermore, the fact that the two voices do not move at the same time means that all vertical intervals will arise through oblique rather than parallel or contrary motion.

In second species, we have learned that two octaves or fifths may produce poor voice leading even if separated by an intervening interval. The same holds true of fourth species, although the criteria differ from those of second species. If two fifths, octaves, or unisons appear in consecutive measures, separated by a dissonant suspension, the voice leading is unacceptable. The dissonance depends upon the framing consonances for clarification of its meaning. It has no independent stability; therefore, it cannot separate the two perfect intervals but instead draws them together and accentuates them. The progressions 8 9-8, 5 4-5, 8 7-8, and 1 2-1 present thinly disguised consecutive octaves, fifths, and unisons (see Example 4-11a to d).

It follows, therefore, as a matter of course that the 9-8 and 4-5 suspensions must never appear in series; the 2-1 and 7-8 fall under the same ban in addition to their general undesirability.

Where fifths, octaves, and unisons in consecutive measures are separated by a consonant interval, the effect is altogether different. The intervening consonance is stable enough to interpose its weight between the two perfect intervals. Progressions, therefore, like those of Example 4-11e and f may occur. One caution must be observed, however. If the perfect interval is approached by leap in one of the voices, it becomes somewhat emphasized. In view of this emphasis, it is best to avoid more than two such intervals in consecutive measures. Since only the 5-6 and 6-5 progressions are in stepwise relationship, only they may properly appear in a series of three.

Syncopated rhythm, in two-part texture, produces only oblique motion. Therefore, the problem of "hidden" fifths and octaves (approaching the perfect interval in similar motion) will arise only when the syncopations are temporarily abandoned.

UNISONS

Unisons can occur more freely in fourth than in any of the preceding species. The reason lies in the oblique voice leading characteristic of syncopation. The two voices do not move at the same time. Therefore, the unison cannot create the disturbing effect of an ending or of one voice suddenly dropping out. If possible, unisons should be avoided as intervals of resolution, that is, in connection with the 2-1 suspension. There is no other general restriction on their use. Example 4-12 presents some typical progressions containing unisons.

In the lower counterpoint, unisons frequently occur on the second beat as a preparation for a 2-3 suspension, as in Example 4-12a.

MELODIC LINE

The nature of fourth species greatly limits the possibilities for melodic development. In particular, the requirement of downward resolution often makes the continuation of a melodic progression a matter of necessity rather than choice among several alternatives. As a result, fourth-species lines tend to consist of downward stepwise motions occasionally varied by upward melodic leaps.

The student must use every opportunity for producing a good melodic line; in particular, consonant first beats should be taken ad-

EXAMPLE 4-11

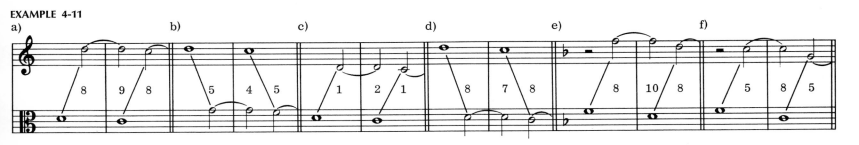

EXAMPLE 4-12

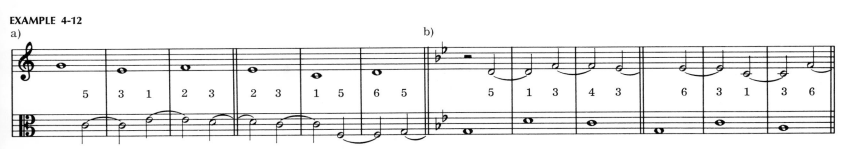

vantage of. It is difficult to give a fourth-species line the flexibility and variety of a third- or second-species counterpoint; nevertheless, it must be made as good as possible.

INTERRUPTION OF SYNCOPATION

One expedient for improving an otherwise poor melodic line consists of interrupting the syncopated rhythm. Instead of tying over the second half note of the measure, it is possible to let it move to a new tone at the beginning of the following measure. This technique, in effect, constitutes the temporary introduction of second species and is called *breaking the species*. As long as unsyncopated half notes occur, the rules of fourth species are set aside and those of second species prevail.

From the pedagogical standpoint, it is best to restrict breaking the species to a minimum. To the extent that we use this expedient, we forego practice in fourth species. It is hardly possible to give precise

rules for the extent to which we may abandon syncopation; it depends on the individual exercise. We may wish to do so for the following reasons:

1. To curtail a suspension series of more than three statements.

2. To provide melodic relief from steadily downward motion.

3. To prevent errors that would otherwise occur.

In Example 4-13, a faulty chain of 9-8 suspensions threatens; only breaking the species can remove this threat.

The progression of Example 4-14 is interesting. A fourth occurs on the first half of measure 3; this fourth, in resolving, will move to a diminished fifth. Since a consonance must appear on the second half note, the diminished fifth is clearly incorrect. The lower voice, however, cannot leap out of the dissonance or ascend. Therefore, we must interrupt the syncopated rhythm.

EXAMPLE 4-13

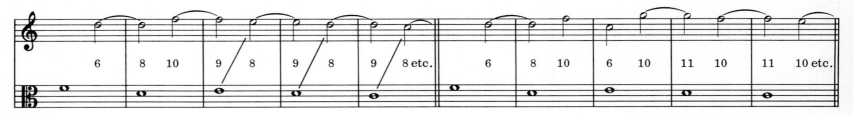

EXAMPLE 4-14

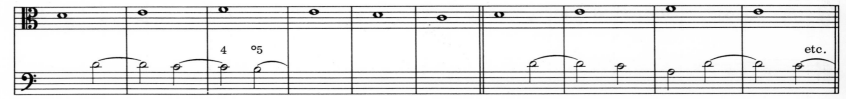

BEGINNING AND ENDING THE EXERCISE

Beginning the exercise offers no new problems. The added voice must always begin with a half rest in order to stress the importance of the second half note at the very beginning. As in all species of two-part counterpoint, we shall use the octave or fifth in the upper counterpoint and the unison or octave in the lower.

Fourth species, like all the others, places a whole note in the final measure. The next-to-last measure, therefore, will contain two half notes of which the first will be tied over from the preceding measures (unless we have broken species), whereas the second will not be suspended into the following measure. The second half note, of course, must be the leading tone. In general, the most effective ending will result when the leading tone constitutes the resolution of a dissonant suspension. In the upper counterpoint, this suspension will be a 7-6; in the lower counterpoint, it will be a 2-3 or 9-10. Approaching the leading tone through a dissonant suspension greatly enhances its motion impulse toward the tonic. Even a cursory examination of the literature will reveal how general was the use of suspension into the leading tone in music from the Renaissance through the nineteenth century. Cantus firmi ending with the scale steps 4 2 1 do not permit suspension into the leading tone in the lower counterpoint. Therefore, it is best to avoid them in fourth species. Example 4-15 demonstrates how to end the exercise. In Example 4-15b, the leap of a fifth continued in the same direction is good. The tone following the leap—the leading tone—has a strong impulse upward to the tonic; this prevents any break in melodic continuity.

Example 4-16 presents additional illustrations of this species.

EXERCISES

1. Play and sing Example 4-16 as suggested in previous chapters.
2. Select four cantus firmi, two in major and two in minor. Write two fourth-species lines above and below each cantus.

EXAMPLE 4-15

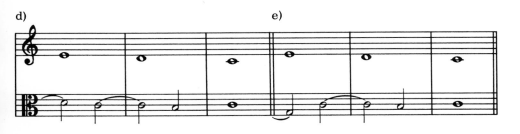

EXAMPLE 4-16

a)

b)

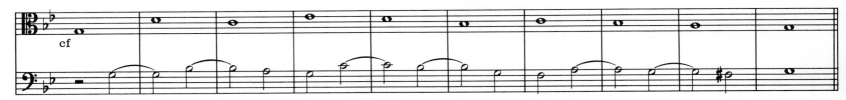

c)

d)

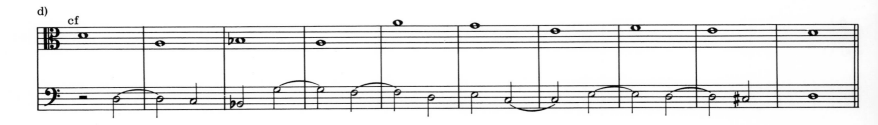

EXAMPLE 4-16 (continued)

e)

f)

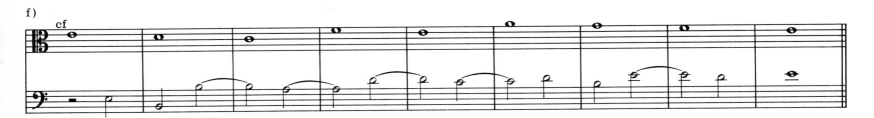

g)

Schenker

h)

Schenker

3. As a supplementary exercise, write a fourth-species part against a whole-note line of your own composition.

2. THREE-PART COUNTERPOINT

GENERAL OBSERVATIONS

The addition of a third voice in whole notes creates more new considerations in fourth species than in second or third. To be sure, the basic requirements are those of fourth species in two voices and the fundamental considerations of three-part texture in general. These requirements may be formulated as follows:

1. The first-species voice must be consonant with the cantus.

2. The second half note of the fourth-species part must form a consonant combination with both the cantus and first-species voice.

3. If the first half note forms a dissonant suspension with one or both of the whole-note voices, the dissonance must resolve by step and down.

Rules 2 and 3 occasionally work at cross purposes. Sometimes, in attempting to resolve a dissonance with one whole-note voice, we move into a dissonance with the other. Example 4-17 demonstrates this unhappy possibility; obviously we must avoid the combinations $\frac{7}{5}$, $\frac{6}{5}$, and $\frac{6}{2}$ in fourth-species three-part writing.

DISSONANT SUSPENSIONS IN THE TOP VOICE

The dissonant suspensions of fourth-species three-part counterpoint simply add a third tone to the familiar progressions of two-part writing. When the syncopations occur in the top part, suspensions result primarily from interaction with the bass voice; the added, complementary tone occurs in the middle part. The exercise, therefore, becomes more difficult when the cantus occurs in the middle part; it is then necessary to conceive both outer voices simultaneously. The suspensions themselves, however, take the same form regardless of the position of the cantus.

Let us now determine the possible added tones for each of the dissonant suspensions of two-part counterpoint. If possible, it is best to let the suspension resolve into a complete chord. Where this is not possible, for reasons of voice leading, the added tone may double the bass. However, it must *never* double the resolution of the suspension. The student will remember from his study of two-part fourth-species writing that doubling and anticipating the tone of resolution spoils the effect of the suspension. Note Example 4-18.

The 7-6 suspension must be accompanied by a third or tenth above the bass if a complete, consonant chord is to result. An octave doubling of the bass is less desirable because of the incomplete chord. Neither the fifth nor the sixth above the bass will be possible. The former does not allow a consonant resolution, and the latter doubles the tone of resolution (Example 4-19).

The 4-3 suspension can be accompanied by two tones: a fifth or a sixth above the bass. The first produces a resolution into a $\frac{5}{3}$; the second

EXAMPLE 4-17

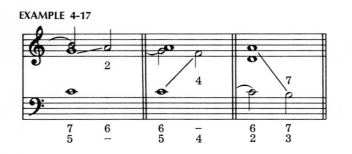

$$\begin{matrix} 7 & 6 & & 6 & - & & 6 & 7 \\ 5 & - & & 5 & 4 & & 2 & 3 \end{matrix}$$

EXAMPLE 4-18

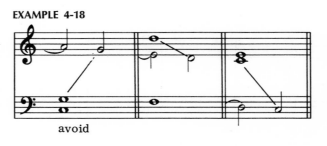

avoid

resolves to a $\frac{6}{3}$. Incidentally, the latter possibility represents the first appearance in species counterpoint of a $\frac{6}{4}$ sonority on the first beat of the measure. The $\frac{6}{4}$, of course, is not a chord of independent vertical identity but results entirely from rhythmic displacement. The $\frac{5}{4\text{-}3}$ contains a more energetic impulse forward than the $\frac{6}{4\text{-}3}$ because the former contains two dissonances as compared with one for the latter. Again, it is possible, though not particularly desirable, to double the bass. Doubling the tone of resolution, of course, is incorrect (Example 4-20).

The 9-8 suspension must resolve to an incomplete chord in three-part writing. The best added tone is the third or tenth above the bass; this produces a resolution to an $\frac{8}{3}$. The sixth is also possible; the fifth, though less good, is not to be altogether excluded. These will produce

$\frac{8}{6}$ and $\frac{8}{5}$ chords. Doubling the bass is incorrect; the resolution would be to a single tone tripled (Example 4-21).

DISSONANT SUSPENSIONS IN THE MIDDLE VOICE

Middle-voice suspensions, like those in the top voice, function essentially with respect to the bass. As a result, precisely the same suspension forms occur in this arrangement as when the suspensions are in the top voice. Now, however, the added, complementary tones appear in the top part and are above the suspensions rather than below them. If the student will compare the progressions of Example 4-22 with the corresponding progressions in the three preceding examples, he will discover that they are the same except for the relative position of the syncopations and the added whole notes.

Although the suspensions themselves and their accompanying tones

EXAMPLE 4-19

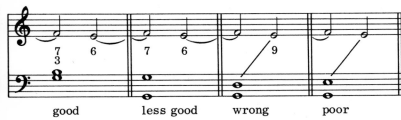

good   less good wrong poor

EXAMPLE 4-20

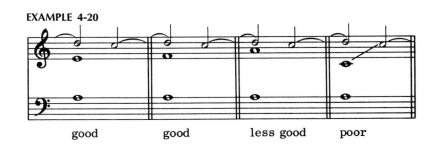

good   good less good poor

EXAMPLE 4-21

good   good less good poor

EXAMPLE 4-22

are not new, the total effect differs markedly from that of suspensions in the top voice. In this permutation, the middle voice becomes the most active rhythmically and contrapuntally. Therefore, it assumes greater significance than is usually accorded a middle part. At the same time, the added tones occur in the prominent top voice; they too acquire greater importance than when they occupy the middle voice. Every voice has a differentiated but equal role to play; the contrapuntal texture is extremely well balanced. Perhaps for this reason, middle-voice suspensions (usually in the voice nearest the top if there are more than three parts) occur very often in compositions of a variety of styles.

Example 4-22 requires little comment. As in the case of top-voice suspensions, the preferred forms are those resulting in complete chords of resolution. The student will note that some suspensions involve two dissonant relationships: a 2-3 with respect to the top part as well as the primary relationship with the bass. These suspensions, particularly the $\frac{5}{4\text{-}3}$, contain an unusually powerful kinetic impulse.

DISSONANT SUSPENSIONS IN THE BASS

As we have seen, when the suspension occurs in one of the upper parts, it relates primarily to the bass. When the bass voice itself contains the suspension, the primary relationship involves the upper part with which the bass forms a dissonance. In Example 4-23 the principal relationship is first to the middle voice and, in the second progression, to the top voice. For in the first progression, the middle voice forms a 2-3 suspension with the bass, whereas the top voice forms a consonant 5-6. In the second progression, the consonant-dissonant relationships are reversed.

The basic dissonant syncopation of the lowest part is the 2-3 or its expansion the 9-10. In Example 4-23, this suspension is accompanied by a sixth above the tone of resolution; the chord produced, therefore, is a $\frac{6}{3}$. In Example 4-24, the added tone is a fifth above the tone of resolution. Here, there are two dissonant suspensions: the 2-3 or 9-10 and the 4-5. The 2-3 constitutes by far the stronger and hence the primary suspension. Notice that the presence of the strong 2-3 or 9-10 removes the otherwise weak effect of the 4-5 with its resolution to a perfect consonance. The 4-5 becomes acceptable when it occurs as a secondary suspension in three-voice texture.

The 7-8, on the other hand, does not fare so well in three voices; the anticipated doubling of the tone of resolution remains a problem here as elsewhere. In general, incomplete chords of resolution are less satisfactory when the bass has the suspension than when one of the upper parts is syncopated. The best possibility consists of a doubled third above the tone of resolution (Example 4-25a). The progression of b is poor; without an accompanying imperfect consonance, the 4-5 reverts to the condition of two-part writing; the doubled fifth adds to the thin, static effect; c doubles the tone of resolution by means of a secondary 7-8 suspension; it is not to be recommended.

CONSONANT SYNCOPATION

The 5-6 and 6-5 consonant syncopations are most practicable in the top or the middle voice. The added tone should be a third or tenth above the bass if complete chords are to result; doubling the bass gives a far less satisfactory sound (see Example 4-26).

EXAMPLE 4-23

EXAMPLE 4-24

EXAMPLE 4-25

a)   b)   c)

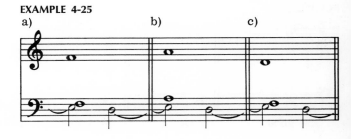

In attempting to use the 5-6 and 6-5 in the bass part, we shall discover that it is impossible to obtain complete and consonant chords. If we double the upper tone, the chords, of course, are incomplete. The voice leading is not incorrect, but the sound is poor, as Example 4-27 demonstrates.

The 6-5 cannot give rise to complete chords. It is obvious that both attempted solutions of Example 4-28 contain faults of voice leading. In the first, we have a dissonant fourth on the first beat followed incorrectly by upward motion. In the second, we find a dissonance on the second beat of the measure, where, of course, consonances must occur.

The 5-6 can be accompanied by a third or tenth above the tone of resolution. However, this tone forms a dissonant 2-3 or 9-10 with the bass; it is the dissonant suspension that we hear as primary; the consonant 5-6 recedes into the background (see Example 4-29).

Disjunct consonant syncopations are possible in all voices. There are no new considerations except that it is best to have the complete chord on the first rather than the second half note. This is a preference, not a rule. Example 4-30 demonstrates some of the possibilities.

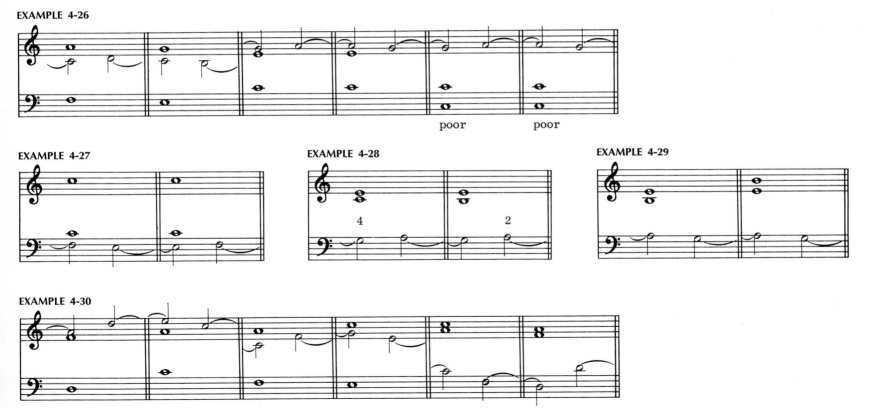

EXAMPLE 4-26

EXAMPLE 4-27

EXAMPLE 4-28

EXAMPLE 4-29

EXAMPLE 4-30

FIFTHS, OCTAVES, AND UNISONS IN CONSECUTIVE MEASURES

In three-part writing, octaves and unisons in consecutive measures require the same treatment as in two-part counterpoint. Those that result from the resolution of a dissonant suspension are incorrect (Example 4-31). Those separated by an intervening consonance are permissible;

it is best to avoid more than two perfect intervals in a row (Example 4-32).

In one characteristic and important progression, a series of 4-5 suspensions can occur between the two top voices; this presents a kind of voice leading quite different from anything in two-part fourth species. Consider Example 4-33. When a series of 7-6 suspensions occurs be-

EXAMPLE 4-31

EXAMPLE 4-32

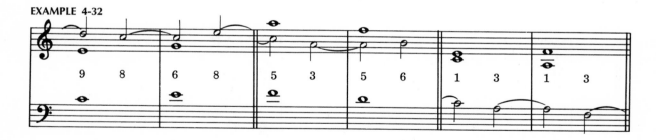

EXAMPLE 4-33

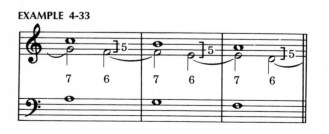

EXAMPLE 4-34

tween middle voice and bass, the top voice will properly accompany the bass in tenths, thereby producing complete chords. The reader will note the secondary 4-5 suspensions between the top voice and the middle voice. These 4-5's produce fifths resulting from the resolution of a dissonance in consecutive measures. Nevertheless, the progression is good. The ear registers the 7-6 series as the primary event and does not focus on the 4-5.

(In Example 4-34, we see a series of 7-6 suspensions in the top voice with the thirds or tenths in the middle part, fifths occur on the first half of each measure. These fifths are separated by consonant fourths; their validity, therefore, does not even come into question.)

The oblique motion characteristic of fourth species makes it impossible to provide contrary motion against hidden fifths and octaves in the whole-note parts. The approach to the fifth or octave in similar motion, therefore, should be avoided if possible. Where the fourth

species has a dissonant syncopation, however, the effect of the perfect intervals is somewhat mitigated. Therefore, if it is necessary to use this voice leading in order to avoid more serious errors, the fourth-species part should contain a dissonant suspension. (See Example 4-35.)

SUSPENSIONS IN SERIES

A series of 7-6 suspensions is best accompanied, as we have seen, by parallel thirds or tenths between the whole-note parts (Example 4-36).

The consonant 5-6 and 6-5 series will be similarly accompanied. As we have seen, these series are only possible when the syncopations occur in the middle or the top voice (Example 4-37).

As Example 4-38 shows, the 4-3 series can accompany the lower part in parallel sixths; this will give rise to a series of $^6_{4\text{-}3}$ progressions.

EXAMPLE 4-35

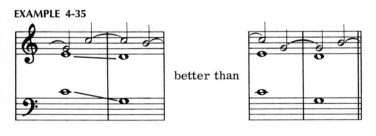

better than

EXAMPLE 4-36

EXAMPLE 4-37

EXAMPLE 4-38

A series of $\frac{5}{4\text{-}3}$ progressions with the added voice a fifth above the bass is incorrect, of course, because of the parallel fifths. Example 4-39 illustrates.

A mixture of fifths and sixths, on the other hand, is possible (see Example 4-40).

A 2-3 or 9-10 series in the lower counterpoint can be accompanied by sixths above the tones of resolution. The $\frac{5\text{-}6}{2\text{-}3}$ series produced thereby is good only when the upper parts form fourths, as shown in Example 4-41a; otherwise a series of parallel fifths results. The fourths of Example 4-41a are consonant because of the support of the tone of resolution. Their rhythms contrast much more than is the case in an unsyncopated setting. The syncopated bass tends to accentuate the fourths. For this

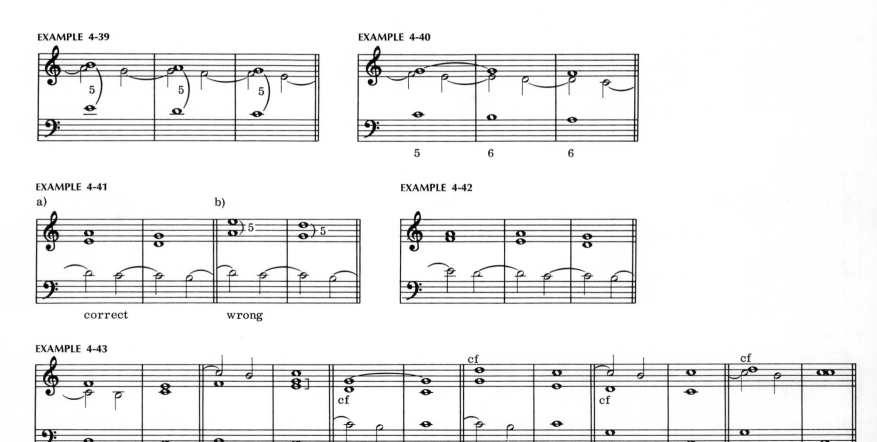

EXAMPLE 4-39

5

5

5

EXAMPLE 4-40

5   6   6

EXAMPLE 4-41

a)   b)

5   5

correct   wrong

EXAMPLE 4-42

EXAMPLE 4-43

cf   cf

cf   cf

cf

cf

reason, it is best not to prolong this series beyond two statements.

As in the 4-3 series in the upper parts, it is possible to alternate fifths and sixths above the tones of resolutions (see Example 4-42). This will produce alternating $\frac{5\text{-}6}{2\text{-}3}$ and $\frac{4\text{-}5}{2\text{-}3}$ progressions. Of course it is not possible to employ the $\frac{4\text{-}5}{2\text{-}3}$ progressions consecutively because of the fifths.

THE FIRST-SPECIES VOICE

The exigencies of this combination make it difficult to construct an ideal first-species part. The need to avoid doubling the tones of resolution and the desirability of obtaining complete chords of resolution limit the possibilities. Nevertheless, the student must attempt to create as good a line as possible; occasionally breaking species in the syncopated voice will prove helpful. The student must avoid the continual doubling in thirds or tenths of the cantus.

EXAMPLE 4-44

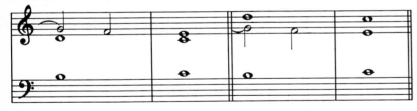

BEGINNING AND ENDING THE EXERCISE

The syncopated voice, as in two-part counterpoint, will begin with a rest. The tones of the first measure will follow the usual procedure of three-part counterpoint beginning with a rest.

As in two-part writing, a dissonant suspension into the leading tone enhances its drive to the tonic and produces a very strong cadence. The leading tone itself must, as always in three parts, form part of a complete, consonant chord. Example 4-43 demonstrates the typical cadence forms; note that the harmonic V–I necessarily occurs when the first-species part is in the bass and the syncopated voice makes a dissonant suspension into the leading tone.

Should a stepwise bass be desired at the cadence, it will be necessary to forego the dissonant suspension. Example 4-44 shows the best solution. The dissonance on the second half of the measure is only possible because that tone is not tied over; in effect, we revert to second species. This cadence, though correct, lacks the forceful, driving quality evoked by the dissonant suspension resolving into the leading tone.

RESOLVING INTO THE DIMINISHED TRIAD

Some counterpoint texts recommend a resolution into a root-position diminished triad in the next-to-last measure. In close position (with the fifth in the top voice), this chord permits a stepwise motion into the final measure of the highest part. Resolution into a $\frac{6}{3}$, on the other hand, requires disjunct continuation or a tie (see Example 4-45).

EXAMPLE 4-45

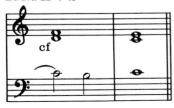

instead of

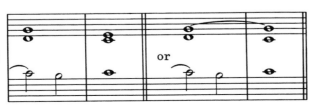

or

EXAMPLE 4-46

The diminished triad is a comparatively mild dissonance; following the suspended second, it forms a quasi-resolution of strong dissonance to milder dissonance rather than the true resolution of dissonance into consonance. This extension of the principle of resolution represents prolonged rather than elementary counterpoint. If this fact is understood by the student, the use of the progression is justified.

THE TIED FOURTH

Another progression of prolonged counterpoint often finds its way into texts. This technique, as seen in Example 4-46, involves tying over a fourth with respect to the bass; it requires that the bass be sustained for two measures. Here, the fourth functions as an upper neighbor to

EXAMPLE 4-47

a)

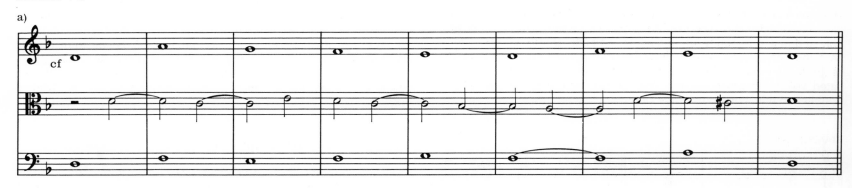

b)

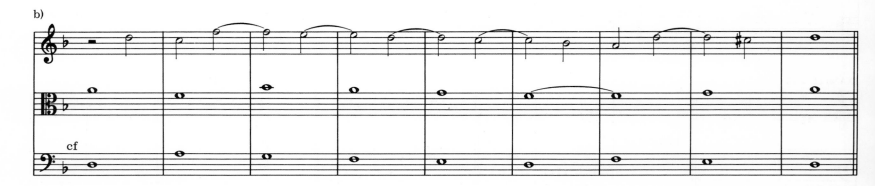

EXAMPLE 4-47 (continued)

c)

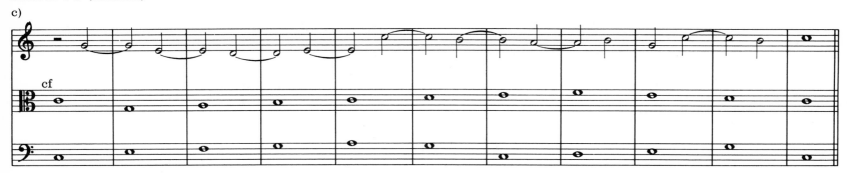

d)

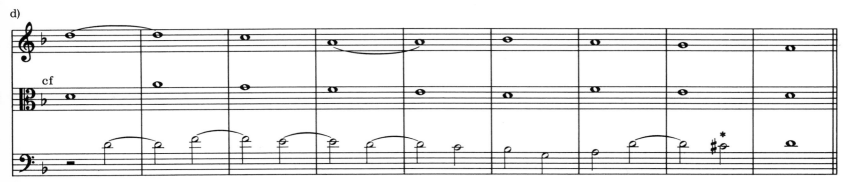

* Resolution to diminished 5th

e)

Schenker

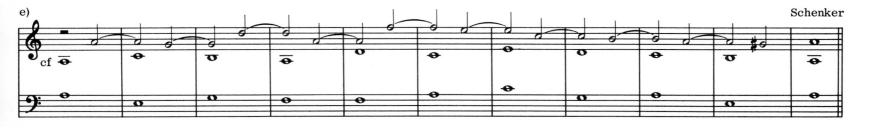

the third; the neighbor is suspended into the following measure before resolving. The suspension of a neighbor combines two dissonant types and as such constitutes a prolongation of fundamental contrapuntal procedure. A second aspect of prolonged counterpoint is revealed in this progression. The function of the dissonance becomes clear only within a framework of two measures; the time scale of the species exercise expands from one measure to two.

This tied fourth is sometimes called the *consonant fourth*. This term is incorrect. Certainly the fourth is not so strong a dissonance as the second or seventh; compared with the dissonant suspension between the top voices in the second measure, the fourth is mild. But it is a dissonance nonetheless.

Example 4-47 will illustrate fourth-species writing in three parts.

EXERCISES

1. Play and sing Example 4-47 as suggested in earlier chapters.
2. Select two cantus firmi, one major and the other minor. To each cantus write exercises in each of the six permutations.
3. As a supplementary exercise write a three-part setting consisting of a fourth-species part and two original whole-note parts.

5

FIFTH SPECIES

1. TWO-PART COUNTERPOINT

GENERAL OBSERVATIONS

The purpose of the fifth and last species is not to introduce any fundamentally new concept of voice leading and dissonance treatment but rather to combine the materials and procedures of the preceding species into coherent and logical wholes. In fifth species, the note values of second, third, and fourth species occur in various mixtures; half notes, quarters, and tied halves can all appear. These note values are governed by the procedures of the species in which they belong, halves by second species, quarters by third, etc. In addition, eighth notes are introduced. Only the whole note of the first species is excluded, or, more correctly, confined to the last measure of the exercise. Appearing at the beginning of an exercise, the whole note would inhibit the development of rhythmic momentum; in the middle of the exercise, it would arrest motion.

The use of contrasting note values makes it possible to construct melodic lines of greater differentiation, complexity, and esthetic quality than in any of the preceding species. It is easier to achieve mere correctness in relation to the cantus in fifth than in the preceding species; the student's main attention should focus on the attainment of a smoothly flowing line. In order to produce such a line, it is first necessary to learn how to organize the variety of rhythmic values now available.[1]

[1] Because of the decorative character of the mixed note values, fifth species is often termed *florid counterpoint*.

Before proceeding to a discussion of specific details of rhythmic organization, let us examine the general principles underlying the treatment of rhythm in fifth-species counterpoint. Our aim will be to produce as unbroken a rhythmic continuity as possible. Just as we have avoided melodic sequences or motivic repetition, so we shall avoid every rhythmic pattern that tends to produce a segmented, articulated line.

UNMIXED NOTE VALUES WITHIN THE MEASURE

In fifth species, a mixture of note values often takes place within the measure. To a limited extent, it is also possible to continue a given note value—for example, halves or quarters—for a whole measure or even longer. The longer a single note value continues unrelieved, the more drastic will be the effect of the eventual change. More than two, or at most, two-and-a-half measures of a single note value will destroy the rhythmic balance of the line. In particular, the slower-moving half notes continued too long will create a rhythmically static section within the exercise.

Even if unmixed note values occur within the two-measure limit, they should be employed sparingly. To construct a line containing first two measures of halves, then two measures of quarters, then two of syncopations is to divide the line into little segments. Too much uni-

6

formity within each two-measure group creates too much contrast between them; instead of a smooth flow, we have a series of stops and starts (see Example 5-1).

MIXED NOTE VALUES WITHIN THE MEASURE

Example 5-1 demonstrates that a mixture of note values should preponderate over single values unmixed. We must now determine what mixtures of note values are most appropriate to the creation of the flowing, continuous lines we wish to produce. In the most general terms, our solution lies in the proper correlation between two factors: duration and metrical emphasis. Let us first examine this correlation with respect to halves and quarters; later we shall take up the use of syncopation and eighth notes.

Where longer and shorter tones occur in close proximity, the long tones naturally receive more emphasis than the short. If these long and short tones unfold within a metrical framework—that is, against a back-

ground of regularly recurring strong and weak pulses—the long values most naturally coincide with the strong pulses, the short values with the weak pulses. In Example 5-2, the half note comes on the strong first beat followed by two quarters in the weaker second half of the measure. The long note fits smoothly into place because the emphasis of duration coincides with emphasis of position.

In Example 5-3, the half note occurs on the weak second quarter. The long note occurring on the weak second half of the first beat interrupts the rhythmic flow. We feel a contradiction between emphasis of duration and of position. The long note coming in the "wrong" place calls attention to itself and stands out from its surroundings; it is not smoothly integrated into the line as is the half note of Example 5-2.

The half note on the second quarter of Example 5-3 creates yet another problem. It constitutes a syncopation within the measure; such a syncopation implies a rhythmic pulse of quarter notes. In fifth species as in the others, a half-note pulse should characterize the exercise. Therefore, syncopation within the measure produces a sudden acceleration of the metrical framework—a procedure too complex for the ele-

EXAMPLE 5-1

EXAMPLE 5-2

EXAMPLE 5-3

EXAMPLE 5-4

EXAMPLE 5-5

mentary species exercise. The rhythm of Example 5-3, consequently, must not occur.

Example 5-4 presents the long note on the second half of the measure preceded by two quarters. This rhythmic pattern, too, interrupts the flow. The second half of the measure should lead into the next strong pulse. Coming after the two short notes, the half note constitutes a static point; it blocks the flow from the two quarters rather than channeling it into the following measure. Once stopped, the motion begins again with a jolt at the next downbeat. Therefore, the rhythm of Example 5-4 must not be employed; it is inappropriate to the uninterrupted flow we are trying to achieve.

If we modify the rhythm of Example 5-4 by tying over the half note, we restore the free flow of the rhythm. Now, the motion does not halt abruptly at the next first beat; indeed, the syncopation carries the momentum across the bar line into the following measure. Therefore, two quarter notes may precede a half within the measure if the half is tied over into the following measure (Example 5-5).

Later in this chapter we shall study in greater detail the use of syncopation in fifth species. At present, it is sufficient to state that a half note can be tied to a quarter as well as to another half, as in fourth species.

The use of eighth notes is unique to fifth species. They represent the quickest note value possible in species counterpoint; they must be used sparingly and carefully if the line is not to become instrumental in character. Three rules govern the use of eighths: they must occur in pairs (two at a time) with only one pair per measure; they may appear only on the second or fourth quarter; they must move by step. The requirement that not more than two eighths may appear in succession prevents the texture from becoming overloaded with quick notes and protects its vocal character. Stepwise motion also helps prevent the line from becoming instrumental. An instrument can easily perform a melodic leap in quick values; this is not natural or easy for the singing voice. In addition, eighths are generally decorative tones, and as such most logically move in stepwise fashion. Very occasionally, it might be possible to precede the first of two eighth notes with a small leap; however, a leap from an eighth should never occur.

The rule restricting eighths to the second and fourth quarters follows from the general principle that longer values should occupy stronger metrical positions than shorter notes. In other words, eighths in relation to quarters behave in the same way as quarters in relation to halves. Example 5-6 summarizes all available rhythms containing halves, quarters, eighths, and tied halves. All of the patterns of Example 5-6 can appear with the first tone tied over from the preceding measure.

These patterns must not become motivic. Immediate repetition or excessive use of a single rhythmic pattern carries with it the danger of segmentation. Example 5-7 shows what is to be avoided in this respect. Of course, the recurrence of a pattern after several intervening measures

EXAMPLE 5-6

EXAMPLE 5-7

does not fall under this restriction. Nor does the persistence for two measures of a neutral, undifferentiated rhythm consisting of a single note value.

In general, smoother continuity results when the prevailing note value changes in the middle of the measure rather than at the beginning. It is relatively easy to change from halves to quarters; the reverse presents more problems. Suspensions provide the best means for broadening the note values without abruptly stopping the forward motion (see Example 5-8).

Eighth notes are used to decorate and intensify quarter-note movement. Therefore, the use of eighth notes does not count as a significant change of note value in relation to the two-measure limit.

DISSONANCE TREATMENT

The treatment of dissonance in fifth species raises no fundamentally new questions and poses no real problems to those who have carefully worked through the first four species. Only the treatment of the dissonant suspension undergoes some elaboration. The mixture of note values allows us to decorate the resolution of the suspension. The preparation of the suspension remains a half note, as in fourth species, and the resolution falls on the second half of the measure. However, it is now possible to shorten the dissonant tone itself to a quarter and to insert between the dissonance and the tone of resolution a decorating quarter or pair of eighths.

Example 5-9 demonstrates the most important possibilities for decorating the resolution. They consist of: pairs of eighths in two step-wise configurations (the first passes to the lower neighbor of the tone of resolution, while the second passes from the upper neighbor of the suspension); lower neighbor of tone of resolution; upper neighbor of suspension tone; anticipation of tone of resolution; and downward leap to consonance. An upward leap between suspension and tone of resolution would not fit as smoothly into the line as the downward leap; therefore, the downward motion is preferred. It should be noted that all quarter-note decorations are consonant tones; to interpose a dissonant quarter between the suspension and its resolution is to becloud the resolution. However, the third and the last progressions contain leaps away from the dissonant suspension. Because of the transient, decorative nature of the tone following the leap, the ear hears the essential continuity from suspension to tone of resolution; it hears through the intervening tone. The principle here is the same as that governing the nota cambiata and double neighbor of third species. On a miniature scale it represents one of the basic premises of prolonged counterpoint: that relationships between non-consecutive tones often take primacy over relationships between immediately consecutive tones.

Some authors allow the dissonant suspension to resolve on the second quarter of the measure. This procedure, while valid in itself, tends to shift the pulse from the half note to the quarter; for this reason, we do not recommend its use in fifth species. The tone of resolution, however, can be shortened to a quarter without quickening the metrical flow; this device can be quite useful (Example 5-10). A consonant syncopation awakens no definite expectancy for a required continuation; therefore, the consonant syncopation can be shortened to a quarter note without any further restrictions (Example 5-11).

For dissonances other than syncopations, the fundamental rule is

EXAMPLE 5-8

as follows: every note value is governed by the procedures of the species to which it belongs. A half note, for example, must be consonant if it occurs on the first beat of the measure; if it appears on the second beat, it may be dissonant but only as a passing tone. A quarter note must also be consonant on the first quarter of the measure; dissonant passing and neighboring notes, etc., may appear on the rhythmically appropriate quarters. Eighth notes present no problems of dissonance treatment. They appear only on the weak quarters, and the requirement for stepwise motion in itself guarantees correctness. Either the first or second note of the pair may be dissonant. Example 5-12 shows various types of dissonance treatment involving halves, quarters, and eighths.

EXAMPLE 5-9

EXAMPLE 5-10

EXAMPLE 5-11

EXAMPLE 5-12

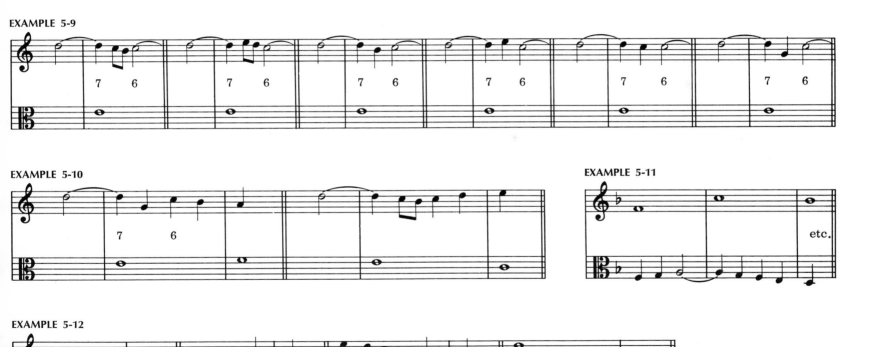

PARALLEL MOTION, UNISONS, ETC.

Other considerations of voice leading, like those affecting dissonance treatment, depend upon the note value and reflect the procedures of the species to which that note value belongs. Octaves and fifths on successive first beats (accented octaves and fifths) are valid when separated by three quarter notes, as in third species. With only an intervening half note (second species), octaves should not occur, fifths must not be emphasized, etc. A mixed rhythm of half, quarter, quarter presents a borderline case. Except where the perfect intervals receive unusual melodic emphasis, these accented fifths and octaves can be allowed. In normal circumstances, the two quarters of the second half of the measure sufficiently separate the perfect intervals. Example 5-13 serves to illustrate.

A consonant suspension of a quarter note gives us the possibility of afterbeat fifths and octaves separated only by a single quarter. Where the second interval is produced by stepwise melodic motion, the afterbeat fifths are good; this will only occur in connection with a 5 6-5 progression (see Example 5-14). When preceded by a leap, the second perfect interval is thrown into relief; these progressions should be avoided (Example 5-15).

Unisons in fifth species create no new considerations. They are permitted on the first beat only through suspension. They may occur elsewhere in the measure if tied over or followed by stepwise motion.

CORRELATION OF MELODIC AND RHYTHMIC MOTION

Fifth species with its mixture of note values gives us the opportunity to shape and control the rate of melodic movement through rhythmic differentiation. Example 5-16 shows a melodic progression traversing an ascending sixth during two measures. We see first how second or third species might accomplish this motion. The later examples indicate some of the possibilities of fifth species. By rhythmic means, different tones

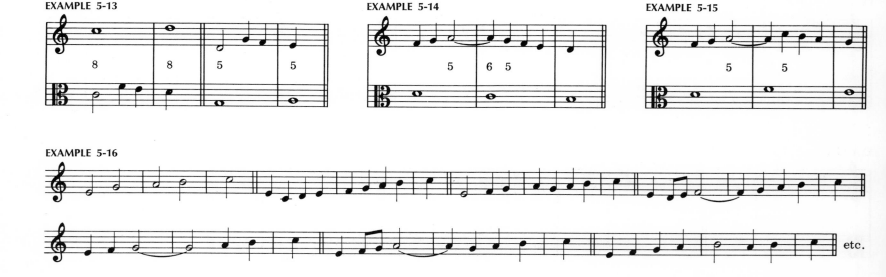

EXAMPLE 5-13

EXAMPLE 5-14

EXAMPLE 5-15

EXAMPLE 5-16

of the ascent can receive stress; the ascent can accelerate or hesitate during its course. No one of these possibilities is in itself better than the others; we must determine which is the most appropriate for a given exercise on the basis of context.

The following guides will be helpful in shaping the melodic contour through rhythmic means:

1. Extended scalewise motion is best entrusted to predominantly small values. Too many half notes will slow the motion to a point where it becomes sluggish (Example 5-17).

2. Motions that decorate a stationary tone should be accomplished by quarters and eighths. Even if half notes yield correct dissonance treatment, they will produce a static effect (Example 5-18).

3. In a series of dissonant suspensions, the total melodic motion traversed is quite small. It is best, therefore, to decorate the resolutions of most of the suspensions. The decorations must vary to prevent melodic sequence (Example 5-19).

4. As a rule, the tone preceding a large melodic leap should be a half rather than a quarter. Of course, exceptions occur; this suggestion is a guide rather than an ironclad rule. However, frequent large skips in quick note values belong to instrumental rather than to vocal writing.

To sing a leap requires time for preparation. The tone following the leap can be short, but the one preceding it will generally be longer.

5. It is best to allow the melodic-rhythmic momentum to develop smoothly and gradually. For this reason, the beginning of the exercise will generally consist of stepwise motion and large values. To begin with quick notes or leaps leaves little room for increasing the intensity. In approaching the climax, however, it is often good to accelerate the note values; here, quarter notes prove useful. Half notes and suspensions begin the exercise best.

BEGINNING AND ENDING THE EXERCISE

For the reason mentioned above, it is best to employ half-note values at the beginning of the exercise. As in the other species, it is preferable to use a rest at the opening. The possibility of employing quarters at the beginning must not be altogether excluded. Again, it will be best to start with a quarter rest preceding the first three quarters.

By far the best ending results from a dissonant suspension into the leading tone as in fourth species. Now, however, it will be possible to decorate the resolution. The progression of Example 5-20 constitutes an

EXAMPLE 5-17

better than ... etc.

EXAMPLE 5-18

better than

EXAMPLE 5-19

etc.

EXAMPLE 5-20

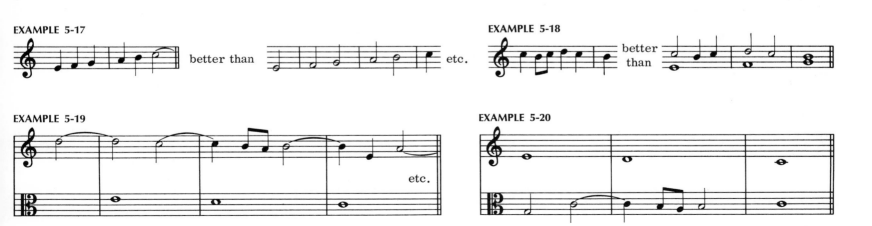

EXAMPLE 5-21

a)

cf

b)

cf

c)

cf

d)

cf

EXAMPLE 5-21 (continued)

e)

f)

g) Mozart[2]

h) Mozart[2]

[2] See Preface, p. ix

exception to the rule forbidding smaller values to precede untied half notes. The powerful melodic impulse of the leading tone into the tonic prevents any impression of arrested movement such as generally occurs with this type of rhythm.

Example 5-21 will serve to illustrate complete exercises.

EXERCISES

1. Play and sing Example 5-21 as suggested in previous chapters.
2. Select four cantus firmi, two major and two minor. Write two fifth-species lines above and below each cantus.
3. As a supplementary exercise write a two-part setting consisting of a fifth-species line and an original whole-note line.

2. THREE-PART COUNTERPOINT

GENERAL OBSERVATIONS

To the student familiar with the principles of fifth species in two parts and practiced in three-part writing in the preliminary species, fifth-species three-part counterpoint should present no problems. At this stage in his studies, the student should have acquired enough technique to write a correct exercise with facility. He must now exert every effort to make his exercises as esthetically pleasing as possible. It is important to gain experience in all permutations of cantus, first species, and fifth species. In particular, the more difficult combinations such as those with the florid counterpoint in the middle part should receive careful attention.

EXAMPLE 5-22

should not become

EXAMPLE 5-23

EXAMPLE 5-24

a)

b)

c)

EXAMPLE 5-24 (continued)

d)

Fux

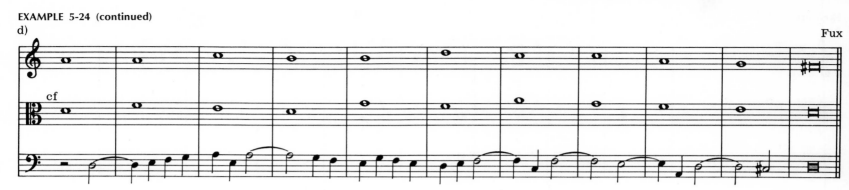

DISSONANCE TREATMENT

No new considerations of dissonance treatment arise through the addition of a third part. Caution is required, however, to ensure that dissonances are correct with respect to the first-species part as well as to the cantus. The decorated resolutions of the suspension dissonances must receive particular attention. It is all too easy to sketch in a fifth species part correct in relation to the cantus and later to add a first-species line involving incorrect dissonances (Example 5-22). It is often best to sketch the suspensions without decoration, leaving the embellishment of the resolutions until after the completion of the first-species part.

PARALLEL MOTION

No new problems arise with respect to parallel, accented, afterbeat, or hidden fifths, octaves, and unisons. Concentration on the fifth-species line to the exclusion of the first-species often leads to an excessive number of parallel thirds or tenths between the whole-note voices. The student is urged to exercise caution in this regard.

BEGINNING AND ENDING THE EXERCISE

As in two-part counterpoint, a half rest followed by a half note makes the best beginning. It is also possible to form an opening measure of a quarter rest followed by three quarter notes. Beginning with a tone rather than a rest, though less productive of independence, is not incorrect. The choice of tones in the initial measure will follow the usual procedures of three-part counterpoint.

The strongest cadence results from a suspension into the leading tone in the fifth-species part. The student can refer to the formulas for cadences in the chapter on fourth species; of course, it is now possible and desirable to decorate the resolution. If necessary, other types of cadence can occur, though none has as much impact as those featuring suspension into the leading tone. Example 5-23 presents some alternative possibilities.

Example 5-24 will serve to illustrate complete exercises in fifth-species three-part writing.

EXERCISES

1. Play and sing Example 5-24 as suggested in previous chapters.

2. Select two cantus firmi, one major and one minor. To each cantus write exercises in each of the six permutations.

3. As a supplementary exercise set a fifth-species line against two original whole-note parts.

PART TWO
THE TECHNIQUES OF PROLONGED COUNTERPOINT

COUNTERPOINT IN COMPOSITION, I

1. THE DIRECT APPLICATION OF SPECIES COUNTERPOINT

GENERAL OBSERVATIONS

Through our study of the five species we have become aware of the basic principles of counterpoint. We are now in a position to understand the application to composition of these basic techniques; we can begin to approach the wide field of prolonged counterpoint.[1] Prolonged counterpoint grows out of the elaboration and manipulation of the fundamental progressions with which we have become familiar. Of course the extent and complexity of this compositional elaboration can vary considerably, even within the framework of a single piece. Sometimes the fundamental progressions lie close to the surface; the relation to species counterpoint, therefore, is readily apparent. Often, however, the use of certain compositional devices, of prolonging techniques, will tend to push the basic contrapuntal progression into the background. In these instances the fundamental voice leading becomes less immediately evident. Its importance, however, is by no means diminished, for it is the underlying voice leading that gives impulse and coherence to the details of the musical foreground.

We shall begin with examples of simpler textures in which the connection with species counterpoint is close and even obvious. Gradually we shall proceed to passages in which the basic counterpoint is ex-

panded and modified by various techniques of prolongation. In order to make more easily apparent the relation between the examples from the literature and the species progressions, we have altered the note values in the graphs to conform with those of the given species. It must be understood that these reductions are solely intended as contrapuntal analyses; they do not attempt to reflect the rhythmic flow of the actual composition. Furthermore, they offer only partial explanations of these excerpts. For the moment we shall concentrate on one aspect alone: the connection between the examples and progressions from species counterpoint. Only later, after we have explored specific techniques of prolongation, will the meaning of certain melodic details, rhythms, and chords become clear. For an explanation of the symbols of graphic analysis in most examples of this book see the glossary of analytic notation (page ???).

PROGRESSIONS OF FIRST SPECIES

In Examples 6-1 to 6-4 the outer voices show intervallic relationships characteristic of first species. Study the outer-voice graphs; they indicate the basic voice leading divested of the individual rhythmic and

---

[1] See explanation of term, p. xviii.

EXAMPLE 6-1 Bach, Chorale 142

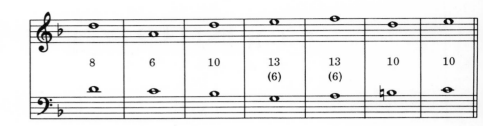

EXAMPLE 6-2 Bach, Chorale 298

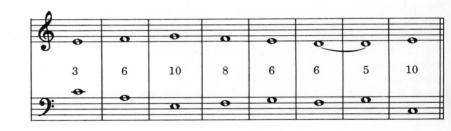

EXAMPLE 6-3 Bach, Chorale (with figured bass) 53

textural features of the actual composition. The connection with first species is evident; indeed, these reductions might well appear in first-species exercises. Play, in close succession, the excerpt and the reduction. Note to what extent the two-part counterpoint of the outer voices gives direction to the musical contour and determines the vertical sonorities and their succession.

Example 6-5 presents a very different surface texture. The outer voices are no longer in a note-against-note relation; the soprano line contains ten tones as against the four of the bass. The ten tones of the soprano, however, are not of equal significance. Quite instinctively the ear interprets the melodic progression D–E–F sharp as the essential motion of this excerpt. This progression shapes and directs the melodic line; the other tones constitute figurations or prolongations subordinate to the basic motion of an ascending third. These melodic figurations decorate the repeated D of the first two measures and separate the E and F sharp of the last two. The separation, however, does not at all cause the basic tones to lose contact with each other. If tones form a stable melodic structure, the ear can easily perceive their connectedness, even though they may be separated by the interpolation of other tones.

EXAMPLE 6-4   Beethoven, Piano Sonata, Op. 14, No. 2, 2nd movement

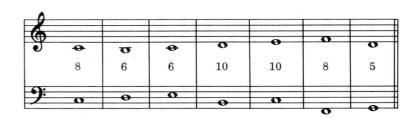

EXAMPLE 6-5   Handel, Chaconne in G major (Var. 6)

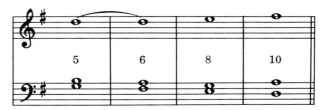

If the tones of the melody are of different orders of significance, so too are the intervals between the melody and the bass. The intervals formed by the main melodic line constitute the basic contrapuntal progression 5-6-8-10; this progression, of course, belongs to first species. This simple example leads to a conclusion of great importance for the understanding of voice leading: the relevance of species counterpoint to composition in no way depends upon a superficial resemblance between the texture of the composition and that of a given species. In Example 6-5 the outer voices are not in a note-against-note relationship; yet the underlying counterpoint relates to first species.[2]

Example 6-6 also presents a figurated melody as counterpoint to a more slowly moving bass. Graph a attempts to indicate, with quarter

[2] For the seeming parallels of measure 1 see chap. 7, Octaves and Fifths.

notes, the basic direction of the outer voices; the eighth notes and the stemless notes represent the figurating or prolonging tones (suspension A flat, neighboring note F, embellishing tone E flat, and appoggiatura D flat). Graph b, a further reduction, relates the motion of the outer voices to first-species counterpoint.

Example 6-7, a longer and more complex excerpt, is drawn from the beginning of the second movement of Beethoven's Piano Sonata, Op. 31, No. 1. In the next chapter we shall attempt to clarify the nature and function of melodic prolongations like those found in this phrase. At this point in our investigations it is more important for the reader to learn to distinguish between principal tones and figurating tones than to attempt to explain the specific functions of the latter. The reader should try to grasp the underlying first-species progression by separating the basic contrapuntal progression, with its forward movement, from

EXAMPLE 6-6   Beethoven, Piano Sonata, Op. 26, 1st movement

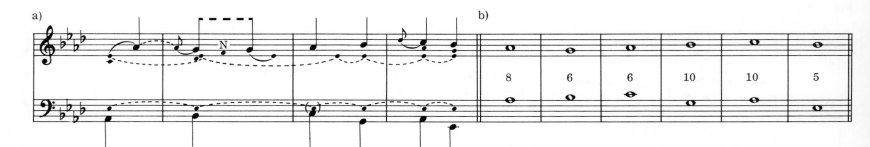

EXAMPLE 6-7 Beethoven, Piano Sonata, Op. 31, No. 1, 2nd movement

EXAMPLE 6-8   Bach, Chorale 103

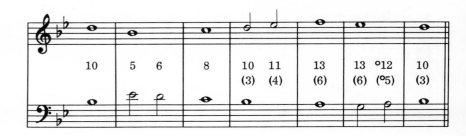

EXAMPLE 6-9   Bach, Chorale 353

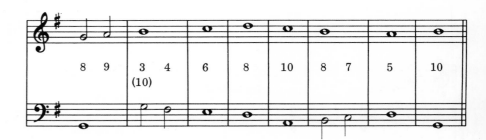

EXAMPLE 6-10   Brahms, Intermezzo, Op. 76, No. 7

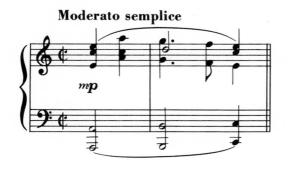
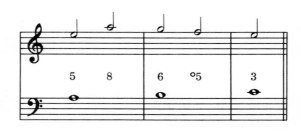

the delaying tones of melodic prolongation. The wide arabesques of the prolonging motions make possible the slow pace of the fundamental melodic progression in measures 1-4. In measure 5 figuration virtually ceases; only the grace notes at the lower octave echo the ascending scales of measures 2 and 4; this absence of figuration accelerates the motion of the basic melodic tones. As in Example 6-5 the musical ear perceives the continuity of the ascending line C–D–E through the interpolated tones of figuration.

In summing up we can state that the music of these last three examples can be understood as the motivic and rhythmic individualization of basic progressions studied in first-species counterpoint. The relation to first species does not depend upon the literal presence of note-against-note texture in the actual music. By reducing the counterpoint of the outer voices to its essential movement, we arrive at note-against-note progressions similar to those of first species and of great significance for the musical direction of the passage. As he gains experience in contrapuntal analysis, the reader will discover that outer-voice

progressions of this sort occur frequently in many compositions of widely varying styles and surface textures.

PROGRESSIONS OF SECOND SPECIES

In presenting examples related to second species, we shall again proceed from simple and obvious excerpts to those in which the basic contrapuntal progression is embedded in the deeper levels of the musical structure. We shall concentrate mainly upon the most characteristic feature of second species, the dissonant passing tone. Examples 6-8 and 6-9 require little comment. The reader will note that progressions from first and second species appear in alternation. Such mixtures of elements from different species occur frequently in composition.

The dissonant passing tone featured in the preceding examples also plays an important role in Example 6-10.

In Example 6-11 dissonant passing tones appear alternately in the

EXAMPLE 6-11   Beethoven, Piano Sonata, Op. 2, No. 1, 3rd movement

bass and the top voice. This distribution of melodic activity between the parts contributes to the fine balance of the texture.

As we have seen, the progressions of elementary counterpoint may serve as the basic voice leading of excerpts from the literature. This basic voice leading is given individuality and esthetic quality through the manifold possibilities of prolongation. Our next few examples show us that these techniques of prolongation are themselves frequently grounded in the familiar procedures of the species exercises. In second species, for example, we learned that large leaps effect changes of register and thereby add variety to the line. In Examples 6-12 to 6-14, transfers of register are used to elaborate melodic passing motions.

In Example 6-12 the basic motion of the right-hand part consists of a descending third, F–E flat–D. This motion appears in our final analytic

reduction, graph c. Bach prolongs this progression in the following way: the initial F is transferred down an octave; the lower F moves up a seventh to E flat. The downward octave and upward seventh are incidental detours prolonging the motion from the upper F to the passing tone E flat. It would be wrong, therefore, to interpret the outlined melodic seventh as an infraction of a contrapuntal rule or as an example of "free" counterpoint. Rather, it represents one of many possible expansions of the passing-tone principle first presented in second species.

In Example 6-13, from a recitative of Bach's *St. John Passion*, the transfer of register radically influences the contour of the phrase. In the previous passage transfer of register was applied in such a way as not to modify the relationship between the main tones F–E flat–D. In Example 6-13, however, the initial register does not recur. The first melodic tone,

EXAMPLE 6-12 Bach, Well-Tempered Clavier I, Prelude XI

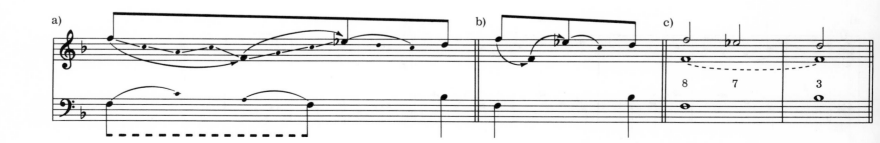

F sharp, is transferred to a lower register that is retained for the rest of the phrase; the main line F sharp–E–D, therefore, begins and ends in different registers.

Variations provide excellent illustrations of melodic prolongations. The theme often presents simple, direct motion that will be elaborated and prolonged in the subsequent variations. Example 6-14 is cited as confirming evidence that melodic progressions outlining sevenths (as in Example 6-12) or ninths (as in Example 6-13) often constitute the inversion or expansion of stepwise passing motions. In Mozart's Variations on *Lison dormait* the first phrase is varied as in Example 6-14.

The reader will observe that the descending third of the theme's top voice (Example 6-14a) appears in Variation II (measures 2-4) in the indicated prolonged form (Example 6-14b). The aware listener relates

the outlined interval of a seventh to the simple, stepwise progression of the theme.

In concluding this section we present another example drawn from a recitative of the *St. John Passion* (Example 6-15). Here we glimpse a new technique of far-reaching importance. By now the reader should have no difficulty in grasping the main melodic progression from C sharp through D sharp to E, and thence down through D natural to C sharp. Attentive listening reveals that this melody contains a secondary linear continuity: A–B–C sharp. Thus the vocal line in itself expresses an underlying two-part setting. We refrain from a detailed explanation of the melodic figurations, except to point out that the B which ends measure 1 anticipates the inner-voice tone of the following E major sixth chord.

EXAMPLE 6-13   Bach, St. John Passion, No. 16, Recitative

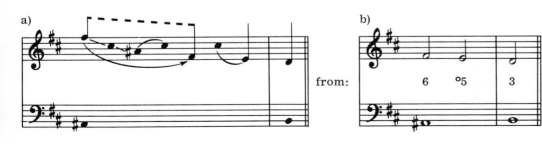

EXAMPLE 6-14 Mozart, Variations on Lison dormait

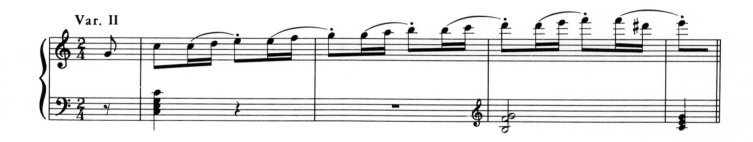

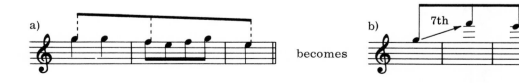

a) becomes b)

PROGRESSIONS OF THIRD SPECIES

The reader will remember that third species embodies melodic motions of varying types; direct progression between two different tones alternates with neighboring and embellishing motions. Procedures characteristic of third species occur with great frequency in compositions of many styles; study again Examples 6-5, 6-11, and 6-15, and note the compositional use of embellishing techniques similar to those of third species. Again we see that species counterpoint presents an abstraction of compositional procedures and helps us to understand the voice leading of music whose outward appearance may bear no resemblance to the species progressions.

Examples 6-16 and 6-17 are simple and require no comment.

Example 6-18 applies successive reduction to a phrase of Brahms. Graph a shows the "surface" counterpoint of the outer voices which demonstrates characteristics of third species in $\frac{3}{4}$ meter. Graph b omits the incomplete neighbor, F sharp, of the first measure and the passing tone, D, of the second. This reduction shows a progression similar to second-species writing; note that the ascending third, C sharp to E, is answered by D to B, the same interval in descending direction. Graph c removes the embellishing thirds and reveals the basic voice leading of the passage as it relates to first-species counterpoint. If it is to yield meaningful insights, this process of analytic reduction must not be ap-

EXAMPLE 6-15 **Bach, St. John Passion, No. 43, Recitative**

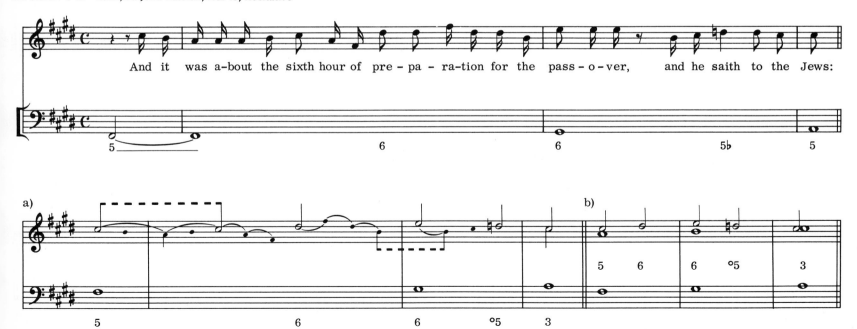

plied in a haphazard or arbitrary way. The first reduction omits tones of purely local significance, tones completely dependent upon their immediate context for their meaning and function. This will reveal a somewhat broader pattern within which we must again distinguish between principal and dependent tones. The final reduction will not necessarily contain the most prominent tones of the musical foreground; in Example 6-18, the highest tone, F sharp, is clearly a dependent tone of figuration.

The purpose of the final reduction, rather, is to show those tones that enter into the broadest and most far-reaching connections within the context under view. The procedure of successive reduction becomes much more difficult when applied to the analysis of longer and more complex musical continuities; but the basic principle remains the same.

Examples 6-19 and 6-20, also by Brahms, reduce themselves to progressions similar to rhythmically expanded third-species counterpoint

EXAMPLE 6-16 Schütz, Sacred Cantata

EXAMPLE 6-17 Fauré, Les Berceaux

Le   long du quai,____ les grands____ vais-seaux,

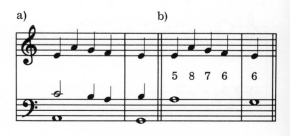

EXAMPLE 6-18   Brahms, Trio, Op. 114, 3rd movement

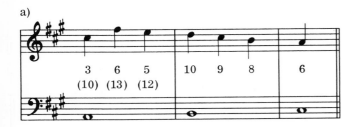

a)

b)

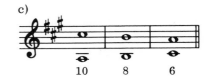

c)

EXAMPLE 6-19   Brahms, Piano Concerto No. 2, 3rd movement

(six and eight notes against one). They also indicate the possibility of emphasizing dissonant tones in a compositional framework. Note in particular the accented quality of the passing and neighboring tones.

Example 6-21 presents the opening of Chopin's Twenty-fourth Etude. The arpeggiated chords are not intended as a mere vehicle for pianistic display. As so often with Chopin—a contrapuntist of daring originality—the pianistic figurations embody voice leading of great economy and force. As in Example 6-18, a thorough analysis requires several reductions. The immediately apparent counterpoint between the outer voices resembles a third-species setting in $\frac{6}{4}$ meter (graph *b*); this setting in turn prolongs a second-species progression that determines

the essential motion of the top voice (graph *c*). Musical hearing depends upon conceiving the foreground texture as the imaginative prolongation of the underlying voice leading. The reader is advised to play in immediate succession graphs *c, b, a,* and then to play or listen to the Chopin phrase.

PROGRESSIONS OF FOURTH SPECIES

The syncopated progressions of fourth species (and the delayed, decorated resolutions of fifth) occur frequently in all compositional styles from the fifteenth through the nineteenth century. Fourth-species tech-

EXAMPLE 6-20 Brahms, Piano Quartet, Op. 60, 2nd movement

EXAMPLE 6-21   Chopin, Etude, Op. 25, No. 12

niques—even in prolonged form—are often easier to recognize than are the progressions of first, second, and third species. In later chapters we shall present excerpts in which the presence of syncopation is not immediately apparent. The examples in the present section, however, should offer the student no difficulty. As with the previous examples of this chapter, we shall not attempt to define the specific techniques of prolongation, although the added voice-leading graphs may indicate them. Our purpose here is solely to show the various categories of syncopation as they appear in composition. Some of the analyses show successive reductions; the final graphs will most clearly present the underlying syncopated progressions.

Our first four examples present a technique of great importance; the ascending series of consonant syncopations, 5-6 ⌢ 5-6. In three-part counterpoint we have learned that the 5-6 progression is best accompanied by tenths or thirds moving parallel to the bass. In Example 6-22 the outer voices move in tenths. The middle part clearly embellishes a 5-6 progression against the bass. Notice that the fifths at the head of each bar, although definitely implied by context, are not actually present; in the reduction, therefore, we have put the implied tones in parentheses.

A passage from Haydn's Piano Sonata, No. 44 (Example 6-23) shows a more elaborate version of the same voice-leading progression. Note the transfers of register in the top voice as well as the decorative tones—similar to those of fifth species—interpolated between the

EXAMPLE 6-22 Couperin, Ordre No. 5, Les Agréments

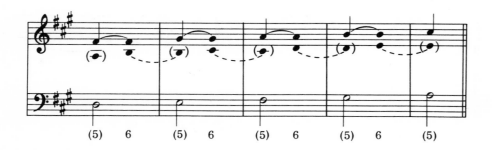

EXAMPLE 6-23   Haydn, Piano Sonata No. 44, 1st movement

fifths and sixths of the middle voice. On the third beat of the second measure the reader will notice a diminished chord. We shall frequently observe the use of diminished chords in sequential passages from the literature, especially where leading-tone impulse is required, as here.

Example 6-24, from C. P. E. Bach's Fifth Prussian Sonata, expresses the underlying three-part counterpoint in two voices (compare Example 6-15). Through techniques to be described in Chapter 7 the sixths of the 5-6 progression are transformed into dissonant $\frac{6}{5}$ chords (see graph a); this is an important technique of frequent occurrence.

In Example 6-25 the two notated voices again express three. Here the bass is prolonged; the brackets of graphs a and b indicate that the tones B flat and C on the first beats of measures 9 and 10 anticipate the thirds of the following chords. These bass tones are not the "roots" of seventh chords; for it is the bass tone, not the seventh of the top voice, that creates the dissonance.

When we studied fourth species, we learned that the descending progression 6-5̑ 6-5 emphasizes the fifths more than does the 5-6. For this reason, perhaps, 6-5 progressions occur much less frequently in the

EXAMPLE 6-24   C.P.E. Bach, Prussian Sonata No. 5, Finale

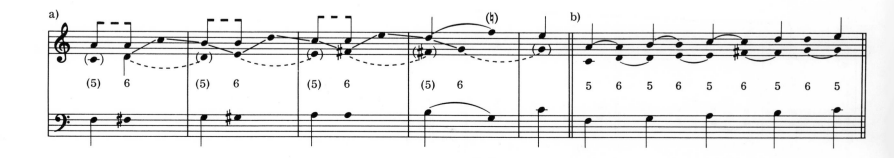

literature than do the 5-6's. We present two examples, widely divergent in style and texture. Example 6-26 contains a literal embodiment of the progression and needs no comment. In Example 6-27 the 6-5 succession appears literally only in the inner voice. The ear, however, also connects the downbeats of the top voice with the second beats of the middle voice, as shown in graph a.

We now proceed to illustrations of dissonant syncopations with their characteristic downward resolutions. In Example 6-28 we see a highly typical use of a 7-6 series with the outer voices moving in tenths.

The first seventh is prepared by a tied sixth that in turn originates from a fifth. Very often, as here, a 7-6 series is introduced by a single 5-6 progression. The reader will note the transfer of register in the top voice of measures 3 and 4.

In Example 6-29 the prevailing 7-6 progression is clearly evident. In this example the student should try to explain the functions of all the embellishing tones of the top voice up to measure 26. The brackets point out the parallelism between the broad melodic descent of measures 21-26 and its brief echo in measure 27.

EXAMPLE 6-25   Bach, Little Prelude No. 8

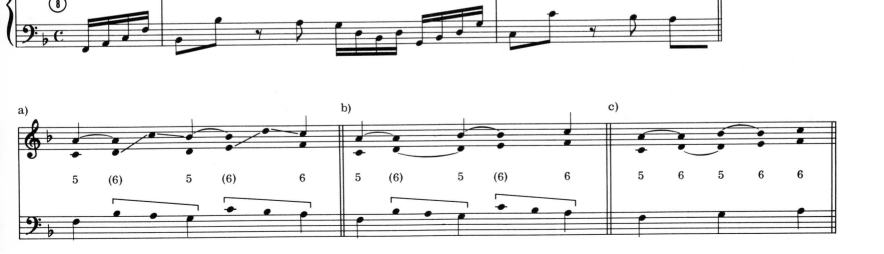

EXAMPLE 6-26 Arcadelt, Amour ha pouvoir

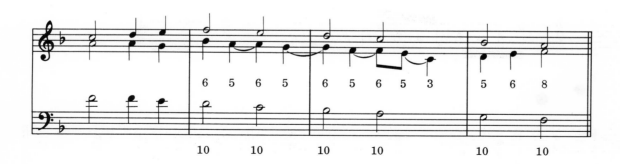

EXAMPLE 6-27   Brahms, Intermezzo, Op. 117, No. 3

EXAMPLE 6-28 Handel, Chaconne (Trois Leçons, No. 3), Var. 9

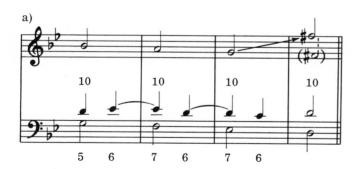

EXAMPLE 6-29   Scarlatti, Sonata No. 7 (Kirkpatrick, Vol. I)

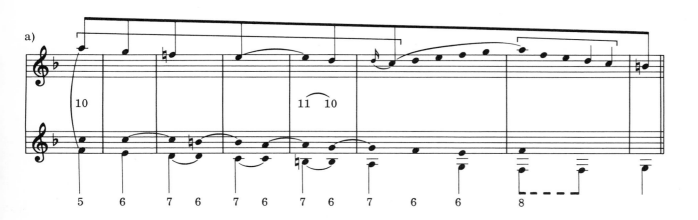

Example 6-30 is of great rhythmic interest. Here the normal metrical position of the suspension becomes reversed. The rhythmic grouping, therefore, contradicts the underlying meter; as a result, the dissonance appears on the accented third quarter, and not on the first, as would usually be the case. Instances of rhythmic manipulation or rhythmic prolongation are frequently to be found in the literature. The crossed lines of graph *a* point to the well-known device of *Stimmtausch*, or voice interchange (see Chapter 7).

In Example 6-31 the underlying 7-6 progression is interrupted by the embellishing thirds of top voice and bass. Here again, note the use of the diminished triad in measure 3.

In concluding this section we present excerpts from works of Mattheson and Bach. Example 6-32 shows the use of the 11-10 (or 4-3) syncopation; Example 6-33 demonstrates the important 9-10 (or 2-3) bass syncopation.

EXAMPLE 6-30 Haydn, Piano Sonata No. 51, Finale

a)

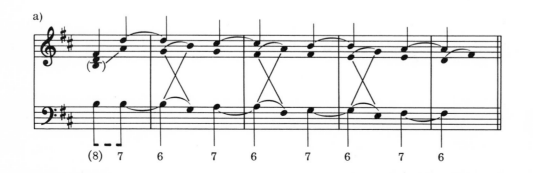

b)

EXAMPLE 6-31   Schumann, Waltz (Albumblätter, Op. 124, No. 4)

a)

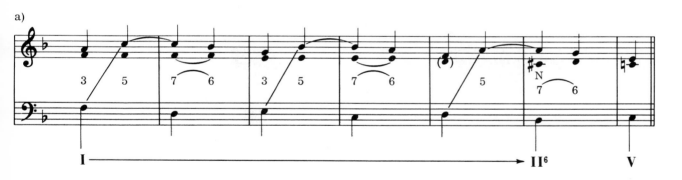

b)

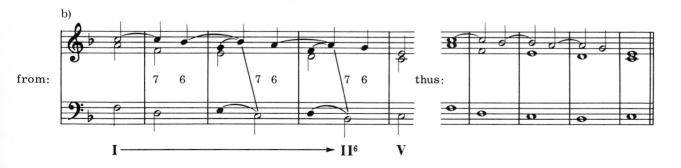

EXAMPLE 6-32   Mattheson, Minuet

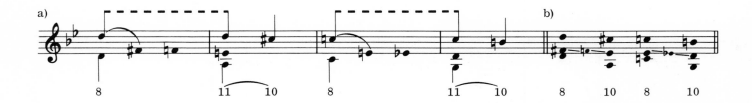

EXAMPLE 6-33   Bach, Well-tempered Clavier I, Prelude II

a)

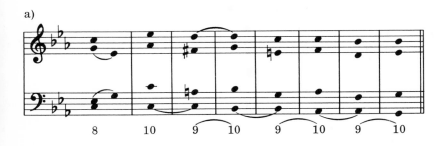

2. TWO MAJOR INFLUENCES ON CONTRAPUNTAL TEXTURE

CHORD PROLONGATION

We have now studied a number of examples showing the procedures of species counterpoint at work in excerpts from the literature. As we mentioned earlier, the reductions to progressions of elementary counterpoint were not intended as complete analytical explanations of these excerpts. And indeed, before we can deepen our understanding of the prolonged counterpoint of composition, we must explore two compositional principles which have had a profound impact on contrapuntal textures.

As early as the twelfth century, composers must have felt the need of going beyond the concept of contrapuntal motion for its own sake, of the movement of lines regulated by the desire for consonance and predominantly contrary motion. In the music of these composers larger continuities appear, and purposeful musical direction begins to be evi-

dent. A higher, more inclusive concept of musical organization becomes necessary, once the artistic will is directed toward creating greater units of musical continuity. In the course of striving for an organic whole—for the tonal organization of sections or of an entire piece—composers became aware of, and began to exploit, an architectonic factor which we shall call *chord prolongation*. (This will serve as an English equivalent for Heinrich Schenker's term *Auskomponierung eines Klanges*.) Centuries later, and conceivably out of chord prolongation, a second concept developed, that of harmonic progression. We follow the historical sequence in first introducing chord prolongation.

The basic idea of chord prolongation is the elaboration in time of a governing vertical sonority—a chord or an interval. Chord prolongation can be achieved by means of several techniques. The most significant of these techniques is the *horizontalization* of intervals belonging to the prolonged chord. When an interval is horizontalized, its tones unfold against a background determined in the vertical dimension by the governing sonority of which it is a part. Horizontalization, therefore,

EXAMPLE 6-34   Bach, Chorale 6

EXAMPLE 6-35   Bach, Chorale 54

EXAMPLE 6-36   Bach, Chorale 63

EXAMPLE 6-37

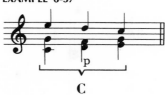

draws into close interrelation the two dimensions of music, the vertical and the horizontal.

Melodies often horizontalize intervals of the governing sonority, thereby prolonging it. Let us study the opening phrases of three chorale tunes (Examples 6-34 to 6-36). The reader will easily perceive that these melodic lines move within intervals of the governing F-major, G-major, and A-major triads. The tones belonging to the triads, of course, need not appear in immediate succession; they may be connected by passing tones or decorated by neighbors.

The process of horizontalization is by no means confined to a single melodic line. In textures of two, three, or more parts, horizontalized intervals can unfold simultaneously in several voices. In this case chord prolongation gives rise to a succession of intervals or chords, all of which are subordinate to the inclusive, governing sonority. Examples 6-37 and 6-38 present prolongations of the C-major triad; the factor of chord prolongation is indicated by the brackets under the progressions. In these examples the outer voices horizontalize intervals of this chord, thereby expanding it in time. The second chord in each example results from the passing tones of the outer voices; it is therefore a passing chord *within* the prolonged C triad. (In these examples the outer voices exchange tones between the first and the last chord. Thus in Example

6-38 the soprano moves from C to E while the bass makes the complementary move, E–C. This illustrates the technique of voice interchange referred to above.)

Chord prolongation also results if only one of the outer voices fills in the horizontalized interval with a stepwise passing progression. In Example 6-39 the A of the bass, supporting the passing tone C of the top voice, is an incomplete neighbor of the following B flat. The chord it supports results from both neighboring and passing tones; we therefore call it a *neighbor-passing chord* within the prolonged B flat triad. Incomplete neighbors like that of Example 6-39 often substitute for the more direct passing tone; in this sense the A of Example 6-39 can be understood as a substitution for C. The reader will remember from second species that a leap of a fourth often substitutes for direct stepwise progression.

In Example 6-40, as in Example 6-39, the top voice fills in the intervals of the governing chord while the bass outlines a chordal interval only with its first and last tones. The bass moves down a sixth from A to C sharp; the sixth is subdivided into a third plus a fourth by means of the F sharp of the third beat. The third, A–F sharp, is then filled in with a passing tone. The technique of interval subdivision, like that of substitution, is known to us from second species. In Example 6-40 the

EXAMPLE 6-38 Scheidt, Das Görlitzer Tabulaturbuch (1650), No. 95

C

EXAMPLE 6-39 Bach, Chorale 27

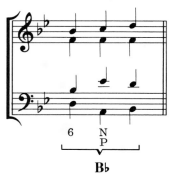

6   N
     P

B♭

EXAMPLE 6-40 Bach, Chorale 35

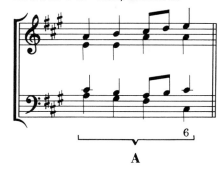

6

A

a)

A

chords of the second and third beats arise from the contrary motion of the bass to the ascending top voice.

Neighboring and embellishing chords play a significant role in chord prolongation. The reader will remember from third species that neighboring and embellishing tones, from which these chords arise, extend the domain and enhance the value of the main tones they prolong. The voice leading of Example 6-41 is determined by neighboring tones; in the graph the downward transfer of register between the

lower-neighbor F sharp and the upper-neighbor A has been omitted in order to clarify the basic voice leading.

In Example 6-42 the subdominant chord results from the neighboring tone of the top voice and the embellishing tone of the bass; this subdominant, in consequence, functions as a neighbor-embellishing chord ($\begin{smallmatrix}N\\EM\end{smallmatrix}$).

The C^6 chord in Example 6-43 is also a neighbor-embellishing

EXAMPLE 6-41 Bach, Partita No. 6, Toccata

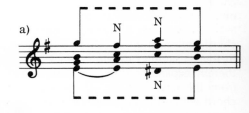

EXAMPLE 6-42 Schein, Die Nacht ist kommen

EXAMPLE 6-43 Scheidt, Das Görlitzer Tabulaturbuch, No. 43

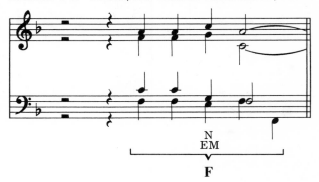

EXAMPLE 6-44 Scheidt, ibid., No 28

chord, only here the neighboring tone appears in the bass and the embellishing tone in the top voice.

Examples 6-44 to 6-46 require no further written explanations.

The preceding examples illustrating chord prolongation are short and simple. As we shall see later, composers have used this technique to create much larger contexts and to unify much larger spans than those illustrated in this section. Indeed, the broadly inclusive use of chord prolongation represents one of the most significant factors distinguishing the counterpoint of composition from the abstract techniques of the five species. In species counterpoint we study the elements of voice leading: the characteristics and behavior of the consonant intervals, the three fundamental types of dissonance, and general aspects of linear motion and of the combination of voices. In the species exercises—especially in some of the embellishing motions of third species—we sometimes encounter progressions that resemble rudimentary chord prolongations. However, chord prolongation on a large scale would be contrary to the purposes of species counterpoint;

embellishing progressions, therefore, must occur within a single measure or from one downbeat to the next. In species counterpoint the all-important problem of direction must be solved in terms of motion to and from climactic points; aside from these factors no broad organizing principle is evident.

In becoming aware of chord prolongation we begin to study the elements of voice leading in their compositional environment. In all of the preceding examples techniques of species counterpoint are evident, and in some of them the interval movement relates closely to procedures of the species exercises. These procedures, however, take on an enhanced meaning when deployed within prolonged chords. The musical listener relates the immediate event—the passing, neighboring, or embellishing chord—to the governing sonority; in so doing he hears, as it were, two events at the same time but on different levels of perception. The underlying chord, though not always acoustically present, functions as a background against which other tones and sonorities unfold.

EXAMPLE 6-45 Palestrina, Motet, Salvator mundi

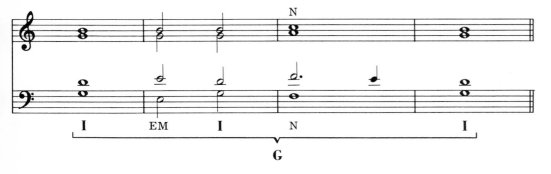

EXAMPLE 6-46 Gastoldi, Balletto

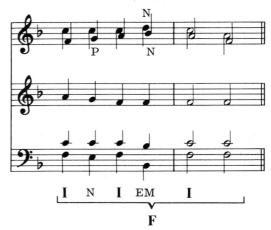

HARMONIC PROGRESSIONS

Considerably after the appearance of chord prolongation a second element emerged out of the contrapuntal voice leading that had evolved through centuries of rich experience. This new element was harmony. Harmonic progressions begin to appear in the music of the late Middle Ages and early Renaissance, but they develop into a powerful organizing force only during the later fifteenth and the sixteenth centuries.

At this time we shall present only the basic principles of harmony; later musical examples will throw further light on particular harmonic influences on voice leading (see Chapters 7 and 8). Harmony and counterpoint represent fundamental architectural forces in our music; these two forces act upon and react to each other, and sometimes become very closely interconnected. However, the harmonic and the contrapuntal concepts differ markedly in their essential characteristics; only if we are clear about the essential nature of each will we understand the various ways in which their cooperation and fusion organize musical textures.

In its essence the harmonic concept is based upon the relationship subsisting between chords with roots a fifth apart. Placed within the framework of tonality this relationship expresses itself most completely by means of the chord progression I–V–I (Example 6-47). The bass of this progression unfolds horizontally the fundamental, fifth, and upper octave of the tonic chord; it is therefore a partial horizontalization of the triad, or a complete horizontalization of the $\frac{8}{5}$ chord, the primary sonority of medieval music and the progenitor of the triad (Example

6-48). The I–V–I progression results when triads crystallize above these bass tones.

The fundamental I–V–I progression is frequently elaborated through the interpolation of another chord between I and V; because of their frequent association with the tonic-dominant relationship, we accept these intervening chords as harmonies. Example 6-49 presents some of these expanded harmonic progressions. I–III–V–I results from the horizontalizing or arpeggiation of the complete triad. The frequently heard I–IV–V–I molds the fifth relationship below as well as above the tonic into a single harmonic progression. In I–II–V–I the V is preceded by its own upper fifth, and in I–VI–V–I the opportunity is given to approach the V from above.[3]

Despite the harmonic character of the progressions of Example 6-49, the contrapuntal implications of the stepwise motion from IV to V, from I to II, and from VI to V must not be overlooked.[4] Counterpoint makes itself even more strongly felt by introducing II^6, II^6_5, or, less often, IV^6 on the way from I to V. The absence of the fifth relationship in the bass weakens the harmonic function of the intervening chord, but because of the overriding motion to the V we accept these chords as members of harmonic progressions I–II^6 or II^6_5–V–I, and I–IV^6–V–I.

The basic tonic-dominant principle can also be applied to non-

[3] For more on the harmonic concept see Felix Salzer, *Structural Hearing* (2d ed.), New York, 1962, Part 2, chap. 4.

[4] See Schenker, *Der freie Satz* (Vienna, 1935), vol. I, pp. 55–57.

EXAMPLE 6-47

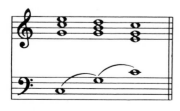

EXAMPLE 6-48

tonic chords; that is, such chords can be preceded or followed by temporary dominants. We call these temporary dominants *applied* or *secondary* dominant chords.[5] Related to applied dominants are incomplete harmonic progressions such as II–V–I or I–IV–V.

The harmonic nature of a progression—whether of the fundamental I–V–I or any of its elaborations and derivatives—is essentially dependent upon the use of the V in root position. Only then is the fifth relationship directly expressed in the bass part, the foundation of the musical texture. When the V appears in inversion it generally demonstrates a neighboring or passing function; it is then a contrapuntal rather than a harmonic dominant. We employ the letters N, EM, and P under

bass notes to indicate the contrapuntal character of the sonority they support (neighboring, embellishing, or passing chord). Example 6-50 contrasts a harmonic progression with one containing a neighboring dominant chord. The II, III, IV, and VI chords should be considered harmonic chords or harmonies only if they are used in connection with the tonic-dominant relationship as in Example 6-49; that is, if they form part of a progression from I to V. If they occur between two tonics, their contrapuntal role as neighboring or embellishing chord is the predominant one. Whereas I–V–I indicates a harmonic progression, I–EM–I and I–N–I are contrapuntal progressions.

The crucial bass voice is the deciding factor in determining the presence or absence of harmonic function. If the bass, as in Example 6-51, shows a neighboring or embellishing motion, the progression is contrapuntal; if, however, the bass indicates a harmonic progression,

---

[5] See Mitchell, *Elementary Harmony* (3d ed.), Englewood Cliffs, 1965, chap. 17. Also Salzer, *Structural Hearing*, Examples 292–303.

EXAMPLE 6-49

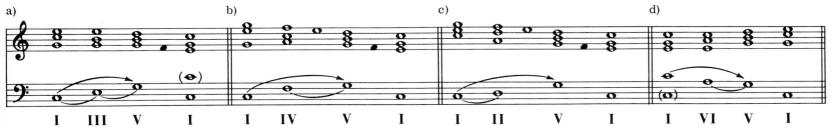

a) I III V I   b) I IV V I   c) I II V I   d) I VI V I

EXAMPLE 6-50

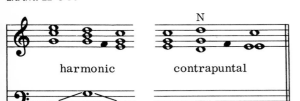

I V I   I N I

harmonic   contrapuntal

EXAMPLE 6-51

I EM I   I EM I   I EM I   I N I

the embellishing or neighboring motion of the top voice does not change the harmonic function of the chords (Example 6-52).

The reader will have noted that the view of harmony expressed in this section differs from those generally held. We do not consider all vertical sonorities to be harmonies, nor do we regard all successions of such sonorities as harmonic progressions. According to our view, counterpoint is the more inclusive, harmony the more restrictive, principle of musical organization. The harmonic element in a progression is the relationship between chords as such. If a harmonic progression is to be realized in sound, we must have voice leading. Therefore, no har-

monic progression can be embodied in an actual musical setting without the participation of counterpoint.

CONTRAPUNTAL CHORD PROLONGATIONS WITHIN HARMONIC FRAMEWORKS

As harmonic progressions became part of the compositional fabric, composers began to employ a variety of means for integrating contra-

EXAMPLE 6-52

EXAMPLE 6-53   Févin, Agnus Dei from Missa Mente tota

puntal and harmonic procedures. One of the most important of these means of fusion is the use of a harmonic progression as the structural framework within which the contrapuntal texture takes shape. We begin with an early example of contrapuntal motion within the harmonic framework I–V–I (Example 6-53). The opening imitation serves to prolong tonic harmony until measure 6. (We shall see in Chapter 10 that imitation constitutes a powerful means of prolonging chords.) In measure 6 the bass begins a brief passing motion down to the V (indicated by the straight arrow); the V appears as a minor chord supporting an embellishing tone of the top voice. The minor V occurs frequently

in the modal repertory and is found in later music as well. The lack of a leading tone lessens the forward impulse to the tonic; this weakens somewhat but does not impair completely the harmonic function of this chord.

Three excerpts from Beethoven's work follow; all of them show a prolongation of the initial tonic chord of a harmonic progression. Frequently, as in these examples, the end of a chord prolongation falls on a weak part of the measure; this helps link the prolonged chord to the following sonority. In Example 6-56 the melody clearly prolongs the tonic in the first two measures, the bass counterpointing with a motion

EXAMPLE 6-54 Beethoven, Sonata for Violin and Piano Op. 96, 2nd movement   **EXAMPLE 6-55** Beethoven, Trio, Op. 97, 3rd movement

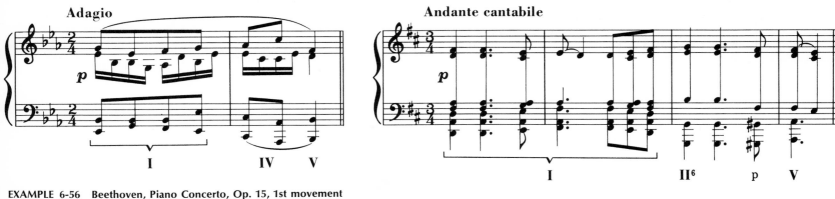

EXAMPLE 6-56 Beethoven, Piano Concerto, Op. 15, 1st movement

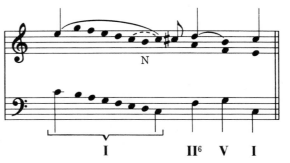

within a descending octave C–C. Consequently the chords of measures 1 and 2 are passing chords within the prolonged tonic; the technique of consecutive $\frac{6}{3}$ chords is familiar to us, of course, from three-part counterpoint. The tonic is of a structurally higher order than the passing chords moving within it; as the governing sonority it creates the musical space within which the passing chords move. The harmonic movement proceeds to II^6–V and I; the progression I–II^6–V–I, therefore, constitutes the structural framework of this brief example. In hearing this we realize a distinction not only between harmonic and contrapuntal chords but, even more importantly, between the tones that form the basic direction or structure and those that elaborate or prolong this structure. (As we shall see in Chapters 7 and 8, harmonic progressions can also fulfill prolonging functions.)

As a final example we show a chorale setting of the early eighteenth century (see Example 6-57). The contrapuntal techniques within the prolonged tonic are indicated in graph a. The small notes show a realization of the figured bass.

The foregoing discussion enables us to formulate a conception of chord function as distinct from chord grammar, the labeling of each simultaneity according to component intervals and position within the scale. Function depends first of all upon the structural or prolonging value of the chord within the context under view. Function also results from contrapuntal activity; a passing chord is significantly different from a neighboring or embellishing chord even when the two chords contain the same tones and bear the same grammatical label. Other contrapuntal procedures, such as interval subdivision and the techniques of suspension and anticipation, also influence chord function. Finally, function arises from harmonic relationships and from harmonic influences upon voice leading.

The preceding chapter has presented a brief introduction to prolonged counterpoint. At the present stage it would be premature to introduce written exercises of a quasi-compositional nature. Such exercises will be helpful only after the student has learned more about specific techniques of prolongation. Written exercises of various kinds will be presented after Chapters 7, 8, and 9.

EXAMPLE 6-57   Freylinghausen, Figured-bass chorale, Lobe den Herren

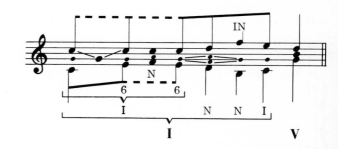

7

COUNTERPOINT IN COMPOSITION, II

1. MELODIC-CONTRAPUNTAL PROLONGATIONS

POLYPHONIC MELODY (THE UNFOLDING OF INTERVALS;
MOTIONS TO AND FROM INNER-VOICE TONES)

In the preceding chapter we observed the use of progressions from species counterpoint in compositions of varying styles and textures. Our principal aim was to discover the basic voice leading; we touched only lightly upon the processes through which the contrapuntal outline becomes living music. In this chapter we shall follow the complementary procedure. We shall concentrate upon the techniques of prolongation that are used to manipulate the progressions of elementary counterpoint. Each example has been chosen to illustrate a specific technique. However the reader must do more than merely recognize the given technique. He must try to achieve contact with the total voice-leading fabric of each example; only by so doing will he begin to understand the manifold possibilities of prolonged counterpoint.

Some of the most obvious contrasts between elementary and prolonged counterpoint lie in the realm of melody. Among the important attributes of compositional melody is its ability to suggest two or more voices moving in counterpoint to each other; such melody is no longer confined to the horizontal dimension but contains important vertical implications. In Chapter 6 we presented an example showing how a single melody (a recitative from Bach's *St. John Passion*) can embody two linear continuities (see Example 6-15). Let us now investigate this compositional resource in greater depth.

Our first example is drawn from a theoretical work of the eighteenth century, from Johann Mattheson's *Der vollkommene Capellmeister* (1739). Mattheson presents a short two-voice setting and shows how it can be transformed into various single melodies. We give Mattheson's model and two of his derivatives; a few obvious misprints are corrected (Example 7-1).

Mattheson's examples, of course, are designed to serve a pedagogic rather than an artistic purpose; they demonstrate with admirable clarity the possibility of incorporating two distinct lines within a single melody. We refer to such melodies as those of Example 7-1 as *polyphonic melodies*. The implied polyphony results from an oscillation between the upper and lower components of the melody. The vertical intervals of the underlying two-part setting are *unfolded* into the horizontal dimension. This unfolding of intervals can give rise to apparent melodic dissonance. Note the sevenths of Example 7-1*b* and *c* (see asterisks); they result from suspensions in the underlying two-part counterpoint. The suspensions are prepared and resolved regularly (the resolution of the first seventh to a tenth will be explained in connection with combined species). Polyphonic melodies are more highly organized, more complex, more differentiated than are the simple melodic lines of elementary counterpoint. Their use of dissonant leaps constitutes an evolution from rather than a violation of the principles embodied in the species exercises. Incidentally, species counterpoint gives a faint foreshadowing of polyphonic melody in the embellishing leaps of third species and the decorated resolutions of fifth.

Example 7-2, from one of Mendelssohn's *Songs without Words,* shows a more refined and subtle use of polyphonic melody than do Mattheson's simple illustrations. At first acquaintance the texture seems to resemble a slightly elaborated mixture of first and second species (graph *a*). In terms of elementary counterpoint, however, one would naturally question the leap of a diminished fifth in the first measure of

the melody. Like the sevenths of Mattheson's examples, this diminished fifth results from the unfolding of an essentially vertical interval; the two component tones belong to different "voices" of the implied polyphony. Graph *b* demonstrates the polyphonic character of the melody. The upper component proceeds from A through G to F sharp, while the lower begins on F sharp, skips down to C sharp, and from there moves up by step until both "voices" meet on F sharp. Here, of course, the polyphonic melody is supported by a bass; the lower segment of the melody, therefore, functions as the inner voice of the underlying three-part setting (graph *c*) which prolongs the D-major chord.

EXAMPLE 7-1   Mattheson, from Der vollkommene Capellmeister

a)

becomes:

b)

or:

c)

Example 7-3 presents in abstract form some of the possibilities for unfolding a succession of intervals. The notation of the horizontalized thirds in Example 7-3c and *d* indicates not only the existence of two implied voices but also the manner of their connection. In c the motion proceeds from the top voice to the inner voice and from the inner voice back to the top voice. In *d* we see a less frequently encountered pattern; the melody begins with two tones of the inner voice before turning to the top voice of the underlying setting.

EXAMPLE 7-2   Mendelssohn, Songs without Words, Op. 85, No. 4

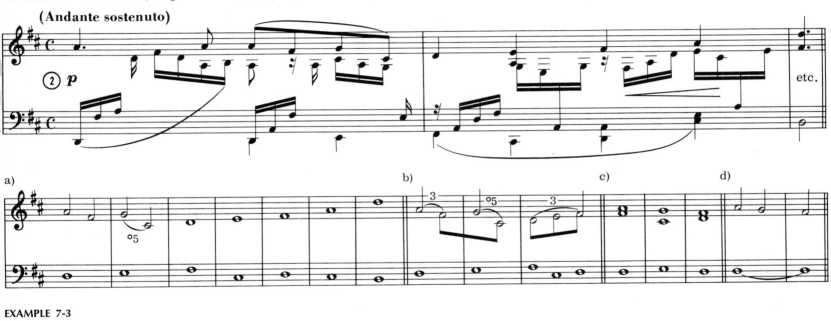

EXAMPLE 7-3

Let us now examine several excerpts of great diversity illustrating the technique of unfolding. A short passage from a sonata by C. P. E. Bach (Example 7-4) shows the possibility for polyphonic implication in a rapidly moving figuration.

In Example 7-5 unfolded intervals shape the basic melodic contour.

Note the clearly implied sustaining of E-flat as the first inner-voice tone of measure 3.

We turn now to a phrase by Mendelssohn in which the unfolded intervals are partially filled in (Example 7-6). This example also indicates that unfolded intervals may appear in the bass and in middle voices. In

EXAMPLE 7-4   C. P. E. Bach, Prussian Sonata No. 4, 1st movement

EXAMPLE 7-5   Haydn, Trio No. 29, 1st movement

the left-hand part, measure 4, G, the fifth of dominant harmony, appears before the true bass tone, C.

The unfolding of intervals, whereby the melody moves to and from the inner-voice region, creates a hierarchy of tonal significance. All the tones of the unfolded intervals belong to the melody; but they are not all of equal significance. We must distinguish the main tones that form the basic melodic direction from the prolongations that separate these main tones from one another. This is especially true where the melody, after completing the first unfolding, begins the second one with an inner-voice tone of a new chord before returning to the top-voice

EXAMPLE 7-6   Mendelssohn, Songs without Words, Op. 85, No. 1

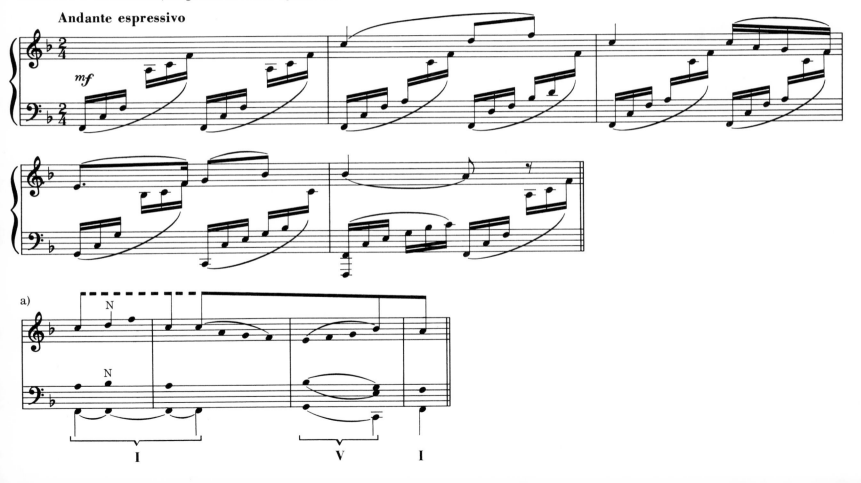

region. Here the separation of the main tones creates tensions that must be carefully observed in analysis and in performance. Bear this in mind when studying Example 7-7, the opening theme of the *Andante* from Mozart's Piano Concerto, K. 467.

In the phrase by Haydn, Example 7-8, a dissonant neighboring note A, skips to D, a tone of the inner-voice region. A stepwise ascent from

EXAMPLE 7-7   Mozart, Piano Concerto, K. 467, 2nd movement

the inner voice then leads to the G of measure 2, the delayed resolution of the dissonance.

A melodic progression strikingly similar to the example by Haydn is found in the excerpt (see Example 7-9) from a counterpoint treatise by the sixteenth-century composer and theorist Vincenzo Galilei.[1] Galilei

[1] Cited in Claude V. Palisca, "Vincenzo Galilei's Counterpoint Treatise," *Journal of the American Musicological Society*, vol. 9, no. 2, p. 90, 1956. The analytic explanation is ours, not Galilei's.

EXAMPLE 7-8   Haydn, Piano Sonata No. 40, 1st movement

EXAMPLE 7-9   Vincenzo Galilei, Discorso intorno all'uso delle dissonanze

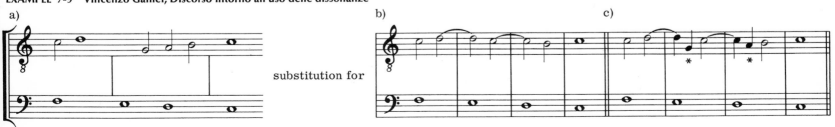

substitution for

suspends the neighboring tone D so that it becomes a dissonant seventh. Instead of resolving the seventh by stepwise descent, Galilei allows it to leap to the inner-voice tone G. From G the melody ascends to the top-voice tone C. Note that the motion out of the inner voice uses tones that would appear in the decorated resolutions of fifth species (Example 7-9c). Both the Haydn and the Galilei examples illustrate the prolonged use of dissonance, a topic that will be discussed later in this chapter.

The polyphonic character of a melody can be indicated by the use of two terms: *unfolding* and *motion to and from the inner voice*. To a certain extent these terms overlap. In general we shall use the expression *unfolding* to denote a succession of two or more intervals, whereas single leaps and motions filling in the horizontalized intervals will be termed *motions to and from the inner voice*.

THE MANIPULATION OF REGISTER (TRANSFER OF REGISTER; SUPERPOSITION OF INNER-VOICE TONES)

The manipulation of register constitutes an important compositional resource; registral contrast can help to shape both the detail and the large section. Our present concern is to investigate the impact of registral manipulation upon melody—especially upon instrumental melody with its wide ranges and often rugged contours. As the reader will recall (review Examples 6-12 to 6-14), a *transfer of register* occurs when a tone is placed in significant juxtaposition with its upper or lower octave (or, on occasion, multiple octave). Closely related to the tech-

nique of octave transfer are the inversion to a seventh and the expansion to a ninth of stepwise progression. Example 7-10 illustrates these latter techniques schematically and shows their relationship to octave transfer.

Transfers of register vary in dimension and in significance. Sometimes they create merely a fleeting play of color. At other times they form the basis of extended musical development. Later—especially in Chapters 8 and 10—we shall have occasion to observe large-scale register transfers. In this section we shall concentrate upon smaller details. In a close context transfers of register—in particular, interval expansion and inversion—can lead to direct or slightly elaborated melodic dissonance. In Example 7-11, interval inversion accounts for the melodic seventh; the diminished fifth results from an unfolding above the basic line of the melody.

Next we present an excerpt from Handel containing both inversion and expansion (Example 7-12). The inverted progressions (the sevenths) are filled in with passing tones; the ninths, on the other hand, are stated directly. The large ascending leaps emphasize the basically upward direction of the melodic line. As a whole the progression of parts expresses the A major triad by means of the familiar 5-6 technique of fourth species.

Example 7-13 is also from Handel. Here a basic progression in seconds (shown in the *Air*) is manipulated in the variation into filled-in ninths. A sensitive performer will project the underlying progression through the cascading thirty-seconds.

EXAMPLE 7-10

A. Interval expansion

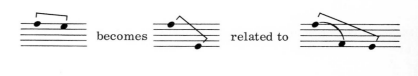

B. Interval inversion

EXAMPLE 7-11   Bach, St. John Passion, No. 41

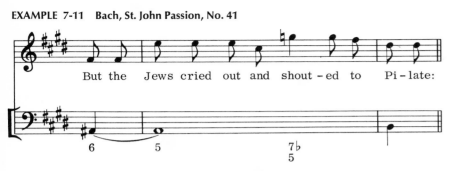

But the   Jews cried out and shout – ed to   Pi – late:

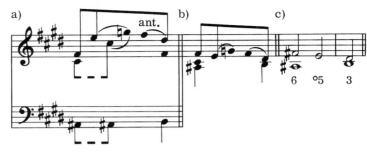

EXAMPLE 7-12   Handel, Violin Sonata XIII, 1st movement

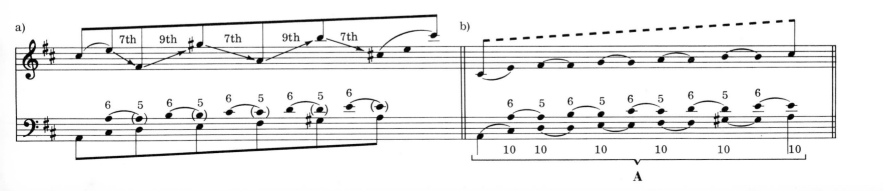

We now turn to two examples from the *Prussian Sonatas* of C. P. E. Bach. In the first, Example 7-14, the close juxtaposition of two registers (measures 3-4) produces a sixth as inversion of a third; this in turn motivates another interval inversion resulting in the leap of a seventh.

In Example 7-15, from the fifth *Prussian Sonata,* a neighboring motion is expressively manipulated.

A more indirect use of interval inversion can be observed in the excerpt given in Example 7-16. Graph *b* omits the change of register in order to reveal the underlying progression. Comparing this reduction with the composition we note that the inverted progression between the high E and its neighbor, F, is subdivided by a melodic unfolding,

E–G, and an embellishing motion A–F. The second interval inversion is also subdivided, but it aims more directly at its goal. Note the beautiful repetition in measure 4 of the G–G sharp–A of measure 2. The meaning of the repeated tone group changes according to context; in measure 4 the A is a dissonant incomplete neighbor.

The reader should remember that not all melodic sevenths and ninths result from transfer of register within a single linear continuity. Many arise out of the unfolding of intervals in a polyphonically conceived melody (cf. Example 7-1).

Our next examples introduce a new technique, the *superposition of inner-voice tones.* This technique consists of the shift of an inner-voice

EXAMPLE 7-13   Handel, Suite V, Air

EXAMPLE 7-14   C. P. E. Bach, Prussian Sonata No. 6, 1st movement

(meas. 3–6)

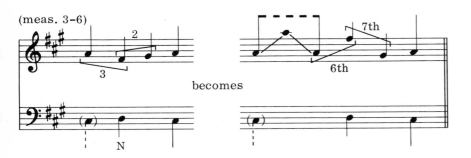

becomes

EXAMPLE 7-15   C. P. E. Bach, Prussian Sonata No. 5, 2nd movement

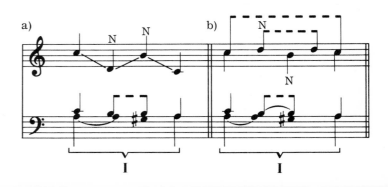

EXAMPLE 7-16   Haydn Trio No. 27, 1st movement

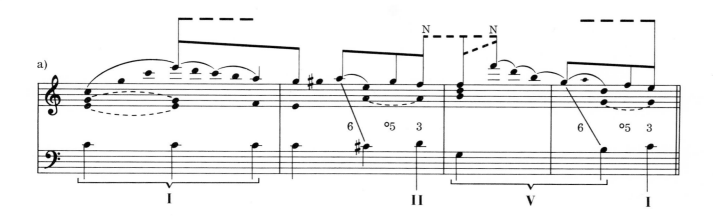

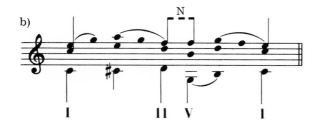

tone above the previous tone of the top voice. In its simplest, most obvious, and probably original form, superposition results when an actually notated inner voice crosses above the upper voice. This occurs in Example 7-17, from a trio sonata of Corelli. In the first measure the second violin is above the first; after resolving its suspension, however, the first violin leaps above the second. This process continues; each lower voice is shifted above the previously higher one until the second violin arrives at high A. A larger melodic continuity emerges out of the two overlapping parts; the ear perceives a melodic ascent C–D–E–F–G–A; this motion, of course, does not belong to either of the parts singly but arises out of their combination. Incidentally the voice leading of this example relates to combined-species counterpoint and will be taken up again in Chapter 9.

In Example 7-18, as in the Corelli excerpt, superposition results from the crossing of voices. Here the inner-voice shifts are accomplished by means of transfers of register; seconds are expanded into ninths. In the measure preceding the quoted passage the D chord appears with D in the top voice; this is shown by the tones in parentheses at the beginning of graphs a and b. Graph b shows the underlying stepwise progression; graph c removes the pedal point in order to clarify the relationship with second species.

Example 7-19 presents a short but complex excerpt from the intro-

duction to the last movement of Beethoven's Piano Sonata, Op. 101. Unlike the Brahms and Corelli examples there is no crossing of separately notated voices; however the melodic skips result from the shift, an octave upward, of inner-voice tones. We have indicated B as the top-voice tone of graph a, the basic progression as it would appear without superposition; we have done so because B begins the passage as cited. If he consults the score, the reader will observe that the climactic F enters into a broad melodic connection with E in the same register four measures later.

Let us now turn to a passage from C. P. E. Bach's *Fourth Prussian Sonata* (see Example 7-20). In this excerpt superposition takes place between the implied voices of a polyphonic melody. Graph b shows the melodic unfolding, first in its simplest form and then as transformed by superposition. In this example the melodic leaps do not originate from actually sounding tones of the inner voice; they stem from tones implied by context and latent in the sonorities (see the tones in parentheses, graph a). The upward shifts throw into relief a two-note motive; these sequential superpositions occur frequently in the literature. Observe the descending direction of the two-note figure; as in species counterpoint the leaps are followed by stepwise motion in the opposite direction. Note the register transfers.

EXAMPLE 7-17   Corelli, Sonata da Camera, Op. 4, No. 1, Allemanda

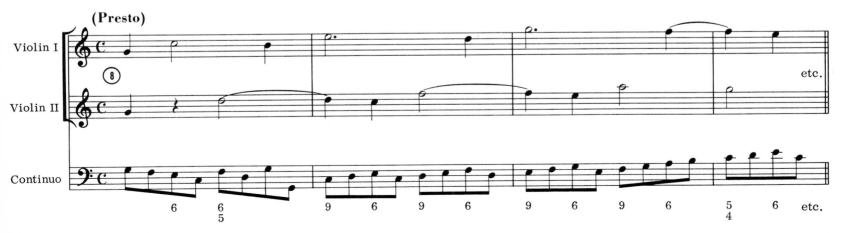

EXAMPLE 7-18 Brahms, Romanze, Op. 118, No. 5

EXAMPLE 7-19 Beethoven, Piano Sonata, Op. 101, Introduction to last movement

Langsam und sehnsuchtsvoll

EXAMPLE 7-20   C. P. E. Bach, Prussian Sonata No. 4, 1st movement

a)

b)

becomes

EXAMPLE 7-21 Brahms, Quintet, Op. 111, 3rd movement

The upward shift of inner-voice tones often motivates embellishing progressions of the top voice. In an excerpt from Brahms' Quintet, Op. 111, two melodic events overlap (see Example 7-21). The top voice (first violin part) begins with a descent D–C–B flat. The descent is completed in measure 4; but the completion is obscured by the upward shift of the inner-voice G. This shift, accomplished by transfer of register, initiates the second melodic event: an embellishing motion from high G down to D.

MOTIONS TRANSFERRED FROM ONE VOICE TO ANOTHER; THE INTERCHANGE OF VOICES

In Example 7-17 we observed that a melodic line—an ascending stepwise progression—arises out of the combination of the two violin parts. That example leads us to an important general principle: a coherent linear progression need not be confined to a single voice; it can migrate from one part of the texture to another. In Example 7-22, from

EXAMPLE 7-22   Schumann, In der Fremde, Op. 39, No. 1

a *Lied* of Schumann, the B sharp of the bass is a chromatic passing tone; it continues a motion that originates in the C sharp of the inner voice and moves to the third of tonic harmony. In an almost literal sense this is a motion out of the inner voice down to the bass.

Later in this chapter we shall observe the significant effect on dissonance treatment of transferred motions. Let us now turn our attention to another technique whereby two voices become closely interconnected. This technique is the *interchange of voices* often referred to by the German term *Stimmtausch*. We have called attention to this device in the preceding chapter (see page 140); we shall now present two additional examples.

Voice interchange is a very old technique and occurs in music as far back as the thirteenth century. In medieval polyphony the exchanged tones are frequently in the same register; in later music they are more often in contrasting registers. Example 7-23 is from a *Bagatelle* of Beethoven. The soprano unfolds two thirds, D to B flat and E flat to C. The bass makes the complementary moves B flat to D and C to E flat. By exchanging tones with the soprano the bass helps to avoid incomplete chords on the second and fourth quarters; the first unfolding of the bass also prevents parallel fifths with the alto. The crossed diagonal lines,

EXAMPLE 7-22 (continued)

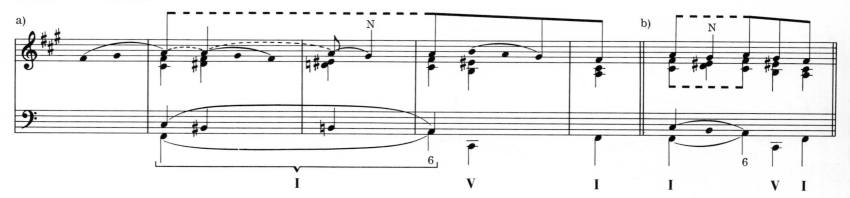

EXAMPLE 7-23 Beethoven, Bagatelle, Op. 119, No. 11

here and elsewhere in this volume, point to the technique of voice interchange.

Stimmtausch can occur between any pair of voices. In Example 7-24, from a quartet of Haydn, the viola executes the complementary motion to the first violin's descent B flat–A flat–G. Here the voice interchange is prolonged by means of the passing $\frac{6}{4}$ of the second bar. Sometimes two voices interchange a group of tones rather than a single tone (see Example 7-66).

2. COUNTERPOINT WITHIN PROLONGED CHORDS

In the first section of this chapter we mentioned the close relationship between polyphonic melody and chord prolongation; by unfolding intervals of the underlying chord a melody extends that chord in time. In this section we shall examine in greater detail the interconnection between the horizontal and vertical dimensions of composition. We shall observe how prolonged chords define the tonal space within which melodic lines move; they form a stable background that gives guidance and direction to the details of melody. And, conversely, melodic lines provide the kinetic impulse through which chords can be extended in time.

In the following group of examples stepwise motions are used to fill in chordal intervals. These stepwise progressions derive ultimately from the passing motions of second- and third-species counterpoint. But in these compositional settings the passing motions are deployed within intervals of underlying vertical sonorities. The beginnings and ends of the motions are closely related, for both belong to the same chord. The stabilizing influence of chord prolongation permits the melodic lines to become longer and more complex without losing their directional quality.

EXAMPLE 7-24   Haydn, String Quartet, Op. 17, No. 4, 1st movement

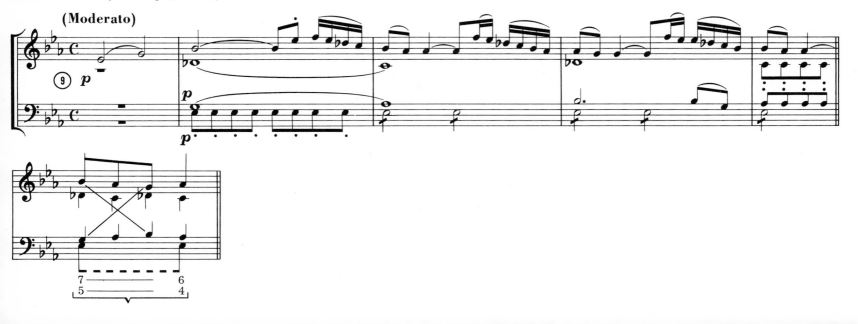

Our first excerpt, Example 7-25, is from Mozart's Violin Sonata, K. 481. The unfolding of the fifth E flat–A flat and the gradual stepwise ascent from the inner to the top voice require no further comment. The stepwise ascent fills in and balances the descending arpeggio in a manner familiar to us from species counterpoint. The ear connects the goal of the ascent, E flat, with the initial tone of the melody and hears the intervening tones in relation to the framing E flats. Within a broad context, therefore, E flat functions as the top-voice tone of the underlying A flat chord; it maintains its structural significance until the prolongation has run its course. Therefore we refer to the E flat as a *retained*

tone; in so doing we point to its structural meaning rather than to a literal sustaining of the tone. The principle of the retained tone is an important one accounting for many large-scale musical connections. In graphs *a* and *b* the dotted beams indicate the structural retention of E flat.[2]

The melody moves between the fundamental and fifth of the A flat chord; the bass counterpoints this motion with a descent from A flat to

[2] Compare this melody with that shown in Salzer, *Structural Hearing* (2d ed.), New York, 1962, Example 203.

EXAMPLE 7-25 Mozart, Violin Sonata, K. 481, 2nd movement

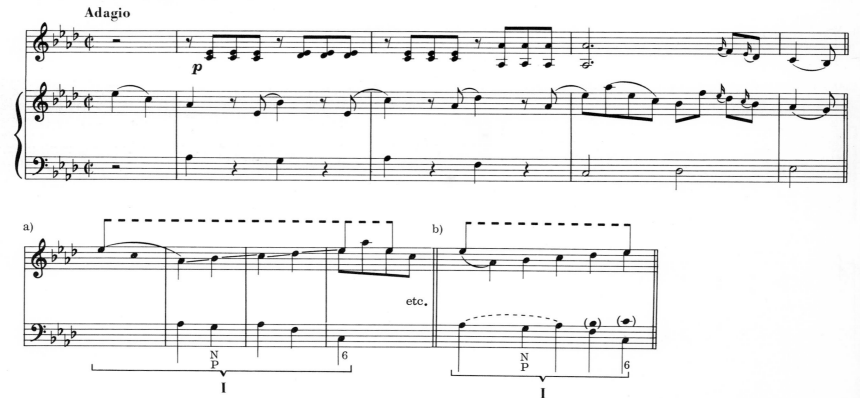

C, the third of the chord. Together the outer voices give horizontal expression to the A flat triad. The bass requires some comment. Direct progression from A flat to C would traverse an ascending third through B flat (see graph *b,* tones in parentheses). Instead of an upward third, Mozart moves down a sixth, supporting the passing tone, D flat, of the top voice with F. The sixth chord defined by F and D flat fulfills several contrapuntal functions. Since it supports a passing tone of the top voice, it is a passing chord. The passing tone, D flat, is a dissonance with respect to its larger environment, the A flat triad. The use of F in the bass makes consonant the D flat. The transformation of a dissonant passing tone into a consonant one is a significant technique of voice leading; it gives a temporary stability to active melodic tones. We shall encounter this technique in combined-species counterpoint. Within the bass line itself the F fulfills a melodic function; it subdivides the sixth

A flat–C into a third and a fourth. In addition to its passing quality, therefore, the chord can also be termed a *subdividing chord.* The reader will remember that the subdivision of a large interval into two smaller ones constitutes one of the functions of the second half **note** in second species.

In Example 7-26 the transfers of register make it difficult to hear the underlying melodic continuity. For this reason the reader should first consult graph *b,* in which the main melodic events are placed in a single register. In addition, we should like to stress the importance of hearing a large-scale melodic progression in a most challenging kind of setting. The sixteenth notes must not be heard—or played—as mere passages; musical perception hears a melodic line through the pianistic figuration. The line moves into the inner voice of the governing tonic before the voice leading proceeds to the II⁶; an artful transfer of register

EXAMPLE 7-26   Haydn, Piano Sonata No. 47, 1st movement

shifts this motion above the top-voice C. The main top-voice progression is a descending fifth C–B flat–A–G–F; the C is separated from B flat by the above-mentioned motion into the inner voice. The B flat is preceded by a motion in thirds down from F. In the last measure the main melodic tones appear on the second sixteenth of each group; indeed the second sixteenth serves throughout to initiate important melodic

events (see graph a). In this example, the retained tone C moves to its continuation without being restruck. This makes demands on our ability to hear large connections, but it does not weaken the structural significance of the C.

A very instructive example can be found at the beginning of the Duet, No. 11, from *The Magic Flute* (see Example 7-27). Here the main

EXAMPLE 7-26   (continued)

prolongation of tonic harmony is achieved by a stepwise motion *above* the main melodic tone E. The stepwise unfolding to G is followed by downward unfolding, a leap to C. The structural continuation of E is the D of measure 6. As counterpoint to these melodic evolutions we find a descending sixth in the bass; all sonorities between measure 2 and the middle of measure 4 are passing chords within the prolonged tonic. Thereafter the melody begins to unfold an interval of dominant harmony, B–D supported by D–C–G of the bass, in bars 4-5. The G

EXAMPLE 7-27   Mozart, The Magic Flute, No. 11

Be-wah-ret euch   vor Wei – ber – tück – en;   dies ist des Bun – des er – ste   Pflicht!

chord of measure 2 makes consonant the otherwise dissonant passing tone D; in itself, the G substitutes for the direct passing tone B. Observe the parallelisms of the two descending thirds E–D–C; also note how the ascending third E–F–G of measures 2-4 is echoed by the B–C–D of measures 5-6. A beautiful detail is the neighboring note E in the middle voice at the beginning of measure 3; this tone creates a fleeting A minor sonority.

In Examples 7-25 to 7-27 chord prolongation arises—at least in part—out of stepwise motion within an interval of the chord. In the next two examples neighboring and embellishing progressions serve to prolong chords. We present first (Example 7-28) two phrases from a chanson of Lassus; the second is a variation of the first. In the first phrases two neighboring progressions are contracted into a single one. In the second, the insertion of the top-voice tone A brings about the use of a D major chord for support; this in turn results in a harmonic progression I–IV–V–I; contrapuntal implications are still present, of course, particularly in the neighboring A and F chords.

In Example 7-29 the D chord of measures 5-8 arises out of a neighboring note in the top voice counterpointed by an embellishing progression in the bass. The duration of this chord, of course, is con-

EXAMPLE 7-28 Lassus, Bonjour, mon coeur

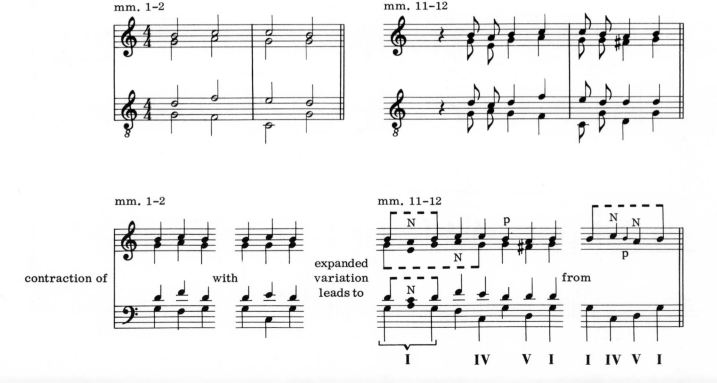

EXAMPLE 7-29 Beethoven, Bagatelle, Op. 33, No. 3

siderably longer than in the Lassus. The chromatic inflection of F to F sharp creates a striking contrast of sonority. The prolonging use of the harmonic progression I–V–I in the first phrase will be taken up in Chapter 8.

In closing this section we present an example illustrating the prolongation of chords through an arpeggiated motion. In species counterpoint, it will be remembered, the use of broken chords is restricted to subdividing a large interval into two smaller ones. In composition, on the other hand, broken chords occur freely as a consequence of chord prolongation. In an excerpt from Bach's first *Partita for Clavier* (Example 7-30), the top voice unfolds the sixth between A and F ascending and descending. Within the unfolding occur arpeggiations on two levels, indicated in graph a by stemmed and stemless quarter notes. One aspect of dissonance treatment can be touched on here, for it relates to the next section of this chapter. At first hearing the leap from C to F, second measure, second quarter, might seem to constitute a skip out of a dissonance. In reality the dissonance is caused by the passing tone D of the bass. C forms part of the tonic arpeggio and must be considered a stable, consonant tone. In the first two measures the broken tonic of the right hand is equivalent to a single tone of the cantus firmus in a species exercise (see graph c).

3. THE EVOLUTION OF DISSONANCE

In the prolonged counterpoint of composition, dissonance treatment undergoes a process of evolution that leads to many differentiated and often complex usages. The simple procedures of the species exercises offer the best point of reference for the prolonged use of dissonance in composition. Comparison with species counterpoint will help us to become consciously aware of details that at first hearing we might take for granted. Moreover the more complicated and individual usages will only reveal their meaning when heard in relation to the simpler forms out of which they developed.

A simple but important development of dissonance is the skipped passing tone—the use of a single passing tone, rather than two—within the interval of the fourth. In species counterpoint such a passing tone—preceded or followed by a leap—must, of course, be consonant. In

prolonged counterpoint the tone may be dissonant, since the ear can be relied on to fill in the missing tone. In Example 3-26 we showed the use of the abbreviated passing motion in a fifteenth-century composition. Example 7-31 now presents an excerpt from the works of Chopin in which the passing tone E is slightly ornamented.

Another simple manipulation of dissonance brings about the various types of *incomplete neighboring note*. In these the neighbor has only one stepwise connection with the main tone rather than two as in the complete neighboring progression. The familiar *appoggiatura* can be understood as an accented incomplete neighbor. Excerpts from the literature illustrating incomplete neighbors will be found throughout this chapter and in the following one.

Example 7-9, from a theoretical work of Vincenzo Galilei, showed a motion out of the inner voice substituting for the normal resolution of a suspension. Our next illustration, Example 7-32, shows an even bolder treatment of suspended tones. Here the suspensions in the upper parts involve tones of the unfolded A minor chord; instead of resolving these by step, the composer skips down to the main tones A and C. This example also shows the use—frequent at cadences—of the dissonant anticipation. Here the anticipation in the top voice coincides with the resolution of the 4-3 suspension in the middle voice, giving rise to parallel seconds. These consecutive dissonances result from prolongation and do not involve the basic voice leading.

In composition dissonances frequently occur in a note-against-note setting. Such dissonances often result from the *contraction* of a passing motion; the initial tone of the motion is omitted. This technique was well known to the thorough-bass theorists of the Baroque period. Our next illustration, Example 7-33, is drawn from a treatise by Johann David Heinichen; it shows how note-against-note dissonances arise out of the elision of the consonances from which passing tones would move in a simpler setting. The dissonances form seventh chords in various positions. The origin of the chordal seventh is usually to be found in such contracted passing motions in those cases where the seventh is not a normal passing tone, neighbor, or suspension.

In Example 7-34 the $\frac{4}{2}$ chord results from contraction. Here the omission of the "original" F permits a steadily descending bass and enhances the directional quality of the motion from F down to C.

EXAMPLE 7-30   Bach, Partita I, Sarabande

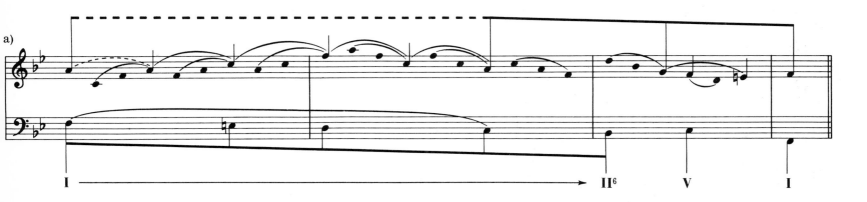

a)

I $\longrightarrow$ II^6 V   I

b)

c)

EXAMPLE 7-31   Chopin, Ballade, Op. 38

EXAMPLE 7-32   Marco da Gagliano, Alma mia, dove t' en vai

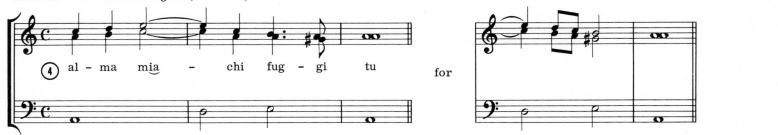

EXAMPLE 7-33   Heinichen, from Der Generalbass in der Composition

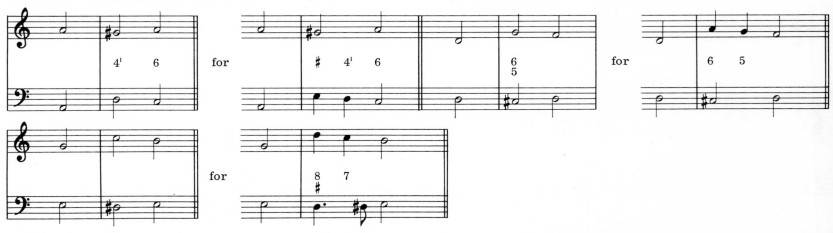

The two following excerpts require little comment. In Example 7-35, the impact of the dissonance underscores the emphatic second quarter of the measure. In the *Menuet,* Example 7-36, the broken chord of the right-hand part is decorated by appoggiaturas.

The opening phrase of Beethoven's Piano Sonata, Op. 110 (see Example 7-37) contains several vertical dissonances that require explanation. In measure 3 the tenor contains B flat on the second half of the second beat. This tone, foreign to the prevailing subdominant harmony,

EXAMPLE 7-34   Bach, Chorale No. 6

EXAMPLE 7-35   Anna Magdalena Bach Book, Marche

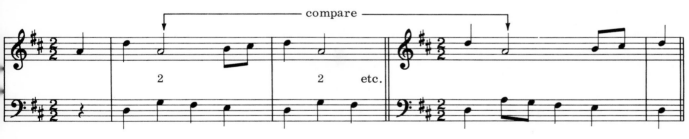

EXAMPLE 7-36   Anna Magdalena Bach Book, Menuet

EXAMPLE 7-37   Beethoven, Piano Sonata, Op. 110, 1st movement

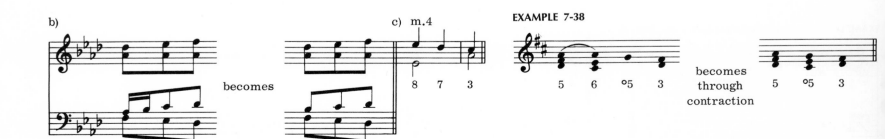

is also dissonant with the A flat of the alto. As graph *b* indicates, this dissonance arises from contraction; A flat, the beginning of an ascending passing motion to D flat, is elided. The full passing motion would require the use of sixteenth notes; this would disturb the tranquilly flowing rhythm. Contraction is often employed, as here, to maintain a consistent rhythmic movement. The elision of A flat, allowing the B flat to occupy a full eighth note, develops a pattern of parallel tenths between tenor and soprano.

In measures 1 and 2 the simultaneous unfoldings in the top voice and the bass produce part interchange. The basic voice leading moves in parallel tenths; the true bass of the first three measures is A flat–B flat–C. In measure 2 there is an apparent leap into the dissonant bass tone D flat. This tone is the result of unfolding and does not belong to the fundamental voice leading. Furthermore it is prepared, in a higher register, by the D flat of the top voice.

In measure 4 the dissonant passing tone, D flat, of the melody is

EXAMPLE 7-39 Mozart, Ave verum Corpus, K. 618

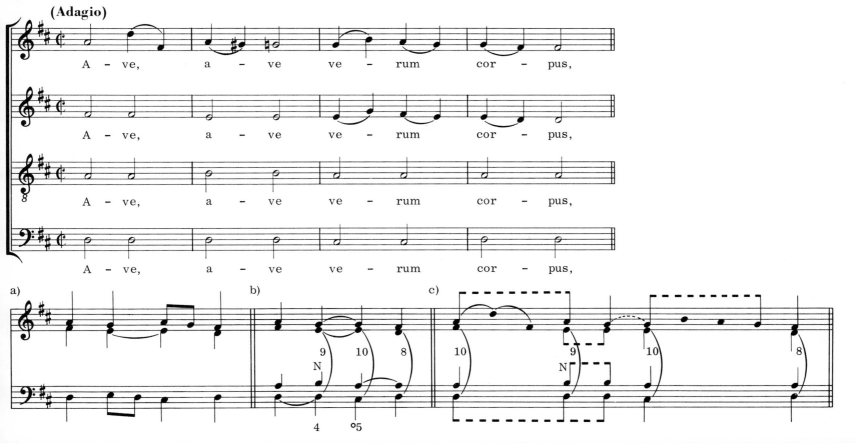

prolonged, retarding the resolution to C and briefly heightening tension. The brackets in graph a point out the melodic parallelisms that cause the embellishment of the dissonance. A previous example, from Mozart's Piano Concerto, K. 467 (Example 7-7), also features the pro-

longation of a dissonance, again the dominant seventh.

An important compositional use of contraction produces an interval succession of perfect fifth–diminished fifth–third (Example 7-38).

Examples 7-39 and 7-40 are based on the progression of 7-38. The

EXAMPLE 7-40   Bach, Well-tempered Clavier II, Prelude IX

contrapuntal progression underlying the Mozart phrase can be seen in graph *a*. As graph *b* indicates, the dissonant chord of the second measure results from the suspension of the bass tone, D; this creates a ninth against the alto and an eleventh against the G of the soprano. In measure 3 the ninth resolves to a tenth, in accordance with the procedures of fourth species, but the outer voice fourth (eleventh) gives way to a diminished fifth. The more dissonant $\frac{4}{2}$ makes a quasi-resolution into the less dissonant $\frac{6}{5}$ before consonance is established in the fourth measure. The prolongation of the diminished fifth in measure 3 relates to the embellished seventh in the previous Beethoven excerpt.

Comparison of graphs *a* and *b* reveals that the suspensions in this excerpt are derived from contracted passing motions. In this connection we should like to mention that Heinrich Schenker held that the origin of the dissonant suspension lies in such contracted passing motions (see *Kontrapunkt* I, p. 342). This, however, must not be taken as an account of the historical evolution of the suspension, which arose out of late medieval rhythmic manipulation (ars nova).

The Bach excerpt (Example 7-40) presents the same basic progression. Bach notates two distinct voices in the upper staff. The two lines, with their beautifully interlaced thirds, move in alternation rather than at the same time. They create the impression, therefore, of a single polyphonic line.

As we have seen, the contraction of a passing motion, by suppressing the initial tone, can allow the dissonant passing tone to fill an increased amount of time. This technique, therefore, often influences

rhythmic movement. Sometimes a tone will be altogether displaced from its original position in the texture; we refer to such an event as a *rhythmic displacement* or a *shift of tones*. The shift of tones can occur in species counterpoint as a consequence of combining two species of different note value; we shall take up this technique, therefore, in combined-species counterpoint. In the next chapter we shall discuss the use of rhythmic displacement in chorale setting. Here we present three examples only.

In the Bach excerpt (Example 7-41) the A of the alto would normally extend through the fourth quarter. The extension of A is elided; as a consequence the G is shifted from the fifth to the fourth quarter. Both the G and the F sharp occupy a full quarter note rather than an eighth as they would in less evolved voice leading.

The shift of tones sometimes results from the simultaneous use of figuration in two or more voices. In the first measure of Example 7-42, from a sonata of Scarlatti, the resolution of a suspension in the top voice coincides with the appearance of a passing tone in the bass (see graph *b*). The second measure shows displacement of a different sort. Note the downward stem of the B in graph *b*; it indicates that this is an activated middle-voice tone that has been shifted so as to appear on the second beat at the same time as the passing tone A of the bass. The descending progression of the bass is ornamented by incomplete neighbors. Note the use of the consonant neighbor B as decoration of the dissonant A (second measure, second quarter). Fleeting consonances often prolong dissonances when the latter form part of large-scale musical connections.

EXAMPLE 7-41   Bach, French Suite No. 5, Loure

from

EXAMPLE 7-42 Scarlatti, Sonata No. 37 (Kirkpatrick, Vol. II)

a)

b)

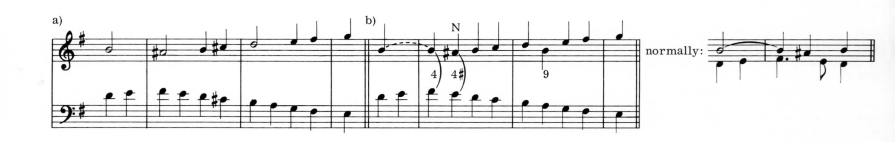

normally:

c)

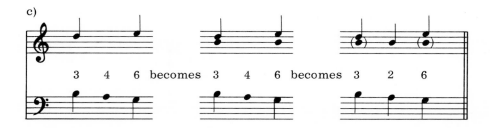

Example 7-43 is from a *Lied* of Schumann. The voice leading is complex and difficult to grasp, but it is of such visionary beauty that it amply repays careful study. The texture is highly dissonant; indeed from the second half of measure 10 to measure 14 there is not a single wholly consonant sonority to be found. Some of the dissonances are caused by the inner-voice pedal point on C (tenor part); but most result from the shift of tones. Graph a removes the pedal point and clarifies the surface texture by putting the displaced tones into their normal contra-

EXAMPLE 7-43   Schumann, Auf einer Burg, Op. 39, No. 7

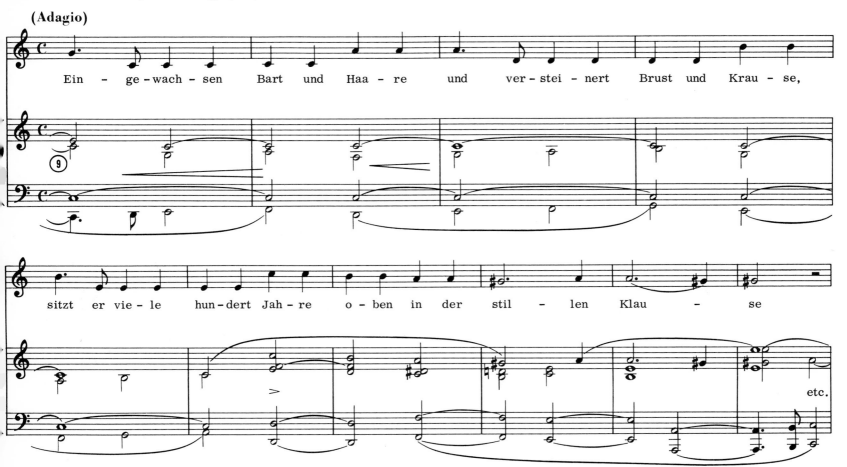

puntal context. If Schumann had continued the rhythmic pattern of the bass of the first measure, the displacements would not have arisen; this insight provides a clue to the meaning of measures 9-14. In measure 17 the dissonances arise through a fusion of the tonic and dominant chords. The bass enters "prematurely" with the motivic leap of a de-

scending fifth E–A while the upper parts still express dominant harmony.

Graph *b*, a further reduction, reveals the underlying two-part counterpoint of the vocal line. This leads us to graph *c*, which indicates that measures 9-14 constitute a 5-6 suspension series transformed by techniques of prolongation.

EXAMPLE 7-43   (continued)

a)

b)

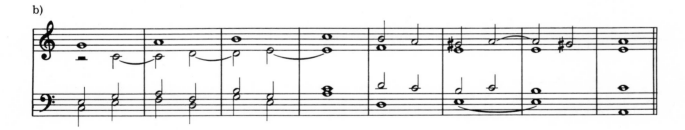

c)

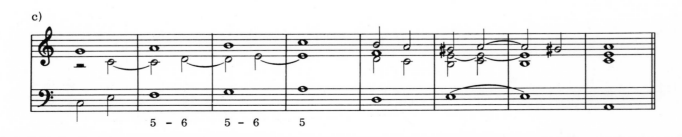

5 – 6   5 – 6   5

Let us close this section with yet another aspect of the prolonged use of dissonance. Earlier in the present chapter we learned that significant musical connections can transfer from one voice to another. In regard to dissonance treatment this means that a dissonant tone can move from or to a tone belonging to another part of the texture. Like the contraction of passing motions, this technique is cited in the works of thorough-bass theorists. Example 7-44, by J. D. Heinichen, is drawn from the same treatise as Example 7-33. It indicates clearly that the top-voice B flat continues to and is resolved by the A of the bass.

A fragment from Purcell's *Four-part Fantasia, No. 7* (see Example 7-45) illustrates Heinichen's example. Here the suspended F of the top voice is followed by a leap of a descending fifth. However the resolution is not altogether omitted, as, for instance, in Example 7-32. The two inner voices supply the expected E flat, but in a lower register. The brackets point out the motivic repetition that causes the irregular suspension. The influence of repetition on voice leading will be taken up in the following section.

4. REPETITION AND ARTICULATION

In species counterpoint directed motion takes the form of progressions using the basic elements of voice leading. Such progressions occur within a narrow frame of reference, the distance between beginnings and goals of motion being relatively short. Within this restricted setting the principle of repetition can operate only to a very limited degree;

EXAMPLE 7-44   Heinichen, from Der Generalbass in der Composition

EXAMPLE 7-45   Purcell, 4-part Fantasia, No. 7

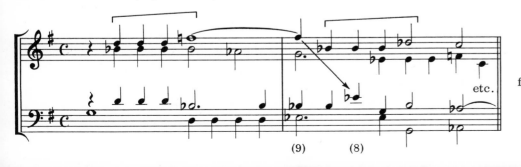

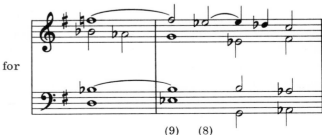

otherwise monotony would result. Therefore only two or three identical intervals will appear in immediate succession; the same holds true for interval progressions such as the various suspension series. The brevity of the exercises makes impossible the use of motivic development which, of course, is based upon repetition. Similarly the articulation of the musical flow into sections of varying dimension will be consciously avoided.

Composition expands the scope of motion. Beginnings and goals become more widely separated. The larger frame creates a compositional problem: how to organize in a convincing manner motion to a distant goal. It is intriguing to observe that a possible source of monotony in species counterpoint becomes, in a compositional setting, an important tool of musical direction. For composers learned to apply repetition—and articulation caused by repetition—in such a way as to produce purposefully directed musical motion.

The following examples illustrate at once the relationship and the contrast between species counterpoint and composition. The first excerpt is from the second movement of Schubert's Symphony No. 9 in C major (Example 7-46).

What makes this beautiful theme and its convincing contrapuntal setting so different from species counterpoint, although growing out of some of its basic principles? In species counterpoint, first of all, a series of seven tenths, five of them consecutive, would be meaningless. Secondly, a species exercise would not contain the similar motion into the fifth between bass and middle voice at the downbeats of measures 2 and 3. And finally a specific progression (7-46c) is repeated twice on different pitches (a sixth is interpolated on the second eighth note of measure 3); in species counterpoint such repetition would not occur.

In composition, however, the repetition of the outer-voice interval of the tenth occurs within a larger whole; the descending series of tenths performs a definite function within that whole. The tenths create passing chords unfolding and prolonging the F major triad. As details of a more inclusive whole, the parallel tenths no longer create monotony. Together with the 5-6 alternation of the two lower parts, the repeated tenths form a sequential progression of chords. The resultant pattern punctuates slightly the descent to the I^6 and softens the impact of the similar motion into the fifths. In species counterpoint each interval or

chord is exposed by the bareness of the setting; the manner of their connection, therefore, is a very sensitive factor. In the Schubert phrase, however, the vertical sonorities no longer stand on their own; they are details within a larger whole. The repetition of the same progression on different pitches adds to the kinetic impulse of the motion down to the 6th chord (I^6); this kind of organization, of course, contrasts with species counterpoint. Nevertheless, and this is most significant, the contrapuntal origin of the motion in tenths lies in the passing motion of second species (Example 7-46d); the dissonant passing tones are made consonant by the bass in a manner explained earlier.

The reader should also note how much Schubert's rhythmic organization offsets any impression of monotony which might otherwise have arisen through the use of so many consecutive tenths. For the first two measures the melody and its counterpointing bass move in even quarters; the syncopated cellos provide an unobtrusive subdivision into eighths. In the third measure all voices break into eighth notes; this leads into the ornamental sixteenths of the fourth measure. The drive to the goal of the voice leading is thus enhanced by a kind of rhythmic accelerando.

What functions are fulfilled by the chords on the second and fourth eighths of measure 3? The first results from incomplete neighbors; it serves to prepare the subsequent ascent of the melody as well as the sonority of the sixth. The D chord of the last eighth has a different meaning. In determining chord function, one comes across contrapuntal sonorities that are neither passing, neighboring, nor embellishing chords. Some of these are required for purposes of voice leading—for example, to break up fifths or octaves. Others support a melodic tone for added chordal color, or rhythmic activity, or both. The D chord in the Schubert phrase belongs to the latter category. It is not needed for reasons of voice leading, since the composer could have proceeded as in Example 7-46e; the result, however, would have weakened the rhythmic momentum, as all voices would no longer move in eighth notes. To parallel the unfolded third at the beginning of the measure, the solution of Example 7-46f might have proved acceptable. However, by using the D chord Schubert gave added emphasis of rhythm and color to the F of the melody; his solution is undoubtedly the most beautiful. We shall term such sonorities *chords of melodic emphasis*.

EXAMPLE 7-46   Schubert, Symphony No. 9 in C major, 2nd movement

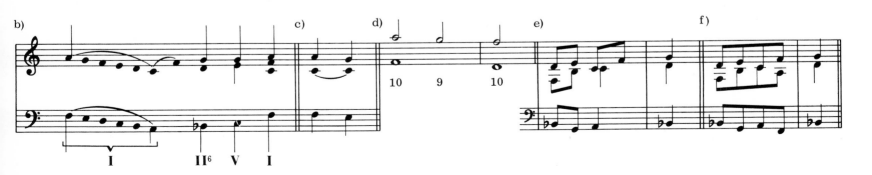

The illustration from Chopin's *Etude* Op. 25, No. 9 (Example 7-47) shows a marked structural identity with the Schubert excerpt. Once one has recognized the great similarities between the two phrases, their different "appearance" becomes all the more fascinating. Unlike Schu-

bert, Chopin covers the second, fourth, and sixth tenth by means of the embellishing chromatic top-voice motive. In graph *a* we have indicated these covered tenths by the use of parentheses.

The same contrapuntal technique is at work in Example 7-48. Again

EXAMPLE 7-47 **Chopin, Etude, Op. 25, No. 9**

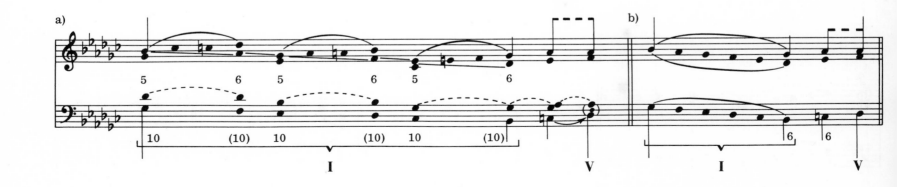

some of the thirds and tenths are covered by the recurring motivic ascending sixths.

An interesting variant of the same principle of voice leading is shown in Example 7-49. Here the tenths occur between bass and middle voice, while the 5-6 alternation takes place between top voice and bass. The underlying counterpoint in this example is the same as in the preceding ones, but the highest and the middle voices have exchanged positions. The leap into the fifth becomes slightly more prominent, since it now occurs in the top voice.

EXAMPLE 7-48   Mozart, The Magic Flute, No. 12

EXAMPLE 7-49 Mozart, The Magic Flute, No. 5

a)

10ths in outer voices, 5–6 between bass and inner voice.

b)

5–6 in outer voices, 10ths between bass and inner voice.

EXAMPLE 7-50

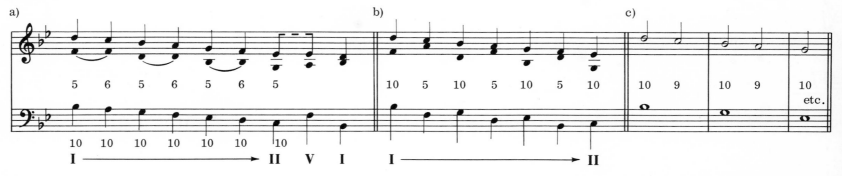

In large-scale passing motions of this sort we frequently encounter progressions in which every chord appears in $\frac{5}{3}$ position. Example 7-50 shows that such progressions originate out of the same contrapuntal technique as do the four examples we have just presented. Through a kind of exchange the $\frac{6}{3}$ chords of Example 7-50a become transformed into the $\frac{5}{3}$'s of 7-50b. This results in less stepwise progression and offers the possibility for some contrary motion.

It would be meaningless to label the second, fourth, and sixth chords as dominants of the chords they follow. From the point of view of chord grammar this labeling is correct, but it disregards the primary function of these chords. They are the result of counterpointing the passing tones of the top voice thereby making them consonant. In Example 7-51 the above progression is decorated by suspensions in the middle voice.

EXAMPLE 7-51 Monteverdi, Si ch'io vorrei morire, Madrigals, Book 4

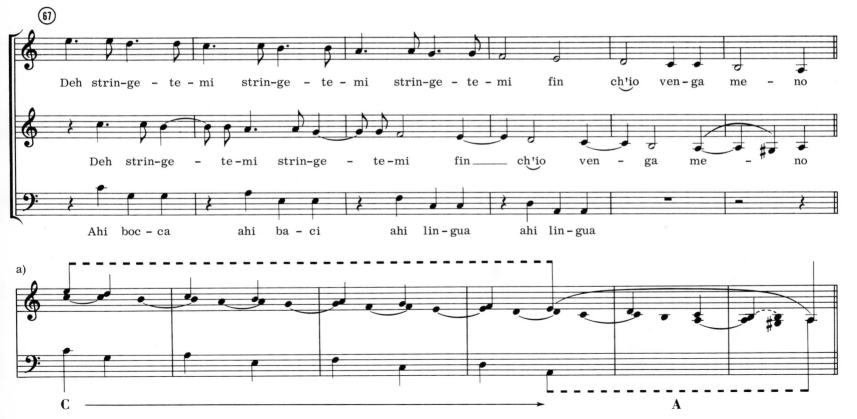

A rather complex but most instructive example is taken from Mozart's cadenza to the first movement of his Piano Concerto, K. 450 (Example 7-52). A gradual reduction to the essentials of this passage leads us first to graph a. There we note that the octave leaps expand an essentially stepwise melodic line. The sixteenth notes of the bass give expression to an ascent from B flat to C, subdivided into sixths. Graph *b* indicates that the stepwise melodic line fills in a descending octave,

and that the wide range of the bass, which appears in the composition as an upward ninth plus octave, is the inversion and elaboration of a descending seventh expressed as a motion in thirds from B flat to C. The seventh itself, of course, represents the inversion of a stepwise ascent from B flat to C. In both top voice and bass, therefore, we see registral manipulation on a larger scale than in any of the preceding illustrations of this chapter. By now the reader will have realized that

EXAMPLE 7-52   Mozart, Piano Concerto, K. 450, Cadenza to 1st movement

graph *b* is identical with Example 7-50*b*. In closing we cite another excerpt from the works of Mozart (see Example 7-53). Here an underlying progression in tenths receives a most imaginative elaboration. The repeated intervals help to orient the listener to the basic direction of the descending motion.

In this section we have shown instances of the repetition of intervals and of progressions; these repetitions can lead to the interior articulation of a motion without in the least disturbing the continuity of the motion's flow. In Chapters 8 and 10 we shall discuss motivic and sectional repetition, both direct and disguised. And in both of these chapters—especially Chapter 8—we shall attempt to show that large-scale continuity of voice leading need not be impaired by the strong articulations that occur at the ends of phrases and even of sections, and that an underlying continuity makes itself felt through the surface divisions.

EXAMPLE 7-52 (continued)

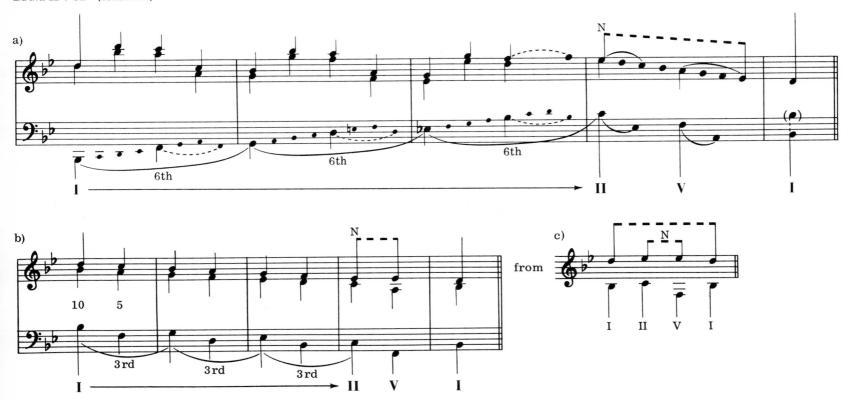

EXAMPLE 7-53   Mozart, Fantasy, K. 396

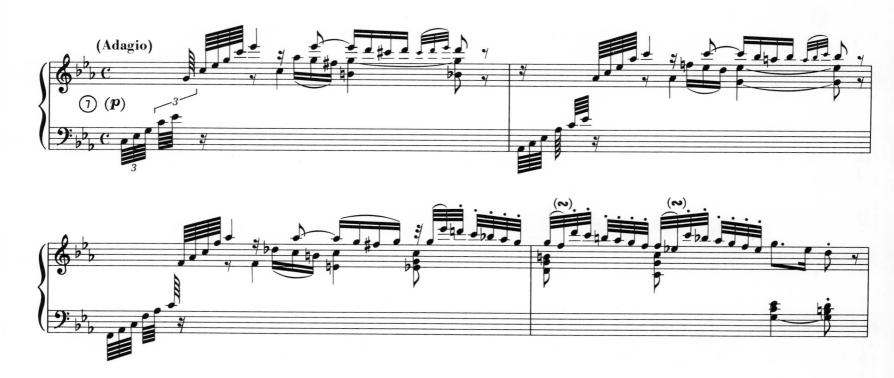

EXAMPLE 7-53 (continued)

a)

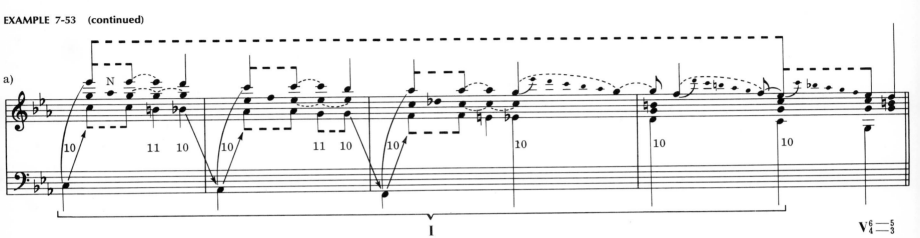

b)

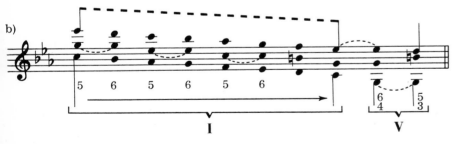

5. HARMONIC INFLUENCES ON VOICE LEADING (HARMONIC PROLONGATIONS)

In most of the examples shown so far in this chapter harmonic progressions have acted as structural frameworks influencing the large-scale movement of the melodic lines. The influence of harmony also makes itself felt on the prolonging level. Harmonic prolongations act directly upon details of voice leading, and only indirectly upon the broad contrapuntal flow.

The simplest type of harmonic prolongation results from the use of a dominant chord of purely local effect (see Example 7-54). When such chords relate to the tonic, we call them prolonging dominants; when they refer to non-tonic chords we use the term applied dominant (⌐↗) already introduced in Chapter 6, section 2.

The harmonic impulse of the applied dominant adds emphasis to the chord it prolongs. In addition to this harmonic function, applied dominants can accomplish a number of contrapuntal tasks; these chords, therefore, frequently show overlapping or double function.[3] In Example

[3] For more about double function, see Salzer, *op. cit.*, pp. 162–169.

7-55 the applied dominants give consonant support to the passing tones of the top voice; consequently they are also passing chords. Furthermore, they help to produce good voice leading by breaking up the unisons on consecutive downbeats between the second violin and the viola. In this excerpt we are confronted with two passing motions on different structural levels. The main passing motion occurs in the bass and leads from I downward to V (see graphs *b* and *c*). Within this progression the second from C to B flat is inverted into an ascending seventh; at the same time the top voice, in moving from E flat to D, assumes the form of a stepwise passing motion also up a seventh. The second, fourth, and sixth tones of this progression are supported by the applied dominant chords.

When applied dominants appear in inversion rather than in root position, their harmonic impact is weakened but not necessarily extinguished. In Example 7-56 the leaps in the bass at once arise from and emphasize the harmonic implications of the applied dominants. Two of these leaps take the form of a melodic dissonance, the diminished fourth. In prolonged counterpoint, melodic dissonances other than those resulting from unfolding or registral manipulation often arise out of harmonic inflection. Such dissonances are not due to the breaking of a contrapuntal rule but to the addition of a new element—harmony. In

EXAMPLE 7-54

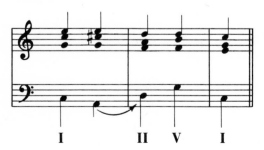

I   II   V   I

EXAMPLE 7-55   Mendelssohn, String Quartet, Op. 44, No. 3, 2nd movement

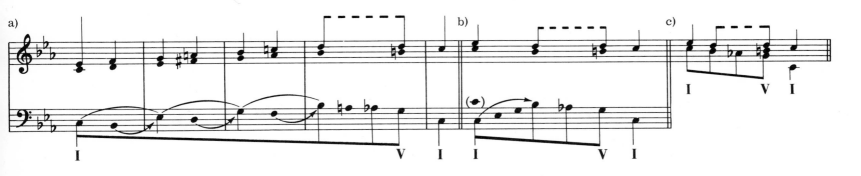

the Beethoven excerpt the contrapuntal origin of the applied dominants can be seen in Example 7-56b. The chords, like those of the preceding example, help to avert impending parallels. The stepwise motions of the bass (F sharp–G, D–E flat, etc.) constitute a series of incomplete neighbors moving to their main tones.

If the bass is entirely stepwise, the labeling of certain chords becomes nothing more than an exercise in chord grammar, for the contrapuntal, passing function of such chords is unequivocal. Such is the case in Example 7-57, where an underlying three-voice progression is "dis-solved" into scalewise arabesques. Inversions and transfers of register play a major role here.

Next we cite the concluding passage from Gibbons' *Pavane Lord Salisbury* (Example 7-58). As in the preceding example, a grammatical analysis of some of the chords as applied dominants would be correct in itself, but essentially irrelevant to the musical contents of the excerpt. Here a prolonging dominant is extended by means of a large-scale passing motion; within this motion consecutive octaves are prevented by sequential 8-9-10 progressions.

EXAMPLE 7-56 Beethoven, Piano Sonata, Op. 31, No. 3, 1st movement

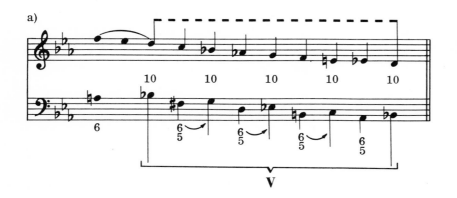

EXAMPLE 7-57   Mozart, Piano Sonata, K. 576, 2nd movement

(Adagio)

EXAMPLE 7-57 (continued)

a)

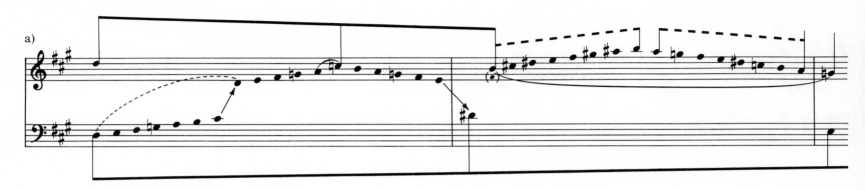

b)

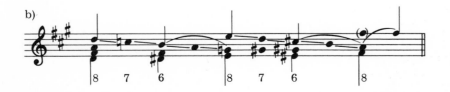

EXAMPLE 7-58   Gibbons, Pavane Lord Salisbury

a)

b)

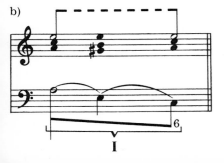

A second widely used harmonic technique is a series of descending or ascending fifths in the bass; of course the fifths can be expressed as fourths, ascending or descending. Whereas the essence of contrapuntal movement lies in stepwise progression, the basis of harmonic movement is the fifth relationship, whose most direct expression is the leap of a fifth or fourth. A bass moving contrapuntally from G to B flat, for example, would proceed through A. As Example 7-59 shows, the same goal can be reached by means of descending fifths, or ascending fourths, or a mixture of both. (The ascending fifths of progression e occur much less often; see, however, Examples 8-106 and 8-107.)

The technique of descending fifths frequently appears in composition as the harmonic enrichment of a stepwise passing motion. In Example 7-60 we find a stepwise motion leading from the G minor sonority to C. The accented fifths between the lower voices are quite prominent despite the intervening sixths (progression a). In progression b the 7-6 syncopations eliminate the fifths. Progression c shows a series of descending fifths woven into the fundamentally stepwise bass. The suspended sevenths now move to tenths instead of sixths; at the same time the skipping bass creates dissonances with the top voice; the entire texture consists of dissonant sonorities between the consonances of beginning and goal. The heightened sense of direction and the enrichment of chordal color achieved in progression c are evident.

We now offer three examples from the literature, Examples 7-61 to 7-63. The fusion of counterpoint and harmony in these examples is obvious. By now the reader should be able to comprehend all explanations from the voice-leading graphs alone, thus making added comments superfluous. He should carefully study the graphs so that he may use these progressions in the exercises following this chapter.

EXAMPLE 7-59

EXAMPLE 7-60

EXAMPLE 7-61   Couperin, Ordre No. 8, Gigue

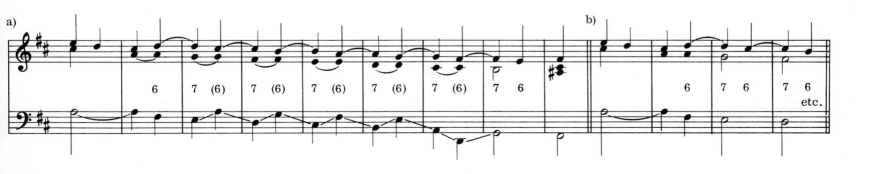

EXAMPLE 7-62   Mozart, Overture, K. 399

(Allegro)

a)

b)

becomes

EXAMPLE 7-63   Bach, Partita No. 1, Allemande

a)

b)   c)

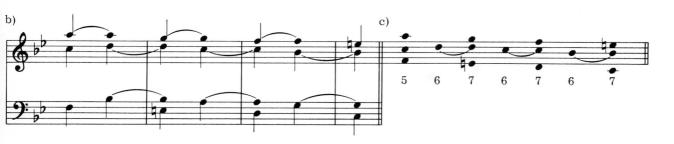

In this section we have seen voice-leading techniques originating out of harmonic relationships. Sometimes the resultant patterns of voice leading clearly reveal their harmonic origin; at other times the harmonic element becomes subordinated to the contrapuntal flow. In the following chapter we shall take up yet another significant technique of harmonic prolongation. We shall observe that complete or incomplete harmonic progressions can function as the prolongations of a sonority of higher structural order:

$$\underbrace{\text{I II V I}}_{\text{of I}} \quad \text{or} \quad \underbrace{\text{IV V I}}_{\text{of VI}} \quad \text{etc.}$$

6. CHROMATICISM; CONTRAPUNTAL LEADING-TONE CHORDS

Applied dominant chords generally require the use of chromatically altered tones, and series of ascending or descending fifths often do so.

Chromaticism, however, is by no means always associated with the expression of harmonic relationships; it frequently grows out of purely contrapuntal usages. Most chromatically altered tones fall into two categories: *inflection* and *substitution*. A tone is chromatically inflected if it precedes or follows the diatonic form of the scale step bearing the same letter name; in F major the progressions C–B natural–B flat and G natural–G sharp–A show chromatic inflections of B flat and G natural. A tone is a chromatic substitution when it replaces the normal diatonic tone with the same letter name. Thus in G major the progressions B–C sharp–D and E–F natural–E contain chromatic substitutions; C sharp replaces C natural and F natural replaces F sharp.

Inflection and substitution frequently produce chromatic passing and neighboring tones. In Example 7-64, from Mozart's String Quartet, K. 428, both passing and neighboring tones can be observed. The C flat of the viola seems at first to be a main tone, the seventh of a diminished seventh chord. But it eventually resolves to the B flat of measure 17 and

EXAMPLE 7-64 Mozart, String Quartet, K. 428, second movement

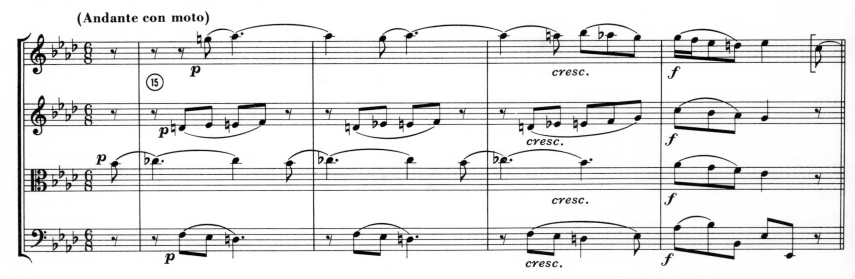

is therefore a chromatic upper neighbor of that tone. The E natural of the second violin is a chromatically inflected passing tone; note the voice interchange between cello and second violin. The chromatically filled-in third of the second violin prepares the similar but expanded idea of the first violin in measures 16-17. These expressive chromatic ascents are derived from the cello part of the opening phrase of the movement, measures 2-4 (this opening phrase is quoted in Example 9-70).

Chromatic alteration sometimes produces chords that function as contrapuntal equivalents of the applied dominant. Triads (usually in first inversion) and seventh chords built on leading tones achieve a forward impulse similar to that of the applied dominant but without explicitly harmonic character; we shall refer to them, therefore, as *contrapuntal leading-tone chords*. In a phrase from Chopin's *Ballade in G minor* (Example 7-65), an applied diminished seventh chord, resulting from contraction and chromatic substitution, leads to the dominant of

the B flat chord. The contrapuntal outline of the phrase is a quasi-second-species progression 8-10-8-7-10.

In Example 7-66, from Mendelssohn's Piano Sonata, Op. 6, two diminished seventh chords intensify a passing motion to the V. (More about the applied diminished seventh chord in the following chapter, Examples 8-40 and 8-41.)

Like the applied diminished seventh, the various augmented sixth chords can function as contrapuntal analogues to the applied dominant. Usually, though not always, they move to and emphasize dominant harmony. In Example 7-67 the augmented sixth results from the substitution of F sharp for the diatonic "original," F natural.

Example 7-68 is taken from the prologue to Wagner's *Die Götterdämmerung*. Here the augmented sixth arises out of a chromatic inflection in the bass. Although the internal structure of the augmented sixth chord is similar to that of the chord shown in Example 7-67, its function within the larger context is different. This excerpt is centered on the tone

EXAMPLE 7-65 **Chopin, Ballade, Op. 23**

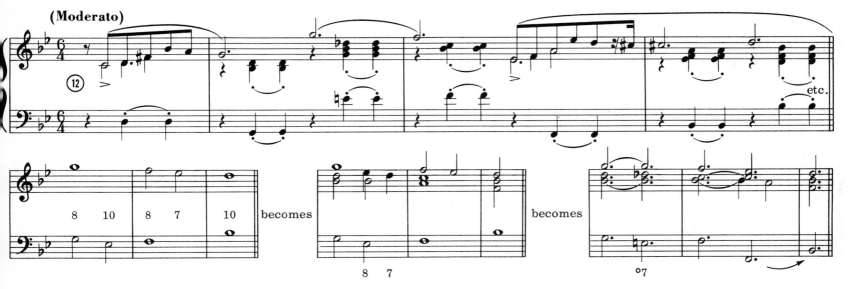

EXAMPLE 7-66   Mendelssohn, Piano Sonata, Op. 6, first movement

(Allegretto con espressione)

EXAMPLE 7-66 (continued)

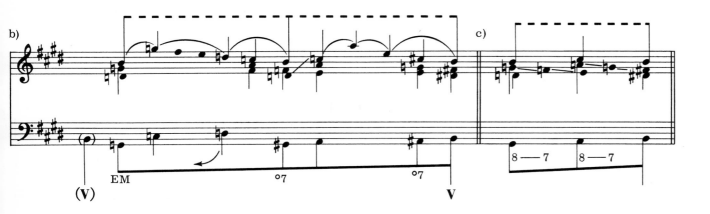

G; G supports first a minor triad, then a dominant seventh chord leading to C minor. (The C minor has not been shown in the illustration.) Broadly viewed, the A in the bass of measure 3 is a neighbor decorating G; the progression from G to A has been inverted to a seventh, and the seventh subdivided into three thirds. The inflection of A to A flat (measure 3) adds the impulse of a passing motion to the return to G; the use of A flat also reinforces the "dominant" quality of the G chord of measure 4 and points to the C minor to come.

In a well-known passage from Strauss's *Till Eulenspiegel* (Example 7-69), the interval of the augmented sixth characterizes a neighboring

EXAMPLE 7-67 Beethoven, Piano Sonata, Op. 10, No. 1, Finale

EXAMPLE 7-68 Wagner, Götterdämmerung, Prologue

EXAMPLE 7-69 Strauss, Till Eulenspiegel

chord that decorates tonic harmony. Unlike most chords containing an augmented sixth, this one has a minor, rather than a major, third. Every tone of the chord moves by half-step to a tone of the tonic chord. The neighboring function of the chord, its pervasive half-step attraction to tonic harmony, and the pungency of its intervallic combination—these are all more significant than any grammatical label. Those who like to dig for chord roots would probably consider this chord a diminished seventh in $\frac{4}{3}$ position with chromatically raised sixth.

Chromaticism often arises out of the *mixture of modes,* that is, the use in a single context of elements from the two modes—major and minor—centering on a given tonic. A striking use of mixture contributes to the tragic intensity of our next excerpt, the conclusion of a chorale prelude of J. S. Bach (Example 7-70). Both the II^6 of the final cadence and the submediant that precedes it occur in the forms characteristic of E flat minor, rather than E flat major. (The symbol "M" under the II^6 in the detailed graph signifies mixture.) The quiet return to major at the cadential $\frac{6}{4}$ follows a melodic detail of extraordinary beauty. The F, top voice of the II^6, moves to E flat through a chromatic passing tone, F flat; the progression from F flat to E flat is interrupted by the interpolation of D, lower neighbor to E flat.

The use of mixture at the cadence is foreshadowed by the G flat that initiates the chromatically ascending bass line. This ascent of the bass points up an obvious but often overlooked aspect of chromaticism. Chromatic progression adds to the number of tones between the beginning and the goal of a passing motion. Chromaticism, therefore, can retard the tonal movement without slackening the rhythmic impulse. Compared with a diatonic progression, a chromatic one moving at the same rate of speed traverses only about half as much ground; as a result, the listener's temporal perspective is altered.

Example 7-71 illustrates a chromatic technique widely used by composers of the nineteenth century. The bass of measures 1-7 extends the E flat tonic by means of a series of descending major thirds, E flat—C flat-(B natural)-G-E flat. The underlying motion is clearly a descending octave (see graph a); but manipulations of register in both the vocal and the instrumental bass divert the E flat of measure 7 into a higher region and motivate the subsequent descent to the V. Subdividing an octave

into equal (or enharmonically equivalent) intervals creates a pervasively chromatic tonal environment. Thus although it might seem plausible to explain the C flat of measure 3 as a substitution for C natural, the evidence of our ears does not confirm such a theoretical construct. We register the equal intervallic progressions without referring them to a supposed diatonic original. This temporary lack of a diatonic frame of reference creates, as it were, a suspension of tonal gravity. Two additional features of Example 7-71 deserve mention. Note the whole-tone scale in the bass resulting from passing whole steps within the major thirds. And observe the altogether surprising effect of the use of minor triads on C flat (B natural), G, and the second E flat; a bass moving chromatically in thirds usually supports major triads.

Example 7-72 also contains a chromatic progression in thirds. Here, however, the thirds are minor rather than major (one of them, F–G sharp, is expressed as an augmented second). And the progression unfolds within an ascending rather than a descending octave. The triads on the downbeats are connected by applied dominants which, because they support passing tones in the top voice, simultaneously function as passing chords. The applied dominants provide smoother immediate connections than in the Schubert excerpt where harmonically unrelated chords are juxtaposed. The persistent use of tenths between the outer parts relates this example to some of those studied earlier in this chapter (see Examples 7-46 to 7-48).

Next we present a celebrated excerpt from Wagner's *Die Walküre.* In Example 7-73 the outer-voice motion is also organized into chromatic progressions of thirds. The motion does not unfold within the space of an octave, however, as in the two previous examples. The fundamental movement is a diminished fourth (major third) from A flat down to E (graph a). This progression is expanded into a diminished eleventh, which is in turn subdivided into two minor sixths, A flat–C–E (graph b). Each of these sixths is again subdivided into descending thirds A flat–E–C–G sharp–E; C is the pivotal point of the motion (graph c). The crucial importance of the C is confirmed by a change in orchestration (woodwinds give way to strings) and by the resumption of a low register in the bass. Graph d shows passing tones that fill in the thirds of the top voice; these are supported by bass tones that suggest applied dominants. In graph e, which shows Wagner's actual bass registers, the passing motions of the top voice are enriched by chromatic passing tones; the chromatic progressions that result are counterpointed in the bass by

EXAMPLE 7-70   Bach, O Mensch bewein' dein' Sünde gross (Orgelbüchlein)

EXAMPLE 7-71 Schubert, Mass in E flat, Sanctus

EXAMPLE 7-71   **(continued)**

a)

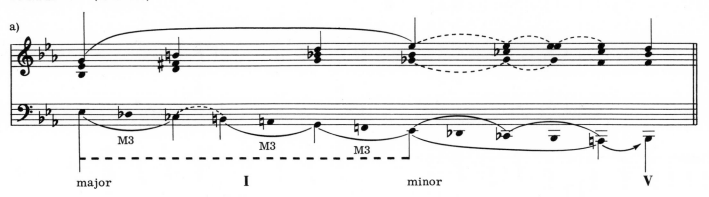

major   **I**   minor   **V**

EXAMPLE 7-72   **Chopin, Mazurka, Op. 50, No. 3**

a)

motions from the fundamental to the third of the applied dominant chords. The passing chords at the beginning of measures 2, 4, 6, and 8 (see asterisks) are emphasized by rhythmic position and consequently weaken the harmonic force of the applied dominants within which they move, and strengthen their contrapuntal significance.

In this section we have been able to explain and illustrate only a

EXAMPLE 7-73   Wagner, Die Walküre, Act III

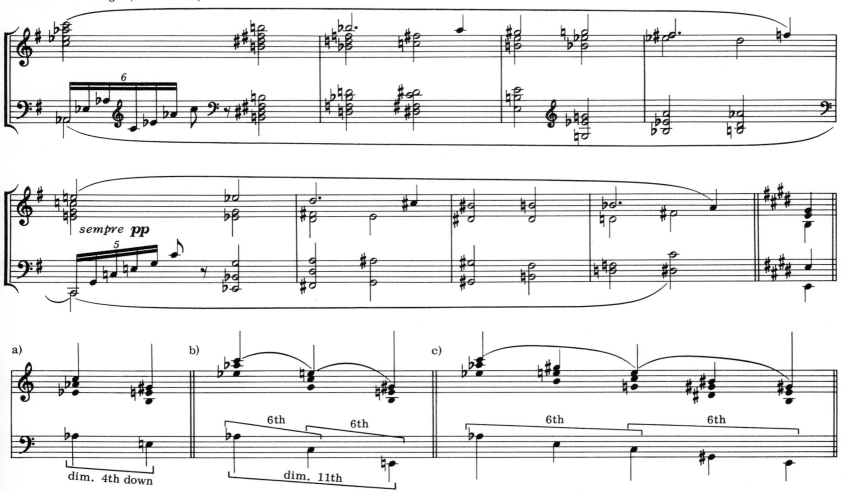

few of the manifold possibilities of chromatic counterpoint. In Chapters 8 to 10 additional chromatic examples will be discussed.[4] Before proceeding to the next section, let us briefly mention one further chromatic technique. Composers from the Baroque through the Romantic periods have been able to produce colorful and surprising yet logical and coherent progressions by chromatically inflecting one or more of the voices of a suspension series. A passage from Schumann's *Kreisleriana* (Example 7-74) ascends from B flat to F sharp; the motion is organized into two major thirds, B flat–D–F sharp (graph a). The top voice and bass progress in parallel tenths; the middle voice shows the familiar 5-6

---

[4] Also see Salzer, *op. cit.*, Examples 350–386.

consonant suspension series (graph *b*). The bass line is chromatically inflected, producing leading tones to C, D, E, and F sharp (graph *c*). Graph *d* shows prolonging motions of a descending third (see brackets) at first in the lowest part, later in the middle-voice region. The presence of prolonging tones below the main bass line creates a dense, opaque texture. This texture is further complicated by the contraction of the three-note descending figure to a two-note group owing to the elision of the first note; the dissonances thus produced make it very difficult to hear through the clouded surface to the underlying $\begin{smallmatrix}10 & 10\\5\text{-}6 & 5\end{smallmatrix}$ progression (graph *e*).

In Chapter 10 we shall present several examples showing the chromatization of a suspension series. See in particular Examples 10-13 to 10-17.

EXAMPLE 7-73 (continued)

EXAMPLE 7-74   Schumann, Kreisleriana, Op. 16, No. 2

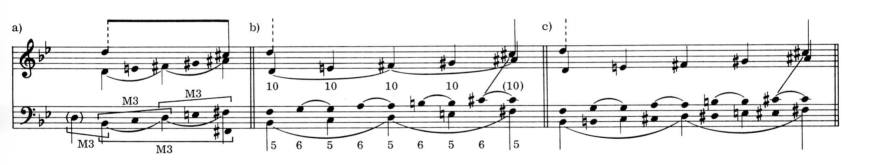

7. OCTAVES AND FIFTHS

Understanding the distinction between elementary and prolonged counterpoint helps to clarify the meaning of the parallel octaves and fifths that appear in the literature. These are often wrongly cited as violations of the rules of counterpoint. Actually the contrapuntal rules about fifths and octaves retained their relevance to composition until the end of the nineteenth century. The fifths and octaves that occur may on occasion result from an oversight on the part of the composer. Generally, however, they are due to various techniques of prolongation; they belong to the surface rather than to the basic setting and represent convincing and valid voice leading.

In Example 6-5, fifths (C–G and B–F sharp) occur between the middle and top voices of the first measure. The musical ear easily perceives that the middle voice figurates B with neighboring notes; the fifths arise out of this figuration. In the excerpt from a Chorale Prelude of Brahms,

EXAMPLE 7-75   Brahms, Es ist ein Ros' entsprungen (Chorale Prelude)

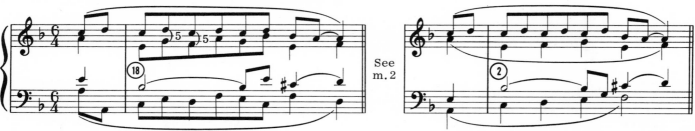

EXAMPLE 7-76   Mozart, Piano Sonata, K. 576, Finale

Example 7-75, the first quotation is a variation of the second. The prolonging thirds of the alto produce fifths with the repeated neighboring notes of the soprano.

A more complex illustration can be found in the last movement of Mozart's Piano Sonata, K. 576 (see Example 7-76). The underlying voice leading consists of a series of 5-6 syncopations. This progression is individualized by the chromatic passing tones and rhythmic displacements; these lead to the fifths.

Surface octaves occur less frequently than fifths; of course we do not refer to doublings of a single voice. In the excerpt from an Impromptu by Schubert (Example 7-77) the F of the soprano is an embellishing tone that reinforces the dominant of the bass. The fundamental voice leading, again, does not contain parallels.

In Mozart's Rondo, K. 494, octaves apparently occur. At this point in the composition the left-hand part is not a single line but a three-voice broken-chord progression. Therefore the succession F–E flat (second measure) results from the alternation of the two implied voices; it should not be heard as a melodic progression. The octaves, therefore, are illusory. (The rhythmic contrast between the left-hand and right-hand parts helps to clarify the voice leading.)

We remind the reader that prolongations often improve voice leading by separating parallel octaves and fifths that would otherwise occur at deeper levels of structure. Composers have found many ways of averting faulty parallels; the efficacy of these techniques depends in large measure upon such features as rhythm, tempo, and density of texture. Fifths are most frequently broken up by means of suspended or passing sixths; octaves are usually avoided by means of the interpolation of tenths. Examples of the 5-6 5 suspension technique are found throughout the book; for passing sixths, review Examples 7-46 to 7-49. For the use of tenths to break up octaves see Example 7-58.

In Example 7-79 fifths between the outer parts occur at the beginning of each two-measure group. The fifths, beginning with the one on C (third measure) are anticipated on the last quarter of each group. The bass shows an interesting use of interval inversion; descending seconds are stated as ascending sevenths, and the sevenths are subdivided into three thirds. Root position triads built on these subdividing bass tones interpose their weight between the fifths and successfully break them up (graph a). Without the registral manipulation of the bass the progression would have taken the form shown in graph b; this in turn reveals itself to be a manipulated consonant suspension series (graph c).

The problem of fifths and octaves will be continued in the following chapter.

EXAMPLE 7-77 Schubert, Impromptu, Op. 142, No. 3   EXAMPLE 7-78   Mozart, Rondo, K. 494

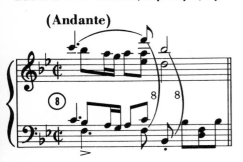

EXAMPLE 7-79   Schubert, Piano Sonata in B flat, D. 960, Finale

(Allegro, ma non troppo)

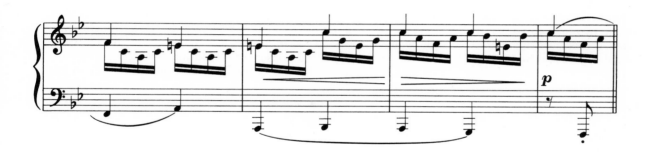

EXAMPLE 7-79 (continued)

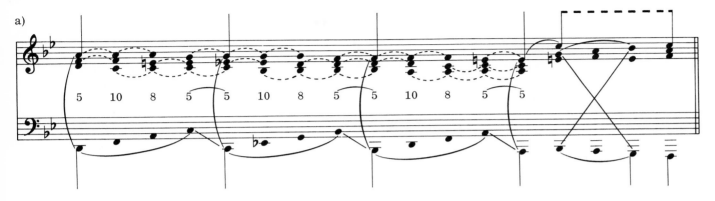

EXERCISES

A. EXERCISES IN MELODIC-CONTRAPUNTAL PROLONGATION

As the basis for the following exercises we shall present a number of progressions, many of them based on previously discussed examples from the literature. In all cases the given model is a reduction of the original, which has been divested of its rhythmic and textural individuality. The progressions contain three voices; the upper two are to be dissolved into a single polyphonic line through the use of unfolding. Transfer of register and superposition can also be used. In a sense these exercises are based upon the principle of variation—the fundamental constructive principle of music. Of course the point of departure is an abstract progression rather than an individual theme. In the first few exercises the student should restrict himself to simple and clear patterns and should avoid the use of rhythmic, motivic, and textural complexities. For some of the exercises we present sample solutions to which the student should add several of his own. The student should be able to define the types of prolongation he uses and to explain the function of every tone. These exercises, incidentally, are similar in conception to Mattheson's illustration of polyphonic melody presented as Example 7-1.

A-1. This simple progression lends itself well to the technique of unfolding. Let us attempt a sample solution. We unfold the first two intervals without filling them in, beginning with the upper voice (see Solution A-1a). The third interval, however, we fill in with a passing motion out of the inner-voice region; this separates the G of measure 2 from its continuation, F sharp, but the ear easily perceives their connection. We elaborate slightly the bass of measures 3-4. Instead of the sustained D of the model, which would produce a static effect if held for two measures, we introduce a bass progression complementary to the soprano's. By means of this interchange we avoid a bare octave at the beginning of measure 3 and gain the contrapuntally better sixth.

Solution A-1b is similar; here, however, we shift the "inner-voice" F sharp above the A by inverting the initial third into a sixth. In so doing we effect a change of register; the final F sharp is an octave above that of the model.

Another possibility is to fill in the initial third with a passing tone (Solution A-1c). In the second measure we produce a corresponding pattern by means of arpeggiation. The final third of the model is not unfolded. Only F sharp is actually present; the inner-voice D is implied by the context, but it is not realized in sound. The bass unfoldings require no comment; the ninth

EXAMPLE A-1

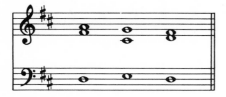

SOLUTION A-1

against the upper voice (second measure, second quarter) results from a passing tone moving against a broken chord.

The student should attempt to write at lease three additional variants of Example A-1.

A-2. Our second progression permits the use of a harmonic bass, or of a contrapuntal one giving rise to a neighbor-passing chord. (The diminished fifth E–B flat results from contraction.) A bass unfolding, of course, could use both tones, E and C. Our first solution needs no comment.

In the next variant, Solution A-2*b*, the filled-in third of the first measure is echoed in the second. What is the function of the dissonant D (second measure, second quarter)?

Another possibility is to bring the initial C down an octave and to unfold upward (Solution A-2*c*).

Solution A-2*d* is slightly more elaborate. Note the motivic correspondence between measures 1 and 3: the ascending fifth of measure 3 answers the descending one of the beginning. The momentum of the bass increases in the third measure; explain the dissonance that occurs on the second beat.

Write at least three additional variants of this progression.

EXAMPLE A-2

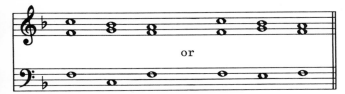

or

SOLUTION A-2

a)   b)   c)

d)

A-3. This is a somewhat longer and more complex progression. We provide only one sample solution. In the last measure the two implied voices of the polyphonic melody have become distinct parts in order to reinforce the cadence.

EXAMPLE A-3

I   V

SOLUTION A-3

a)

A-4. The progression in Example A-4 can be prolonged by means of arpeggiation in the melody. We present three solutions; the dissonances result from the simultaneous presence of the passing bass and the arpeggiated upper voice (or voices). The student should invent additional solutions.

EXAMPLE A-4

SOLUTION A-4

a)   b)

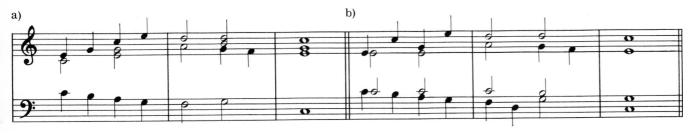

c)

A-5. The progression in Example A-5 can be expanded by using the technique of superposition. Two solutions are offered.

EXAMPLE A-5

SOLUTION A-5

a) b)

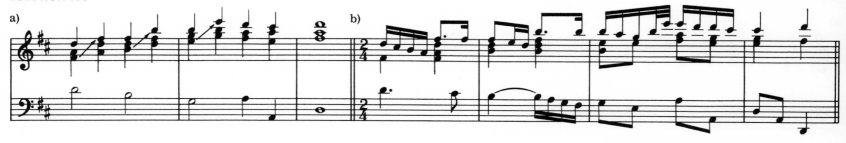

A-6. We present only one variant of this progression. As in Example A-5 the technique of superposition is used, leading here to a rising sequence based upon a two-note figure.

EXAMPLE A-6

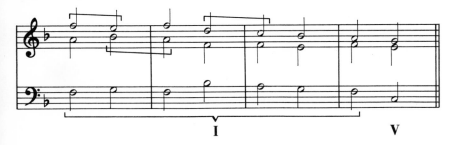

SOLUTION A-6

a)

No sample solutions are given for the remaining progressions (Examples A-7 to A-11). Write at least three variants of each. The last progression is divided into two phrases. Use unfolding and superposition to eliminate the monotonous effect of the given top voice with its limited amount of movement. If unfolding is correctly used, the octaves between the bass and the middle voice (measures 4-5) will be displaced, and the voice leading will be good.

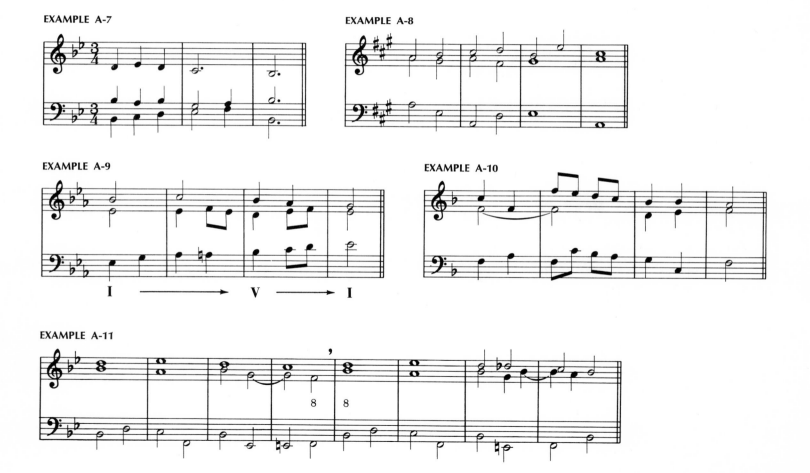

EXAMPLE A-7

EXAMPLE A-8

EXAMPLE A-9

I   V   I

EXAMPLE A-10

EXAMPLE A-11

B. EXERCISES BASED UPON THE OUTER VOICES OF CHORALES

Interesting exercises, slightly different from those of the preceding group, can be derived from progressions adapted from the outer voices of Bach's chorales. The following models lend themselves to melodic-contrapuntal prolongations of varying types, and can be transformed into settings that differ considerably from chorales.

B-1. We offer one variant of this progression. The "first-species" intervals of the model have been expanded through the use of unfolding and superposition. The suspensions should also be noted.

The student should write additional variants of the progression in Example B-1, and should attempt similar solutions for the following exercises (Examples B-2 to B-4).

EXAMPLE B-1

SOLUTION B-1

a)

EXAMPLE B-2

EXAMPLE B-3

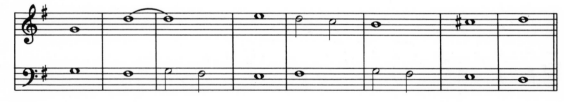

EXAMPLE B-4

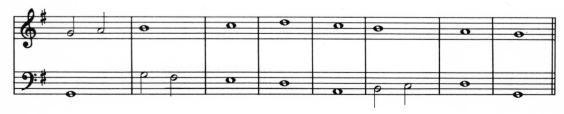

C. EXERCISES WITH SEQUENTIAL PATTERNS

In the following exercises simple sequential patterns are derived from elementary contrapuntal techniques. These patterns form the basis for work with specific techniques of prolongation. The student should play or write the given solutions in several keys; those left unfinished should be completed. The progressions given should be used as models for further variation.

C-1. The given variants use techniques of melodic development which the student should be able to identify. Note the prolonged use of dissonance.

Exercises C-2 and C-3 are similar and require no comment.

The remaining exercises are given without sample solutions.

EXAMPLE C-1

SOLUTION C-1

EXAMPLE C-1 **(continued)** THE TECHNIQUES OF PROLONGED COUNTERPOINT **236**

h)

EXAMPLE C-2

SOLUTION C-2

a)   b)   c)

d)

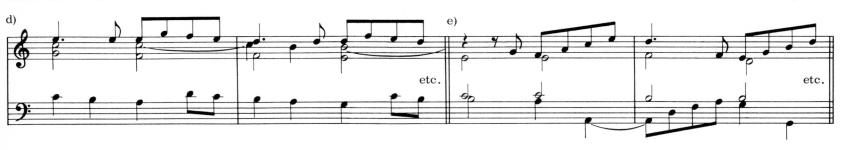

etc.　　　　　　　　e)　　　　　　　　　etc.

EXAMPLE C-3　　　　　　　　　　　　**SOLUTION C-3**

a)

b)

m. 3

avoids

8　　8

SOLUTION C-3 (continued)

c) Explain use of 9th:

d)

e)

f)

g)

h)

i)   j)

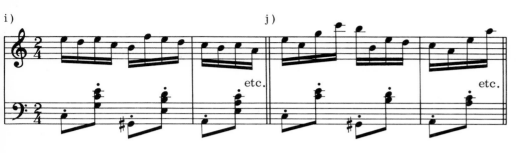

EXAMPLE C-4

EXAMPLE C-5

EXAMPLE C-6

D. EXERCISES IN CHROMATICISM

The following exercises are designed to provide experience in some of the fundamental techniques of chromaticism; chromatic progressions have appeared only to a limited extent in the previous exercises.

Example D-1 shows a consonant neighboring progression often encountered in third species. Many chromatic neighboring chords can be derived from this progression. The given solutions indicate some of the possibilities.

The student should discover additional chromatic derivatives, write them in four parts, and play them in several keys.

Example D-2 shows a dissonant lower neighbor. Like the previous example, this progression can serve as the point of departure for the discovery of chromatic neighboring chords.

Again, look for alternative possibilities.

Examples D-3, D-4, and D-5 should be expanded and varied in the same manner.

Example D-6 shows a passing motion reminiscent of second species. This progression can be transformed into chromatic settings in two, three, and four parts.

The student should find alternative solutions.

For Example D-7 and D-8 no sample solutions are offered. The student should proceed as in Example D-6.

Examples D-9, D-10, D-11, and D-12 contain a chromatic progression in one of the outer voices. Complete the contrapuntal setting in two, three, and four voices. One sample solution is offered.

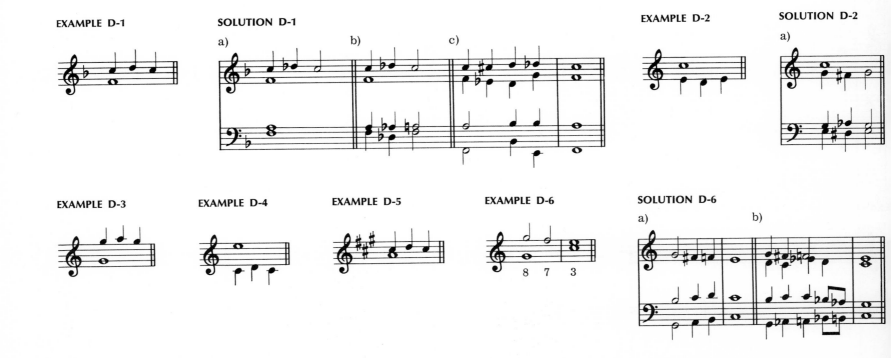

EXAMPLE D-1　　SOLUTION D-1　　EXAMPLE D-2　　SOLUTION D-2

EXAMPLE D-3　　EXAMPLE D-4　　EXAMPLE D-5　　EXAMPLE D-6　　SOLUTION D-6

EXAMPLE D-7

3　4　8

EXAMPLE D-8

6　7　10

EXAMPLE D-9

SOLUTION D-9

a)

EXAMPLE D-10

EXAMPLE D-11

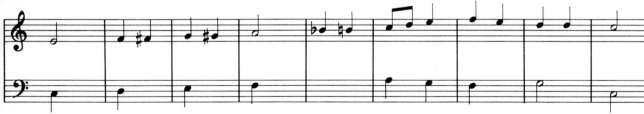

EXAMPLE D-12

Examples D-13, D-14, and D-15 prolong an underlying chord by means of chromatic progressions in the outer voices moving through a complete octave in opposite directions. The solution following Example D-13 adds two inner voices notated in keyboard style. It is best to repeat common tones whenever possible and to use stepwise progressions. The apparent large leaps are caused by transfers of register necessitated by the keyboard setting.

Examples D-16, D-17, D-18, and D-19 are based on suspensions. These can be transformed into chromatic progressions in a variety of settings in two, three, and four parts. Any of the voices can be inflected chromatically and melodically embellished. In Example D-16 the sixths can be realized as $\frac{6}{5}$ chords. In Example D-17 at least three different top-voice versions should be provided. Use chromatically inflected tones in at least one solution of the top voice. Example D-18 should be continued down to the III. Transform it into a progression of descending fifths and chromaticize the upper voices as indicated. We have provided Example D-19 with a solution showing gradually more complex prolongations of the underlying suspension series.

EXAMPLE D-13

SOLUTION D-13

EXAMPLE D-14

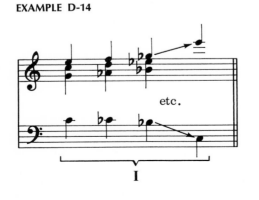

EXAMPLE D-15

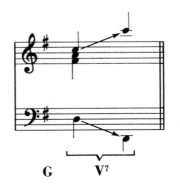

EXAMPLE D-16

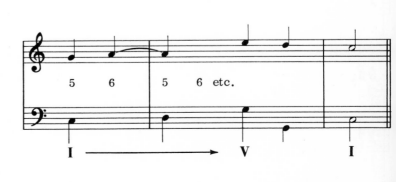

EXAMPLE D-17

EXAMPLE D-18

SOLUTION D-18

a)

etc.

EXAMPLE D-19

E. EXERCISES IN PASSING MOTIONS AND CONTRAPUNTAL CHORD PROLONGATIONS

The use of a bass plan as the foundation for improvised or written work is an old and valuable method of instruction.[5] We have adopted this principle in Examples E-1 to E-4, which contain both passing motions and contrapuntal chord prolongations. The student should set the basses finding the meter, rhythms, chords, and voice leading appropriate to his melodic ideas, and to the contrapuntal or harmonic function of the bass. He should feel free to add further prolongations to the bass as long as he does so within the given structural framework.

[5] See C. P. E. Bach, *Essay on the True Art of Playing Keyboard Instruments*, trans. and ed. by William J. Mitchell, New York, 1949.

EXAMPLE E-1

EXAMPLE E-2

EXAMPLE E-3

EXAMPLE E-4

8

THE CHORALE

1. THE ELEMENTS OF CHORALE WRITING

CHORALE WRITING AND THE STUDY OF COUNTERPOINT

In the preceding chapters of this book we have been concerned mainly with basic contrapuntal techniques and with specific prolongations of these techniques as they appear in excerpts from the literature. We have not yet observed the interaction of counterpoint with other musical forces in the context of setting a whole piece or large section. Chorale writing will allow us to progress gradually to that stage.

In this chapter we shall concentrate upon the voice-leading problems in chorale setting. Therefore we shall refer only in passing to historical development, text interpretation, performance practice, and related matters. The chorale repertory extends through four centuries. Although many composers have written excellent chorales, we shall concentrate upon the four-part settings of J. S. Bach. Bach's chorales are universally regarded as the supreme examples of the *genre;* many are masterpieces whose richness of content and depth of expression belie their brevity.

THE CHORALE MELODY

Chorale melodies are the hymn tunes of the Lutheran church. Some of these melodies were written especially for the Lutheran service by composers of the sixteenth to eighteenth centuries. Others are adaptations of earlier secular or religious melodies; some of these are of great antiquity. Naturally, chorale melodies vary considerably in style and in quality. Some of the earlier tunes are modal; other melodies belong to the major/minor system. Some are beautifully constructed melodies; others have survived because of sacred associations rather than intrinsic musical value.

When we set a choral tune, we use it as a cantus firmus; we cannot change it except by occasionally adding ornamental detail. The chorale tune, however, represents a very different sort of cantus firmus from the simple and abstract given line of the species exercises. The chorale melody is not purely linear, but has strong vertical implications; we must hear groups of tones as the horizontalized expression of underlying chords.[1] Often, these chords enter into harmonic associations; we must therefore realize the harmonic as well as the contrapuntal implications of the melody. Furthermore, many chorale tunes have a distinct individual profile; in our settings we must respect the motivic design and expressive character of the melody. Finally, a stylistic point: we shall follow the procedure of Bach and other Baroque masters by

[1] As discussed in chaps. 6 and 7.

placing the chorale melody in the soprano voice. In the earliest chorale settings, the cantus firmus was generally placed in the tenor. Bach's more elaborate settings, such as the chorale-preludes for organ, sometimes show the cantus firmus in the bass or in an inner part; in his four-part vocal chorales, Bach always places it in the soprano.

RHYTHM AND METER

By the time of Bach, the rhythm of the chorale had become strongly metrical. Rhythmic movement occurs against a background of metrical groups, of strong and weak pulses in regular and periodic succession. Often, important structural events occur on the strong pulses; the final tonic chord, for example, virtually always falls on the accented beat. It is possible, on the other hand, for a metrically weak beat to act as a focal point, as the beginning or end of an important motion. Many chorales begin with an upbeat. Often the upbeat presents the initial

tonic chord and forms the point of departure for the entire chorale; such upbeats must not be heard as merely preparing the subsequent downbeat (see Example 8-1[2]).

A cursory look through the Bach chorales will suffice to indicate that the quarter note represents the usual metrical pulse or beat. In a very few chorales (e.g., Nos. 179 and 194) the half note becomes the metrical unit. Most chorales are in duple meter with a time signature indicating 4/4. Both the first and the third quarter can function as strong beats; quite often the third quarter contains the final chord.

Relatively few chorales are in triple meter; of those that are, most bear a signature of 3/4. These chorales are often characterized by a rhythm of half-quarter (see Nos. 1, 93, and 143). In the chorales with 3/4 meter each measure normally contains only one strong beat. Comparison of Chorales 6 and 316, given in Example 8-2—both settings of the same tune—is instructive. Number 6 has a meter of 4/4; No. 316 is composed in 3/4. Note that two measures of the 3/4 chorale correspond

[2] The numbering of the Chorales follows the Riemenschneider edition (New York, 1941), which retains the traditional numbering found in most previous editions.

EXAMPLE 8-1   Bach Chorale 5

EXAMPLE 8-2   Bach Chorale 6, 316

to one measure of the 4/4; the half notes of 316 represent the accented quarters of 6.

NOTE-AGAINST-NOTE AND FIGURATED SETTINGS

In his chorales Bach employs a variety of texture ranging from simple note-against-note settings to fairly complex figurated writing. This is illustrated in the juxtaposition of the two excerpts in Examples 8-3 and 8-4 (Chorales 108 and 198). Sometimes one of these textures prevails throughout an entire chorale. Chorale 106, for example, shows predominantly note-against-note texture; Chorale 61, another setting of the same melody, is highly figurated. At other times Bach varies the density of a figuration within a single chorale.

In his work the student should confine himself to binary divisions of the beat. Bach uses eighth-note motion freely. Eighth notes occur most characteristically in groups of two (Example 8-5); however, Bach will write as many as fourteen consecutive eighth notes in a single voice (Example 8-6). Bach uses sixteenth notes far more sparingly; he seldom writes more than two consecutive sixteenth notes in a single part. Many chorales contain no sixteenths at all. Syncopations—usually tied eighth notes—occur frequently (see Example 8-4).

At this point it is suggested that the student reduce several figurated chorale phrases to their note-against-note outlines (see Exercises, Nos.

EXAMPLE 8-3 Bach Chorale 108

EXAMPLE 8-4 Bach Chorale 198

EXAMPLE 8-5 **Bach Chorale 68**

EXAMPLE 8-6 **Bach Chorale 45**

EXAMPLE 8-7 **Bach Chorale 151**

EXAMPLE 8-8

A-1 to A-5, pages 312–313). By comparing these outlines with Bach's settings we shall gain insight into both his use of melodic prolongations and his treatment of dissonance. Example 8-7, from Chorale 151, may serve as an example: through elimination of the figurating tones we arrive at the outline given in Example 8-8.

DISSONANCE TREATMENT: RHYTHMIC ASPECTS

If the student, as recommended above, reduces figurated chorale phrases to note-against-note settings, he will observe that some—but not all—dissonances will be removed. We can, therefore, establish a distinction between two types of dissonance: figurated dissonance usually in eighth- or sixteenth-note value, and note-against-note dissonance usually in quarter-note value. The value of the dissonant tone is seldom extended beyond the quarter note; for exceptions, see Chorale 216, bar 2, and Chorale 316, bars 6-8. This distinction is intended only as a preliminary guide; as we shall see, note-against-note dissonances represent prolonged or manipulated figurations.

Dissonance treatment in the chorale stands midway between the rigorous simplicity of the species exercises and the texture—sometimes highly dissonant—of instrumental music. That dissonance arises out of motion against a background of consonant stability is one of the great lessons of species counterpoint. The horizontal origin and transitory nature of dissonance characterize all the music of triadic tonality;

especially since the Baroque period, however, composers have been able to control dissonance through other than purely rhythmic means. Where the need arises, dissonant tones can enjoy long duration without losing their dependent character. Sustained dissonances do not occur in the chorale; however, the use of note-against-note dissonance marks an advance in complexity over species counterpoint.

FIGURATED DISSONANCE

Example 8-9 shows the simple and direct application to chorale writing of the three basic types of dissonance: the passing tone, the neighboring tone, and the suspension. In these excerpts, the treatment of dissonance resembles that of species counterpoint and requires no comment. The 8-7 passing motion is of great importance; Bach often uses it over dominant harmony at cadences (Example 8-9b).

In Example 8-10 we see ornamental dissonances similar to those of fifth-species counterpoint. The use of sixteenth notes is characteristic; like the eighth notes of fifth species, sixteenth notes in the chorale are generally used for decorative purposes.

We have not employed dissonant anticipations in the species exercises. Like the suspension, the anticipation results from rhythmic manipulation; however, it does not represent a fundamentally important type of dissonance, as does the suspension. Usually the anticipation occurs in a weaker metrical position than the tone it anticipates; in this

EXAMPLE 8-9   Bach Chorales 224, 1, 18, 168

respect it is the opposite of the suspension. In chorales, anticipations appear most characteristically in the soprano part. Often the melodic tonic is anticipated at cadential points; Bach sometimes added anticipations of the tonic to chorale melodies, and the student should be allowed to do the same. Example 8-11 presents an anticipated tonic in the soprano.

In example 8-12 we see the anticipation of the next-to-last tone of a phrase, also in the soprano.

Example 8-13, from the same chorale, shows a less frequently en-

countered use of the anticipation. Here a short chain of two anticipations occurs in the course of a passing motion in the tenor part.

The third tone in the soprano voice of Example 8-14 can be understood as an indirect anticipation; it is not repeated in the same voice but forms part of the following chord. Though a dissonance with respect to its immediate context, the tone C belongs to the governing C-minor chord, within which the first four beats of this chorale move.

The student will sometimes encounter other tones of figuration preceded or followed by a leap. Most of these are incomplete neigh-

EXAMPLE 8-10   Bach Chorales 27, 43,

EXAMPLE 8-11   Bach Chorale 207

EXAMPLE 8-12   Bach Chorale 57

bors; that is, neighboring notes with only one stepwise connection instead of the usual two. In Example 8-15 the dissonance is connected to the preceding but not to the following tone; this type of incomplete neighbor is often called the escape tone or *note échappée*.

The escape tone is most appropriately used in the soprano voice, usually at cadences. Sometimes, as in Example 8-16, it is accompanied in thirds by the alto.

In Bach's chorales, the échappée occurs typically as an upper neighbor. The idiom is best explained as the result of the elision of the normal tone of resolution (Example 8-17).

A second type of incomplete neighbor is preceded by a leap and followed by stepwise motion. Whereas the escape tone is most closely connected to the preceding tone, this second type (sometimes confusingly called the cambiata) belongs primarily to the following tone. Dissonances like those of Example 8-18 result from the contraction of a passing motion; by eliding the tone that would normally precede it, we transform the passing tone into an incomplete neighbor.

As in Example 8-18, Bach frequently introduces sevenths as incom-

EXAMPLE 8-13   Bach Chorale 57

EXAMPLE 8-14   Bach Chorale 149

EXAMPLE 8-15   Bach Chorale 28 (figured-bass chorale)

EXAMPLE 8-16   Bach Chorale 156

EXAMPLE 8-17   Bach Chorale 156

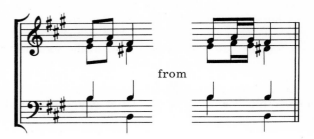

EXAMPLE 8-18   Bach Chorale 210

from

EXAMPLE 8-19   Bach Chorale 191

EXAMPLE 8-20   Bach Chorales 352, 9

plete neighbors where the 8-7 passing motion (Example 8-9b) is impracticable; such sevenths usually occur in one of the inner voices rather than in the soprano.

In Example 8-19 we see a more rarely encountered type of embellishing dissonance. Here the figuration decorates the fifth of a $\frac{6}{5}$ chord—in this context a dissonant tone—by an upward leap of a third followed by a stepwise descent back to the main tone.

In Examples 8-9 and 8-10 we have seen that Bach's treatment of the suspension dissonance resembles very closely that familiar to us from the species exercises. And, indeed, in his chorales Bach generally uses suspensions simply and without much prolongation. It is understood, of course, that a suspension can occur through repetition as well as tying over; the difference is one of articulation rather than contrapuntal meaning. Occasionally Bach introduces more complex suspensions. In Example 8-20a, for instance, a dissonant diminished fifth is repeated. The seeming upward resolution of the suspension in Example 8-20b, however, is illusory. Actually, the suspension resolves downward according to normal procedures; the ascending tone is a decorative interpolation.

Example 8-21 shows a highly atypical 4-3 succession in which the fourth is introduced by leap. This accented incomplete neighbor (or appoggiatura) seldom occurs in chorales; as F occurs in the previous chord the tone receives an indirect preparation.

From his contrapuntal exercises the student will remember that the primary types of dissonances, the passing tone, neighboring tone, and suspension, have their consonant analogs. It goes without saying that consonant figurations appear in the chorale as well. In addition to the types mentioned above, the student will encounter leaps from one to another tone of the same chord. Such chordal skips frequently occur in combination with other figures. Example 8-22 is instructive. The simultaneous presence of a chordal leap in the bass and neighboring, passing, and anticipating figurations in the upper parts gives rise to an apparent $\frac{6}{4}$ chord. In reality this chord, like many others, is solely the product of linear motion.

RHYTHMIC SHIFT; THE DISPLACEMENT OF TONES

The displacement or rhythmic shift of certain tones constitutes an important technique of prolonged counterpoint. As we shall see, this technique appears even within the framework of the species exercises when two species of different note values occur in combination (see Chapter 9). In his chorales, Bach makes very frequent use of displacement; the rhythmic value of the shift is usually the eighth note. By displacing tones from their normal contrapuntal setting, a composer can enhance the interest of his voice leading. Depending upon how they

EXAMPLE 8-21 Bach Chorale 256

EXAMPLE 8-22 Bach Chorale 209

are used, shifted tones accelerate or retard forward motion. They help maintain (or avoid) repeated rhythmic patterns, thus contributing to the motivic design of the piece. The rhythmic shift often places dissonant passing or neighboring notes on the strong part of the beat; these emphatic dissonances tend to create a dense, massive texture and, on occasion, a quality of poignant expression.

In Example 8-23 the bass contains an accented dissonant passing tone on the second beat of the first bar. This accented dissonance results from displacement; in an unprolonged contrapuntal setting, the dissonance would fall on the second half of the first beat.

The accented dissonant neighbor of Example 8-24 forms part of

the decorated resolution of a suspension. The normal values for such a decoration are sixteenth notes; the basic contrapuntal relation between the parts is shown in Example 8-24b. The use of rhythmic shift makes it possible to maintain eighth-note motion until the final chord of the phrase.

The contrapuntal settings of Example 8-25 show displacements similar to those of combined second and third species (see Chapter 9). In order to preserve the flow of eighth notes, the neighboring tones are made to resolve on the following beat. At this time, a new chord enters, creating a dissonance. The third and fourth beats of Example 8-25b show another type of displacement. The dissonant passing tone E flat

EXAMPLE 8-23   Bach Chorale 63

from

EXAMPLE 8-24   Bach Chorale 25

from

is suspended, thus delaying its resolution to D. The suspension of dissonant passing and neighboring tones occurs somewhat less frequently in the chorales than in other types of prolonged counterpoint.

In Examples 8-23 to 8-25 displacement occurs in one voice against a background of quarter-note motion in the remaining voices. In a setting containing figuration in several voices, displacement produces a denser, more complex texture. Example 8-26, from Chorale 315, shows such a case. Example 8-26a shows the basic setting; b adds the figurations of the top voice; c shows the introduction of stepwise motion between G and C in the bass; d presents the actual setting. Keeping the eighth-note motion in the bass shifts the C from the first to the second

half of the second beat and creates two dissonant sonorities (* *). In addition, the domain of the initial tonic harmony is extended by half a beat, and the C chord (IV) reduced to a passing chord between I and V.

Successive dissonances also arise when a neighboring note in one voice counterpoints an embellishing tone in another. In Example 8-27, the bass shows an embellishing motion within the third D–F of the D minor triad. The neighboring notes in the two upper voices coincide with the embellishing tone F; the return of the main tones in the upper voices dissonates with the accented passing tone E in the bass.

The technique of displacement embodies still other means for obtaining immediately consecutive dissonances. Sometimes a passing

EXAMPLE 8-25   Bach Chorales 25, 19

EXAMPLE 8-26   Bach Chorale 315

EXAMPLE 8-27   Bach Chorale 13

tone in one part coincides with the decorated resolution of a suspension in another (Example 8-28a). Sometimes one voice features accented passing tones whose resolutions occur against unaccented dissonances in one or more of the other voices. Example 8-28b presents such a case. The accented passing tones in the soprano create expressive dissonances with the tenor line; Bach's simpler settings of this chorale melody do not add the accented passing tones (see Chorales 88 and 99). The reader should note the sustained E in the alto; by delaying the leap to A, Bach avoids a second with the soprano. In addition, the retention of a tone belonging to the tonic harmony points up the transitory, passing character of the F chord on the second beat.

EXAMPLE 8-28   Bach Chorales 1, 123

a)

b)

The shift of tones can produce consonances as well as dissonances. In Example 8-29 (also from Chorale 123) the eighth note B in the top voice is a neighboring tone decorating the basic melodic progression D–C–B. Therefore the second quarter of the measure does *not* contain a B minor $\frac{6}{3}$ chord; the D chord remains in force throughout the first two beats.

CONTRACTION; NOTE-AGAINST-NOTE DISSONANCE

The important technique of contraction was explained in Chapter 7, pages 178ff. This type of prolonged counterpoint occurs frequently in chorale settings. In Example 8-30, the $\frac{4}{2}$ on the first eighth note results from the elision of the root of the chord, C. A five-note succession, C–B flat–A–G–F, is contracted to four. In this example both contraction and displacement are in evidence.

Contraction also gives rise to note-against-note settings. In Example 8-31a, this technique enlarges the dissonant E flat thereby intensifying the passing motion. In *b*, the technique of contraction shapes the very beginning of the chorale, producing the expressive initial $\frac{4}{2}$ chord and underscoring the large rhythmic design of the piece (every phrase begins with a half note). In *c*, contraction produces three successive $\frac{6}{5}$ chords.

A note-against-note setting sharply increases the impact of a dis-

sonant tone; in addition, the dissonant tone now occupies as much time as the consonant members of the chord. For these reasons many theorists have fallen into the error of assigning to some of these dissonant combinations a vertical origin. In particular the seventh chords and their inversions are explained as arising out of an assemblage of superimposed thirds. Actually these chords result from melodic activity; they originate in contrapuntal materials such as the passing tone, neighboring tone, or suspension. Sometimes the contrapuntal procedure is immediately evident, as in the passing dissonance of Example 8-32. At other times, the origin of the dissonance is veiled through techniques such as contraction or transfer of register. Both in written work and in analysis, knowledge of the specific contrapuntal origin of the dissonance provides the clue to an understanding of its behavior.[3]

In concluding this section we offer a phrase from Chorale 26 (Example 8-33). Out of the seven sonorities, only two—the first and the last —are consonant. The analytic reductions show that the many note-against-note dissonances are grounded in familiar contrapuntal procedures. The most significant determining factors are the passing motion

[3] The linear origin of dissonant $\frac{6}{4}$, 7th and 9th chords receives a clear and cogent explanation in William J. Mitchell's *Elementary Harmony*, chaps. 12, 15, and 16. Before proceeding to the writing of chorales, the student should read these chapters and evaluate the information contained in them in the light of his experience in species counterpoint.

EXAMPLE 8-29   Bach Chorale 123

from

EXAMPLE 8-30 Bach Chorale 311

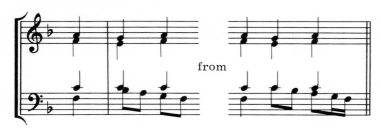

from

EXAMPLE 8-31 Bach Chorales 8, 10, 279

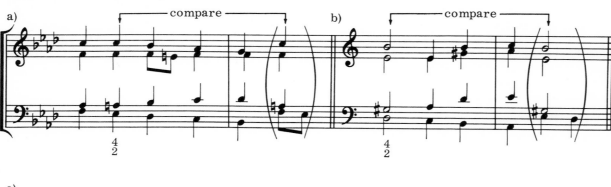

from

EXAMPLE 8-32 Bach Chorale 191

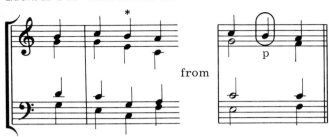

from

EXAMPLE 8-33 Bach Chorale 26

in the bass from F to the dominant of G and its counterpoint in the soprano—a motion out of the inner-voice region prolonging the melodic progression C–B flat (see graphs a and b). Graph c indicates the shift of tones and the interpolated neighbors which increase the density of dissonance.[4]

MELODIC DISSONANCE

In species counterpoint dissonant leaps are not allowed; the abstract character of the species exercises requires the use of only the simplest melodic relationships. Dissonance between successive tones of a single line, therefore, falls within the domain of prolonged counterpoint. The nature and extent of melodic dissonance vary according to medium and style. Broadly speaking, instrumental music offers more scope for its use than does vocal. In the rather severe vocal idiom of the chorale, melodic dissonances occur comparatively seldom. Nevertheless, in certain contexts their use is permitted or even required.

In order to secure a favorable register, it is sometimes necessary to substitute a seventh for a second. This technique of interval inversion

[4] See Exercises, Nos. B-1 to B-6, page 314.

EXAMPLE 8-33 (continued)

a)

becomes

b)

becomes

c)

occurs mostly in the bass line; Bach seldom employs it in the inner parts (see, however, Example 8-34c). A related procedure—the expansion of a second into a ninth—occurs very infrequently. In *d* such a ninth appears. In all probability this chorale has come down to us with the bass of the instrumental accompaniment rather than with the vocal bass part. Disjunct lines of this sort occur frequently in Bach's instrumental music, but they are not characteristic of the vocal parts of his chorale settings (Example 8-34).

EXAMPLE 8-34   **Bach Chorales 58, 346, 339, 131**

stands for

A second cause of melodic dissonance is the desire to obtain a leading tone. Leaps of a diminished fifth occur very often; diminished fourths and diminished sevenths are also characteristic of the chorale style. Typically, the second tone of the interval functions as a leading tone; the dissonant leap downward, therefore, is followed by an upward motion of a half step. This change of direction after the dissonant leap occurs only with diminished intervals, not with their inversions into augmented fourths, fifths, and seconds. Because of the change of direction, the diminished intervals can be more smoothly integrated into the line than can the augmented; in his chorales, Bach seldom uses the augmented forms and excludes one of them—the augmented second—altogether.[5]

Example 8-35 is drawn from Chorale 201; in this piece, the leap of the diminished fifth occurs repeatedly and assumes motivic significance. (The source of this chorale has not survived, and we do not know for which verse of the hymn it is intended. It is possible—though we cannot be certain—that these diminished fifths are intended to be emblematic of the words "great sin" referred to in the title.) Note that the second, lower tone of the diminished fifth is a leading tone supporting an applied dominant chord. Although these local dominants are in inversion, the fact that they are approached by leap throws them into

strong relief and adds a definite harmonic implication to the contrapuntal stepwise progression from leading tone to temporary tonic.

The diminished fourth arises out of a juxtaposition of the third tone and the leading tone of a minor scale. Example 8-36 presents the most common use of this interval; here, the leading tone occurs between the third and the root of the D minor chord. This progression originates in the substitution technique of second-species counterpoint; C sharp substitutes for the passing tone E.

Example 8-37 illustrates a typical use of the diminished seventh. The large leap effects a change in register and emphasizes the harmonic implication of the applied dominant chord.

Diminished leaps, like leaps of sevenths, generally occur in the bass; occasionally, however, they will be found in an inner voice. Example 8-38 shows the leap of a diminished fifth in the tenor. In this case the dissonant leap helps to avoid the parallel fifths that would result from stepwise motion in all the parts.

In this section we have not attempted to discuss all the contexts in which melodic dissonances occur in the Bach chorales; we have had to confine ourselves to the most typical usages. In the exercises following this chapter, Nos. C-1 to C-4, the reader will encounter a few examples that differ slightly from those discussed so far. In attempting to understand and explain the voice leading of these examples, he should be guided by the procedures we have adopted in this chapter, always relating the specific instance of voice leading to general contrapuntal principles as modified by other compositional forces.

[5] There is only one melodic augmented second to be found in the 371 chorales; see Mitchell, *Elementary Harmony*, p. 187–188.

EXAMPLE 8-35 Bach Chorale 201

EXAMPLE 8-36 Bach Chorale 213

CHROMATICISM: CHROMATIC INFLECTION; THE CROSS RELATION

In general, Bach's use of chromaticism is less complex in the chorales than in some of his other compositions. Nevertheless, a few chorales (such as Nos. 216 and 279) are quite chromatic, and many of the simpler ones make some use of chromatic techniques. Perhaps the most frequent cause of a chromatic succession is the upward inflection of a diatonic tone in order to produce a leading tone. In Example 8-39, the chromatic line adds impetus to a prolongation of the V; the basic voice leading within this sonority consists of an embellishing motion (D–A–B flat–C–D) in the bass as counterpoint to the soprano's F sharp decorated by its upper and lower neighbors. In Example 8-6, the chromatic passing tones move within an ascending octave.

Chromatically inflected leading tones also occur in larger values. Example 8-40 presents the opening of a magnificent chorale from the *St. Matthew Passion*. The initial tonic is transformed into an applied $\frac{6}{5}$ to the IV; the IV moves to the V through a chromatic passing chord supported by E sharp in the bass. The passing chord is a diminished seventh, a chord frequently used to connect IV and V in the minor mode.

In descending lines, chromatic inflection often results from contraction. In Example 8-41, contraction eliminates changes of direction in the bass, thereby reinforcing the drive to the dominant. In the second measure of this example we observe another contrapuntal use of the diminished seventh chord; namely, as a chromatic neighboring chord decorating the resolution of the $\frac{6}{4}$ to $\frac{5}{3}$ over the dominant.

Examples 8-39 to 8-41 have featured chromatic inflection, that is, the immediate succession of two chromatic variants of a single tone. In Example 8-41, however, a second type of chromaticism comes into view. The neighboring diminished seventh chord has a chromatic tone, C sharp, for its bass. This C sharp is neither preceded nor followed by the diatonic C natural; C sharp, therefore, is not an inflection of but a replacement for the diatonic tone. This substitution of the diatonic by the chromatic form often serves to create applied dominant chords, so often, indeed, that no examples are needed.

EXAMPLE 8-37 Bach Chorale 108

EXAMPLE 8-38 Bach Chorale 271

EXAMPLE 8-39 Bach Chorale 19

derives from

EXAMPLE 8-40 Bach Chorale 105

EXAMPLE 8-41 Bach Chorale 23 (figured-bass chorale)

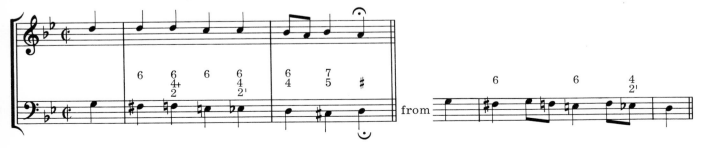

from

Chromatic substitution also frequently occurs in connection with the *mixture of modes*, that is, with the use of a tone or of several tones from one mode in a context principally determined by the other. In Example 8-42a, we see the substitution of D flat for D natural; this substitution produces the II $\frac{6}{5}$ of F minor within an F major context. In Example 8-42b, a prolongation of the V of A major (see section on harmonic prolongation) uses first the minor, then the normal major form of the E chord.

In Example 8-42b the G sharp in the tenor follows closely upon the G natural of the soprano. When chromatic inflection occurs across two voices rather than in a single one, the result is called a *cross relation* (or false relation). As we have seen, the cross relation is not appropriate to species counterpoint (see first-species three-part counterpoint). Composition, however, offers many opportunities for the use of this type of voice leading. In Example 8-43 we see an immediate, uninterrupted cross relation. G sharp in the bass follows the G natural of the alto. The reader will notice that a chromatic tone involved in a cross relation produces a much sharper impact than one introduced in the same voice as its diatonic original. By using cross relations, therefore,

EXAMPLE 8-42   Bach Chorales 6, 2

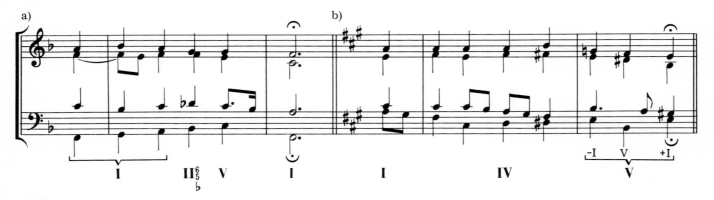

EXAMPLE 8-43   Bach Chorale 217

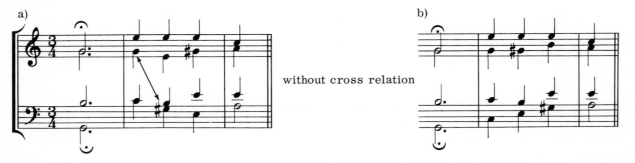

without cross relation

we make the texture less smooth. Smoothness, however, is by no means a constant requirement; and to forbid cross relations, at this stage, would be sheer pedantry. The cross relation of Example 8-43 results from the sudden, climactic use of high register underscoring the appearance of the tonic, C, in the bass. Had Bach wished to write smoothly here, he could have proceeded as in Example 8-43b, but the result is as featureless as it is smooth.

There are no rules for determining in advance when to use and when to avoid cross relations. We can offer only a general guide; use the cross relation only where it is musically appropriate to emphasize and call attention to the inflected tone. Where a smooth, even transition is desired, keep the chromatic succession in the same voice.

MELODIC CHARACTERISTICS OF THE SINGLE VOICES; REPEATED TONES

Many harmony texts present a "chorale style" in which the bass contains so many leaps as to prevent melodic continuity and in which the alto and tenor are so restricted in motion as to lose all linear profile. Nothing could be further from Bach's practice.

To be sure, the chorale bass generally contains more leaps than the upper parts. Sometimes these leaps are caused by the need to express (or imply) harmonic relationships; sometimes they result from the use of arpeggiation. However, Bach always deploys his leaps so as to maintain continuity. In Example 8-35 the diminished fifths are followed by stepwise contrary motion. The same holds true for the diminished fourth of Example 8-36; and the large leaps of Example 8-34 decorate an underlying stepwise progression. In all of these excerpts, repeated tones and conjunct motion in the upper parts compensate for the more widely ranging bass. The alert student will also notice how often Bach fills in contrapuntally the interval between two tones of a harmonic progression. See Example 8-13 with its passing motion from V to I. The frequency with which Bach uses applied dominant chords in inversion rather than in the more explicitly harmonic root position also points up the melodic, contrapuntal quality of his basses.

Bach's inner voices have nothing in common with the inert, aimless "fillers" of the textbook chorale style. Often, the inner voices play an individual and important role. Note the alto of Example 8-35 which gives so much rhythmic life to the phrase, or the tenor of Example 8-33 whose parallel sixths with the soprano underscore by contrast the important descent of the bass. Although Bach frequently lets an inner part move in parallel thirds, sixths, or tenths with one of the outer voices, he offsets any possible monotony through contrasting progressions in the other parts.

Repeated tones appear frequently in the upper parts, less frequently in the bass. These repeated tones often result from the syllabic setting of the chorale text; that is, each syllable normally receives a quarter note. Since each voice must accommodate a set number of syllables, repeated tones must be used in place of long sustained tones. Let us study Example 8-44. The five consecutive D's in the alto represent a textural variant of a whole note tied to an eighth; the single long tone

EXAMPLE 8-44 Bach Chorale 29

without repetition

etc.

is broken up into five shorter values in order to enunciate the first five syllables of the text. Repeated tones (like sustained tones) act as a binding, integrative element in the tonal fabric, and as a stable foil for the motion of the other parts. The reader is advised to sing the entire alto part of Chorale 29 from which our example is drawn. Despite the many repetitions, the line has a distinct profile; note in particular the enlivening effect of the suspensions.

As mentioned above, repeated tones occur less frequently in the bass than in the upper voices. Bach does not hesitate to repeat a bass tone from a strong to a weak beat (see Chorale 113), for such a repetition underscores the accentual pattern of the meter. Bach tends to avoid the repetition (or sustaining) of a bass tone from a weak beat to a strong, except in the case of suspensions. A weak-strong repetition in the bass contradicts the meter by making the strong pulse a mere continuation of the preceding weak one. The one situation in which Bach frequently repeats a bass tone from a weak to a strong beat is where the chorale begins with an upbeat. Bach often fortifies the initial tonic by repeating it from fourth to first quarter (see Chorales 26, 27, etc.).[6] Occasionally, as in Example 8-35, Bach will repeat or tie over a bass tone from a weak to a strong beat in the middle of a phrase. The tied C of Example 8-35 is not a suspension, of course. A static effect is prevented here by the vigorous motion of the upper voices, in particular the alto.

[6] For more information about weak-strong bass repetitions, see Mitchell, *op. cit.,* pp.90–93 and 160–161.

VOICE CROSSING

In general Bach keeps each voice in its normal position within the texture. Sometimes, however, he allows two adjacent parts to cross. In Example 8-45, an excerpt showing an unusual amount of imitation, the tenor crosses above the alto in order to complete a second statement of the motivic ascending fifth; two measures later the voices recross and assume their usual positions.

Voice crossing sometimes improves the counterpoint by averting forbidden parallels. In Example 8-46 the crossing of tenor and alto (by far the most frequently interchanged voices) prevents parallel octaves. This use of crossing in order to prevent parallels is by no means a merely visual trick. In a setting where each part is performed by a separate group of singers and instrumentalists, the listener can easily distinguish the progress of the different voices. On a keyboard instrument, on the other hand, it is much more difficult to project the course of each individual part, and the impression of parallel octaves might easily arise. Note the fifths between tenor and soprano at the point where the voices recross. We shall discuss fifths caused by tones of figuration (in this case, by the chordal leap to B in the tenor) in the next section.

If the tenor and bass cross, the position of the chord changes, at least in so far as the vocal setting is concerned. Sometimes, as in Example 8-47, the crossing of the lower voices creates apparent $\frac{6}{4}$ chords. The reader should remember, however, that Bach conceived his chorales as

EXAMPLE 8-45   Bach Chorale 358

accompanied, not as a *cappella* compositions. In most instances, we can assume that the instrumental bass is doubled at the lower octave. This would remove the $\frac{6}{4}$ chords; nevertheless, the incursion of the vocal bass into the inner voice region does weaken the stability of the chord.

CONSECUTIVE PERFECT INTERVALS

In Example 8-46 we noted the fifths between soprano and tenor caused by the broken-chord motion D sharp–B–F sharp in the tenor against the leap F sharp–C sharp in the soprano. This is an unusual example;

Bach's chorales seldom contain fifths involving only consonant tones of the texture. In this instance, the B of the tenor is an obvious figuration; it is perhaps less obvious that the soprano's C sharp—though a quarter note—also functions as a decoration, for it is part of a motion out of the inner voice prolonging the basic progression F sharp–E (see Example 8-48).

The voice leading of Example 8-49, on the other hand, occurs rather often. Here the fifths arise out of the simultaneous use of a dissonant passing tone and a dissonant anticipation. The listener can easily hear the fundamental voice leading; it is equally evident that no inherent vertical relationship exists between the tones of the second fifth. This coincidence of passing tone and anticipation is probably responsible for the greatest number of apparent fifths in the Bach chorales.

EXAMPLE 8-46   Bach Chorale 4

crossing prevents

EXAMPLE 8-47   Bach Chorale 156

EXAMPLE 8-48   Bach Chorale 4

stands for

EXAMPLE 8-49   Bach Chorale 121

In the printed collections of Bach's chorales, one sometimes encounters fifths between tones of the basic voice leading. Most of these anomalous fifths seem to be misprints. In Example 8-50a, the third and fourth notes of the tenor should be corrected to B and A; Example 8-50b, from a virtually identical setting in B♭, contains what seems to us to be the correct version as shown in some printed editions.

Fifths by contrary motion or antiparallel fifths function more convincingly in the fuller texture of four voices than in two- or three-part writing. In the chorales they sometimes appear at cadences; Example 8-51 shows antiparallels between the outer voices.

In the compact, dense texture of the Bach chorale style, parallel motion in octaves and unisons would be inappropriate even when produced by tones of figuration; the temporary doubling caused by such motion creates a looser web of voice leading and weakens the tonal fabric.

We have seen that figuration sometimes gives rise to consecutive fifths in Bach's chorales; we know from Chapter 7 that the more diffuse textures of instrumental music sometimes allow octaves to arise in a similar fashion. There is, however, a second aspect to the problem of forbidden consecutives: namely, to what extent is it possible to break up fifths or octaves in the basic voice leading through the use of intervening figuration?

EXAMPLE 8-50   Bach Chorales 64, 256

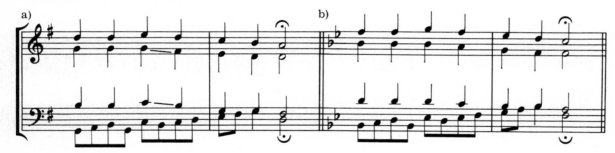

EXAMPLE 8-51   Bach Chorale 114

In Bach's chorales parallels are often separated by a mere eighth note's figuration. It must be remembered, however, that the closely interwoven texture of the chorale gives a certain weight and substance even to the eighth note. Between two octaves, Bach always interpolates a disjunct tone; between two fifths, a simple anticipation suffices (see Example 8-70). In Mitchell's *Elementary Harmony*, Chapters 13 and 14, the reader will find a number of examples illustrating the role of tones of figuration in breaking up fifths and octaves. We add to Mitchell's examples a single excerpt. Here, fifths are prevented not through the use of a tone, but through a rest (Example 8-52). In Example 8-52 the reader will also note that fifths appear on successive downbeats between bass and tenor. These fifths are broken up by embellishing motions producing a 5-10-5 progression. This 5-10-5, in turn, arises out of the prolongation of an underlying 5-6 suspension series through the interchange of the two lower voices.

VOICE LEADING AT THE CADENCE; THE CADENTIAL SUSPENSION

The fermatas to be found in chorale melodies indicate the end of a line of text. Often, but by no means always, they also point out an articulation in the melodic line and thereby show us where a musical phrase ends. We emphasize that not every fermata marks the end of a phrase; furthermore, where the melody alone might suggest a phrase ending, Bach frequently bridges over the articulation in his setting in order to avoid excessive segmentation. It goes without saying that, in a coherent setting, even the most strongly articulated single phrase forms part of a larger whole; just as, in the statue of a human figure, a head or hand, no matter how complex in inner organization, must function within the total design.

We mention this by way of caution, for the student must learn to hear through the surface articulation to the underlying continuity. Unfortunately the student is often advised to determine the cadences first, only then "filling in" the rest, as if the end of a phrase were not the consequence of what has gone on before and the preparation for what is to come. Not all cadences are equally definitive. Some are mere breathing pauses. Others are stronger, and crystallize the preceding flow into a harmonic structure stable enough to serve as point of departure for the next kinetic impulse. It is these more conclusive, harmonically explicit cadences that we shall discuss in this section.

A full harmonic cadence requires a V–I progression with both chords in root position. Bach usually elaborates the dominant contrapuntally. We have already mentioned the 8-7 passing motion (see Example 8-9b); over dominant harmony, this contrapuntal progression gives rise to the so-called dominant seventh chord (Example 8-53).

EXAMPLE 8-52 Bach Chorale 143

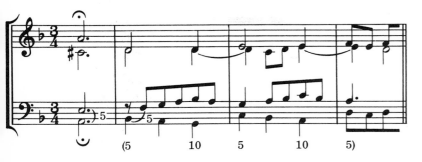

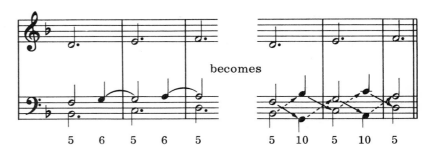

Example 8-54a is drawn from the same chorale. Bach adds an extremely significant voice-leading progression: the leading tone is retarded by a dissonant 4-3 suspension in the tenor. We know from fourth- and fifth-species counterpoint that a suspension into the leading tone powerfully enhances the drive to the goal of motion. Many compositional idioms, in the chorale and elsewhere, arise out of this cadential suspension. When, as in Example 8-54a, the phrase ends with a melodic motion 2-1, with the 2 occupying two beats, a suspension in one of the inner parts creates this frequently used $\frac{5\text{—}}{4\text{-}3}$ progression. In Example 8-54b the repeated C of the soprano permits the same progression with the 4-3 suspension in the top voice. When the leading tone occurs in an inner voice, it frequently leaps to the fifth of the tonic chord (Example 8-54a); when it appears in the soprano, it almost

EXAMPLE 8-53   Bach Chorale 90

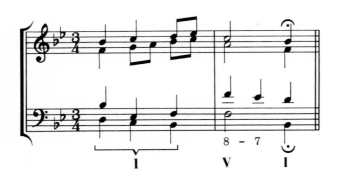

EXAMPLE 8-54   Bach Chorales 90, 277

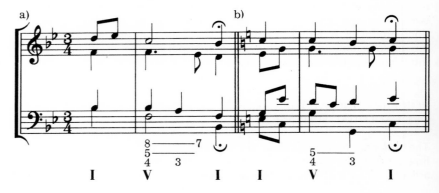

EXAMPLE 8-55   Bach Chorales 271, 17

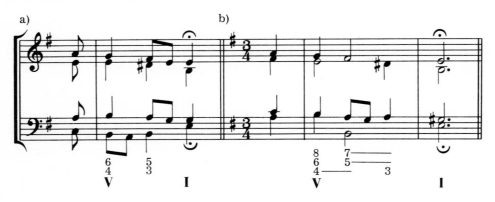

always resolves normally (Example 8-54b).

Often, the cadential suspension occurs in an inner voice against a melodic progression 3-2-1 (the 3 accented) in the soprano. This voice leading produces the important and characteristic V_{4-3}^{6-5} progression. In Example 8-55a also note the use of anticipations of tonic harmony. Although Bach generally introduces the fourth of a cadential $\frac{6}{4}$ as a suspension, he sometimes brings it in as an accented passing tone (Example 8-55b). The fourth, in turn, is suspended over the second beat rather than accompanying the melody in thirds.

We know from Chapters 6 and 7 that complete harmonic progressions often expand the basic I–V–I through the use of an intermediary harmony between the initial I and the V. These intervening harmonies— II, III, IV, or VI—need not appear directly before the dominant; indeed, the III and VI seldom do so. However, the IV and, still more often, the II frequently appear immediately before the V, thus forming part of the cadence. The most important of these harmonically expanded cadences is II_5^6 –V–I. Like the V_4^5 and the V_4^6, the II_5^6 results from the use of the cadential suspension; the contrapuntal origin of this progression lies in a combination of fourth species with second (see Chapter 9), as indicated in Example 8-56. The contrapuntal tension of this voice leading together with the presence of a fifth relationship between II and V makes this a very strong progression. The cadential II_5^6 occurs most characteristically against a melodic progression of 2-1 with the 2 lasting two beats. In Example 8-57 note the expressive descending fourth of the tenor, a melodic idea generated out of the voice leading of the II_5^6–V–I progression.

Example 8-58 shows the IV^7 as a cadential chord. In this case the 7th results from the soprano's repetition of A; it is, therefore, a suspension. When IV^7 moves directly to V, the danger of fifths often arises. Note how Bach avoids the fifths through the use of rhythmic displacement.

EXAMPLE 8-56

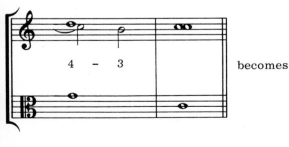

becomes

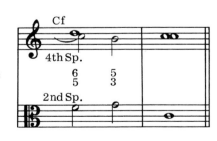

EXAMPLE 8-57   Bach Chorale 271

EXAMPLE 8-58   Bach Chorale 47

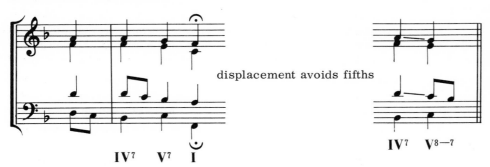

displacement avoids fifths

IV⁷   V⁷   I   IV⁷   V⁸⁻⁷

EXAMPLE 8-59   Bach Chorales 26, 14, 15

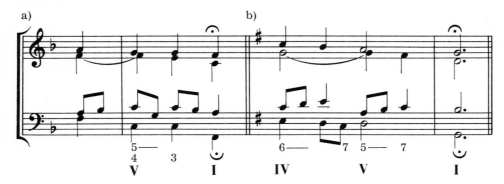

a)   b)

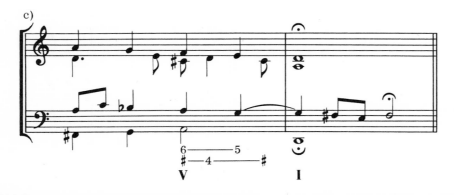

c)

EXAMPLE 8-60

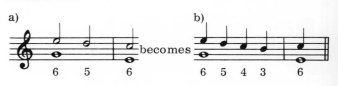

a)   becomes   b)

In Example 8-59 we have assembled three excerpts of particular interest with regard to the leading of the inner voices. In *a*, the tenor counterpoints a 4-3 suspension with an idiom in common use since the Renaissance. The leap into the dissonance with the alto's F represents a voice leading that will be encountered in combined third and fourth species. Example 8-59*b* shows another manner of avoiding fifths in a IV^7–V progression. Note that the seventh over dominant harmony comes from the fifth rather than the octave. This voice leading, by no means infrequent, is a prolongation of the simpler form shown in Example 8-18. Example 8-59*c* presents a cadential $\frac{6}{4}$ chord manipulated by the use of the leading tone as an accented neighbor preceding the fourth (see also Example 8-33).

Our next examples illustrate an important melodic technique. Often a cadential progression $\frac{2\text{-}1}{V\text{-}I}$ is prolonged by a motion into the inner voice of the V chord. Structurally the second step is retained; acoustically it is replaced by the leading tone. This progression occurs in a wide range of literature, and indeed, appears more often in the music of some later composers—e.g., Mozart—than it does in Bach's chorales. As Example 8-60 indicates, the roots of this technique lie in species counterpoint. In second species, a descending third is most directly bridged by a simple passing tone. The same total motion can be accomplished in third species by an ornamental deviation from the straight line of the underlying passing motion.

In Example 8-61*a* we see a clear and simple descent from A, top voice of the II^6, to F sharp, the inner voice of the V, while A acts as a retained tone. The passing tones B flat and G produce a $\frac{6}{4}$ on the dominant. Example 8-61*b* is slightly more complex. Here, the II^6 is prolonged by an embellishing motion in the bass. The passing tone G occurs within this unfolding of the II^6; it is then suspended to create a II$^6_5$.

The voice leading of 8-61*c* is explained in stages. Graph *a* presents the usual motion into the inner voice between II^6 and V, while D acts as a retained tone. Graph *b* shows the contrapuntal support of the melodic C, with F sharp causing a chromatic passing chord. Graph *c*

introduces the anticipation of the coming C at the end of the first complete measure; for contrapuntal support the bass moves into the inner voice A of the coming $\frac{6}{5}$ chord, which then appears in the alto. Thus anticipatory motions in top voice and bass explain the A chord on the third beat. The structural connection of the bass remains, of course, F via F sharp to G.

2. SETTING A SINGLE PHRASE

Before attempting to write all three lower parts, the reader is strongly advised to add middle parts to a given soprano and bass. Bach's figured-bass chorales provide unequaled opportunities for the study of voice leading, both at the keyboard and in written work. A number are suggested in the exercises (D-1 to D-7) at the end of the chapter; the entire collection is easily obtainable and should be in every student's library. In realizing these chorales, the student should make a careful analysis of the contrapuntal setting of the melody and bass and should closely observe the shaping influences of chord prolongation and of harmony. An explanation of the principles of figured bass is outside the scope of this book; we must advise the student, however, that the figures are not to be realized in the mechanical, literal way suggested in most harmony books. Fortunately we have available to us a number of excellent works dealing with figured bass.[7] We suggest that the reader consult these works, for the study of figured bass, properly undertaken, forms an essential part of the education of every serious musician.

After having realized a number of figured-bass chorales, the student can begin to set a chorale tune without a given bass. We suggest that he first attempt single phrases. This is, perhaps, an artificial procedure; as we emphasized in the last section, the phrase takes on its full mean-

---

[7] For a practical workbook we suggest Hermann Keller, *Thoroughbass Method*, trans. by Carl Parrish, New York, 1965; advanced students will wish to consult F. T. Arnold, *The Art of Accompaniment from a Thoroughbass*, London, 1931 (reprinted in facsimile, New York, 1965). Many original sources are now available in reprint, some translated into English. Of paramount importance is C. P. E. Bach, *Essay on the True Art of Playing Keyboard Instruments*, trans. and ed. by William J. Mitchell, New York, 1949.

EXAMPLE 8-61   Bach Chorales 53, 203, 217

a)

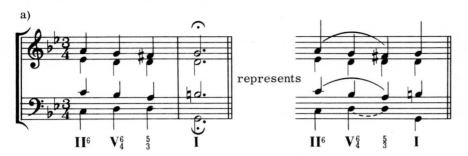

represents

b)

c)

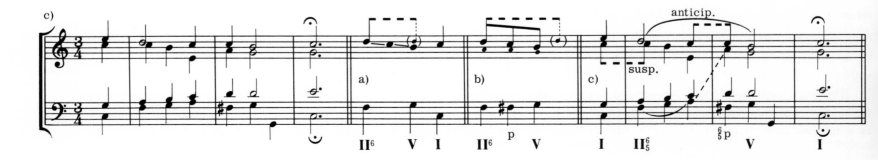

ing only in the context of the whole chorale. However, it is pedagogically sound to begin with small units and gradually proceed to larger ones. It will be difficult enough at the beginning of such study to hear even a single phrase, in all its details, as a coherent whole.[8]

The first step in setting a phrase is to determine the main chord prolongations and the large harmonic framework implied by the melody. We shall thus establish a frame of reference for the specific details of contrapuntal and harmonic organization. In our counterpoint exercises, we have developed the capacity for planning ahead, for mentally grasping continuities instead of working piecemeal, tone by tone. The recognition of inclusive harmonic relationships and, especially, of chord prolongations will enable us to apply this capacity to the more difficult problem of setting a chorale melody. For in the chorale, as in

[8] See Exercises, Group E.

tonal music generally, the prolonged chord with its harmonic associations is the matrix out of which melodic lines originate.

Most chorale phrases lend themselves to several valid interpretations; the student will benefit from comparing Bach's setting of repeated melodic phrases in a single chorale, and his different settings of complete chorale melodies. In setting single phrases, the student should always prepare several contrasting versions embodying a variety of contrapuntal and harmonic interpretations of the melody. We present a few examples illustrating suggested procedures of working; all of them use the last phrase of the chorale tune *Lobe den Herren, o meine Seele.* Our first concern, of course, is to become aware of the functions of each tone of the phrase (see Example 8-62a). Once this has been done, we can outline the harmonic framework in its relation to the melody (see Examples 8-62b and c). Even this simple, brief phrase admits of considerable variety. Setting aside differences in small detail, there are

EXAMPLE 8-62

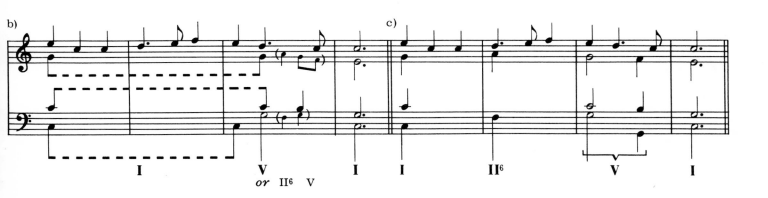

two main possibilities. The first consists of prolonging the C major tonic through the first beat of the third measure (Example 8-62b). The second involves the use of a harmonic framework of I–II^6–V–I (8-62c). In the preliminary sketches we have already indicated some middle-voice motion, including the cadential suspension. We strongly recommend this procedure. Of course, most students will first concentrate upon the bass; and unless they have exceptional powers of mental hearing, they are right in so doing. Even at the beginning, however, the middle voices should receive some attention; it will then be easier to develop them in a purposeful and consistent manner. Examples 8-63 and 8-64 show various solutions to the sketch of Example 8-62b.

First let us realize contrapuntally the prolongation of C. The embellishing progression of the top voice moves within rather narrow limits; by way of compensation, we shall try to achieve greater sweep in the bass. Therefore, we shall apply transfer of register to the retained tone C; this will give the bass room for its motion. Example 8-63a sketches a descending octave; the rhythmic pattern gives consonant support to the tones of the melody. Example 8-63b adds moderately

EXAMPLE 8-63

figurated middle voices. Note especially the increased activity in the second measure to compensate for the sustained dotted notes of the outer voices. Also notice the use of the leading tone C sharp within the unfolded D minor chord. The figurations occupying the last eighth note of the second measure are required in order to break up fifths and octaves with the bass. The use of the leading tone, B, also adds drive to the C chord that ends the prolongation. Most prolongations of the I chord, contrapuntal as well as harmonic, precede the final tonic with the leading tone. As the reader realizes, the fifths between soprano and

alto in the third quarter of the third measure are good, as they result from the combination of a passing tone with an anticipation.

In Example 8-64a we have attempted a similar procedure. Here, of course, the bass moves up rather than down the octave; the harmonic framework is now I–II$^6_5$–V–I. In contrast to the solution of Example 8-63a, the outer voices of Example 8-64 show mainly parallel motion in sixths. Example 8-64b shows the completed setting. Note the disguised parallel thirds between bass and tenor in the second measure.

EXAMPLE 8-64

a)

b)

The framework sketched in Example 8-62b can yield many more settings than the two we have shown. The student should attempt to create solutions using an embellishing rather than a passing bass. We shall now turn to the second plan shown in Example 8-62c. In this sketch each measure contains one of the harmonies of the structural progression. It will be difficult, therefore, to create a bass line of such a wide range as those of Examples 8-63 and 8-64. Nevertheless we must still strive to obtain a good contrapuntal relationship between the bass and the soprano (Example 8-65).

Example 8-66a shows a simple setting, only slightly figured. Note the pervasive use of the dotted rhythms and repeated notes of the melody. Example 8-66b demonstrates more complex figuration. There is not much literal repetition; nevertheless consistency is achieved through the motivic use of neighboring notes and of the melodic interval of the third.

CONTRAPUNTAL CHORD PROLONGATIONS: NEIGHBORING AND EMBELLISHING MOTIONS IN TOP VOICE AND BASS

In the preceding section we discussed procedures to follow when setting a phrase. In this section and in those following, we shall present a number of examples from the Bach chorales illustrating his solutions

EXAMPLE 8-65

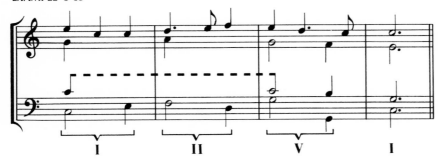

EXAMPLE 8-66

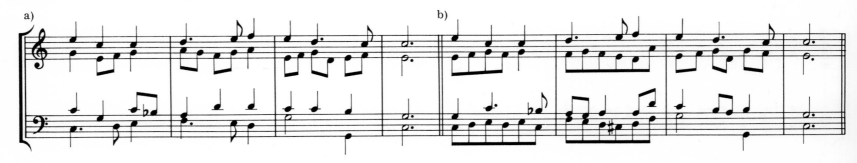

to various technical problems of chorale setting. The reader should study these examples in connection with his own written work.

In Example 8-67 we see four short excerpts containing embellishing and neighboring progressions.

Example 8-68 shows an embellishing progression of the bass in the context of a whole phrase. The bass counterpoints the soprano's ascent from D to A with an embellishing motion around the tonic. The second half of this prolongation begins an upward motion-impulse that motivates the subsequent passing progression from II to V.

Frequently we encounter contrapuntal prolongations of chords other than the tonic. In Example 8-69a an embellishing motion within I is followed by an unfolding of II^6_5. In 8-69b the V is prolonged by chords produced by the upper and lower neighboring notes of the bass.

EXAMPLE 8-67   **Bach Chorales 103, 29, 206, 231**

EXAMPLE 8-68   **Bach Chorale 44**

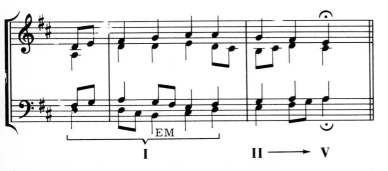

The unfolding of the fourth in Example 8-70 helps to create the neighboring chord of measure 1; the embellishing motion to the I^6 is a secondary prolongation. In moving from IV^7 to V, Bach breaks up fifths between tenor and soprano by means of the anticipation A.

In the following excerpt the main prolonging event is the G minor chord, emphasized by duration, rhythmic position, and the use of the leading tone, F sharp. Subdominant chords frequently and characteristically support neighboring notes in the top voice. Observe also the motivic relationship between measures 1 and 3 of the bass; also note the suspensions in the alto and the tenor's expressive leap to the high D.

The preceding examples have mainly featured contrary motion between the outer voices. Sometimes, however, the bass and soprano will execute similar embellishing progressions in parallel motion. In Example 8-72 the outer voices move in tenths embellishing G in the bass and B in the soprano. Note the somewhat unusual bass repetitions from third to first beat.

PASSING MOTIONS WITHIN AND BETWEEN CHORDS

One of the most important goals in the study of chorale writing is the ability to shape a flowing, melodic bass line, one that has linear as well

EXAMPLE 8-69   Bach Chorales 149, 176

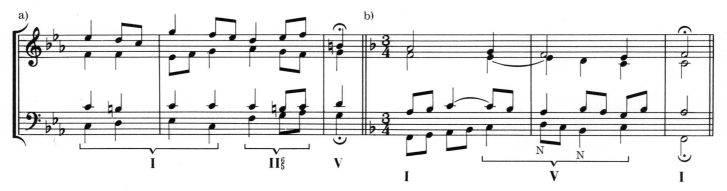

EXAMPLE 8-70   Bach Chorale 297

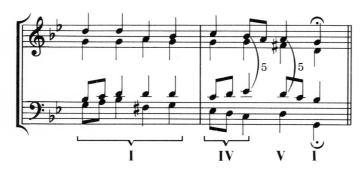

as harmonic direction. In order to achieve such a bass, we must think and hear in terms of directed motion progressing logically from point of origin to goal. We know from second species that the prototype of directed linear progression is the passing motion. In this section we shall see how Bach applies this fundamental musical motion to his chorale basses. The examples are not intended to form an exhaustive compilation; they illustrate some typical usages and should stimulate the student to find others.

MOTIONS OF A THIRD AND SIXTH WITHIN A CHORD

In the chorale—and indeed in tonal music generally—bass progression between the root and the third of the underlying chord forms an important type of chord prolongation. Motions of a third occur so frequently, and we have already shown so many in previous examples, that one illustration will suffice here (Example 8-73).

The third is often inverted to a sixth in order to provide space for

EXAMPLE 8-71   Bach Chorale 207

EXAMPLE 8-72   Bach Chorale 1

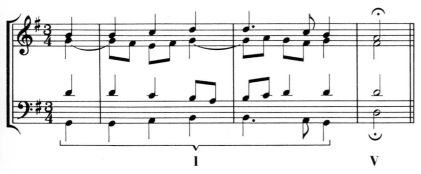

EXAMPLE 8-73   Bach Chorale 179

EXAMPLE 8-74   Bach Chorale 239

EXAMPLE 8-75   Bach Chorale 183

EXAMPLE 8-76   Bach Chorale 217

EXAMPLE 8-77   Bach Chorale 223

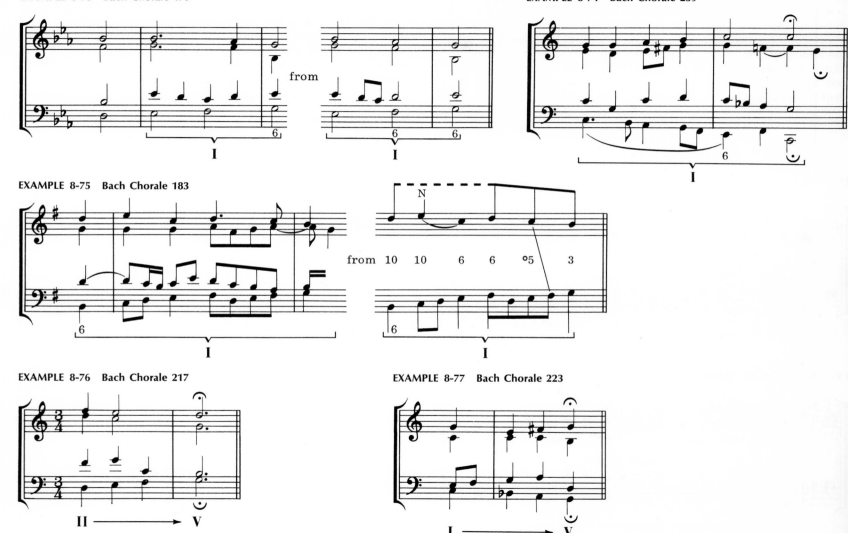

a larger passing motion. In Example 8-74 we see such a motion within a prolonged C major tonic. Motions of a sixth often counterpoint smaller progressions in the top voice; here, for example, the soprano moves only a fourth. The repeated notes of the melody make it possible to accomplish these two motions in the same span of time. The adjustment between the two outer-voice progressions relates to first- and second-species counterpoint; essentially contrapuntal considerations determine the rhythm of the bass. The F chord preceding the final tonic is a contrapuntal sonority composed of a neighboring tone in the bass and passing tones in the inner voices.

Passing motions also occur within ascending sixths. In Example 8-75 the bass line moves up from the third to the root of the G major tonic. The figuration of F sharp decorates the progression.

MOTIONS OF A FOURTH AND FIFTH: PASSING MOTIONS BETWEEN CHORDS

In Examples 8-73 to 8-75 the passing motions all take place within a single prolonged chord. The following examples show passing motions in the bass from a tone of one chord to a tone of another. Unlike motions traversing thirds and sixths, passing motions of fourths and fifths usually move between two chords; often they form a linear connection between members of a harmonic progression. In Example 8-76 we see a passing motion between II and V. Similar progressions appear frequently at cadences, usually in counterpoint to a descending motion in the top voice from the fourth to the second step of the scale.

Example 8-77 shows a descending fourth connecting I with V. The use of B flat would seem to indicate an impending G minor, but Bach moves to the normal, major form of the dominant.

Many chorale phrases move within a harmonic framework I–II^6–V–I, or, with the cadential suspension, I–II^6_5–V–I. Frequently, the bass passes down a fifth, thereby connecting the bass tones of I and II^6 or II^6_5. In Example 8-78 we see such a passing motion of a descending fifth. Note the $^6_4$ chord on the fourth beat. Why does Bach use this chord instead of the $^6_3$, usually the ideal sonority for parallel motion but unconvincing in this context? The $^6_4$ prepares the cadential suspension, but it has a second, more important meaning. The ear connects it with the F minor chord of the first beat; this connection produces, as it were, an atmosphere of F minor through which the passing motion to II^6_5 takes place. This phrase, therefore, shows a prolongation of the tonic within a larger passing motion to II^6_5.

EXAMPLE 8-78 Bach Chorale 8

Example 8-79 shows an ascending fifth in the bass; this unified linear motion encompasses three harmonies. The $\frac{6}{3}$ over D is not merely a passing chord; it clearly functions as a II^6 of harmonic as well as contrapuntal significance. (The reader will remember from Chapter 6 that the stepwise bass in a II^6–V progression results from the cooperation of harmonic and contrapuntal forces.)

Example 8-80 shows a similar progression executed in a somewhat more complex manner. Note the initial prolongation of I with its embellishing motions of a third in the bass. The motivic use of the descending third generates the D chord of the third beat, a chord that also serves to break up octaves $\begin{smallmatrix}A\\A\end{smallmatrix}$ and $\begin{smallmatrix}B\\B\end{smallmatrix}$ between the outer voices. Here the V is preceded by an applied dominant rather than by a diatonic II as in Example 8-79. We include the first chord of the following phrase to show the larger melodic connection A–B–C sharp of the top voice.

EXAMPLE 8-79   Bach Chorale 146

EXAMPLE 8-80   Bach Chorale 189

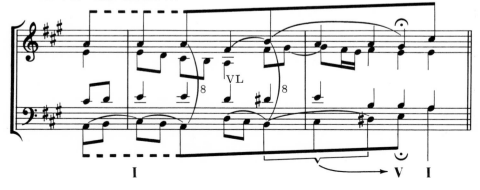

MOTIONS OF AN OCTAVE

Passing motions within the octave represent extended transfers of register. Such motions are often useful for phrases in which the melody contains many repeated tones or protracted embellishments. Example 8-81 shows the motion of a descending octave in two characteristic contexts.

In Example 8-82 we see a motion of an ascending octave within a prolonged V. By emphasizing F natural, Bach weakens the implication

of dominant harmony within the prolongation of G, and creates a strong expectation for the C major tonic that appears in the subsequent phrase.

MOTIONS OF A SEVENTH

The reader will remember that melodic sevenths often result from the inversion of seconds. The seventh, covering as it does a large span, can be filled in by a rather extensive passing motion. In Example 8-83 we see the ascending second, F–G, inverted to a descending seventh. The

EXAMPLE 8-81   Bach Chorales 167, 158

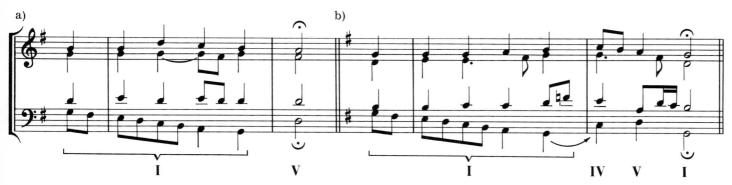

EXAMPLE 8-82   Bach Chorale 268

inversion produces contrary motion with the top voice and gives rise to the D minor chord, the passing $\frac{4}{2}$ on C, and the brief prolongation of the G minor chord. Graph a shows that the G chord results from a prolonged passing motion from F to A; in graph *b* we see that this motion of a partially inverted third belongs to a more inclusive ascending fifth from I to V.

Example 8-84 shows a descending seventh in the context of a harmonic progression I–II⁷–V⁷–I. Here melodic inversion provides room

for a sweeping line that compensates for the repeated tones of the melody. The E minor chord, fleetingly prolonged, results from the counterpoint of the outer voices and has no harmonic significance. Before moving to the II, the bass touches the I⁶; therefore, this passing motion contains an activated· prolongation of the tonic. In the last half of the first measure, displacement shifts the chord tone, B, to the last eighth note, creating an uninterrupted drive through the prolonged I into the II⁷.

EXAMPLE 8-83   Bach Chorale 303

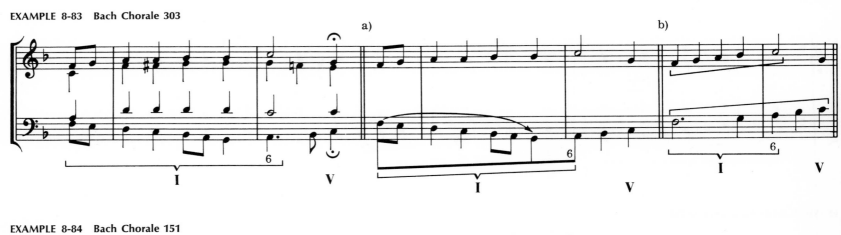

EXAMPLE 8-84   Bach Chorale 151

DISJUNCT MOTIONS WITHIN AND BETWEEN CHORDS: SUBDIVIDING AND PASSING CHORDS

As we know, melodic motion is essentially stepwise; therefore, the melodic quality of a bass line depends greatly upon stepwise progressions like those discussed in the previous section. However, it would be incorrect to assume that the frequent leaps found in Bach's chorale basses result in all instances from harmonic causes. For even in purely melodic terms, some disjunct motion is necessary to create variety and contrast. In this section we shall discuss some of these disjunct melodic progressions, reserving those of harmonic origin for the following section.

INTERVAL SUBDIVISION WITHIN PROLONGED CHORDS

In second species we learned that a tone on the second half note of the measure can subdivide a large interval into two smaller ones; we have seen the compositional use of this technique in Chapter 7. In the progressions of Example 8-85 we find an important and characteristic type of subdivision; the bass breaks a descending sixth from I to I^6 into a third and fourth. The voice leading of 8-85a shows the most frequent usage; the subdivided bass counterpoints a melody rising by step from the third to the fifth of tonic harmony. The outer-voice counterpoint produces a $\frac{6}{3}$ chord above the subdividing tone of the bass; the lightness of this chord is ideally suited to the connective, transitory function it fulfills. (The precise contrapuntal relation between bass and soprano in Example 8-85a closely resembles a combination of two second species; see Chapter 9 for a systematic explanation.) Example 8-85b shows the same bass with a different melody; note, however, the resemblance between the tenor of 8-85b and the soprano of 8-85a.

Example 8-86 illustrates a much less frequently used subdivision; the descending octave is broken into a fifth and fourth. As in 8-85a, the subdividing tone supports an upward directed passing tone in the soprano.

EXAMPLE 8-85   Bach Chorales 106, 153

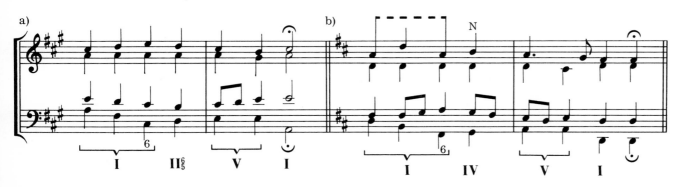

EXAMPLE 8-86 Bach Chorale 232

EXAMPLE 8-87 Bach Chorale 234

from

3 4 6 8

EXAMPLE 8-88 Bach Chorales 185, 184

a)   b)

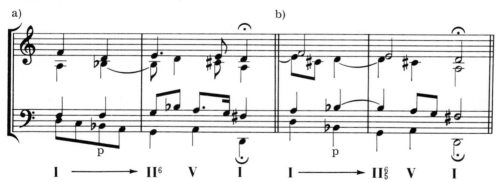

I ⟶ II⁶ V I   I ⟶ II⁶₅ V I

EXAMPLE 8-89 Bach Chorale 62

a)   b)

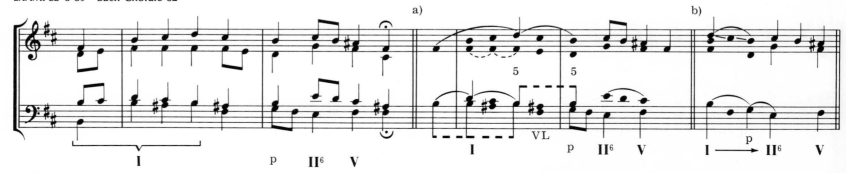

I   p II⁶ V   I VL p II⁶ V   I ⟶ p II⁶ V

DISJUNCT PROGRESSION BETWEEN TWO CHORDS

Disjunct progressions sometimes appear in the course of transition from one chord to another. As a rule these progressions are organized in thirds. Leaps of thirds often result from the omission of a passing tone, as in Example 8-87. Consequently, we have labeled chords supported by such bass progressions as passing chords, reserving the term subdividing chords for those involving larger leaps.

The most important of these passing chords by thirds is the submediant leading from the I to the II^6 (II$^6_5$). In Example 8-88a we find a stepwise passing motion from I to II^6. Example 8-88b is quite similar, except that here the stepwise connections do not appear; the contrapuntal function of the submediant is the same in both excerpts.

Example 8-89 shows a somewhat more complex use of the contrapuntal, passing submediant. In the melody, the high point, D, is a structurally retained tone, its progression to the structural C sharp delayed by a motion into the inner voice. The passing submediant counterpoints this temporary melodic descent. The F sharp chord preceding the submediant breaks up fifths between bass and alto (see graph a) and at the same time provides consonant support for the otherwise dissonant passing tone C sharp.

Example 8-90 contains two passing submediants of different weight and significance. The initial prolongation of the I is achieved through an arpeggiated motion; the two ascending broken chords prolong and

invert a basically descending progression (graph a). This bass progression counterpoints a melodic motion into the inner voice of the melody and thereby prolongs the tonic chord; the B minor chord of measure 1 functions as a passing chord within this prolongation. In measure 3 the top voice returns to the retained tone, D. At the same time, the bass moves to B as a passing chord on the way to G (II$^6_5$). The G supports the second structural tone, E, of the melody. The B chord just mentioned is thus a passing chord of higher structural order than that of measure 1, for it moves between two structural chords.

HARMONIC PROLONGATIONS

So far our discussions of harmony have concentrated upon the use of harmonic progressions to create the structural frameworks within which the counterpoint moves. It is also possible to prolong a chord harmonically, that is, by means of a harmonic progression subordinate to the governing sonority. In Bach's chorales, harmonic relationships permeate the musical fabric, from the structure of the whole to the shaping of many details; they do so, however, without impairing the melodic, contrapuntal flow of the texture. Harmony and counterpoint assert their roles in cooperation, on a prolonging as well as on a structural level.[9]

[9] See chapter on harmonic prolongations in Salzer, *op. cit.*, vol. 1, pp. 148ff.

EXAMPLE 8-90 Bach Chorale 334

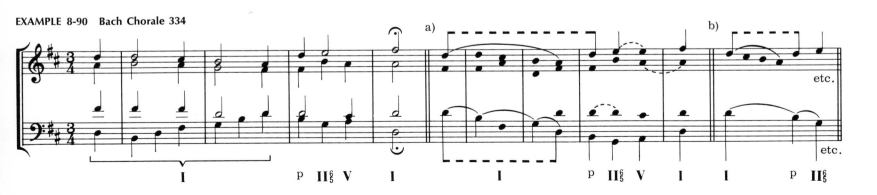

COMPLETE HARMONIC PROGRESSIONS

In Example 8-91 we encounter harmonic progressions on two levels. The inclusive, structural progression is a movement from I to V. The I is itself prolonged by a complete progression (I–II^6_5–V–I) supporting an embellishing motion around C sharp in the soprano. The harmonic prolongation also serves a linear function, since it helps to effect the upward transfer of the bass tone, A, and thus motivates the subsequent passing motion down to V. If we abstract the harmonic quality from the prolongation of I, we see that the outer voices resemble a first-species progression. (In Example 8-91 we have indicated the structural and prolonging harmonies by large and small Roman numerals.)

Example 8-92 shows an overlapping between a contrapuntal and a harmonic prolongation, both supporting an embellishing motion around E. The prolongations overlap because the final chord of the contrapuntal motion is at the same time the beginning of the harmonic progression. Again the harmonic prolongation gives rise to a transfer of register; the C resumes its original low register in preparation for the low G of the structural dominant.

Sometimes harmonic and contrapuntal impulses become so fused that they completely overlap. In Example 8-93 the stepwise descending octave in the bass seems entirely to govern the prolongation of I. The V of measure 3, however, subdivides the octave harmonically, and must not be heard as a purely contrapuntal passing chord.

INCOMPLETE HARMONIC PROGRESSIONS

In Example 8-94 we observe a characteristic technique of tonal music: the prolongation of a cadential goal by an incomplete harmonic progression. At the same time these excerpts illustrate the possibility of applying harmonic prolongations to chords other than the tonic. In Example 8-94a, measure 1, the bass contains two embellishing tones; the G belongs to the preceding E, and the C belongs to the following E. In his own settings, the student should carefully observe opportunities for stabilizing non-tonic chords through complete or incomplete harmonic progressions.

Incomplete harmonic progressions may follow as well as precede the chords they prolong. Such progressions relate back rather than point forward, as do the incomplete progressions of Example 8-94. In Example 8-95 the prolonging IV and V refer back to the opening I; this structural harmony proceeds to II at the beginning of the next measure.

EXAMPLE 8-91 Bach Chorale 169

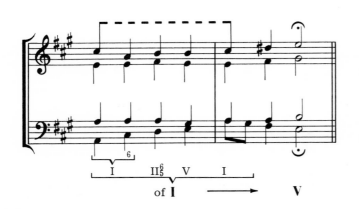

EXAMPLE 8-92 Bach Chorale 298

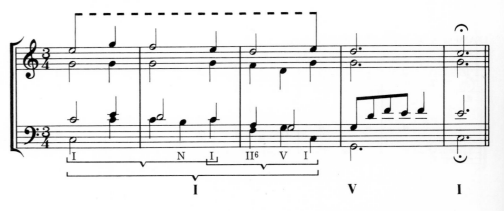

EXAMPLE 8-93 Bach Chorale 90

EXAMPLE 8-94 Bach Chorales 138, 18

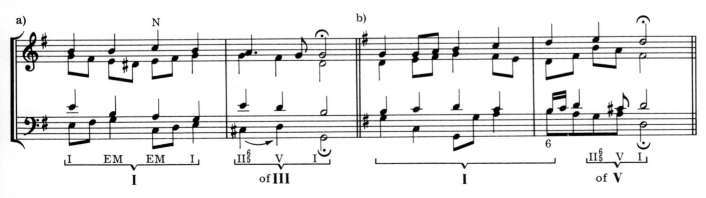

Example 8-96 contains the same melody, now in $\frac{4}{4}$ meter, as Example 8-90. By changing one bass tone, by using D instead of G on the fourth beat of measure 1, Bach creates a radically different setting from that of Example 8-90. The line of the bass now proceeds up to the submediant of measure 2, which now forms part of the structural progression I–VI–V–I.

APPLIED DOMINANTS; DOMINANT PROLONGATIONS OF THE TONIC

We have encountered applied dominant chords in a number of our previous examples. These chords represent the simplest form of incomplete harmonic progression; they refer mostly to the following, less often to the previous chord. Sometimes a single tonic is preceded or followed by a dominant. These V chords of purely local, immediate significance resemble applied dominants; however, the term *applied dominant* is obviously not a logical description of these chords. We shall call them *prolonging dominants,* or dominant prolongations of the tonic. In many styles of music, initial upbeats often contain dominant prolongations of the subsequent downbeat. In the chorales we encounter this progression less frequently since the upbeat of the chorale carries the first word of the text and therefore usually contains the tonality-indicating chord (for a chorale beginning with a dominant prolongation, see No. 364).

If the prolonging dominant follows the tonic without returning to it, we have a harmonic motion similar to that in Example 8-95. Example 8-97, from Chorale 102, contains such a backward-referring dominant in measure 4. This example contains many other events of interest to us. The G chord after the fermata of measure 4 is an applied dominant to the IV; at the same time it breaks up octaves and fifths between the first beats of measures 4 and 5. Consequently this chord has a contrapuntal as well as a harmonic function.[10] The G chord of measure 5 has a quite different meaning; it makes consonant the otherwise dissonant passing tone B of the top voice. The structural V is prolonged by an $\frac{N}{P}$ chord resulting from a neighboring note in the bass as counterpoint to the motion into the inner voice in the melody; the A of the top voice is a retained tone (see Example 8-61). In measure 3 we see an applied dominant to the prolonging V of measure 4; this applied dominant is decorated by the cadential suspension of D. Finally the opening measures show a harmonic prolongation of the I while the melody begins its ascent to the first structural tone, D.

[10] For double-function chords, see Salzer, *op. cit.,* vol. 1, pp. 162ff.

EXAMPLE 8-95   Bach Chorale 309

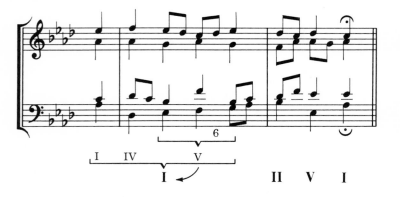

EXAMPLE 8-96   Bach Chorale 14

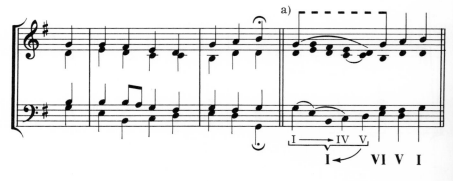

At the fermata the eight-measure section is subdivided into two phrases of four measures each. The two phrases, however, are completely interdependent. In comparing Bach's setting with the voice-leading graph, we see that the main prolongation—the motion to the prolonging dominant—forms the first phrase. This prolongation generates a tension which is resolved in the second phrase; there, the melody undertakes its structural descent from D supported by the harmonic progression IV–V–I. This progression continues the tonic of measures 1-3 and binds the two phrases into a greater whole.

With Example 8-97 we have begun to view sections of two phrases, and to see how the single phrase becomes part of a larger coherent whole. We shall continue this procedure in the following section; as part of this study, new contrapuntal and harmonic techniques will be demonstrated.

3. SETTING GROUPS OF TWO OR MORE PHRASES

Before proceeding to the writing of complete chorales, it is a good practice to set short, relatively self-contained groups of two (or perhaps

EXAMPLE 8-97   Bach Chorale 102

three) phrases. Many chorale melodies are constructed in the so-called *barform,* AAB. The A section of these melodies (in Bach's settings, usually before the first double bar) is often complete enough to allow a logical, coherent setting. We have included a number of these sections in the exercises following this chapter; the reader can easily supplement these with additional melodies.

In setting a group of phrases, planning ahead becomes at once more difficult and more important. We cannot emphasize strongly enough that a chord-to-chord procedure, although possibly resulting in "correct" voice leading, will never lead to a meaningful, coherent musi-

cal texture. In setting chorales, the student must try to stretch his capacity for inner hearing. He will never succeed in this if he adopts a non-directional, purely vertical approach, where the choice of chords is based on pseudo-stylistic considerations rather than on compositional techniques and procedures.

Often the setting of a single phrase becomes unconvincing when heard in a larger context. For this reason we must begin by sketching in the larger, more inclusive relationships before deciding on details. Let us study Example 8-98, a sample setting of the first phrase of *Freu' dich sehr, o meine Seele.*

EXAMPLE 8-98

EXAMPLE 8-99

Taken by itself, the setting is not bad; however, in connection with a setting of the second phrase, it proves unsatisfactory (Example 8-99). There is not enough variety, not enough relief from the constant emphasis on tonic harmony. Let us compare one of Bach's settings of the same four measures (Example 8-100). He has interpreted the end of the first phrase as falling within the sphere of the dominant. This resounding harmonic prolongation of V makes the second phrase a strongly affirmative statement of the tonic.

THE TECHNIQUE OF INTERRUPTION; THE INTERDEPENDENCY OF TWO PHRASES

The technique of interruption constitutes one of the most important form-building devices of tonal music. Through it, an underlying progression is divided into two interdependent parts. The first, the pre-interruption section, is incomplete; it ends, therefore, in a state of tension. The second part, the post-interruption section, begins once more, and this time completes the progression and resolves the tension. Let us study an instance of this technique in Example 8-101. The point of interruption is indicated by the sign ||.

These phrases show the division of a structural melodic and harmonic progression into two parts (Example 8-102).

In the melody, the first period ends on the supertonic, a tone with a marked tendency to proceed to the tonic. This tone is supported by V, a chord with a strong harmonic impulse to the tonic. In the second period, both the melodic line and the harmonic progression begin anew; this time, however, they move to a definite conclusion on the tonic. One must not interpret the first melodic supertonic of Example 8-102 as a neighboring note to E, for its tendency is to move on to C rather than to return to E. The interruption prevents the immediate motion to C; with the tone D, a specific motion comes to its end, if only temporarily. When the melody resumes with the tone E the structural line begins again and moves to its conclusion. The two periods are interdependent precisely because the second completes what had been initiated by the first. The letter D under the first V denotes *dividing dominant* or *divider*; this chord effects the structural division. The technique of interruption can also be applied to progressions showing a descending fifth in the top voice (see Example 8-111).[11]

In setting a group of two phrases, the student should study the implications of the melody to determine whether interruption might be a possibility. As we can see from Examples 8-101 and 8-103, the motivic correlation between the two phrases need not be absolute; considerable variation in detail may exist, so long as the structural line fulfills the necessary conditions. Often, however, in other styles, the post-interruption part repeats the beginning of the unit.

[11] For more on interruption see Salzer, *op. cit.*, pp. 145–147.

EXAMPLE 8-100 Bach Chorale 64

PROLONGATIONS MAY BIND TWO PHRASES INTO ONE SECTION

Two phrases may be fused into a unity if a prolongation begun in the first continues into the second. In Example 8-104 the melody ascends from G, a tone of the inner-voice region, to E flat, the first structural tone. This melodic event is supported by a harmonic prolongation of the tonic, a progression I–V–I. The end of this prolongation occurs at the downbeat of measure 3, after the first fermata. This example shows us that a prolongation can reach further than the phrase ending and fuse two phrases into an organic whole.

Example 8-105 presents overlapping even stronger than in our previous illustration; in this excerpt the structural V arrives at the first fermata and is prolonged through most of the second phrase. Observe

EXAMPLE 8-101   Bach Chorale 217

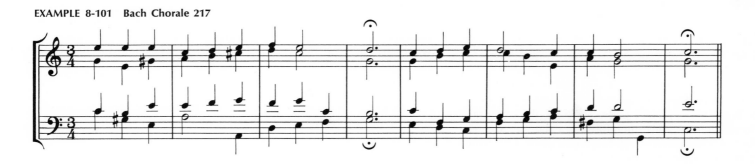

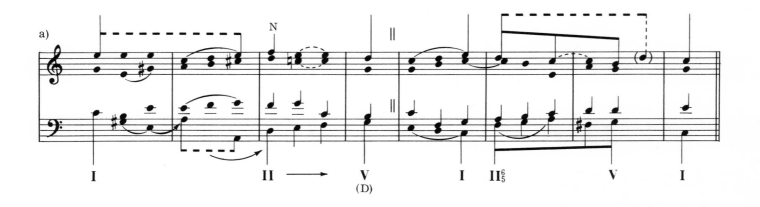

the inversion of the upward second, B flat–C, to a descending seventh in measures 1-2.

In the following examples, the coherence between, or even fusion of phrases will be evident. In addition they feature an important technique, the use of the mediant as a contrapuntal, embellishing chord. The reader will remember from Chapter 6 that the secondary harmonies, II, III, IV, and VI fulfill a harmonic function only within the framework of the tonic-dominant relationship. In Examples 8-106 and 8-108, the mediant constitutes an embellishment of the tonic since it moves between two I chords, rather than between I and V. We shall indicate this contrapuntal progression by the symbols I–EM–I. Such progressions occur more frequently in the chorales than in most other music of the eighteenth century; they have a long history reaching back into the modal tonality of the middle ages.

EXAMPLE 8-102

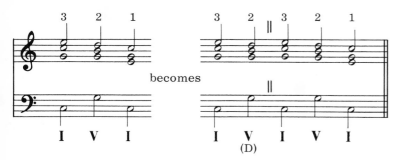

becomes

$$\text{I} \quad \text{V} \quad \text{I} \qquad \text{I} \quad \text{V} \quad \text{I} \quad \text{V} \quad \text{I}$$
(D)

EXAMPLE 8-103   Bach Chorale 1

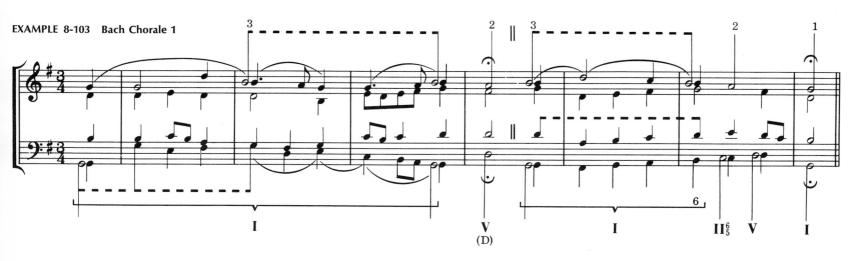

$$\text{I} \qquad \text{V} \qquad \text{I} \qquad \text{II}^{6}_{5} \quad \text{V} \quad \text{I}$$
(D)

EXAMPLE 8-104 Bach Chorale 244

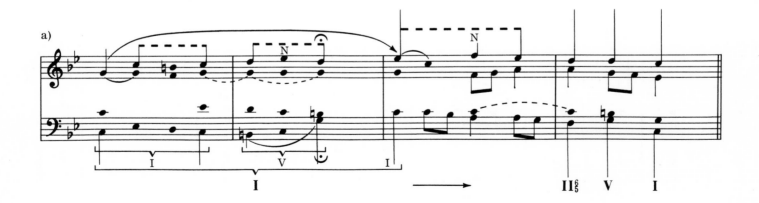

EXAMPLE 8-105 Bach Chorale 252

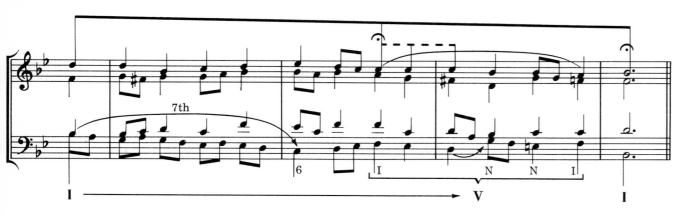

EXAMPLE 8-106 Bach Chorale 31

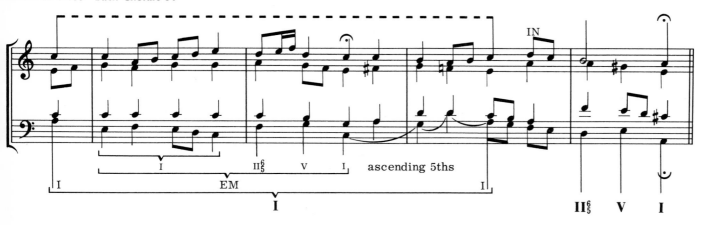

We have observed a series of descending fifths in Chapter 7. Ascending fifths (or descending fourths) occur much less frequently. In Example 8-106 they serve to connect the EM sonority with the I. Again note the fusion between the two phrases.

Of course the mediant also appears in the chorale repertory as a harmonic chord. The excerpt from Chorale 41 given in Example 8-107 shows the harmonic use of the mediant as well as a different application of the technique of ascending fifths. Here the ascending fifths occur in such a manner as to elaborate harmonically a contrapuntal progression. The main line of the bass between III and V consists of a passing motion, C–D–E; the D supports a neighbor-passing chord, since its top voice is the incomplete neighbor, D.

We return now to the contrapuntal, embellishing use of the mediant. A most original example occurs at the beginning of Chorale

EXAMPLE 8-107 Bach Chorale 41

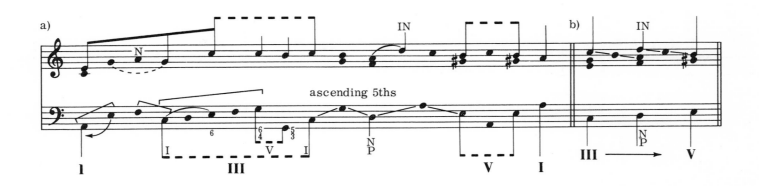

249 (see Example 8-108). The basic prolonging idea is the inversion of a third to a downward-moving sixth. This sixth is subdivided by the E minor chord. Subsequently the bass returns to G, this time by an ascending sixth; this upward-moving sixth is subdivided in the same manner, bringing the I–EM–I progression to its conclusion. The descending sixth of the first phrase is prolonged by what is basically a series of descending fourths (see graphs c and a). Again a single prolongation, I–EM–I, ties two melodic phrases into a larger whole.

In conclusion we quote two excerpts, from Chorales 61 and 83, showing different settings of the same melody (Example 8-109). Here several new techniques make their appearance. In Chorale 83 the EM sonority appears at the very beginning of the composition; it functions

EXAMPLE 8-108   Bach Chorale 249

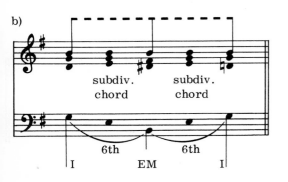

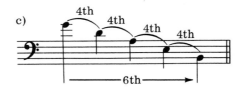

as an extended quasi-upbeat to the tonic.[12] In both excerpts the $\frac{6}{5}$ at the end of measure 2 acts as an applied dominant to the subdominant. Careful study of the graphs, however, will reveal why the subdominant belongs to the harmonic framework in Chorale 61, whereas it has a contrapuntal function in Chorale 83. In Chorale 61 the subdominant moves on to V; in Chorale 83 it is an $\frac{N}{P}$ chord within the contrapuntal prolongation of I.

In these two excerpts, we first wish to remind the reader that the letters DF under the IV in Chorale 61 indicate the *double function* of that sonority. The IV has a structural meaning as part of the inclusive

[12] This type of non-tonic beginning can be traced back to the fourteenth century.

harmonic framework; but since it supports a prolonging tone in the top voice, it has a prolonging meaning as well.

The sign (II) indicates the chord of *harmonic emphasis* which often occurs between III and V, IV and V, or VI and V. It acts as an additional harmonic reinforcement of the coming V; lacking a leading tone it is, of course, not an applied dominant.

In both the chorale sections of Example 8-109, the applied-dominant character of the $\frac{6}{5}$ chords helps to fuse the two melodic phrases into a unified polyphonic whole. The $\frac{6}{5}$ chords appear at the fermatas and strongly impel the motion into the subsequent phrase. This brings us to the question of the musical meaning of the fermatas in Bach's chorales. Older generations of performers tended to take them

EXAMPLE 8-109   Bach Chorales 61, 83

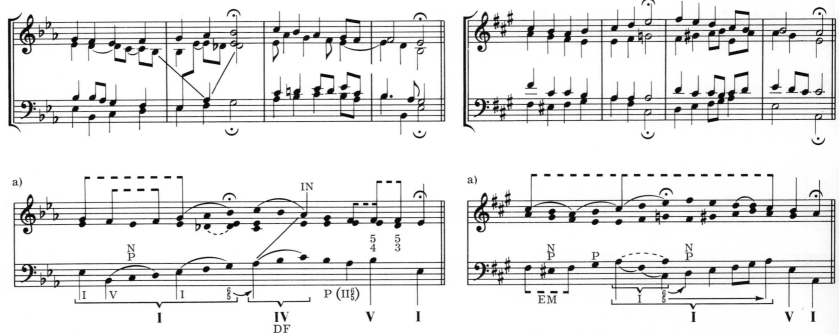

at face value as marking the ends of musical phrases; generally they held them beyond the notated value of the tone. Nowadays, performers tend to ignore the fermatas completely, treating them simply as conventional signs marking the end of a line of text and, perhaps, helping to orient the singers. This is not the place to discuss details of performance practice. However, we can make one general observation: it is of the greatest importance that performers understand that some fermatas definitely mark the end of a musical thought; this would make ob-

EXAMPLE 8-110   Bach Chorale 217

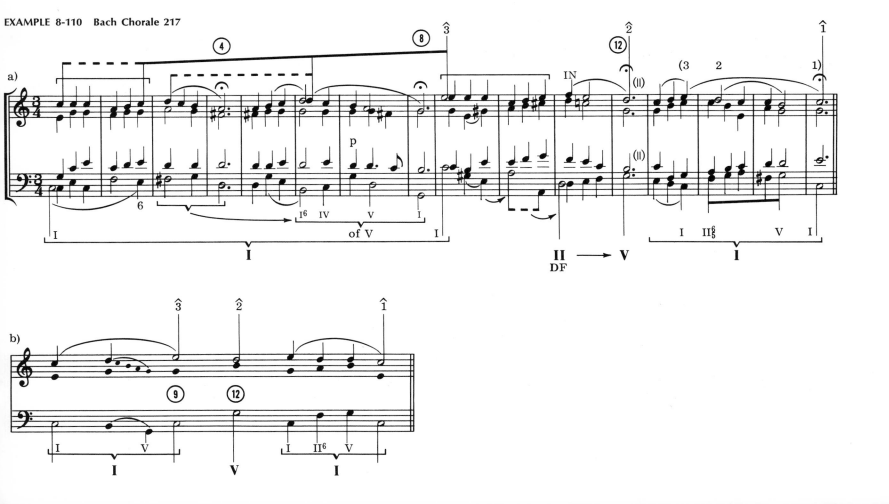

EXAMPLE 8-111   Bach Chorale 44

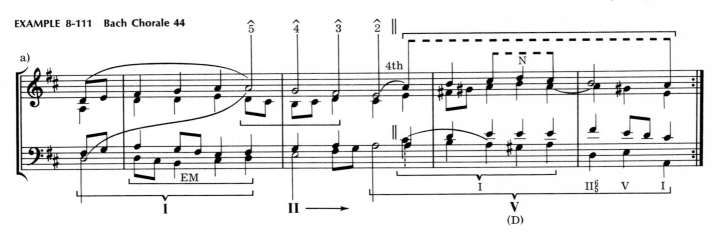

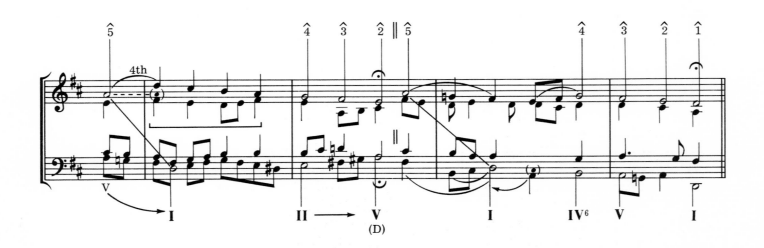

servance of the fermata at least logical. In other situations (see Example 8-109) Bach's compositional procedures make the fermatas musically meaningless; any holding, or strongly marked articulation would interrupt the continuity and interfere with the musical direction to the goals of motion.

4. THE COMPLETE CHORALE

In this section we present analyses of a number of Bach's complete settings. The reader should consult these in connection with his own settings of whole chorale melodies. By carefully studying Bach's inexhaustively inventive writing, we are stimulated to stretch our own capacities to their fullest. In particular we must strive to understand Bach's more unusual procedures. Nothing could be more stifling to musical development than to restrict the student to the most typical, frequently encountered usages.

We begin with Chorale 217, a setting of *Ach Gott, wie manches Herzeleid* (Example 8-110). We have already cited excerpts from this chorale in Examples 8-43, 8-61c, 8-76, and 8-101; the reader should refer to these examples. Note how Bach's setting underscores and supports the broad melodic ascent C–D–E of measures 1-9; these measures

are fused into a unified section by means of a large-scale harmonic prolongation. The climactic thrice-stated E of measure 9 caps the ascent and coincides with the end of the prolongation of the I. Although this third phrase consists of an intensified repetition, a third higher, of the opening melodic idea, Bach's setting does not echo the first phrase. Leaving tonic harmony after only one quarter (in contrast to two measures of tonic prolongation in the first phrase), the bass moves, by way of applied dominants, to II and thence to V. The II represents the goal of the preceding harmonic and contrapuntal movement; it is clearly a structural harmony. As indicated in the graph, the II supports a prolonging tone, an incomplete neighbor, in the top voice, hence the designation DF (double function). The two final phrases show the technique of interruption (see Example 8-101). Heard within the totality of the chorale, the interruption does not divide the basic structure but rather effects a broadening of the motion to the melodic goal C.

The melody of Chorale 44 permits an interesting and unusual application of interruption (see Example 8-111). Reference to the graph will show that the preliminary, incomplete descent from A to E is stated twice, in the first and third phases. Bach treats the third phrase as a quasi-variation of the first; both have the same essential bass line and top voice. The second phrase serves as an interlude, prolonging the dividing dominant of measure 2 and, in the melody, preparing for the

EXAMPLE 8-111 (continued)

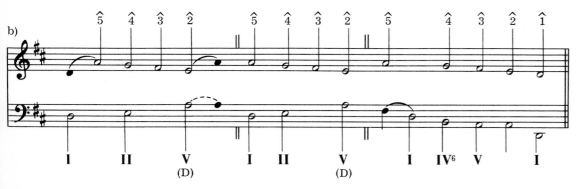

EXAMPLE 8-112   Bach Chorale 151

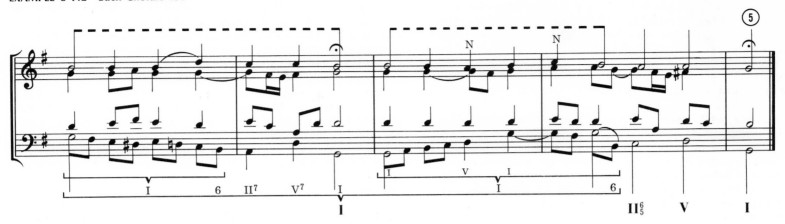

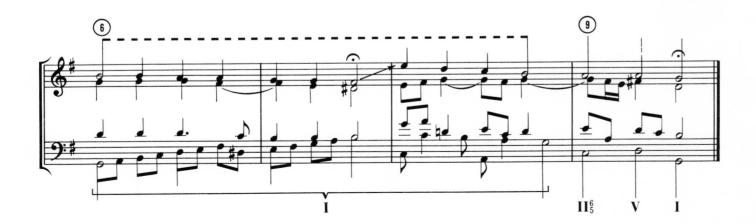

climactic high register of the embellishing motion above A in the third phrase. A high D occurs twice, in measures 3 and 5. The first statement, however, is set by Bach as the upper neighbor of C sharp; the D of measure 5, by contrast, belongs to the underlying tonic chord, which enhances its structural importance.

Chorale 44 shows the familiar and characteristic repetition of the opening section. Repetitions of a less obvious nature permeate this chorale, whose apparent simplicity is deceptive. Note the motive first presented in the bass at the very beginning; it consists of a circling motion of a third, away from and back to its point of origin. The brackets in the graph point up the later appearances of this motive. Of special interest are two statements that, in Bach's setting, emerge out of the chorale melody itself. The entire second phrase presents the idea in broadened time values and decorated by the neighboring tone, D; here, of course, the embellishing motion is above the main tone rather than below it as in the first statement. And in the final phrase, the prolonging motions into and out of the inner-voice region utilize the figure, this time in its original, downward direction.

Example 8-112, Chorale 151, also contains the repeated first section and consequent AAB design. The individual form of this piece, how- ever, differs greatly from that of Chorale 44. Interruption plays no part here; the melody, broadly viewed, consists of two complete and self- contained motions from B down to G. The problem in setting such a melody is that of creating an integrated whole out of the two self- sufficient parts. Bach solves this problem by applying the principle of variation. As was mentioned above, the melodic outline of the two sec- tions is the same. Bach supports both statements of the basic line with the same broad bass motion and progression of harmonies. Both sec- tions, therefore, have the same fundamental structure. In addition there are many similarities of detail that serve to underscore the larger struc- tural relationship. The most obvious of these is the identical voice lead- ing of the two closing cadences; also note the motivic repetition of the bass in the second and third phrases, and—a small but important detail —the binding effect of the many suspended G's resolving to F sharp, mainly in the alto. The detailed graphs of measures 6-8 indicate how Bach fuses the last two phrases into a unified section through the varia- tion of an underlying motion in consecutive tenths.

We conclude this chapter with a few remarks about setting com- plete chorale melodies. In going about his work the student should first analyze the melody in terms of its larger, inclusive motions and of the

EXAMPLE 8-112 (continued)

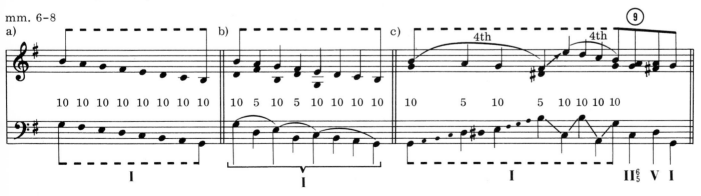

harmonic relationships that they imply. He must also become aware of explicit or latent repetitions and parallelisms, for he may wish to underscore these in his setting. This analysis need not be written out in full, although it often proves helpful to sketch it in roughly.

Example 8-113 shows a preliminary sketch for setting one of the Chorale tunes included in the exercises following this chapter (see Exercise G-6). In Example 8-114 we present two settings, one lightly, the other more densely figurated (Examples 8-114a and b). In the process

EXAMPLE 8-113

EXAMPLE 8-114 (a)

that leads from the first sketch to the final setting, alternative solutions may suggest themselves. Note, for instance, that the prolongation of the initial tonic is shorter in Example *b* than in the sketch. A more radical change occurs in Example *a*; the third phrase ends with the G-chord as a back-relating dominant of C.

An important aspect of setting complete chorales is the treatment of repeated phrases and groups of phrases. In general Bach avoids the exact repetition of entire phrases and sections (of course, we are not referring to the repetition of the first section of chorales showing AAB construction). The student should try to exercise his ingenuity in finding variant solutions. Examples 8-115 and 8-116, from Chorale 327, show a particularly ingenious and unusual treatment of a repeated group of two phrases. Example 8-115 shows the opening two phrases. Bach creates a passing motion in the bass from I to V; the steps of this motion are

the tones D–C natural–B–A in parallel tenths with the melody (graphs *a* and *b*). C natural replaces C sharp in order to avoid the diminished triad of the seventh degree. The first phrase cadences on this C natural. Since this is clearly a transitional tone between D and A, the cadence does not mark an articulation; the two phrases are fused into a single section. Even so the cadencing on C major in the first phrase of a D major chorale is unusual. The meaning of this cadence—its relation to a larger context—defies an explanation in purely harmonic terms. Only an awareness of linear impulse—of counterpoint—helps us to understand it. Incidentally, the emphatic use of the triad on the lowered seventh degree, like the embellishing mediant described earlier, represents a survival from the modal period. Later composers, most notably Schubert, rediscovered and exploited procedures of this sort. Graph *a* indicates that the melodic structure is F sharp–E–D; the descending

EXAMPLE 8-114   (b)

third E–D–C sharp of measures 2 and 3 is a motion into the inner voice of the V. In this example the applied dominant chords also have the contrapuntal function of avoiding fifths and octaves (graphs *b* and *c*).

In Example 8-116 we see how Bach sets the same melodic line at the end of the chorale. Here he interprets the unfolded third F sharp–D of the first measure as implying not the tonic but the submediant, B minor. He carries the prolongation of VI through the second beat of the third measure, again fusing the two phrases into a whole, and also

EXAMPLE 8-115   Bach Chorale 327

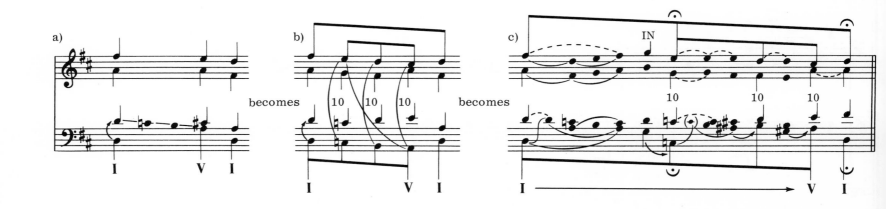

delaying to the last possible moment the V I progression with its effect of completion and repose. Because of the extended prolongation of the B chord, the melody tone E no longer acts as a connective between F sharp and the final D. Instead, the first and last tones of the melodic line are connected by C sharp, the leading tone. Within the frame of the larger melodic structure, this C sharp functions as a substitute for E; the reader will remember from second species that the leap of a fourth can substitute for stepwise progression.

EXAMPLE 8-116

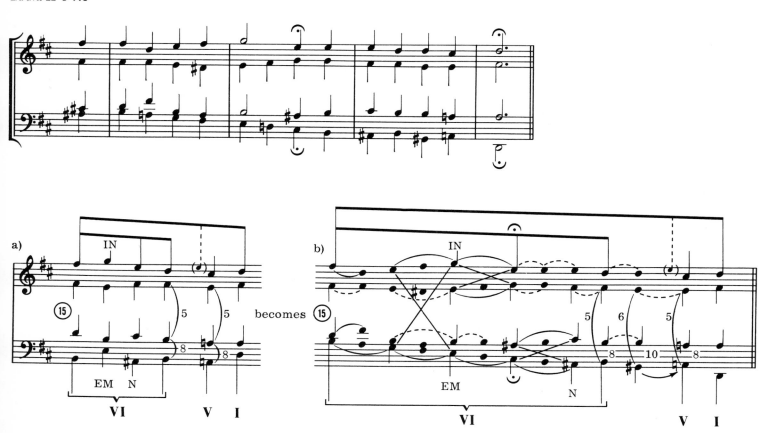

EXERCISES

A. Reduce Examples A-1 to A-5 to note-against-note settings. Compare the reduction with the original setting, and analyze the functions of all dissonant and consonant tones of figuration.

EXAMPLE A-1   Bach Chorale 65

EXAMPLE A-2   Bach Chorale 296

EXAMPLE A-3 Bach Chorale 166

EXAMPLE A-4 Bach Chorale 101

EXAMPLE A-5 Bach Chorale 319

B. Analyze the use of rhythmic shift and of contraction in Examples B-1 to B-6.

EXAMPLE B-1   Bach Chorale 328

EXAMPLE B-4   Bach Chorale 182

EXAMPLE B-2   Bach Chorale 267

EXAMPLE B-5   Bach Chorale 339

EXAMPLE B-3   Bach Chorale 322

EXAMPLE B-6   Bach Chorale 123

C. Explain the use of melodic dissonance in Examples C-1 to C-4.

EXAMPLE C-1   Bach Chorale 336

EXAMPLE C-3   Bach Chorale 107

EXAMPLE C-2   Bach Chorale 314

EXAMPLE C-4   Bach Chorale 113

D. Realize the following figured-bass chorales:
1. Schemelli, No. 48
2.   "   No. 39
3.   "   No. 65*
4.   "   No. 55*
5.   "   No. 22*

6.   "   No. 53*
7.   "   No. 37*

* Compare Bach's four-part settings of these chorales with your realizations. The Schemelli chorales are included in Riemenschneider's edition, and have also been published separately.

E. Set the chorale phrases in Examples E-1 to E-11 in four parts. Follow the sketching procedure illustrated in Examples 8-62 to 8-66. Prepare at least two settings of each phrase, varying the amount and the types of figuration. Not all of these phrases have been drawn from chorale tunes set by Bach, but all of them derive from authentic early Lutheran hymns.

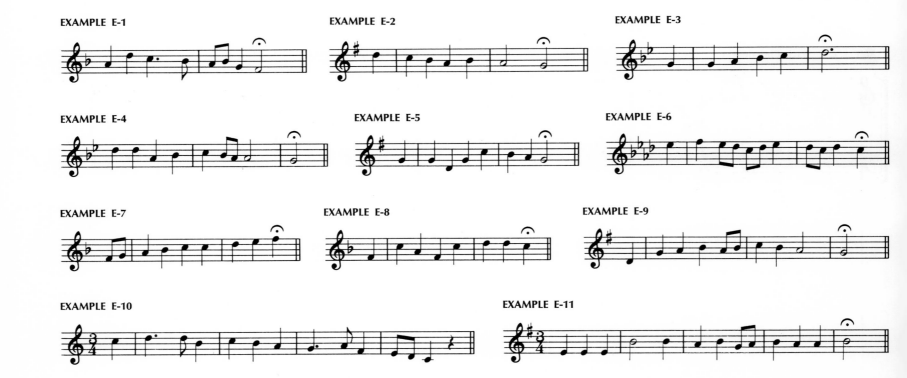

F. Set the groups of two and three phrases given in Examples F-1 to F-14. Not all of these are fragments; those bearing titles are short, complete chorale tunes. Most of these melodies have not been set by J. S. Bach. Prepare at least two settings for each melody given.

EXAMPLE F-1

EXAMPLE F-2

EXAMPLE F-3

EXAMPLE F-4

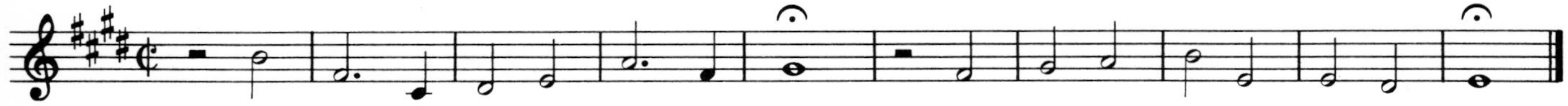

EXAMPLE F-5

EXAMPLE F-6

EXAMPLE F-7

Danket dem Herren

EXAMPLE F-8

Was Lobes soll'n wir dir

EXAMPLE F-9

Den Himmels–Vorschmack

EXAMPLE F-10

Wir waren krank

EXAMPLE F-11

Heiliger Geist Herre Gott

EXAMPLE F-12

Heiliger Geist, du Tröster mein

EXAMPLE F-13

Morgenglanz der Ewigkeit

EXAMPLE F-14

Heiliger Geist, du Tröster mein (Earlier tune set to same text as F-12)

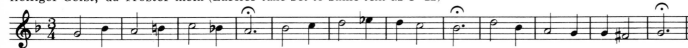

G. Set the chorale melodies, all of which are complete tunes, given in Examples G-1 to G-30. Most of these have not been set by J. S. Bach; a few were written after Bach's death by J. J. Quantz and Bach's son Carl Philipp Emmanuel. The chorales are roughly ordered in terms of increasing length and difficulty. As far as time permits, prepare at least two settings of as many of the melodies as possible.

EXAMPLE G-1

Christus ist erstanden

EXAMPLE G-2

Unser Jesu in der Nacht

EXAMPLE G-3

Ach Gott und Herr

EXAMPLE G-4

Ach wann kommt die Zeit heran

EXAMPLE G-5

Vom Himmel hoch, da komm' ich her

EXAMPLE G-6

Ach, was ist doch unser Leb'n?

EXAMPLE G-7

Jesu, meine Sonne

EXAMPLE G-8

Gott ist mein Lied

EXAMPLE G-9

O Traurigkeit

EXAMPLE G-10

Die Himmel, Herr, preisen sehr

EXAMPLE G-11

Jesu, komm doch selbst zu mir

EXAMPLE G-12

Wie schmeckt es so lieblich

EXAMPLE G-13

Besitz ich nur ein ruhiges Gewissen

EXAMPLE G-14

Auferstehn, ja auferstehn

EXAMPLE G-15

Die Himmel rühmen des Ewigen Ehre

EXAMPLE G-16

Ach wie nichtig, ach wie flüchtig

EXAMPLE G-17

Gedanke, der uns Leben gibt

EXAMPLE G-18

Christ lag in Todesbanden

EXAMPLE G-19

Welt packe dich!

EXAMPLE G-20

O Herr, mein Gott

EXAMPLE G-21

Als Christus mit seiner Lehr

EXAMPLE G-22

Alle Zeit und jede Stund

EXAMPLE G-23

Das alt' Jahr ist vergangen

EXAMPLE G-24

Wie schön leuchtet der Morgenstern

EXAMPLE G-25

Wohl dem, der bess're Schätze liebt

EXAMPLE G-26

Wachet auf, ruft uns die Stimme

EXAMPLE G-27

Mein Gott, verlass' mich nicht

EXAMPLE G-28

Auf, auf, du Christenvolk

EXAMPLE G-29

Mein' Augen schliess ich jetzt

EXAMPLE G-30

O Mensch, bewein dein' Sünde gross

9

COMBINED SPECIES: IMITATIVE COUNTERPOINT

GENERAL OBSERVATIONS

The reader might question why we have separated this chapter on combined species from those concerned with elementary counterpoint in two and three parts. In some respects, to be sure, exercises combining several species form a continuation of elementary counterpoint; they make use of the cantus firmus and of the rhythmic characteristics of the various species. Our reason is twofold. In the first place, combined-species counterpoint offers far greater difficulties to the student than do exercises in elementary counterpoint. And in the second place, the juxtaposition of several species in a single exercise introduces an expanded treatment of dissonance that places combined species, at least partly, in the sphere of prolonged counterpoint.

We believe that the student should acquire some experience in the counterpoint of composition before undertaking these more complex exercises; he will then realize that the procedures of species counterpoint provide us with an invaluable frame of reference for making judgments about such vital matters as dissonance treatment, melodic continuity, and directed musical motion. In Chapters 6 to 8 we have attempted to provide the student with an understanding of the compositional application of species counterpoint. Only after he has learned to relate theoretical abstractions to composition will he be in a position

to benefit from the complex and difficult exercises of combined species.

It was not without reason that we indulged in the above digression at precisely this point. Our present undertaking—the study of combined species—is often considered one of the driest and least rewarding aspects of contrapuntal work. This point of view becomes valid only when exercises in combined species occur in a theoretical vacuum emptied of relevance to genuine musical problems. Once the student becomes aware of the place of these exercises within the discipline of counterpoint as a whole, the very real difficulties will be stimulating rather than tedious.

We shall explore the following five combinations:

1. Two second species

2. Second species and third species

3. Second species and fourth species

4. Third species and fourth species

5. Two fifth species (with imitation)

After having studied combined species, the student will be in a position to undertake work in imitative counterpoint without cantus firmus.

1. COMBINATION OF TWO SECOND SPECIES

In this combination, as indeed in all, the integrity of the species must be maintained. Each voice will preserve the relationship to the cantus firmus appropriate to second species. The first half note of each measure will be consonant with the cantus; the second half note, if dissonant, will form a passing tone. All three voices will unite in a consonant chord at the beginning of each measure.

The relationship of the two species voices to each other is determined essentially by the fact that they form a note-against-note texture. Species counterpoint lacks the means to clarify the function of a dissonant passing or neighboring tone except by relating it to a longer tone sustained in another voice. Except for the suspension, all dissonances require the presence of a stable, held tone. Since the second-species parts move in tones of equal value, it follows as a natural consequence that they must always be consonant with each other. In effect, the two species parts form a quasi–first-species two-part counterpoint. Voice leadings like those given in Example 9-1 should not occur in this combination.

It must be emphasized that the two examples quoted are not in themselves bad. They can both—the first more often than the second—

appear in the compositional framework of prolonged counterpoint. The student should by now be able to analyze the voice leading of Examples 9-1a and *b*. A correct interpretation will indicate the unsuitability of these progressions for our present purposes.

CONSONANCES IN BOTH SPECIES VOICES

The preservation of consonance between the species parts constitutes the main principle of this combination. Within this delimited framework occur three basic voice-leading situations:

1. Two consonances per measure in both species parts

2. Dissonant passing tones in both species parts

3. Dissonance in one part against consonance in the other

We shall now examine the first of these possibilities (see Example 9-2).

In Examples *a, b, c,* and *d,* both second half notes combine to continue or complete the first-beat chord; these represent rudimentary instances of chord prolongation. Examples *e, f,* and *g* present the important interval successions 5-6 and 6-5. In *g,* the succession occurs across the two parts rather than within a single voice; such a procedure is perfectly valid so long as it results from convincing melodic motions. The remaining examples illustrate various possibilities for achieving two distinct chords per measure—chords arising solely out of voice leading. Let us study the last progression, that of Example 9-2*k* (Example 9-3).

EXAMPLE 9-1

As Example 9-3 indicates, the second chord of Example 9-2k shows a passing function. In Example 9-3a, we see a first-species three-part counterpoint. In Example b, a passing tone fills in the leap in the soprano; this progression, of course, belongs to second-species three-part writing. The final example (equivalent to 9-2k) counterpoints the soprano in parallel tenths. In so doing, it destroys the dissonant quality of the passing tone without in the least disturbing its passing function. Giving consonant support to a dissonant tone, as we have already noted, is an important technique with far-reaching implications for composition (see Chapter 7, pages 173 and 190–197).

EXAMPLE 9-2

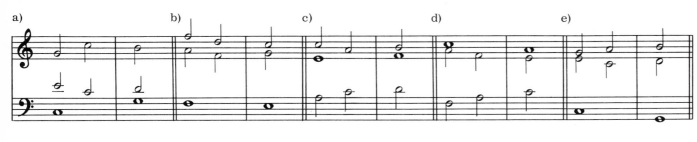

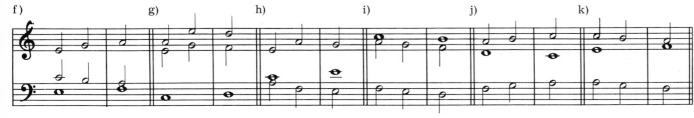

EXAMPLE 9-3

DISSONANT PASSING TONES IN BOTH SPECIES VOICES

The requirement that the two species voices remain consonant with one another by no means prevents us from employing the dissonant passing tone in relation to the cantus firmus. We shall now study various possibilities for using the dissonant passing tone in both parts simultaneously. In Example 9-4 the dissonant passing tones form consonant intervals with each other; thirds, sixths, tenths, and octaves occur. The imperfect consonances can result from both parallel and contrary motion; octaves, of course, can occur only through contrary motion. The fifth cannot occur between two dissonant passing tones; the alert student can easily determine why this is so. But what about the fourth between upper voices? Can we employ the voice leading of Example 9-5?

We cannot. The second of the three fourths is not supported by a third or fifth below the middle voice; consequently, it remains dissonant. This contradicts the fundamental condition of this combination:

that the species voices, being in note-against-note texture, must at all times be consonant with each other. We emphasize that parallel fourths as such need not be excluded. In Example 9-6, both fourths receive consonant support; the progression is completely acceptable.

CONSONANCE IN ONE VOICE AGAINST DISSONANCE IN THE OTHER

Here we encounter somewhat more complex voice-leading situations than is the case when both moving voices have a similar relation to the cantus. The least problematic instances occur when the consonant tone on the second beat continues or completes the first-beat chord (Example 9-7).

Where the consonant tone is foreign to the initial chord, the voice leading is often less satisfactory (Example 9-8). Here, the dissonance no

EXAMPLE 9-4

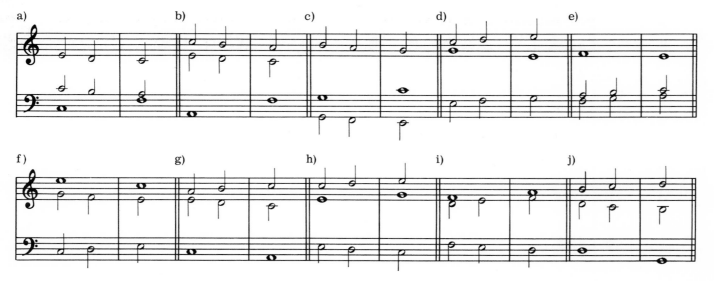

longer moves against a relatively neutral, stable background. The impact of the "new" tone occurring together with the dissonant passing tone produces an impression not unlike that of note-against-note dissonance. Some authors—notably Heinrich Schenker—prohibit the use of this type of voice leading in the context of species counterpoint. An exception might well be made, however, if a fifth in the top voice is followed by a sixth in the middle voice. Here, the impression of a chord change is much weaker, as Example 9-9 shows.

EXAMPLE 9-5

EXAMPLE 9-6

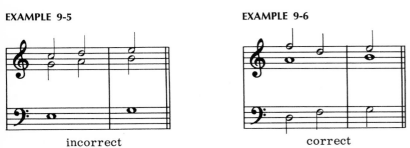

incorrect

correct

EXAMPLE 9-7

a)   b)   c)   d)

EXAMPLE 9-8

a)   b)   c)

EXAMPLE 9-9

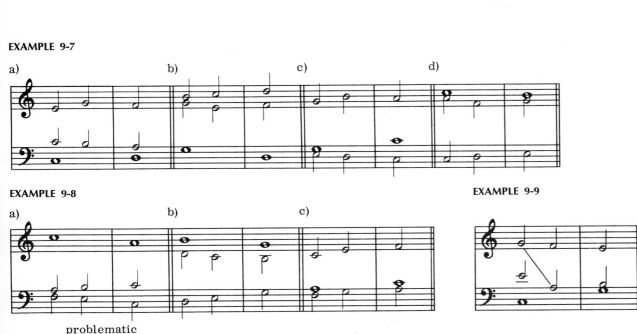

problematic

PARALLEL MOTION AND OTHER VOICE-LEADING CONSIDERATIONS

In this combination, it is quite difficult to avoid the excessive use of parallel thirds, sixths, and tenths. In the interest of independent part-writing, however, the student must make every effort to avoid more than three (or at the very most, four) consecutive intervals. Approaching the fifth or octave in similar motion from first to second beat is a new possibility. (See Example 9-60a, bars 6-7). The perfect interval is less emphasized when it occurs on the weak beat; as a result, the relief of contrary motion in the remaining part is no longer necessary. "Hidden" fifths and octaves between outer voices should not occur even in this new metrical configuration. We refrain from presenting examples for beginnings and cadences, as they follow the principles outlined in Chapters 1 to 5. Example 9-60, illustrating complete exercises in combined-species counterpoint, will be found on pages 354–357.

To several cantus firmi write exercises in all permutations of this combination.

2. COMBINATION OF SECOND AND THIRD SPECIES

Here, we combine two different species in a single exercise. Consequently, there are six possible permutations rather than three as in the preceding combination. The permutations are the following:

CF	CF	2	3	2	3
2	3	CF	CF	3	2
3	2	3	2	CF	CF

As in the previous combination, the integrity of each species part must be preserved. In its relation to the cantus, each part must follow the specific procedures appropriate to its species. The relationship between the two species voices—no longer note-against-note—now becomes highly complex. Possibilities of dissonance treatment are manifold; this combination offers a spectrum of contrapuntal progressions ranging from a totally consonant measure to a measure three-quarters dissonant. Some of the more complex progressions seem to fall within the realm of prolonged counterpoint; it is difficult, however, to draw a hard and fast line between what is possible in the exercises and what should be reserved for composition. We shall demonstrate the various possibilities and indicate our own preferences. Others may perhaps wish to adopt an approach that is either more restrictive or more inclusive than ours.

We shall begin by investigating the voice-leading situations that occur when the second species contains two consonances per measure. We shall then proceed to the more complicated situations arising out of the use of the dissonant passing tone in second species. Finally, we shall discuss the use of the nota cambiata and double-neighbor figures in the third species.

EXAMPLE 9-10

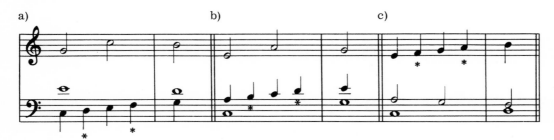

TWO CONSONANCES IN THE SECOND SPECIES VOICE

Where the second species contains only consonances, the density of dissonance remains fairly low; dissonance will occur only in the relatively fleeting quarter-note value. The third-species voice can contain dissonant passing tones on the second and fourth quarters (Example 9-10).

Neighboring notes can also occur, together with passing tones (Example 9-11).

The passing tone can also occupy the third quarter; its relatively accented position gives it greater impact but does not alter its passing function. In Example 9-12, we have a simple instance of an important prolonging technique discussed in Chapters 7 and 8: rhythmic shift or displacement. Example 9-12b shows the basic voice leading of this passage; it proves to be a progression familiar to us from the combination of two second species. Here, the tone C (top voice) occurs at the same time as the C of the middle voice. In a, the passing tone B displaces the C, so that it occurs only on the fourth quarter. (Concerning the apparent leap into a dissonance, see the next section.)

The neighboring note can also appear in relatively accented form on the third quarter. Unlike the passing tone, the neighboring note does not carry the line forward; it decorates a stationary point. Because of its ornamental character, this type of dissonance occurs most naturally in unstressed metrical position. In combined species, the third quarter has greater impact than in simple three-part counterpoint; this is because of the presence of the second half note in the second-species part. Therefore, we shall use the relatively accented neighbor sparingly; its occasional appearance, however, is permissible. Example 9-13 gives an illustration.

EXAMPLE 9-11

EXAMPLE 9-12

from

EXAMPLE 9-13

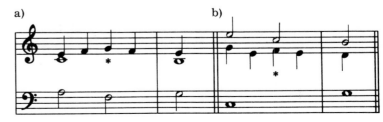

In this combination, situations frequently arise in which two consecutive dissonances occur, on the second and third quarters. In Example 9-14, the dissonances are both passing tones; the voice leading is a somewhat more complex development of progressions like Example 9-12a. (See Examples 9-14c and d, which reduce the progressions of a and b to the underlying voice leading; compare Example 9-12.) Since both dissonances show the same contrapuntal function, and since the melodic direction does not change, the ear can easily hear through the two passing tones to the consonance on the fourth beat. Consequently, we recommend the inclusion of progressions like these.

Example 9-15 reveals a more complicated tangle of contrapuntal relationships. In a, the dissonance on the second quarter seems to be a neighboring note. The return to the original tone on the third quarter, however, brings a dissonance. If we interpret the second quarter as a neighbor, the third note should be consonant. If we interpret the third quarter as a passing tone, the second should be consonant. As neither interpretation is possible, the function of the dissonant tones is unclear. In Example b, the situation is similar; here, the quasi-neighbor occurs on the third quarter rather than on the second. Here, too, the dissonances lack clarity of function. To be sure, these progressions can be explained by an extension of the concept of rhythmic shift (see Examples 9-16a and b, which show the basic voice leading of Examples 9-15a and b). The degree of displacement, however, is greater than in Examples 9-12 and 9-14; we are of the opinion that these examples

EXAMPLE 9-14

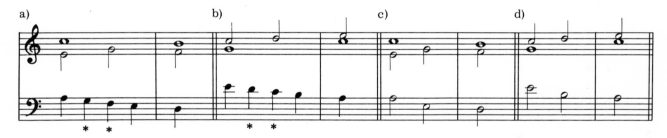

EXAMPLE 9-15

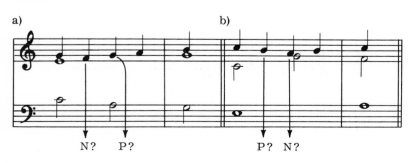

EXAMPLE 9-16

belong to prolonged counterpoint. As a general procedure, then, the neighbor (when dissonant) should be framed by consonances on either side.

MELODIC LEAPS

As we know, the stepwise introduction and quitting of dissonance represents one of the most important basic principles of elementary counterpoint. In this connection, nothing really new is involved here. However, many students become confused about the application of this principle to the relationship between the two species voices. In particular, leaps in the second-species voice often seem to break this important rule. In Example 9-17, the middle voice seems to be leaping out of a ninth with respect to the soprano. (Also see Examples 9-10 to 9-12, where the seeming violations involve leaping into, as well as out of, dissonances.)

These leaps are perfectly valid; they follow basic contrapuntal principles. The dissonances of species counterpoint arise out of the motion of a voice in small rhythmic values against a slower-moving voice. The agent of dissonance is *always* the voice in smaller values. Example 9-18 returns to second-species two-part counterpoint. Nobody will accuse the cantus firmus of "leaping out of" the dissonant seventh; it is the second-species part that is responsible for the dissonance and that must quit it by step. Now the relation between the third- and second-species parts in Example 9-17 resembles that between the second-species part and cantus in Example 9-18. The third species must not approach or leave by leap any dissonance with respect either to the second-species voice or the cantus. (We shall examine in a later section the special cases associated with the cambiata and upper and lower neighbor.) The second-species part will maintain conjunct treatment of dissonance in relation to the cantus; seeming violations such as those of Examples 9-17 and 9-12 are, in fact, no violations at all.

Example 9-19 demonstrates various correct possibilities for the use of leaps in the third-species part.

Example 9-20 contains leaps incorrectly employed in both second- and third-species parts.

EXAMPLE 9-17

EXAMPLE 9-18

EXAMPLE 9-19

NB no dissonances

THE DISSONANT PASSING TONE IN THE SECOND-SPECIES VOICE

Employment of the dissonant passing tone in the second-species part greatly increases the concentration of dissonance in the measure. The third and fourth quarters will contain dissonance as a matter of course; if the second note of the third-species part is dissonant, three quarters of the measure will be in a state of dissonant tension. Some theorists —especially those following the practice of Palestrina—prohibit the use of half-note dissonance in combination with quarter-note motion. In this combination of species, therefore, they would require the second-species part to restrict itself to consonances. Such a restriction is appropriate only when the principal goal of contrapuntal study is the imitation of Palestrina's style. Within the context of the present approach, elimination of the half-note passing tone would be meaning-

less; it would force us to ignore a number of interesting and suggestive voice-leading possibilities used in styles other than the Palestrinian.

For the first time in our study of counterpoint, we encounter dissonance moving on two different levels simultaneously. The second-species line creates a relatively long dissonance against the cantus; the quicker-moving third species can dissonate against both cantus and second species. Let us examine several possibilities.

In all the progressions of Example 9-21, the third-species part is dissonant only in the second half of the measure. It is instructive to sort out the relationships of consonance and dissonance in the second halves of the measure. In many cases, the third quarter note will be dissonant with the cantus; at the same time, it is consonant with the second half note of the second-species part. The fourth quarter will show the reverse relationship; it will be consonant with the cantus and

EXAMPLE 9-20

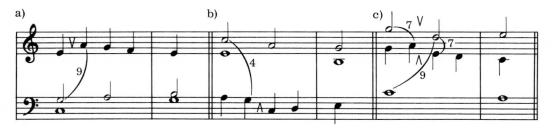

EXAMPLE 9-21

dissonant with the other species part. The ear is quite capable of disentangling the various strands of this contrapuntal web; the passing nature of the dissonances allows no doubt as to the function of the various tones (Example 9-22).

Sometimes the third quarter will be consonant with the cantus and dissonant with the second species (Example 9-21*b*). And, very occasionally, the third quarter will be consonant with both voices and the fourth quarter dissonant with both (Example 9-21*c*). Neither of these possibilities offers any new problems.

The dissonance in the second-species line imposes limitations on the freedom of the third species to move by leap. It is easy to use a disjunct interval from the first to the second quarter—when the second species is consonant (see Example 9-21). The presence of the dissonant passing tone in the second species narrows the number of possibilities

for melodic leaps later in the measure; such leaps, of course, can only occur between two tones consonant with both the cantus and the second-species tone. Example 9-23 indicates some of the possibilities.

We turn now to progressions with a greater concentration of dissonance. Here, the third-species line employs the dissonant passing tone on the second quarter as well as on the third or fourth quarter. Of the third and fourth quarters, one will usually be dissonant with the cantus and consonant with the second-species part; the other will show the reverse relationship. In these progressions, the situation is complicated further by the dissonance on the second quarter. Only the first quarter of the measure contains a consonance; the tension of the several dissonances accumulates until the next first beat, where a new consonance appears. In certain respects, the voice leading of these progressions (Example 9-24) reveals as much complexity as the excluded

EXAMPLE 9-22

EXAMPLE 9-23

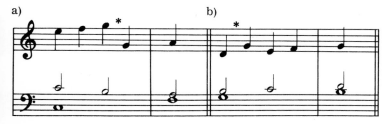

progressions of Example 9-15. We believe, however, that an important distinction between the two types of progression justifies the inclusion of Example 9-24 (and similar cases). The passing-tone function is so readily intelligible that the contrapuntal meaning of the dissonant tones is never cast in doubt; these progressions contain none of the ambiguity encountered in Example 9-15. Clarity of function has greater significance than density of dissonance.

In our next example, the dense saturation of dissonance combines with ambiguity of function. In these progressions, a dissonant neighboring note precedes or follows a dissonance. Such progressions, even more than those of Example 9-15, belong in the domain of prolonged counterpoint. We suggest that the student avoid using them in his exercises (see Example 9-25). An exception might well be made in those cases where the student indicates his correct understanding of the voice leading by providing an explanation of the functions of the various tones. (See Example 9-26 for one possible way in which to present such an explanation.)

For the most part, the dissonant neighboring note will not occur in the same measure as a dissonant passing tone in the second-species voice. An exception might well be made in cases like Example 9-27, where the note following the neighbor is consonant with both the cantus and the passing tone of the second species.

THE NOTA CAMBIATA AND THE DOUBLE NEIGHBOR

As we know, third species provides the opportunity for the use of two idioms or ornamental figures: the nota cambiata and the four-note group consisting of main tone, upper neighbor, lower neighbor, and main tone (see chapter on third species). These idioms can occur in the context of combined species; certain conditions, however, must obtain.

In the cambiata group, the third tone begins a subsidiary melodic

EXAMPLE 9-24

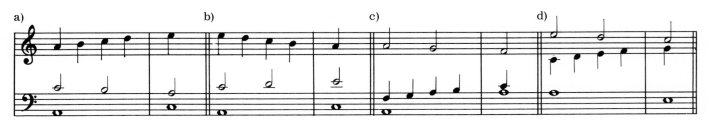

progression interpolated between a passing tone and its melodic goal. In order to allow the tones to reveal their melodic functions, it is important that the third tone be consonant. Otherwise, the progression from the second to the fourth tone will be obscured. In Example 9-28a

we see a correct and in *b* an incorrect use of the cambiata.

The double-neighbor idiom, of course, represents the decoration of a single tone. In simple two- and three-part counterpoint, the third quarter as well as the second can be dissonant. In combined spe-

EXAMPLE 9-25

EXAMPLE 9-26

EXAMPLE 9-27

EXAMPLE 9-28

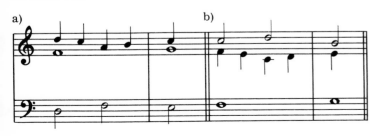

cies, however, the impact of the second half note of the second species adds emphasis to the third quarter. It is better, consequently, to use this figure only where the third quarter is consonant with the second half note of the second-species voice. The student should compare Examples 9-29a, b, and c. In the first two, the third quarter is consonant with the second half note; in the third, it is dissonant.

Example 9-30 might at first seem correct. Careful examination, however, reveals that the leap in the bass is to a tone dissonant with C, the main tone in the soprano. In effect, the bass leaps into a dissonance; the third species line represents the elaboration of a sustained C.

To several cantus firmi write exercises in all permutations of this combination. For illustrations of this combination see Example 9-60.

3. COMBINATION OF SECOND AND FOURTH SPECIES

In this combination, we bring together for the first time two moving parts, one syncopated, the other in normal rhythmic progression. This juxtaposition creates an interesting problem in the distribution of consonance within the measure. The second-species part must be consonant with the cantus on the first beat; the fourth-species part must be consonant on the second beat. As we know, fourth-species dissonance occurs on the first beat; second-species dissonance occurs (as a passing

tone) on the second. If both species are allowed unrestricted freedom in the use of dissonance, many measures will have no consonance at all; the first half will contain a dissonant suspension, while the second half is taken up with a dissonant passing tone in the second-species voice. If we are to achieve the necessary presence of consonant stability, we must avoid the use of dissonance in one of the species parts. A moment's reflection will convince us that it is the second-species part that must sacrifice the use of dissonance. A fourth-species line without the dissonant suspension is a virtual impossibility. To produce such a line, we would have to break the species so often that the part would be more second than fourth species.

On the first beat of the measure, therefore, the fourth-species part may be dissonant with the cantus, with the second-species voice, or with both. It must resolve (downward by step, of course) to a tone consonant with both voices on the second beat. The second-species part must be consonant with the cantus on the first beat; it must combine with both other parts into a consonant chord on the second beat.

The chief difficulty of this combination is in creating a second-species line with a sufficient proportion of stepwise progression to ensure melodic continuity. The student must take advantage of every opportunity to achieve stepwise motion within the measure without the use of the dissonant passing tone. The adjacent consonances—fifth and sixth, and between upper parts, third and supported fourth—will prove of great help. The difficulties of this combination require us to be somewhat tolerant of sequential progressions in the second-species part.

EXAMPLE 9-29

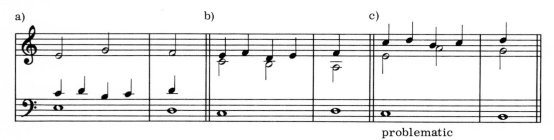

problematic

EXAMPLE 9-30

wrong

THE SECOND-SPECIES VOICE IN THE BASS

The two permutations with the second-species part in the bass produce the most interesting voice-leading progressions of this combination. Many of these progressions occur in direct or ornamented form in compositions of various styles. Let us study some of the possibilities.

The progressions of Example 9-31 represent elaborations of the $\frac{9\text{-}8}{3\ -}$ suspension of simple three-part counterpoint; our next illustrations derive from the $\frac{5\ -}{4\text{-}3}$ progression (see Example 9-32).

It is also possible to elaborate a 7-6 suspension; here, however, the third part (cantus) must double the first note of the bass. If the cantus were a third or tenth above the bass, the second tone of the second species would be a dissonance approached by leap (Example 9-33).

In the preceding examples, the suspension chord on the first beat was a sonority familiar to us from our work in simple three-part counterpoint. Our next example is interesting in that the $\frac{6}{5}$ chord of the first beat has not been hitherto available; in simple counterpoint, it would result in a faulty progression to a $\frac{6}{4}$ chord. (See Example 9-34c.) The progression of Example 9-34a is particularly significant because of the frequency with which it appears in composition. Often this voice-leading progression combines with a harmonic impulse in the fa-

EXAMPLE 9-31

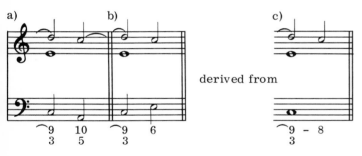

derived from

EXAMPLE 9-32

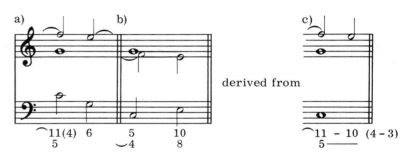

derived from

EXAMPLE 9-33

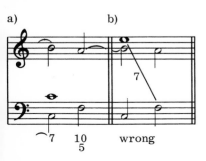

EXAMPLE 9-34

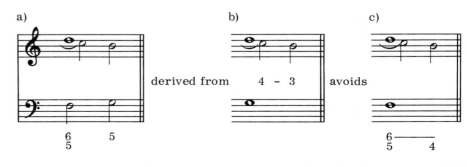

derived from   4 - 3   avoids

miliar II^6_5–V–I cadence; at other times, as here, it results from purely contrapuntal forces.

We shall not list all of the possible voice leadings of this (or any other) combination. It will be valuable for the student to make some discoveries for himself. In particular, the progressions resulting from consonant syncopations combined with half notes offer few problems. We shall illustrate only one example, the decoration of the 5-6 consonant suspension series. The resulting progression (see Example 9-35) also appears with frequency in composition. It illustrates the fact that a root-position chord (in three-part writing represented by the $^8_5$) can de-

rive from an "inversion"; in most harmony textbooks only the opposite derivation is presented as a possibility.

THE CANTUS OR THE FOURTH-SPECIES VOICE IN THE BASS

The remaining four permutations, for the most part, show less change from the patterns of simple three-part writing than is the case when the second species takes the lowest part. Here too, however, we encounter certain suspension chords not previously available. In both the progressions of Example 9-36, the presence of a second moving part is required

EXAMPLE 9-35

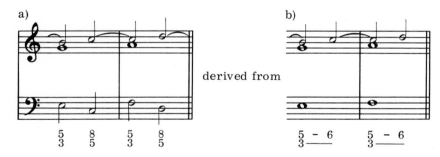

derived from

EXAMPLE 9-36

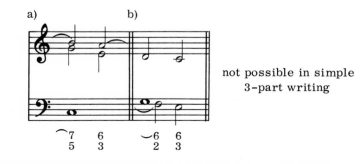

not possible in simple
3-part writing

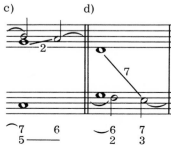

to prevent the "resolution" of the suspension into a dissonance. The student will note that the $\frac{7}{5}$ and $\frac{6}{2}$ of Example 9-36 as well as the $\frac{6}{5}$ of Example 9-34 resemble incomplete seventh chords in root position or inversion. This resemblance is not wholly coincidental; the dissonance of the seventh chord results from voice leading. Often, the causal agent is a passing tone; often, as here, it is a suspension.

The progressions of Example 9-37 require no special comment.

ANTICIPATING THE TONE OF RESOLUTION

The student has learned in fourth-species simple three-part counterpoint that it weakens the resolution of the suspension to anticipate the tone of resolution in any voice other than the bass. The same principle holds good in combined species. Example 9-38 gives illustrations of progressions to avoid.

EXCEPTIONAL USE OF THE DIMINISHED TRIAD

The total avoidance of the dissonant passing tone makes it very difficult to achieve a satisfactory second-species line. We might, therefore, justify the occasional use of the diminished fifth as a passing tone in the second-species part. In combination with the cantus and tone of

resolution, the diminished fifth produces a diminished triad in root position. Although the chord is of course dissonant, the dissonance lies between the second species and cantus alone and is passing; it does not involve the tone of resolution of the fourth species, which is consonant with both other parts. This progression, of course, represents prolonged rather than elementary counterpoint. The occasional use of progressions from prolonged counterpoint can be allowed, as we have mentioned, when the student is fully aware of the voice-leading implications of the particular progression. Example 9-39 occurs with considerable frequency in composition.

To several cantus firmi write exercises in all permutations of this combination. For illustrations of complete exercises see Example 9-60.

4. COMBINATION OF THIRD AND FOURTH SPECIES

As in the last combination, the presence of the syncopated voice requires us to achieve a consonant chord in the second half of the measure. The third-species line, therefore, must be consonant with the cantus on the first quarter and consonant with both cantus and fourth-species part in the latter half of the measure. (As we shall see, this consonance can occur on the fourth as well as on the third quarter.)

Example 9-40 compares a few measures combining second and fourth species with a related passage employing third instead of second.

EXAMPLE 9-37

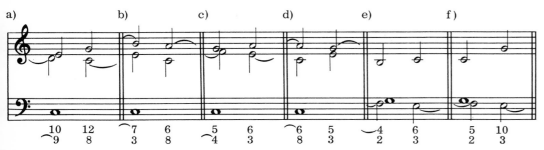

EXAMPLE 9-38

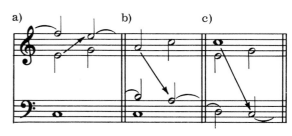

The student will easily see the facility with which the third-species line can achieve stepwise motion without interfering with the resolution of the dissonances in the fourth-species part. Because of its quicker motion, the third-species voice need not at all forgo the use of passing and neighboring dissonances.

CONSONANCE ON THE THIRD QUARTER

Example 9-41 illustrates a number of possibilities in which the consonant part of the measure occurs on the third quarter. This is the most usual (though not the only) distribution of consonance and dissonance in this combination. The second and fourth quarters of the third-species voice can contain dissonant passing tones and neighboring notes.

CONSONANCE ON THE FOURTH QUARTER

The third-species voice can place an accented passing tone on the third quarter. Then, the consonant chord will appear on the fourth quarter. As in the combination of second and third species, the concept of rhythmic shift or displacement is at work here. Example 9-42 shows a few possibilities; the analytic reduction indicates that a combination of second and fourth species represents the fundamental voice leading of these progressions.

The student must take care to secure the presence of a consonant

EXAMPLE 9-39

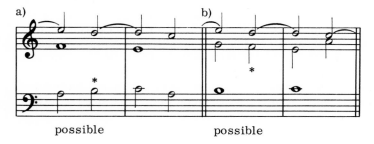

possible   possible

EXAMPLE 9-40

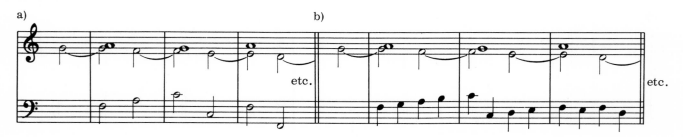

chord on the fourth quarter. Example 9-43 is incorrect because it lacks the necessary consonant sonority.

As in the combination of second and third species, the accented neighbor (on the third quarter) should occur seldom (Example 9-44).

In Example 9-45, the neighbor follows a dissonant passing tone or returns to a tone dissonant with the resolution of the suspension. Like

EXAMPLE 9-41

EXAMPLE 9-42

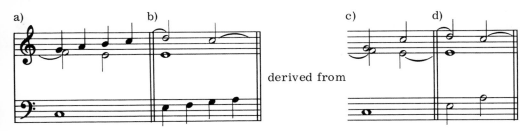

derived from

EXAMPLE 9-43

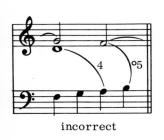

incorrect

EXAMPLE 9-44

EXAMPLE 9-45

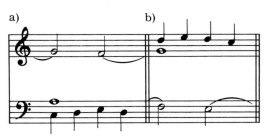

the similar progressions discussed in the combination of second and third species, this passage belongs properly to prolonged counterpoint. (See Examples 9-15 and 9-25.) Again we recommend their use only in the event that the student can demonstrate his understanding of the voice leading.

LEAPS IN THE THIRD-SPECIES LINE

Leaps occur easily in the latter, consonant part of the measure. The third-species line will not leap into or out of any tone dissonant with either of the more sustained parts. (We shall discuss on page 349 the cambiata and upper-lower neighboring-note idioms.) Example 9-46 indicates a few of the many possibilities.

Skips offer no difficulty in the first part of the measure, if the fourth-species part contains a consonant tone. The progressions of Example 9-47 illustrate some possibilities; they require no comment.

If the syncopated voice contains a dissonant suspension, the third-species line will have fewer opportunities to leap. Leaps will take place only between tones consonant with both the cantus and the fourth-species part; they should not add a new dissonance to the prevailing dissonant sonority (Example 9-48).

Some textbooks allow an exceptional type of leap in this combination. The third-species part may leap to or from a tone dissonant with the fourth-species dissonant suspension if the tone represents the unison or octave doubling of the cantus. The tone involved in the leap reinforces the stable cantus tone; it adds no new dissonance. Therefore, the dissonance with the fourth species is said to be covered by the process

EXAMPLE 9-46

EXAMPLE 9-47

EXAMPLE 9-48

of doubling; Jeppesen and others call this voice leading the *covered dissonance*. The tone in question can occur only on the second quarter of the measure. Example 9-49 serves to illustrate.

Example 9-50 carries prolongation to a point incompatible, in our opinion, with the purposes of species counterpoint. It is, of course, an excellent example of prolonged counterpoint. Here, the third-species voice presents an arpeggiation; the dissonance arises through the collision of a tone of the broken chord with the suspension.

THE CAMBIATA AND DOUBLE-NEIGHBOR IDIOMS

Correct procedure in this combination resembles that of combined second and third species. In the cambiata figure, the third tone must be consonant with both cantus and fourth species. In the upper-lower-neighbor idiom, the third tone should be consonant with the fourth-species part, though not necessarily with the cantus. The fourth tone, of course, must be consonant with both other voices. (See Example 9-51.)

ANTICIPATING THE TONE OF RESOLUTION

As in the preceding combination (and, indeed, all three-part writing involving dissonant suspensions), avoid anticipating the tone of resolution in any voice but the bass. Example 9-52 illustrates a few such progressions.

To several cantus firmi write exercises in all permutations of this combination. For illustrations of complete exercises see Example 9-60.

EXAMPLE 9-49

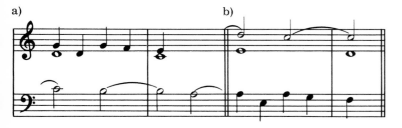

EXAMPLE 9-50

EXAMPLE 9-51

EXAMPLE 9-52

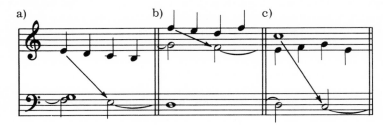

EXAMPLE 9-53

EXAMPLE 9-54

EXAMPLE 9-55

5. COMBINATION OF TWO FIFTH SPECIES

With this combination, we come to the culmination of our studies in combined-species three-part counterpoint. Setting two fifth-species lines to a cantus firmus involves the use of all the voice-leading techniques learned in the preceding four combinations together with a few new procedures. Before discussing this combination in detail, we should like to explain our reasons for omitting a number of theoretically possible combinations.

A combination of two third-species parts is quite practicable. The note-against-note texture, however, would require us to follow essentially the same rules as in a combination of two second-species lines; we would learn nothing really new. A combination of two fourth-species parts, on the other hand, is not practicable. The inflexibility of the syncopated dissonance with its obligatory downward resolution would force us into excessive reliance on parallel thirds, sixths, or tenths between the species parts. The reader should bear in mind, of course, that double suspensions in parallel motion occur frequently in composition. To preserve independence, we should require frequent recourse to the expedient of breaking the species, thus transforming our combination into one of second and one of fourth species. To combine a part in second, third, or fourth species with one in fifth species would be profitless. Since fifth species itself contains elements of all the others, these combinations would present us with no voice-leading situations not also found in a combination of two fifth species. And the esthetic qualities of the latter combination are far more pleasing than is the case when the flexible rhythm of fifth species unfolds against the uniform note values of any of the others.

RHYTHMIC CONSIDERATIONS

The presence of another florid part modifies slightly the rhythmic construction of the single fifth-species line. In general, the single line in combined fifth species will show somewhat less density of rhythm than in simple two- or three-part counterpoint. The principle of complementary rhythm should prevail in most cases. That is, long notes in one voice will occur against quick values in the other. The occasional use of similar values in both moving parts is by no means incorrect. The independence of the parts, however, is most easily secured if the greater part of the exercise contains complementary rhythms. Example 9-53 illustrates this.

In simple fifth-species counterpoint, we have used note values larger than the half note only in the form of syncopated notes. We have tied half notes to halves or quarters in the next measure; we have not, however, employed dotted halves or whole notes within a single measure (except, of course, for the final whole note). This restriction on unsyncopated long notes arises from the need to maintain a certain rhythmic propulsion. This propulsion or momentum requires a melodic motion, in at least one voice, on each half-note beat.

Now that we are combining two florid parts, we can make use of unsyncopated long notes without impeding the rhythmic flow. We need only take care that quicker notes, marking the beat, occur in one voice against the long note in the other. We may employ the dotted half note followed by a quarter or two eighths. (See Example 9-54.)

Obviously, the dotted half can occur only on the first beat of the measure. The part of the note symbolized by the dot (i.e., the third quarter of the measure) should not be dissonant with either of the remaining voices. Dissonance on the third quarter will create the impression of an irregular suspension within the measure (Example 9-55).

The dotted half works to particularly good advantage when the quarter (or eighths) following introduces quick note values in the next measure. Short notes are always more smoothly introduced on a pulse other than the first in the measure.

CONSONANCE AND DISSONANCE

A fifth-species line results from the amalgamation of elements of second, third, and fourth species. A combination of two such lines, therefore, brings together types of voice leading from all the combinations of species we have previously studied. Problems of dissonance treatment must be referred back to the combination of species corresponding to the note values involved. If both voices move in half notes, for example, the rules for a combination of two second-species parts come into play; quarter notes against suspensions will be governed by the requirements of third species combined with fourth.

We have not considered the combination of two third species. As mentioned above (see preceding page), the note-against-note texture requires us to follow the same rules as for a combination of two second species. In other words, the quarter notes must be consonant between themselves although one or both may be dissonant with respect to the cantus. We may now use simultaneous neighbors (Example 9-56a); the dissonant neighbor in one part can sound against a passing tone in the other (Example 9-56b); the cambiata idiom can also combine with other dissonant figurations (Example 9-56c).

The upper-lower-neighbor idiom can also coexist with other types of dissonance (Example 9-57).

In three-part texture, it is best to use syncopation in only one voice at a time. If two parts contain displaced accentuation and only one part shows normal accentuation, the rhythmic balance of the whole can suffer. Double suspensions, therefore, are more appropriately employed in textures of four or more parts. (These observations refer of course to contrapuntal exercises, not to composition, where double suspensions in three-part writing may serve a valid expressive purpose.) When they occur, double suspensions must be consonant between themselves and must both resolve (stepwise and down) to consonant chords. It follows, therefore, that dissonant double suspensions will necessarily consist of parallel thirds, sixths, or tenths.

Mixed note values within the measure create no new problem. The

EXAMPLE 9-56

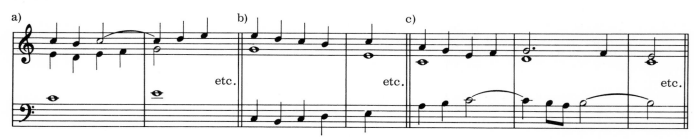

EXAMPLE 9-57

EXAMPLE 9-58

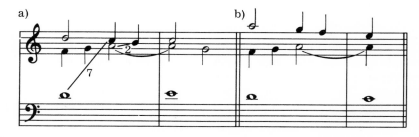

voice leading must be compared with the combination (or combinations) of species associated with the given note values. In Example 9-58a, the top voice is clearly incorrect. The tied note in the middle part requires a consonant chord in the second half of the measure; the dissonances of the soprano frustrate this requirement. Example 9-58b demonstrates correct voice leading. Note the overlapping and the alternating suspensions.

IMITATIVE COUNTERPOINT

A combination of two fifth species may begin in one of two ways. Either the florid parts both begin in the initial measure or one begins in the first measure and the other slightly later. If the second means is adopted, the two voices must show imitation; that is, the second voice will repeat the initial idea of the first. It is only necessary to repeat as much of the first voice as sounds before the second voice enters. It is by no means incorrect, however, to carry the imitation further if the cantus permits. The second voice need not imitate the first at the unison or octave; indeed, it will seldom be possible to do so. Imitation is said to occur at a given interval—octave, second, fifth, etc.—if that interval separates corresponding tones of the two parts. Example 9-59 should be studied here.

Imitation must not be confused with sequence. The latter occurs within a single part; the former, between two different parts. We must still guard against the use of close repetition, sequence, and rhythmical motive within the single line.

Imitative counterpoint forms one of the most important branches of polyphonic writing. Such procedures as canon and fugue are direct outgrowths of imitative techniques. Furthermore, imitation, sometimes disguised, often plays a vital role in shaping the design of compositions not usually considered polyphonic.

In some cases the imitation constitutes an exact duplication of the original idea. Such imitation can be termed *strict*. In other cases, however, the imitating voice may show deviations from the original. This may be termed *free imitation*. Sometimes the qualities of intervals change in order to preserve tonal unity; e.g., a major third may be changed to a minor third, a whole step to a half. Such changes almost invariably occur when the imitation is at the intervals of the second, third, sixth, and seventh; but it may also with imitations at other intervals.

In imitations at the fifth above or fourth below, the fifth step of the scale is often answered by the first step in accordance with the principle of the *tonal answer*. This, of course, will lead to the skip of a fifth being answered by that of a fourth, and possibly to other changes in intervallic size.

For illustrations of combined fifth species see Example 9-60.

To several cantus firmi write exercises in all permutations of this combination. For exercises in imitative counterpoint without cantus firmus see pages 380–394.

EXAMPLE 9-59

a) Imitation at second   b) Imitation at fifth

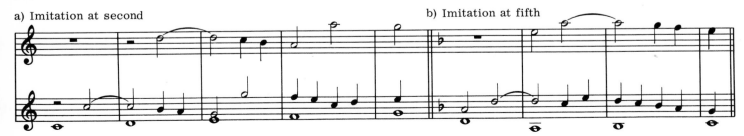

EXAMPLE 9-60

a) 2 + 2

b) 2 + 2

Schenker

c) 2 + 3

EXAMPLE 9-60 **(continued)**

d) 2+3 with more prolonged use of dissonance

e) 2+3   Bellermann

f) 2+4   Schenker

EXAMPLE 9-60 (continued)

g) 2+4

h) 3+4

i) 5+5 without initial imitation

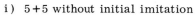

EXAMPLE 9-60 (continued)

j) 5+5 with imitation

k) 5+5

6. PROGRESSIONS FROM COMBINED SPECIES IN COMPOSITION

COMBINATION OF TWO SECOND SPECIES

The most significant voice-leading technique of this combination is the use of a tone in one voice to provide consonant support to an otherwise dissonant passing tone in another. The literature offers countless instances of this technique, and we have already offered a number of examples illustrating it. The reader should reexamine the examples of Chapter 7, section 4, in the light of his experience with this combination.

The above-mentioned technique frequently occurs in a texture showing parallel tenths or thirds between the moving voices. However, a disjunct line can fulfill the same function. The subdividing bass progressions discussed in Chapter 8 frequently make consonant a passing tone in the soprano; these progressions, therefore, also relate to a combination of two second species.

In the species exercises, the cantus firmus provides the stable background to the moving voices. In composition, of course, it is usually the prolonged chord, rather than a single tone, that assumes this function. In the literature, we frequently encounter progressions within prolonged chords that are closely related to this combination. We need not expect literal quotations; we shall find neighboring notes as well as passing tones, and long prolongations will feature more than two moving tones against the stable background.

We offer two examples in different styles. Our first consists of the

EXAMPLE 9-61   Byrd, The Woods so Wild

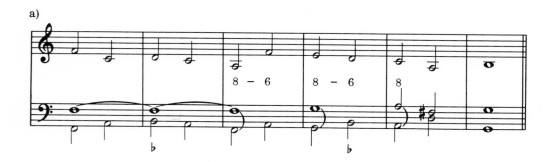

second phrase of William Byrd's setting for virginal of *The Woods so Wild* (Example 9-61). The melody implies a movement from an F chord to a G chord; both the prolongation of F and motion to G reflect a combination of two second species. In this example, unlike most of our others, the basic voice leading deals only with consonant sonorities.

Example 9-62, from a Mozart piano sonata, is slightly more complex. In the tonic prolongation of measures 1-4, the two A's of the bass make consonant the passing C's of the top voice. Note the rhythmic accelerando of the basic outer-voice motion. The motion is first in whole bars (measures 1-2), then half bars (measure 3), then quarter bars (measure 4).

COMBINATION OF SECOND AND THIRD SPECIES

The most characteristic application of this contrapuntal texture is the use of rhythmic shift or displacement. We have illustrated this technique in Chapters 7 and 8. The analyst will seldom encounter extended musical spans directly relating to this combination. However, many details of voice leading, in the most various styles, can best be understood in its terms. Often a chord prolongation will show embellishment in one part against a slower passing motion in another; such progressions often resemble second and third species in combination.

We offer three excerpts in addition to those cited in the chorale

EXAMPLE 9-62   Mozart, Piano Sonata, K. 570, 3rd movement

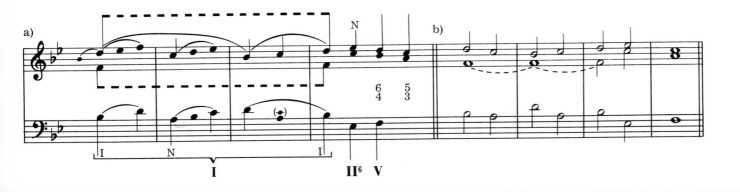

chapter. Our first, Example 9-63, is from a Monteverdi madrigal; it requires no comment.

Our next is from the G major *Partita* of Bach (Example 9-64). Note that the top voice, corresponding to second species, moves in quicker note values than does the bass, which corresponds to third species. The sixteenth notes of the upper voice embellish A and G; they do not influence the underlying pace of the melody.

Finally we cite the opening of the single A flat major Prelude (1834) of Chopin. The voice leading is as closely knit as that of a Bach chorale. But we glimpse it through a veil of pianistic figuration (Example 9-65).

COMBINATION OF SECOND AND FOURTH SPECIES

In the literature we frequently find extended series of suspensions counterpointed by another moving part. These passages often relate directly, even obviously, to fourth species combined with second. As the following examples indicate, the progressions of this combination can be embodied in the most various textures and rhythms. Example 9-66 is drawn from a harpsichord piece of François Couperin. The right-hand part is a polyphonic melody; it implies two lines of which the higher contains suspended dissonances. In combination with the bass, the

EXAMPLE 9-63   Monteverdi, E così poco a poco, Madrigals, Book 5

EXAMPLE 9-64   Bach, Partita V, Sarabande

EXAMPLE 9-65   Chopin, Prelude No. 26

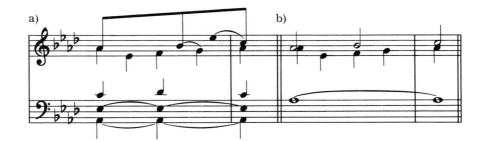

EXAMPLE 9-66   Couperin, Ordre No. 1, La Milordine

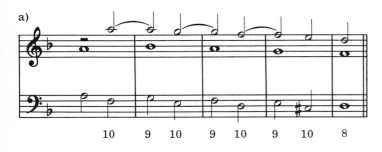

right-hand part gives rise to an important progression of combined fourth and second species. In the bass, the eighth notes D, C (first measure), and A (second measure) add a harmonic impulse to this contrapuntal progression.

Next, Example 9-67 presents a beautiful suspension series from Bach's E major Fugue, in Vol. II of the Well-Tempered Clavier. The bass rests from measure 38 to the entrance of measure 40; the function of lowest voice is therefore assumed by the tenor. In this example, the outer parts produce a 9-10 series counterpointed by the "second-species" progression of the alto. As graph *b* indicates, the contrapuntal progres-

EXAMPLE 9-67   Bach, Well-tempered Clavier, II, Fugue IX

sion occurs within prolonged dominant harmony.

We turn again (Example 9-68) to a work of François Couperin, this time to a passage of much greater complexity than that of Example 9-66. The relationship between the outer voices is fundamentally the same as in the earlier example; the lower part of the right hand presents an additional "second-species" progression (graph *d*). In this example the tenor part is unusual; this voice carries the line that would normally represent the stable "cantus firmus" element of the texture (graphs *a-d*). However, this part becomes syncopated (graph *e*); graph *f* presents a comprehensive plan of the voice leading.

EXAMPLE 9-67 (continued)

a)

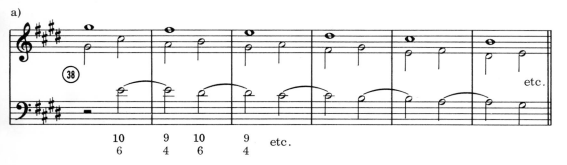

b)

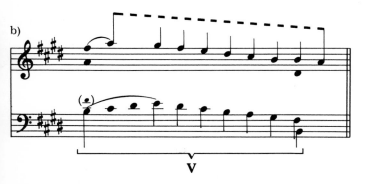

EXAMPLE 9-68   Couperin, Ordre No. 6, Les Baricades Mistérieuses

(Vivement)

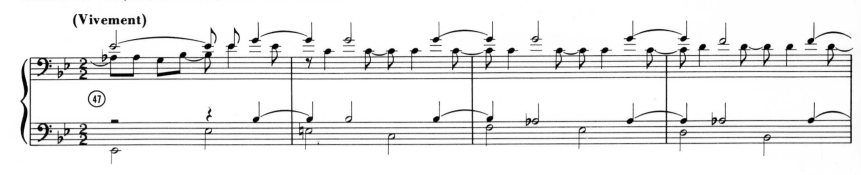

EXAMPLE 9-68 (continued)

a)

b)

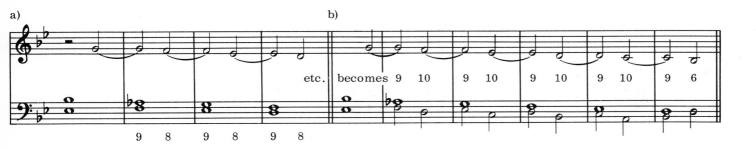

etc. becomes 9 10 9 10 9 10 9 10 9 6

9 8 9 8 9 8

c)

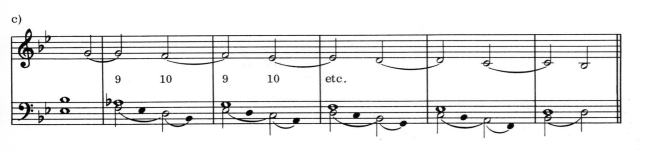

9 10 9 10 etc.

d)

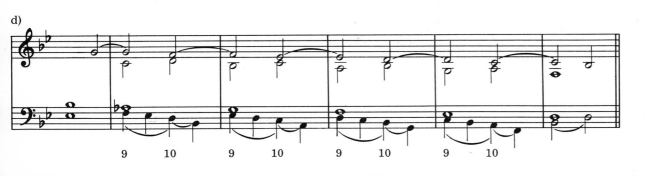

9 10 9 10 9 10 9 10

EXAMPLE 9-68 **(continued)**

e)

f)

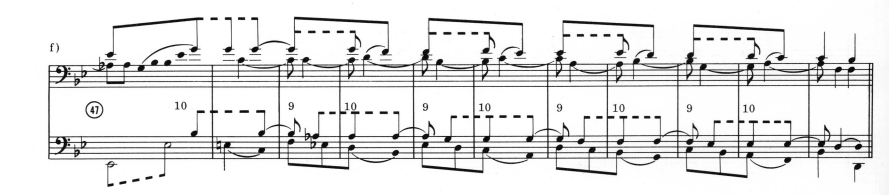

In Example 9-69 we encounter a progression showing similar basic voice leading. Here the stable "cantus" line—also the tenor—is accompanied in parallel thirds by the alto.

In the next illustration—also by Mozart—we encounter a different use of parallel thirds, this time between the parts of the first and the second violin (Example 9-70). In this case, the upper part leads and

EXAMPLE 9-69   Mozart, Mass in C minor, Et incarnatus est

forms the basic suspension series. In the bass part, carried by the cello, the line corresponds to second species; as is normal in supporting a 4-3 or 11-10 series, the basic line is carried by the second tone of each group, the tone that supports the resolution of the suspension. See graphs *b* and *c*.

In Example 9-71 we see a remarkable application of combined

EXAMPLE 9-70   Mozart, String Quartet, K. 428, 2nd movement

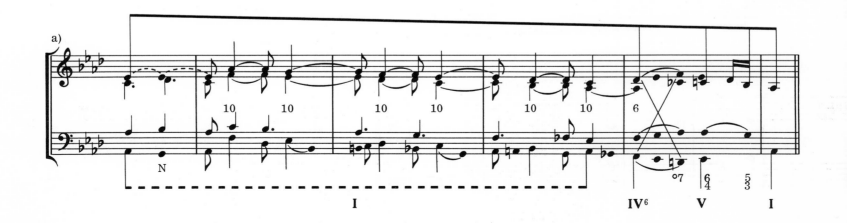

fourth and second species from the development section of the first movement of Beethoven's Piano Sonata, Op. 53. The underlying pro-gression resembles that of Example 9-67, here transformed through the motivic unfolded fourths and the registral transfers of the melody.

EXAMPLE 9-70 (continued)

b)

c)

EXAMPLE 9-71 Beethoven, Piano Sonata, Op. 53, 1st movement

EXAMPLE 9-71   (continued)

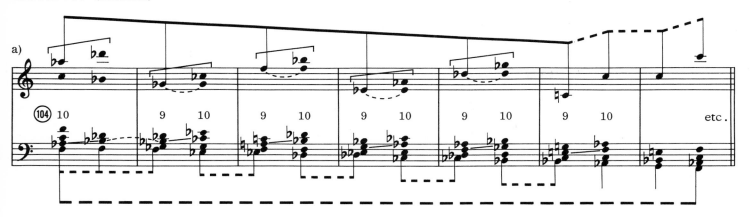

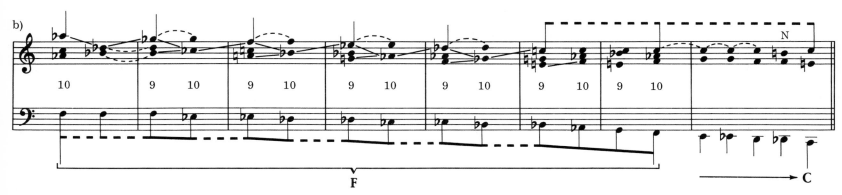

COMBINATION OF THIRD AND FOURTH SPECIES

In basic voice-leading techniques, this combination adds nothing new to the preceding one. In the literature we find analogs to combined third and fourth species when a quicker-moving part counterpoints a series of suspensions. In addition we encounter specific techniques such as the shift of tones (as in third and second in combination) and the so-called covered dissonance. We offer two examples; the first is from Haydn's Symphony in E flat, subtitled *The Philosopher.* Here the viola part adds a fourth voice to the suspensions of the second violins,

the third-species progressions (with downward register changes) of the bass, and the "cantus" progression of the first violins (see Example 9-72).

Example 9-73 belongs to the great chorale setting, the *Duet for Two Armored Men* from Mozart's *Magic Flute.* Notice the chromatic inflection of the top line, and the "covered dissonances" in the lowest voice.

COMBINATION OF TWO FIFTH SPECIES

Since the fifth species contains all the voice-leading possibilities of second, third, and fourth species, all the preceding examples, in a sense,

EXAMPLE 9-72   Haydn, Symphony No. 22, 1st movement

NB Cambiata

also illustrate a combination of two fifth-species parts. One unique feature of this combination consists of the use of alternating and of overlapping suspensions. A few examples follow.

First we see an instance of alternating suspensions with characteristic imitation at the lower fourth. In this progression—a frequently used idiom of the Baroque period—the imitative pattern implies a harmonic background of ascending fifths. In Example 9-74 these fifths are filled in with passing progressions resembling third species. The sevenths in the bass, of course, represent inversions of ascending seconds caused by the need to preserve a consistent bass register.

Overlapping suspensions occur most typically when closely adjacent parts present in alternation a 2-3 series. The suspension, of course, occurs in the lower part; after resolving, that part crosses above the originally higher part, and so on in alternation (Example 9-75).

EXAMPLE 9-73 Mozart, The Magic Flute, No. 21

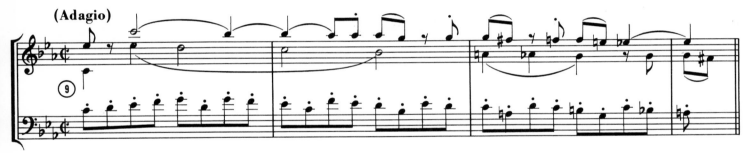

* covered dissonance

In Example 9-76 we see a celebrated application of this progression in the *Recordare* of Mozart's *Requiem*. As in our model, Example 9-75, imitation takes place at the upper second. Note the beautiful poly-phonic melody in the cello part.

Example 9-77 shows the same progression transformed by change of register. Instead of 2-3 suspensions with crossed voices, we here see

EXAMPLE 9-74   Bach, Well-tempered Clavier, I, Prelude XXIV

a)

alternations between 2-3 and 7-6 progressions without crossing.

Finally we show an imaginative prolongation of this contrapuntal idea (Example 9-78). In this case the progression is distributed among three voices, producing graphically expressive dissonant clusters. In the three preceding examples the overlapping voices combine to produce ascending stepwise progressions (compare Example 7-17).

EXAMPLE 9-75

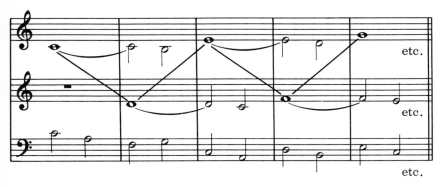

EXAMPLE 9-76 Mozart, Requiem, Recordare

EXAMPLE 9-77   Bach, Goldberg Variations, Var. 6

a)

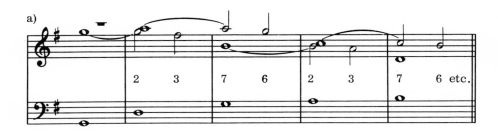

b)

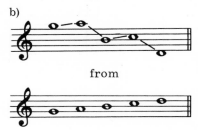

from

c)

EXAMPLE 9-78 Monteverdi, Si ch'io vorrei morire, Madrigals, Book 4

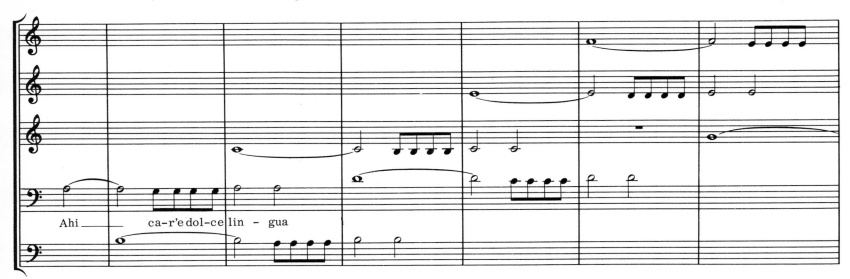

Ahi_____ ca-r'e dol-ce lin - gua

a)

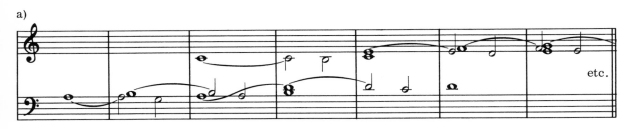

etc.

b)

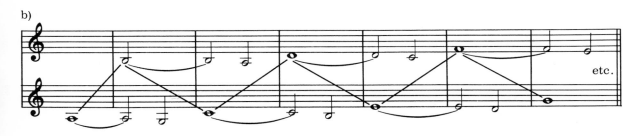

etc.

EXERCISES

A. *SEQUENTIAL EXERCISES.* The sequential written and keyboard exercises presented after Chapter 7, and other similar exercises, can now be prolonged through the use of techniques learned in combined species. In the appended examples, note the use of parallel thirds and tenths (combination of two second species) and rhythmic displacement (second and third). If the student wishes, he may use harmonic progressions, or he may choose consciously to avoid their use.

EXAMPLE A-1

SOLUTION A-1

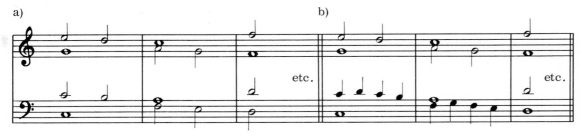

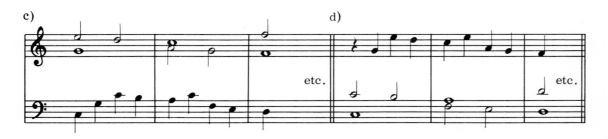

EXAMPLE A-2

SOLUTION A-2

a)

b)

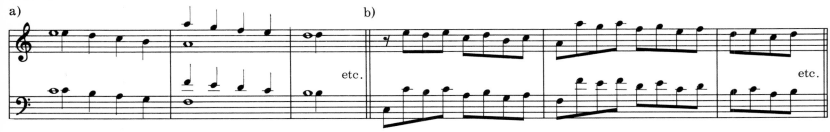

etc.

etc.

c)

etc.

B. *COMBINED SPECIES WITHOUT CANTUS FIRMUS.* Interesting possibilities for voice leading arise out of the combination of certain species without the use of a cantus firmus. Such exercises also provide a convenient introduction to more advanced work in two-part counterpoint. The following combinations are suggested:

1. 2 and 4
2. 3 and 4
3. 5 and 5

A few sample solutions are appended (Examples B-1 to B-4).
Write at least five additional exercises. The exercises combining two fifth species should contain imitation. These will then lead to more advanced work in imitative counterpoint.

EXAMPLE B-1

EXAMPLE B-2

* derived from covered dissonance

EXAMPLE B-3

5 + 5

EXAMPLE B-4

5 + 5

C. *EXERCISES IN IMITATION.* The student should now be ready to write examples of imitative counterpoint in three or more voices. A good point of departure for such exercises is to combine three or more fifth species parts. The voices, of course, will begin at different times with the same initial melodic idea. The imitation can be at any interval, and imitations by different intervals can occur in the same exercise. Imitation by inversion, augmentation, and diminution will also prove useful. In writing for more than three parts, double suspensions become a possibility. Passing chords of three tones against a sus-

EXAMPLE C-1

EXAMPLE C-2

tained tone may be employed. At first the exercise should confine itself to the imitation of one melodic idea.

Sample solutions, not necessarily completed, are offered (Examples C-1 to C-3). The reader will note, especially in C-3, the use of motive repetition and

of repeated tones as well as of phrase articulation and a harmonic framework. Because of the quasi-compositional nature of such exercises, a gradual inclusion of techniques of prolongation is recommended.

EXAMPLE C-3

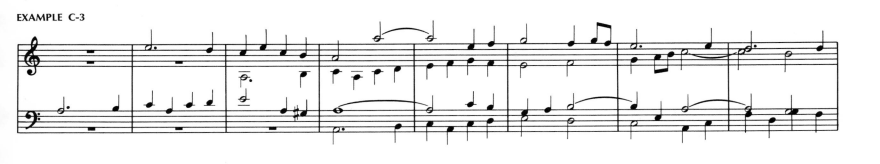

D. *EXERCISES IN IMITATION OUT OF THE ELABORATION OF A SUSPENSION SERIES.* In the literature one frequently encounters passages in close imitation whose underlying voice leading consists of a suspension series. Of course the imitative or canonic effect is achieved by decorating in the same way both the voice with the suspensions and the stable "cantus firmus" voice. The following exercises are classified according to the interval of imitation; the references to the literature indicate similar imitative passages which the student should con-

sult in connection with his written work. In many cases it is possible and desirable to add one or more parts to the ones in imitation; the addition of a bass is particularly instructive. In working out these exercises, the student need not carry through the imitation beyond the opening measures. If, however, the imitation is continuous, a canon will result. A few sample solutions (not necessarily complete) are appended.

1. Imitation at the upper fourth or lower fifth. Elaborate the given progression so that it becomes an imitation at the upper fourth or lower fifth. A suggested bass is given.

Compare Haydn's String Quartet, Op. 1, No. 3, first movement (m. 15ff).

EXAMPLE D-1

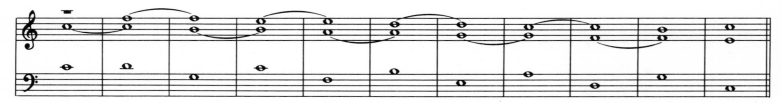

SOLUTION D-1

2. Imitation at the lower third or upper sixth. Elaborate the given suspension series so that it becomes an imitation at the third or sixth; find an appropriate bass.

Compare Bach, *Goldberg* Variations, Var. 18. See solution below.

EXAMPLE D-2

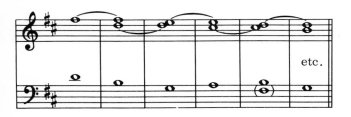

or ... etc.

etc.

SOLUTION D-2

SOLUTION D-2 (continued)

3. Imitation at the lower seventh. The outline below may be expanded in imitative fashion. This pattern derives from 7-6 suspensions; the suspensions are transformed by the unfolded fifths.

EXAMPLE D-3

SOLUTION D-3

4. Imitation at the upper fifth or lower fourth with alternating suspensions. The voice leading below occurs in a combination of two fifth-species parts; it can be expanded into an imitative setting. For an illustration, see Example 9-74.

EXAMPLE D-4

or ... etc.

5. Imitation at upper second or lower seventh with superposed or overlapping suspensions. As in Exercise 4, the voice leading can be traced back to a combination of two voices in fifth species. For illustrations see Examples 9-76 to 9-78, also Solution D-5.

EXAMPLE D-5

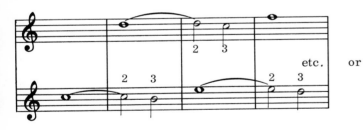

etc. or

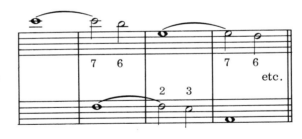

etc.

SOLUTION D-5

Canonic imitation at upper 2nd with bass

E. *EXERCISES IN IMITATION BASED ON SUBJECTS FROM THE LITERATURE.* The student may now attempt to write imitative settings in two, three, or more parts based on motives or themes from the literature. We are therefore offering a number of these which can be developed into points of imitation. We have indicated the location of the second and sometimes of the third entrance. These points of imitation can be set for various vocal and instrumental combinations, and may serve as preparation for later studies in fugue. In this connection, note that some of the excerpts show the use of the tonal answer.

EXAMPLE E-1

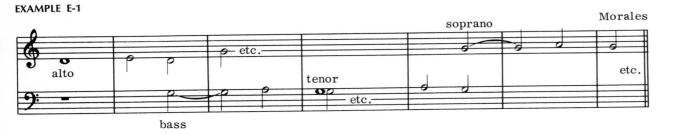

EXAMPLE E-2

EXAMPLE E-3

EXAMPLE E-4

Palestrina

EXAMPLE E-5

Keyboard

G. Gabrieli

etc.

EXAMPLE E-6

Sweelinck

etc.

EXAMPLE E-7

Schein

etc.

EXAMPLE E-8

Purcell

etc.

EXAMPLE E-9

Purcell

etc.

EXAMPLE E-10

Purcell

etc.

EXAMPLE E-11

Caldara

etc.

EXAMPLE E-12

Handel

etc.

EXAMPLE E-13

Bach

etc.

EXAMPLE E-14

Bach

etc.

etc.

EXAMPLE E-15

C. P. E. Bach

Flute

Violin

etc.

EXAMPLE E-16

Haydn

etc.

EXAMPLE E-17

Mendelssohn

etc.

etc.

EXAMPLE E-18

EXAMPLE E-19

EXAMPLE E-20

Brahms

etc.

10

VOICE-LEADING TECHNIQUES IN HISTORICAL PERSPECTIVE (CA. 1450 - CA. 1900)

In this final chapter we attempt to show a variety of voice-leading techniques as they appear in works from around 1450-1900. Unlike the previous chapters, which were organized on the basis of specific procedures, the present one is organized in roughly historical sequence. In this way we hope to show how various voice-leading techniques can be embodied in different and contrasting stylistic personalities. Except for chorales, previous examples have shown passages or sections only. We shall continue to present such examples; however, it now becomes possible to add a number of analyses of complete compositions through which the reader will be able to observe the working of counterpoint within the framework of a complete composition (or large section). By so doing he will be able to relate the detail to the whole musical fabric —surely the goal of all meaningful theoretical work.

If the reader has carefully gone through the earlier sections of this book, he should have no difficulty in understanding the various symbols used in the analytic graphs. It must be stressed that the core of the analysis lies in the graph rather than in any verbalization. We shall use the written word, therefore, only to point up a few salient features of the analyses.

Most of the works analyzed are from the standard repertory, or can be found in readily accessible anthologies. Therefore we have refrained from quoting the musical scores except in those cases where they are not easily available or where a fragment might be difficult to locate. The music for Examples 10-1, 10-2, and 10-5 can be found in Carl Parrish and John F. Ohl, *Masterpieces of Music before 1750* (New York, 1951); see pages 48, 51, 86. The music for Examples 10-3, 10-6, 10-7, and 10-8 can be found in Archibald T. Davison and Willi Apel, *Historical Anthology of Music,* 2 Vols., Revised Edition (Cambridge, 1949 and 1950); see Vol. I, pages 92, 163, 206; and Vol. II, page 144.

BINCHOIS: CHANSON, ADIEU M'AMOUR

This beautiful Rondeau (Example 10-1) is a fine example of early Renaissance polyphony. The partial signature is characteristic of the period and leads to the cross relation of measure 2 and the interesting cadence of measures 9-10. The mode, of course, is Lydian; the frequent use of B flat makes it to all intents and purposes a transposed Ionian. The *superius* (highest part) has the most distinctive melodic profile. However, the lower voices show considerable melodic life and integrity;

EXAMPLE 10-1

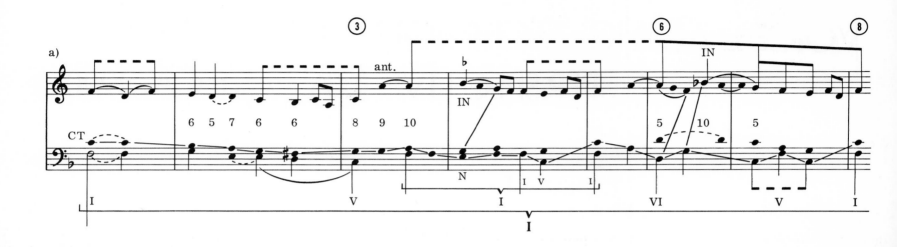

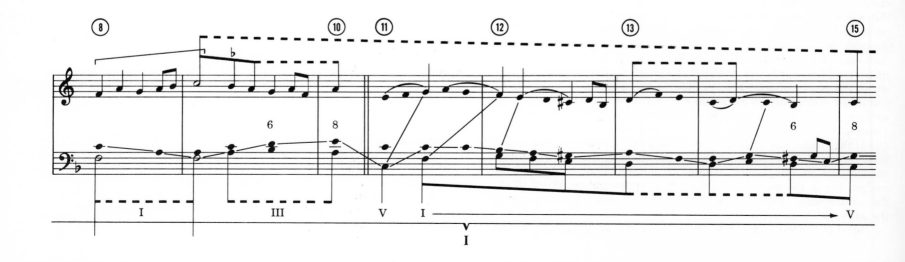

they participate actively in the voice leading. As a matter of fact the voice-leading bass is the result of the cooperation of contratenor and tenor. In the graph the tones of the contratenor are connected by beams.

Reference to the graphs will indicate that stable structural points mainly utilize the perfect consonances. However, the main body of the voice-leading texture makes characteristic and beautiful use of imperfect consonances, especially sixths. The treatment of dissonance is characterized by considerable subtlety and imagination. Particularly noteworthy are the rhythmic shifts, indicated in the graphs by diagonal lines between the voices. The reader should note the interesting effects caused by the anticipating or the delaying of tones. (Extensive use of displacement begins with the ars nova of the fourteenth century.)

Characteristic of Renaissance polyphony is the rhythmic control of dissonance; the reader will observe that dissonant tones are of short duration (in this piece the longest is the minim, here represented by the quarter note). In contrast to much sixteenth-century writing, dissonances sometimes appear on strong pulses. The exploitation of harmonic as well as contrapuntal relationships is quite obvious in this piece. Note, however, that the final cadence—in a manner typical of the early stages of harmonic influence—superimposes the V of the contratenor over the typical 6–8 contrapuntal cadence of tenor and superius.

EXAMPLE 10-1   (continued)

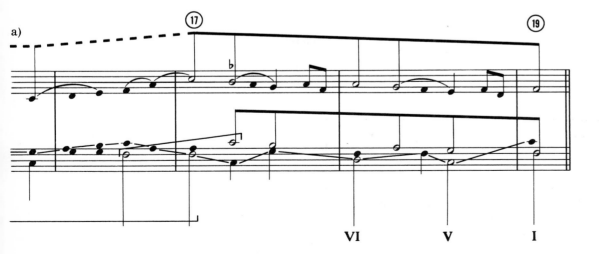

EXAMPLE 10-1   (continued)

c) Decorated cadences (see m. 2)

becomes   becomes

OCKEGHEM: SANCTUS FROM MISSA PROLATIONUM

The first section of the Sanctus from Ockeghem's *Missa Prolationum* (Example 10-2) bears the label *Fuga pausarum ascendendo per sextam*. The superius and tenor following the rests imitate canonically the contratenor and bass at the upper sixth. For an explanation of Ockeghem's ingenious use of the possibilities of the system of mensural notation, see Reese, *Music in the Renaissance*, pages 133-135.[1] Our present concern is rather with the manner in which the composer is able to achieve a fluent and coherent musical texture: so much so that the listener can derive satisfaction without even knowing that canonic imitation is taking place on so vast a scale.

The attentive reader will note that different structural meanings have been assigned to corresponding passages; indeed, one can state as a general rule in canonic and fugal compositions that transposed statements of a subject, or statements in new contrapuntal relationships, acquire a different musical meaning from the original one and must be heard and understood differently. A mechanistic "consistency" can contradict the entire artistic meaning of the composition. A case in point is the section beginning with measure 13; there two new counterpoints make their appearance in the contra and bass, while the superius and tenor present the canonic answer in the sixth to the previous two-part setting of contra and bass. Since the setting of the canonic answers appears now in conjunction with two other voices, the structural meaning of the original two-part setting appears drastically changed. Whereas, for instance, the tone E of the contra in measure 4 is clearly an embellishing tone, the corresponding tone C in measure 16, as preparation of the structural C of measure 19, is a tone of higher structural order. The different interpretation of voice leading is not only conditioned by the definite motion of the bass to C, but also by the following prolongation of the C sonority in measures 16 and 17 preparing the entrance of the structural tonic with C as top-voice tone (measures 16-19). In these changes of voice-leading interpretation the new bass is, of course, a major deciding factor. What functioned as bass in the first twelve

measures is now a middle voice; this has its bearing on the total voice leading. Nevertheless, the individuality of the single voice per se, the middle voice, is still able to express itself. Attention should also be given to the low A in the bass of measure 9 substituting for an expected F; this tone, in the canonic imitation (measure 21), becomes a structurally necessary F; measure 21, one of the culminating measures of the entire section, demands the tonic. The A of measure 9, though unexpected, serves a compositional purpose in that it helps prepare for the cadence in A, measures 12-13.

Careful study of the piece and graphs will reveal similar instances of mutual adaptation between parts and will indicate the amazing degree of mastery shown by the composer. In particular, note the evidence of large-scale planning. Whereas the tonic sonority is only hinted at within the introductory dominant (measures 1-4), it is clearly outlined from measures 4-7. From there on an arpeggio in the bass, F–A–C–F, gives Ockeghem the opportunity for fascinating tonal developments (see graph *b*). The progression from F to A, expressed as a downward sixth, is in itself prolonged by an internal arpeggio, F–C–A, whereby the prolongation of C foreshadows the important A by moving a sixth up to that tone. This gives the entire prolongation of C the effect of oscillating between these two sonorities. All doubts are removed when the four voices intone the A chord in measure 13. This completes the first segment of the large arpeggiation F–A–C–F. The motion from A to C is again prolonged by an internal arpeggiation: A–F (expressed as a sixth up) –C, measures 14-16. The dominant in measures 16-17 with C as top voice leads inexorably to the tonic of measure 19, which serves as conclusion of the arpeggiation that had begun in measure 4. The descending fifths in the superius of measures 22-23 are motions into the inner voice while C acts as the structurally retained tone. The final descent omits B flat and G, an allusion to the previous arpeggiated motions. Observe, however, the beautiful counterpoint in the tenor that in measures 21-25 imitates and elaborates the course of the top voice. It presents a stepwise descending fifth compensating for and, as it were, filling in the chord-outlining motion of the superius. In Renaissance polyphony more often than in later music, voices other than the highest characteristically participate in expressing the fundamental melodic structure (see also the preceding example).

---

[1] Gustave Reese, *Music in the Renaissance*, New York, W. W. Norton, 1954.

EXAMPLE 10-2

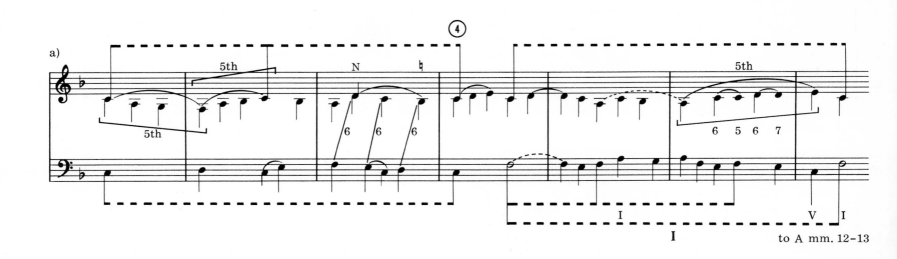

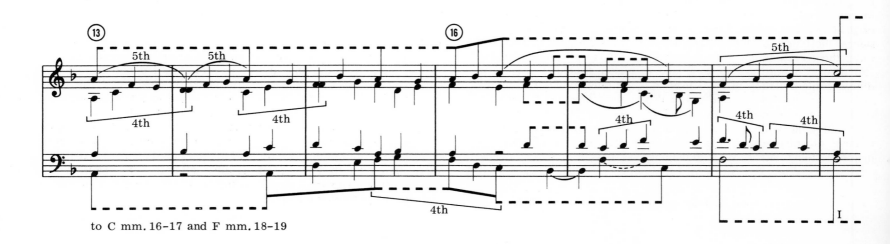

EXAMPLE 10-2 (continued)

EXAMPLE 10-2 (continued)

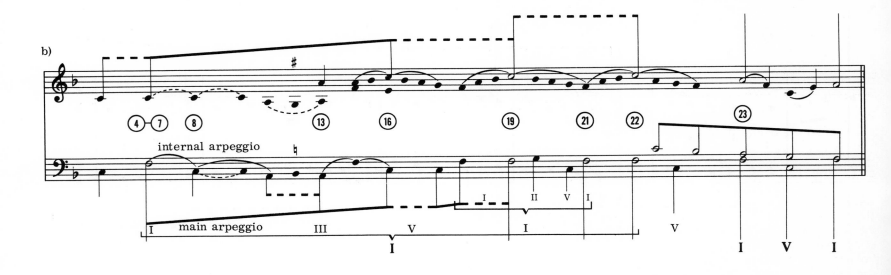

JOSQUIN: TU PAUPERUM REFUGIUM

Example 10-3 analyzes the second part of a motet generally ascribed to Josquin and certainly the work of a great master. This *secunda pars* forms a self-contained and intelligible whole and can be considered apart from the entire motet. It falls into two large sections, measures 1-33 and 34-69. Structural analysis reveals that the second section is an imaginative variation of the first. Each section divides into five phrases: measures 1-5 correspond to 34-37; 6-11 correspond to 38-46; 11-20 correspond to 46-56; 20-27 correspond to 56-60, and 27-33 correspond to 60-69. We present a foreground graph of the entire work and a middleground graph of the first section.

MEASURES 1-5 = 34-37

The relation between both phrases is obvious from the graphs and needs no further comment.

MEASURES 6-11 = 38-46

The main melodic event of measures 6-11, the progression G–C–B–A, is expanded in the variation from six to nine measures. Furthermore, an anticipation of $\frac{EM}{IV}$ takes place within the prolongation of the tonic with a descending fourth plus neighboring note in the top voice.

MEASURES 11-20 = 46-56

The melodic contents of measures 11-20 feature a descending sixth, C–E. The corresponding measures of the second section deal, of course, with the same progression, the descending sixth. In the first section the sixth is subdivided into a fourth and a third; the fourth, of course, derives from the top voice of measures 3-5. In the variation, Josquin dwells upon this motive of the fourth before presenting the descending sixth. Note, furthermore, that the sixth shows prolonging fourths in the course of its descent. Graph c presents a detailed explanation of the contents of measures 50-56. The progression shown is by now well known to the reader (see Chapter 7, pp. 195–197).

MEASURES 20-27 = 56-60

The jagged contours of the two-voice setting of measures 21-27, possibly an expression of the words "path for the erring" (*via errantium*), outline an ascending sixth followed by a descending fourth. This kind of setting would not have been appropriate for the intense plea of the final sentence of the text. Therefore the gradually ascending sixth is drastically shortened in the variation into a single skip, measures 56-57. The descending fourth, by contrast, is given a broad measured setting covering four bars.

MEASURES 27-33 = 60-69

If one compares the final measure-groups of each section, one realizes first that the composer makes a definite distinction between the two-voice setting of the first section, the "temporary" ending, and the full four-voice setting which brings the work in its entirety to a conclusion. The second section, as expression of the anxious: *Ne unquam obdormiat in morte anima mea,* introduces a new motive (measure 60) which is imitated first in the sixth and then (with changes) in the fourth, so that the top voice too brings the embellishing C. And, in another departure from the first ending, the superius is now the structural top voice, thus restoring the original register of the composition. In a short Coda the alto expressively reminisces on the opening neighboring motion B–C–B of the inner voice, using a motive repeated several times in the lowest part beginning in measure 44.

Most of the melodic ideas in this piece can be traced back to the first four measures. Note in particular the use of the embellishing figure G–C–B–A–G. The descending fourth that closes this figure permeates the entire piece, appearing in a variety of rhythmic and melodic configurations. Thus variation techniques underlie the treatment of the detail as well as the total design.

This piece is an outstanding example of the polyphonic use of the Phrygian mode. Because this mode contains a diminished fifth from B, it is incapable of generating a harmonic dominant unless F is raised to F sharp; this would, of course, remove the most characteristic feature of the mode. In both sections Josquin supports the structural top-voice tone F with D in the bass, thus generating a typical modal-contrapuntal progression I–$\frac{N}{VII}$–I. The frequent use of the subdominant is also characteristic of compositions in the Phrygian mode.

EXAMPLE 10-3

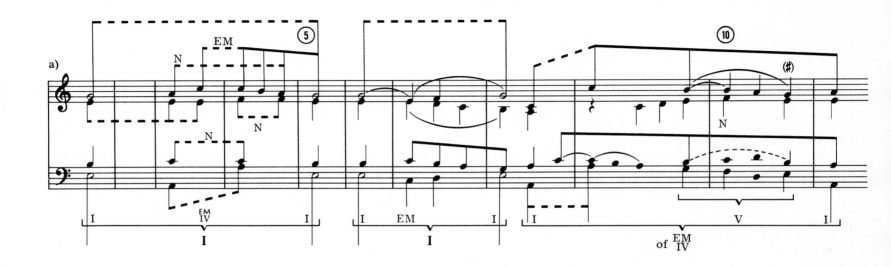

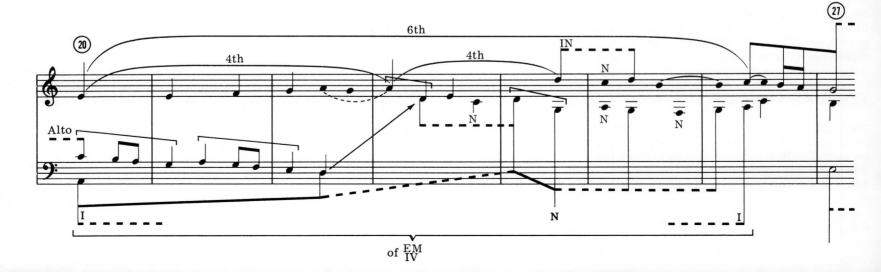

EXAMPLE 10-3 (continued)

EXAMPLE 10-3   (continued)

EXAMPLE 10-3 (continued)

EXAMPLE 10-3 (continued)

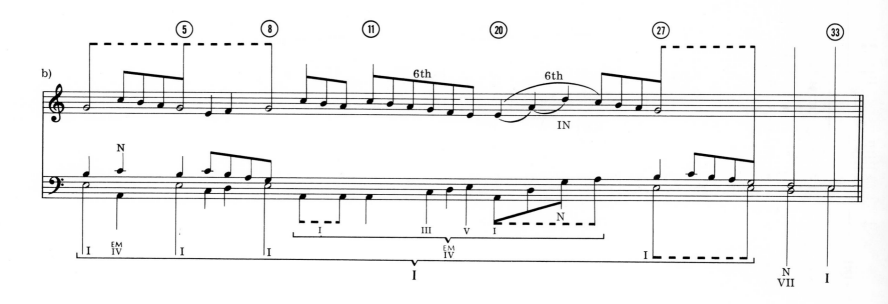

EXAMPLE 10-3 **(continued)**

c)

ISAAC: ASPERGES ME DOMINE FROM THE CHORALIS CONSTANTINUS

Compared with the density of texture of the Ockeghem example, this excerpt from the *Choralis Constantinus* of Heinrich Isaac (Example 10-4) shows a high degree of transparency and lightness. This work dates from the beginning of the sixteenth century and is typical of the period in its imitative setting. The total structure, however, shows features dating centuries back to the Middle Ages. We refer specifically to the top-voice structure of a descending fourth, D–C–B flat–A. This line arises out of the $\frac{8}{5}$ sonority, the basic chord form of the Middle Ages and the predecessor of the triad. This top-voice descent is counterpointed by a progression D–A–G–D in the bass. The consequent use of the dominant (as a minor chord) followed by a subdominant is characteristic of the modal era and is one of the many idiomatic progressions of modal-contrapuntal tonality. Because the principal function of these chords is to support the top-voice progression, we have employed the general term CS rather than EM or N which indicate specific contrapuntal functions.

The slurs and brackets in graph *a* point to the two main motivic features of the piece. Note how imitation, here as in other examples, is put to the service of chord prolongation and results in a terraced unfolding of the D minor tonic and its subsidiary G chord. Note the change of texture at the structurally important A-chord of measure 12 and the ensuing implication of triple rhythmic grouping.

EXAMPLE 10-4   Isaac, Choralis Constantinus, Asperges me Domine

A-sper-ges me

EXAMPLE 10-4 (continued)

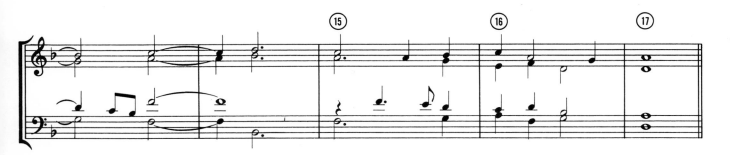

EXAMPLE 10-4   **(continued)**

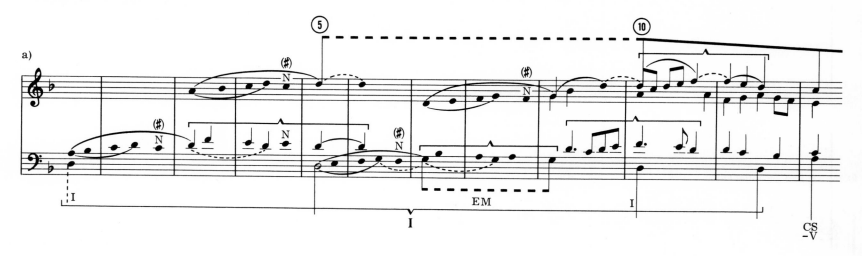

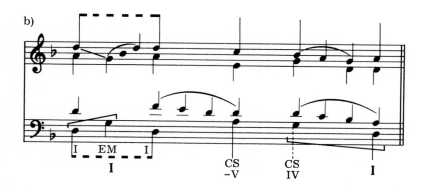

EXAMPLE 10-4 (continued)

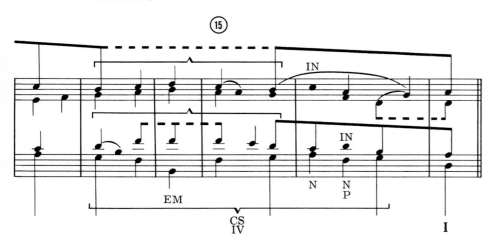

PALESTRINA: AGNUS I FROM MISSA VENI SPONSA CHRISTI

Palestrina's compositions are often held up as the epitome of contrapuntal writing. Without in any way disputing his mastery of counterpoint we bring an example that, like many others, demonstrates the impossibility of understanding this composer in purely contrapuntal terms (see Example 10-5).[2] For the piece as a whole is based on a large-scale harmonic framework, I–IV–V–I. Measures 14-31 are completely grounded in a long prolongation of IV; this is followed by a structural V of only one measure's duration. The consequent emphasis on the IV in this Mixolydian piece is characteristic of the modal concept of tonal organization.

The melodic materials derive from the plainchant antiphon that gives its name to the mass (*Liber Usualis,* page 1214). The graph indicates the free use of imitation; only the soprano brings the significant prolonging tone E flat of measure 5 (not appearing in the chant) which is later to play such an expressive role (measures 26-30). It is also the soprano which, in measures 8-12, anticipates the structural descending fifth of the piece as a whole. The alto and bass imitate the first four

measures of the soprano but, in contrast to the soprano, begin and end on the same tone. The tenor brings a fragment only and continues freely. The brackets in graph c point to the section of the melody used by all four voices. As in previous examples, imitative texture is used to prolong contrapuntally various sonorities. These sonorities unfold progressively rather than being stated at once. Note the thematic relation between the opening measures and the "*Miserere,*" measures 19ff.

The reader should observe the absence of strongly marked articulations. The first twelve measures contain not a single cadence; the movement to B flat in measure 14 is bridged over by the soprano entrance of measure 13 before the resolution of the 4-3 suspension and before the arrival of B flat in the bass.

As usual, graph a brings the detailed voice leading. It also presents incipits of the three principal melodic ideas as found in the chant. Brackets indicate complete or incomplete quotations of these ideas.

[2] In *Masterpieces of Music before 1750* this piece appears in F rather than the original G. To facilitate reference to the score, we follow the same procedure.

EXAMPLE 10-5

a)

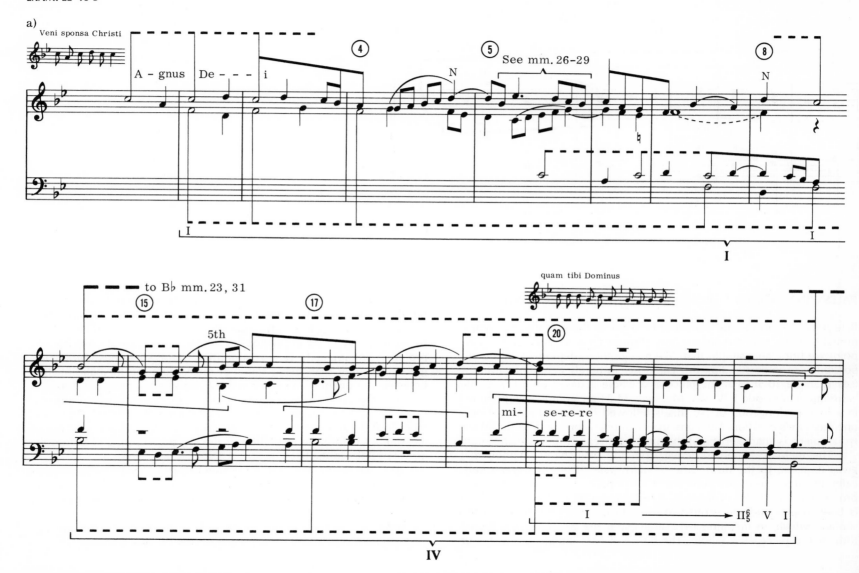

EXAMPLE 10-5 (continued)

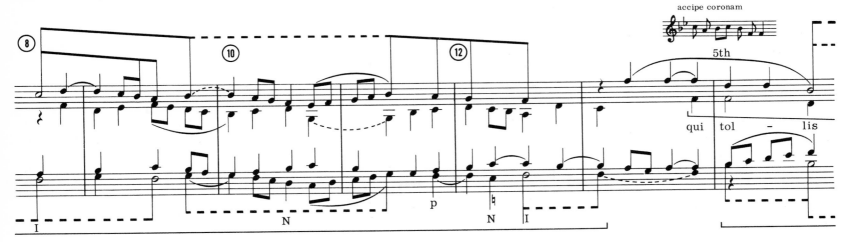

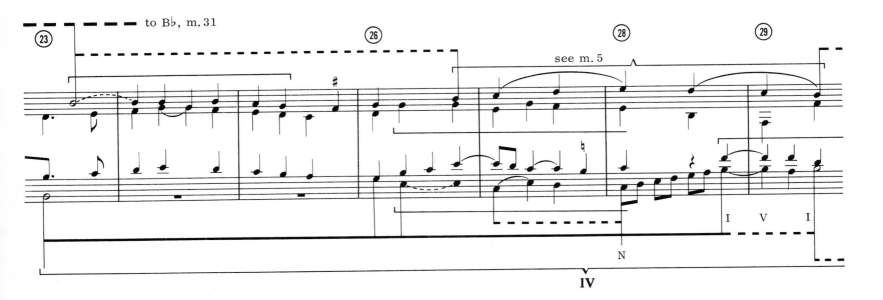

EXAMPLE 10-5   **(continued)**

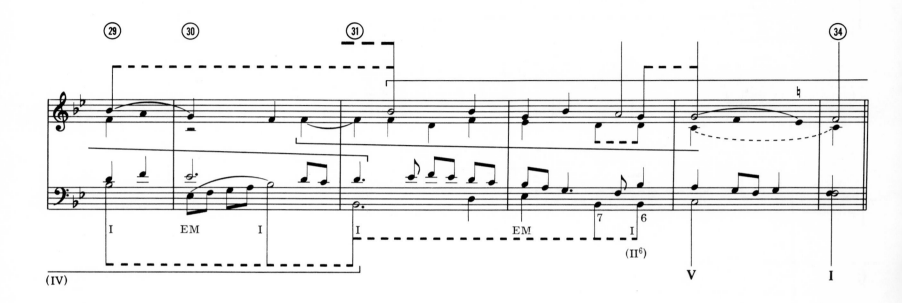

EXAMPLE 10-5 **(continued)**

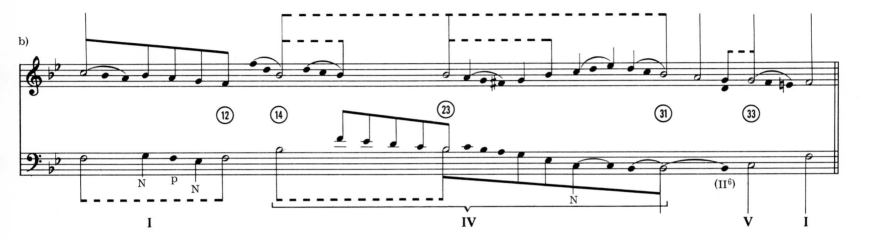

EXAMPLE 10-5   (continued)

c)

Soprano

This prolongation
in Soprano only

Alto

Tenor

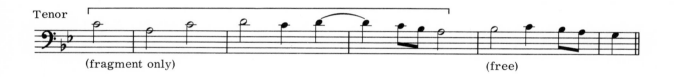

(fragment only)   (free)

Bass

VICTORIA: O VOS OMNES

This magnificent setting of the words of Jeremiah (Lamentations 1:12) appeared in 1572 (see Example 10-6).

A   O vos omnes
      qui transitis per viam } subsection *a* (measures 1-16)
      attendite, et videte

      si est dolor similis } subsection *b* (measures 17-33)
      sicut dolor meus

B   Attendite universi populi } subsection *c* (measures 34-51)
      et videte dolorem meum

      si est dolor similis { subsection *b'* (measures 52-68)
      sicut dolor meus

As the above chart indicates, this work falls into two main sections each of which is in turn divided into two subsections. Subsections *b* and *b'* have essentially the same music and are set, to the same words.

Reference to the graphs will reveal the strongly linear character of the voice leading. The leading melodic idea is first contributed by the tenor; not only does the tenor begin the composition, but its line has the greatest rhythmic and melodic profile. Note that the tenor melody is taken over, in varied form but with the characteristic leap to the structural F, in the soprano of measures 34ff. just at the beginning of the second form section. This new presentation of the initial tenor idea in the highest possible register forms the climax of the composition, motivates the ensuing structural descent, and is made to coincide with the climactic words, *Attendite universi populi*, etc. Whereas both subsections of the first part end on the V, the corresponding subsections of the second part end on the I. The first subsection of the second part brings the structural ending of the piece; what follows is a repetition with altered ending of measures 17-33. Note the changed meaning and expressive quality of this subsection when it returns after the outcry of the soprano and the structural descent in high register. The process of listening is now different, and even the same tones show a changed function since the main story has already been told. The effect of measures 52-68, therefore, is like that of a Coda. We have included these measures in graph *b* only.

EXAMPLE 10-6

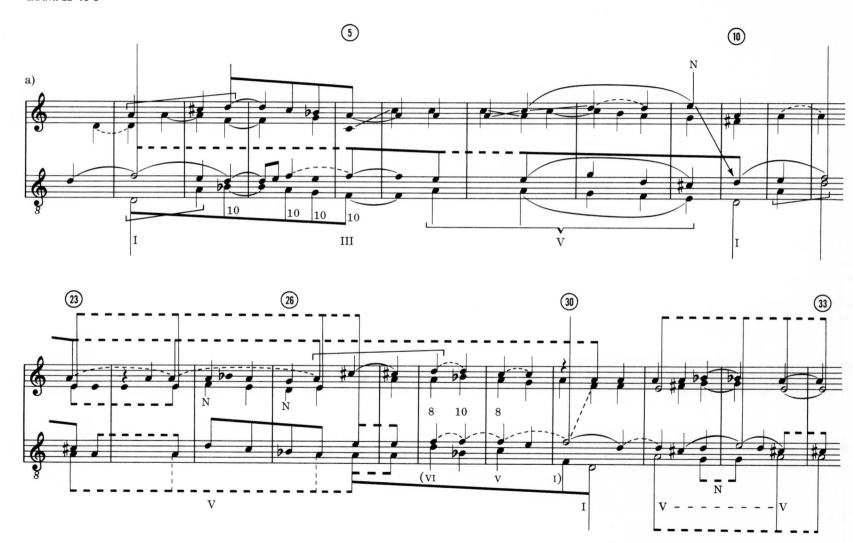

EXAMPLE 10-6 (continued)

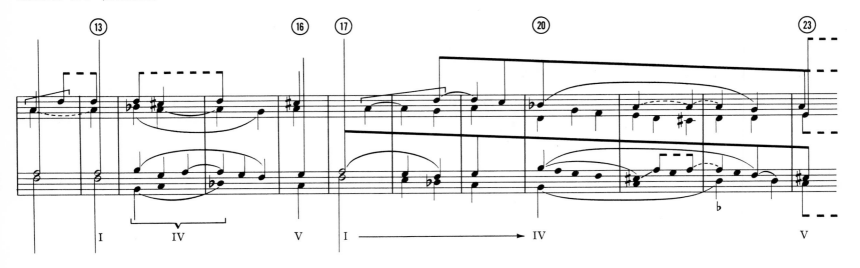

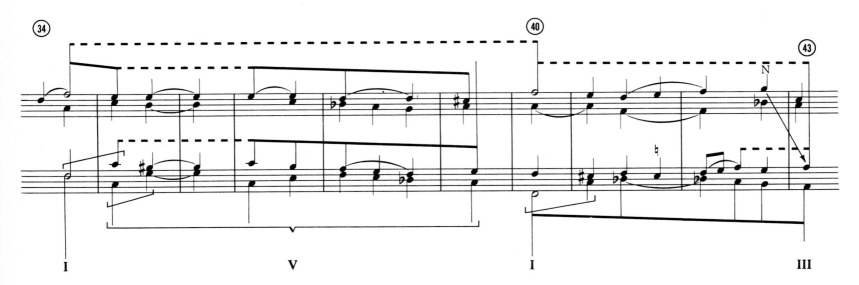

EXAMPLE 10-6   (continued)

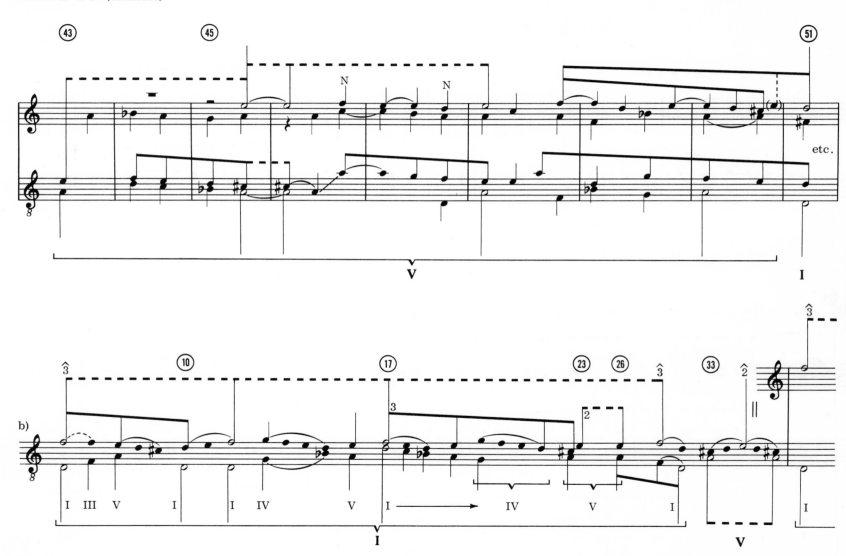

EXAMPLE 10-6 (continued)

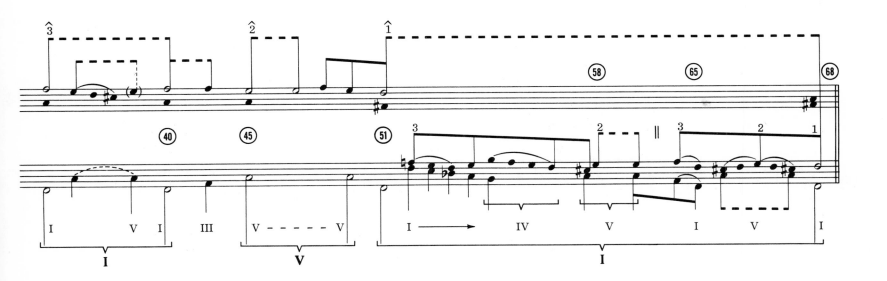

EXAMPLE 10-6   (continued)

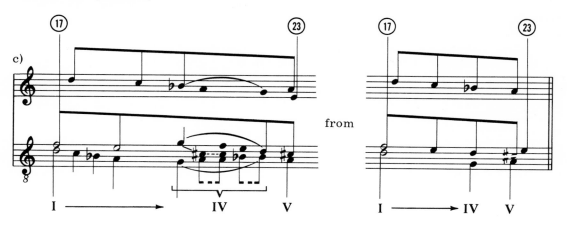

from

EXAMPLE 10-7

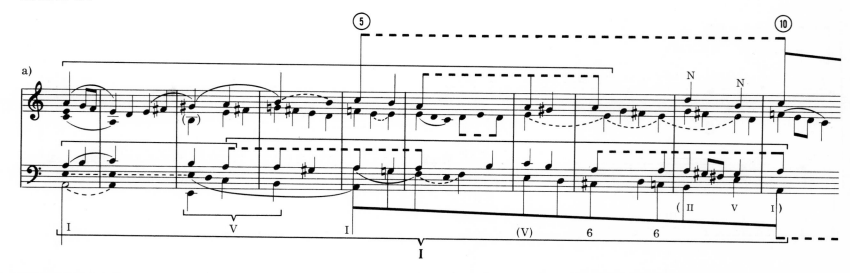

GIBBONS: PAVANE LORD SALISBURY

The three sections of this work (see Example 10-7) may seem at first hearing rather disconnected. They are, however, remarkably well co-ordinated, and the reader is advised to concentrate first on graph *b*, which will provide general orientation. The first section prolongs the I with a top-voice motion from A to C and back to A. The second section drives the top voice up to E, measure 23 (which will later act as structural tone). This E acts as an embellishing tone between two C's supported by a prolonging dominant. The third section—after the C major embellishing chord—again moves to E over V in measure 40 and, as remarkable parallelism to the second section, repeats in varied form the descending sixth, E–G sharp. But then in a rapid ascent E is reached for the third time; now, however, over the I (measure 48), and from here the structural progression takes its course, following a prolongation of V which brings the E down an octave (see graph *a*).

The structural progression shows an amazing distribution of voices. If we compare Gibbons' setting with the end of graph *a*, we shall realize that the graph shows the "normal" arrangement of the voices, which would have Gibbons' tenor act as top voice and the actual top voice as tenor, ending on C sharp. An exchange of voices takes place (measure 53) which veils the structural descent underlying these measures, and allows the major third to appear in a prominent way.

The entire piece is thus characterized by a very gradual ascent to the structural E (measure 48); the first two sections deal with and prepare important items of this ascent and the tonal structure as a whole. Much of the inner tension is created through the fact that the top-voice C, reached and structurally retained from measures 5-10, is taken up again and continued to E in measures 47-48. Once one has grasped this "interruption" of the ascent to the structural tone E (A B C C D E), the intervening processes within the prolonged V receive additional meaning with their preparatory, tension-creating, and, at the same time, delaying activities.

In studying graph *a* one should realize the pervasive use of imitation in the musical foreground. The various brackets give a clear indication of this technique.

Gibbons is also a master of motion intensification by means of intervals made successively larger. This can be observed especially in the beginning of sections 2 and 3, see graph *c*.

EXAMPLE 10-7 (continued)

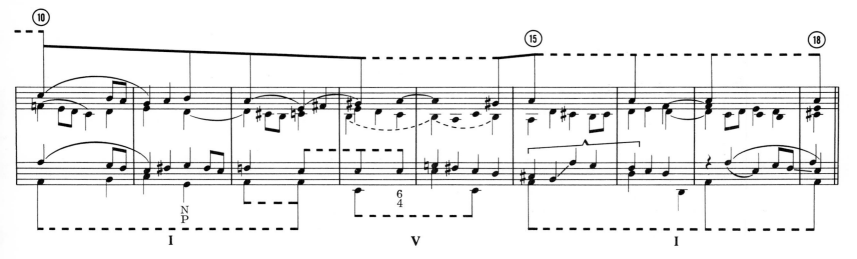

EXAMPLE 10-7   **(continued)**

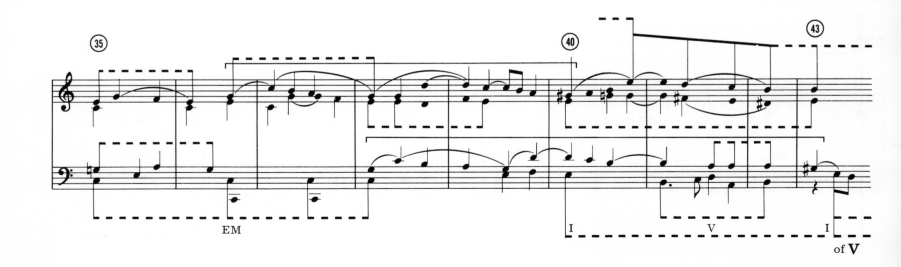

EXAMPLE 10-7 (continued)

EXAMPLE 10-7 (continued)

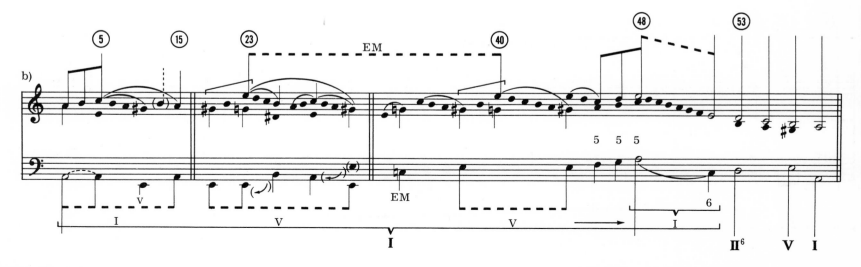

EXAMPLE 10-7 **(continued)**

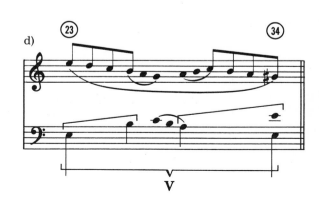

PURCELL: DIDO'S LAMENT

Dido's Lament (see Example 10-8), like several other numbers from *Dido and Aeneas,* uses Purcell's favored ground-bass procedure. The Lament is preceded by a recitative which anticipates the chromatic descent of the repeated bass. The bass progression spans five measures, beginning with an upbeat and ending with a downbeat. In order to prevent an overly segmented design Purcell has the upper voices bypass the articulations of the bass at a number of points. See in particular measure 13, where the vocal line comes to a phrase ending in the middle of the bass progression. The top-voice descent from D is anticipated by the second-violin line that begins in measure 5, thus creating yet another overlap. Pay particular attention to the orchestral postlude in which the bass descent is imitated in the upper voices leading to a climactic statement in the first violins, beginning on high G (measure 38). The motions to and from the High G were foreshadowed in the vocal part, measures 31–33.

EXAMPLE 10-8

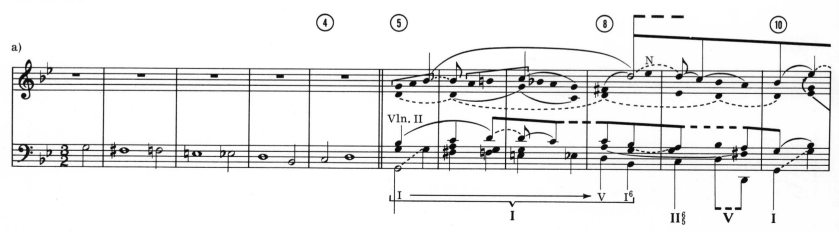

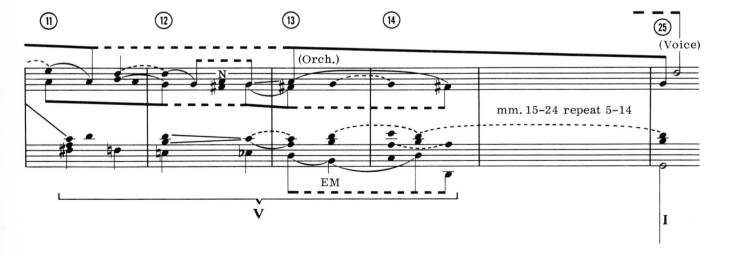

EXAMPLE 10-8   (continued)

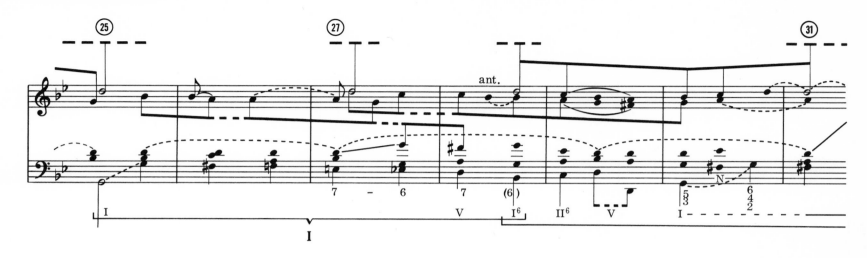

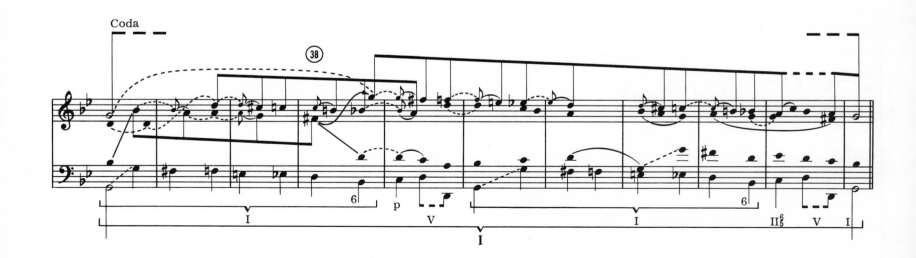

EXAMPLE 10-8 **(continued)**

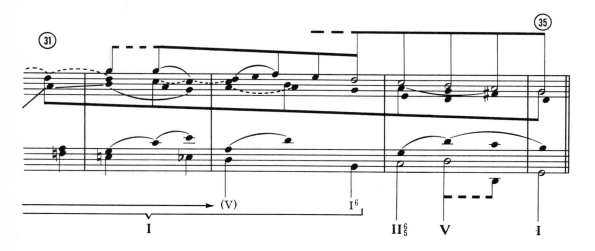

BACH: TWO FRAGMENTS FROM WORKS FOR SOLO VIOLIN AND CELLO

To supplement our earlier examples by J. S. Bach let us turn to two fragments from his works for solo violin and cello (Examples 10-9 and 10-10). To understand these compositions we must be able to hear the contrapuntal background which in the foreground is dissolved into the most imaginative and complex horizontal configurations. It is no easy task to discover the vertical implications behind the seemingly pure horizontality of this style.

EXAMPLE 10-9   Bach, Partita for Violin No. 1, Double of Courante

EXAMPLE 10-9 (continued)

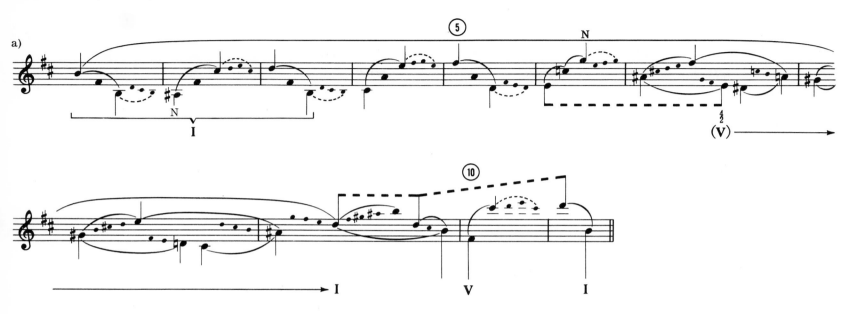

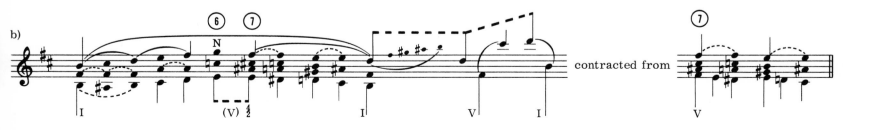

contracted from

EXAMPLE 10-10   Bach, Suite for Cello No. 3, Prelude

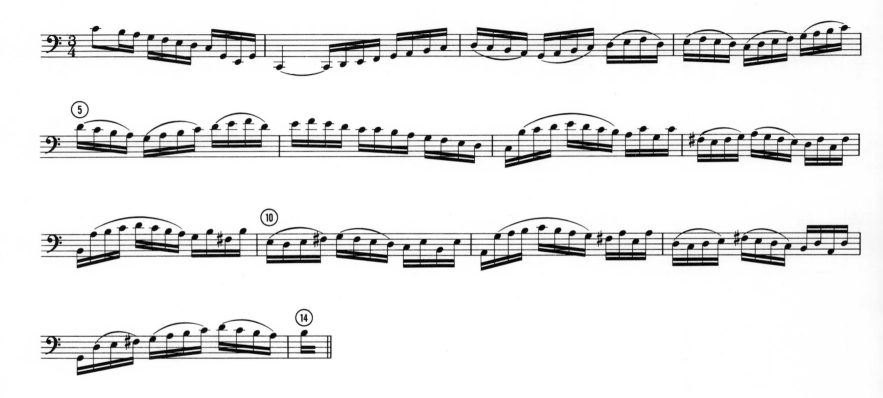

EXAMPLE 10-10 (continued)

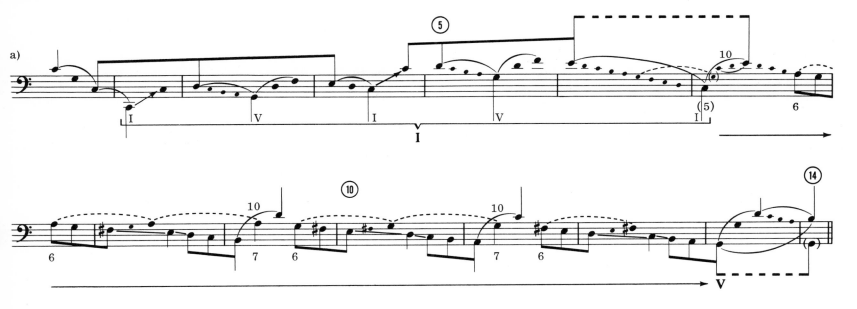

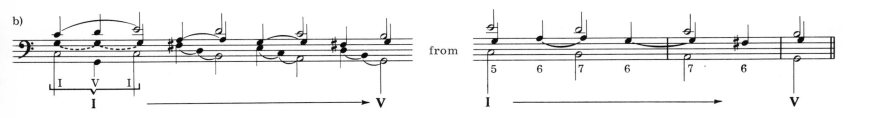

BEETHOVEN: PIANO SONATA, OP. 14, NO. 1; DEVELOPMENT OF FIRST MOVEMENT

The analysis of development sections frequently makes great demands on the musicianship and insight of the analyst. Owing to their transitional nature, development sections must be approached within the context of the totality. The reader is therefore urged to study the entire movement from which the excerpt in Example 10-11 is taken. The very opening of this development offers a problem in hearing. The composer "feigns" a return to the opening measures. However the E-chord turns out to be an applied dominant to the A minor $\frac{6}{3}$ chord of measure 65, which in turn forms part of a large-scale passing motion originating in the B major harmony that closes the exposition. This passing motion ascends to the G of measures 73-74, the applied dominant to the neighboring chord C. The C chord is the goal of the entire previous motion and the structural fulcrum of the development section. This development, like many others, is essentially a prolongation of the dominant through a neighboring motion. Note the pervasive use of the neighboring motion B–C natural–B in various strata of the texture: in bass, top voice, and middle voice. The detailed graphs of measures 61-65 offer a concentrated study of contrapuntal prolongation in its step-by-step evolution.

EXAMPLE 10-11

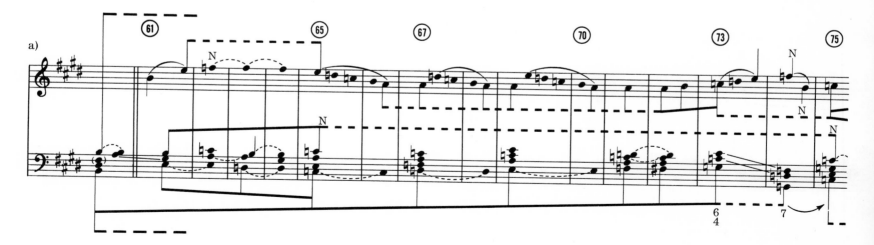

EXAMPLE 10-11 (continued)

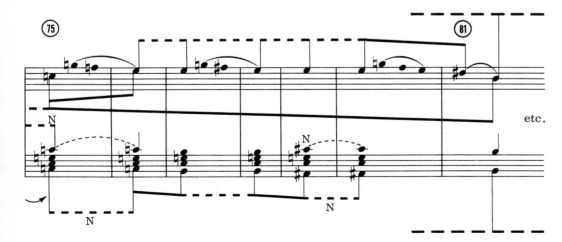

EXAMPLE 10-11 **(continued)**

b)

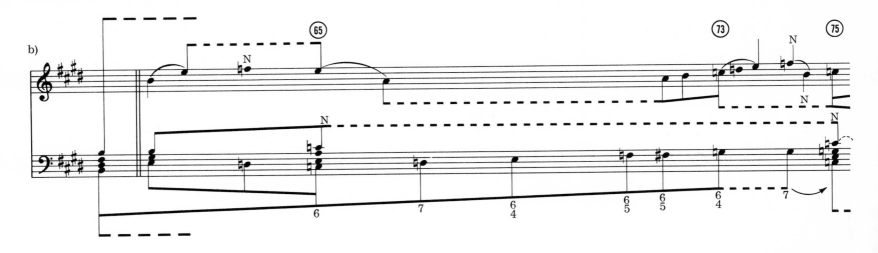

c)

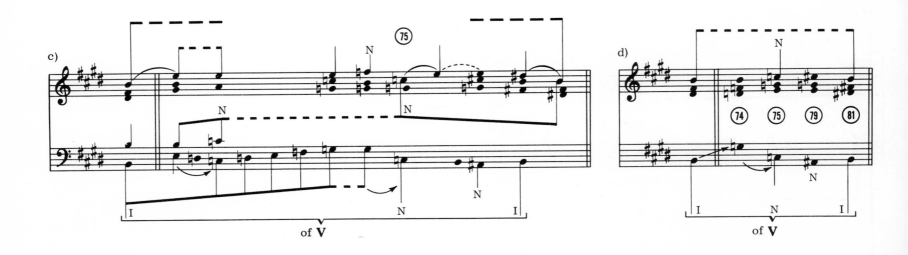

EXAMPLE 10-11 (continued)

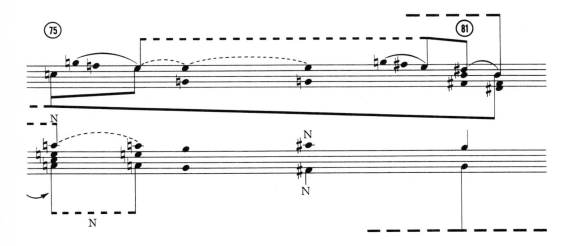

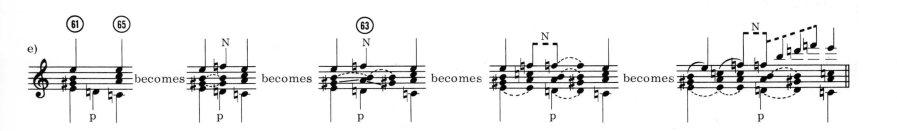

SCHUBERT: PIANO SONATA IN D MAJOR: TRIO OF THE SCHERZO

The outstanding feature of this trio, Example 10-12, is the wide frame of reference determined by basic contrapuntal techniques: the passing motion and the neighboring tone. In the first section Schubert reaches the interrupting dominant (divider), which he prolongs harmonically and contrapuntally (note the beautiful chromatic neighboring chord of measures 131–132) until the double bar. The section after the double bar is subdivided into two segments in the manner characteristic of the rounded binary construction. The first of these segments is transitional: the bass shows (in its last analysis) a passing motion from V down to I. The most significant feature of this passing motion is the bold prolongation of the passing tone C. As the graph indicates, C is fundamentally prolonged by its lower neighbor, B. Schubert reaches this B by two descending fifths, the first diminished and subdivided into two minor

thirds: C–E flat–G flat. The bass tone C supports an E in the top voice. When the C is regained in measure 153, the top voice begins a descent from E to A. This A is retained from measure 127. Because of the C in the bass the end of the widely prolonged interrupting dominant is on a $\frac{4}{2}$ chord rather than the usual root position. Schubert resolves the dissonant bass tone by the usual stepwise descent; highly unusual, however, is the choice of a B major chord (instead of a tonic $\frac{6}{3}$) at the beginning of the A' section.

The reader will note the parallel fifths between the C, E flat, and G flat chords of measures 140-145. These fifths, of course, are products of prolongation and do not affect the basic voice leading.

EXAMPLE 10-12

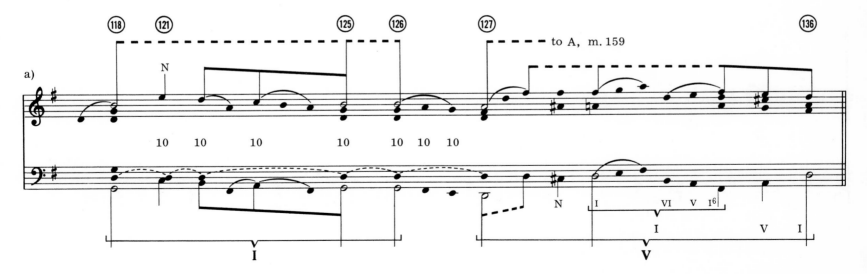

EXAMPLE 10-12   (continued)

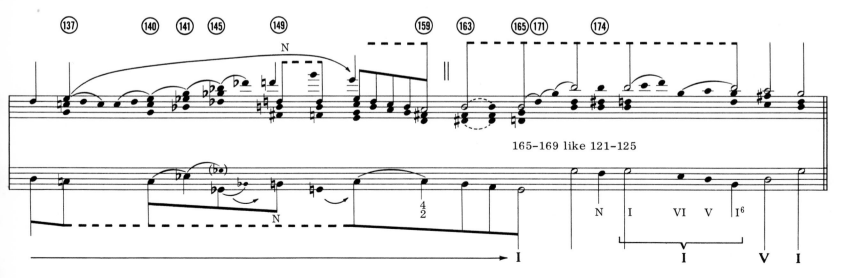

EXAMPLE 10-12   (continued)

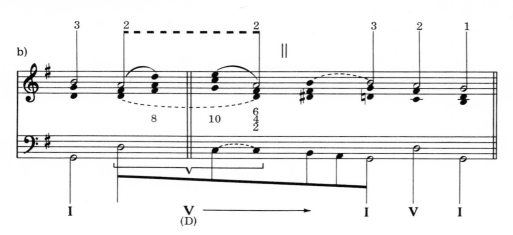

CHOPIN: WALTZ, OP. 64, NO. 2; MEASURES 65-81

In regard to Example 10-13, the reader should first concentrate on the basic direction of the bass voice. By this time he should have no difficulty in recognizing the passing motion from the initial tonic to the dominant, which is arrived at in measure 78. At first hearing the top voice seems to consist of an undulating series of upward and downward motions; out of these motions a group of three tones, F–G flat–A flat, clearly emerges as the primary melodic direction up to measure 73; these tones are supported by the ascending bass in a series of consecutive tenths. After measure 73 the bass continues to rise while the top voice "marks time" by executing a most expressive melodic prolongation of the tone A flat. In a structural sense the A flat is a retained tone,

and the voice leading is the elaboration of the oblique motion familiar to us from species counterpoint (first see graphs c and d). The 5-6 progression between bass and tenor and the register transfers of the top voice emerge clearly from graphs a and b. As counterpoint to the transfers of register, tenor and bass play a quasi-imitative "duet" arising out of the alternating chromatic passing tones of both voices (see graph a). A more hidden parallelism is revealed in graph d; after measure 73 the bass ascends the same third, chromatically elaborated, that the top voice had done from measure 65 to measure 73; we are confronted with imitation on an intermediate structural level. Finally we call attention to graph e which indicates the beautiful rhythmic and melodic manipulations used by Chopin to add impetus to the sequence of the top voice. Note the relationship to the opening melodic idea of the Waltz.

EXAMPLE 10-13

a)

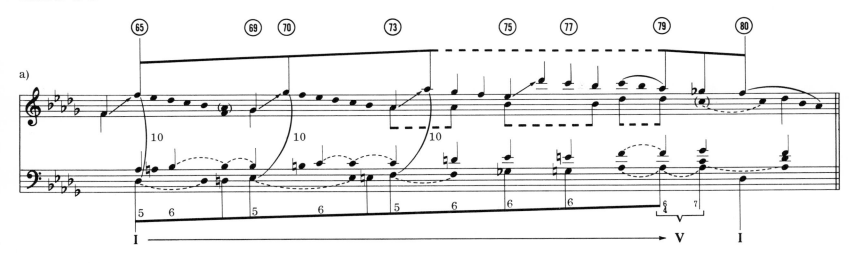

b)

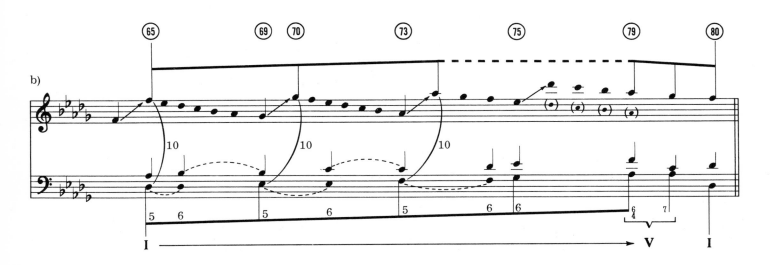

EXAMPLE 10-13 **(continued)**

CHOPIN: PIANO SONATA, OP. 35;
DEVELOPMENT OF FIRST MOVEMENT,
MEASURES 137-161

The passage analyzed in Example 10-14 forms the climax of the development section of the first movement of Chopin's second Piano Sonata.

The bass descends from B flat (supporting a G minor sixth chord) to E flat before turning to the structural V of measure 161. This passing motion supports an elaborate series of 6-5 suspensions which are chromaticized in a non-sequential manner; each pair of chords is unique. Note that the goal dominant is reached only in measure 161. The F major chord of measure 151 forms part of the 6-5 series.

EXAMPLE 10-14

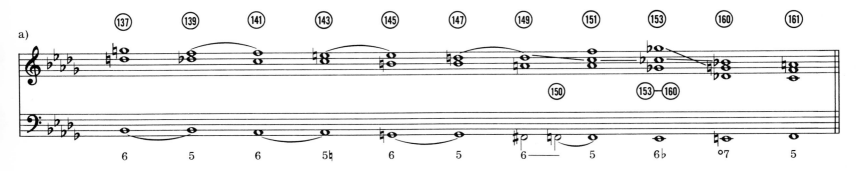

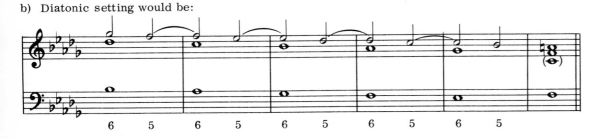

b) Diatonic setting would be:

WAGNER: TRISTAN UND ISOLDE, INTRODUCTION TO ACT III

This excerpt (see Example 10-15) illustrates the chromaticization of a syncopation series, in this case of 7-6 suspensions. The governing sonority is the V of F minor; within this chord the bass effects a stepwise descent from C to E natural (the C in measure 15 results from the entrance of a new voice part, given to the violas in the orchestral setting). The top voice decorates the suspension series; graph a reduces the melodic figuration to show the essential progression. The enharmonic notation (using sharps instead of flats) of measures 13-14 serves

for ease in reading; it has no further musical significance. In graph a, therefore, the "correct" notation has been restored in order to clarify the meaning of the voice leading. This is shown to consist of a 7-6 series with chromatically inflected bass and chromatically lowered top voice. Graph b shows the diatonic bass that underlies and controls the chromatic progression; graph c shows the top voice as it would be without the chromatic lowering. A "harmonic" analysis of this passage—that is, one that attempts to label each chord according to root function—would be meaningless.

EXAMPLE 10-15   Wagner, Tristan und Isolde, Act III, Introduction

(Mässig langsam)

EXAMPLE 10-15 (continued)

a)

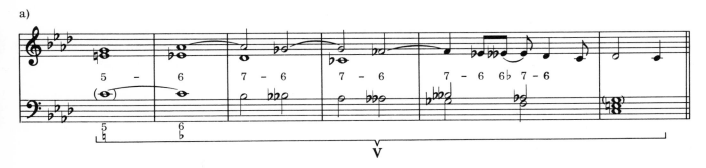

b)

c)

WAGNER: TRISTAN, ACT III, SCENE I (DURCH ABENDWEHEN)

Example 10-16 represents a kind of fantasy on the unaccompanied English horn solo from the beginning of the act; much of that solo is reproduced unaltered (or slightly altered rhythmically) in the accompanying parts. The orchestral top voice (sometimes played by the off-stage English horn) is a polyphonic melody; as indicated by graph *a*, the upper stratum of the polyphonic line leads. Against this line the bass moves in tenths, somewhat disguised through rhythmic displace-

ment. This displacement gives the foreground effect of 9-10 syncopations with the top voice (graph *a*); but the guiding and controlling voice leading consists of a 7-6 series disguised through chromatic alteration and displacement (graph *b*). The harmonic framework, in relation to larger context, is a progression $I–II^{6b}–V^{5b}$ within C minor functioning as the V of F minor, The use of a V with lowered fifth results from the frequent and characteristic diminished fifths of the English horn solo.

EXAMPLE 10-16   Wagner, Tristan und Isolde, Act III, Scene 1

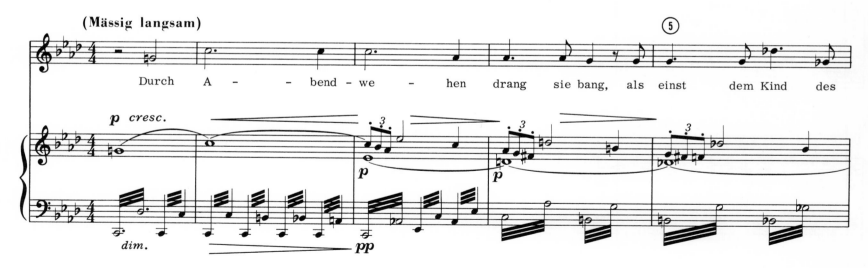

EXAMPLE 10-16   (continued)

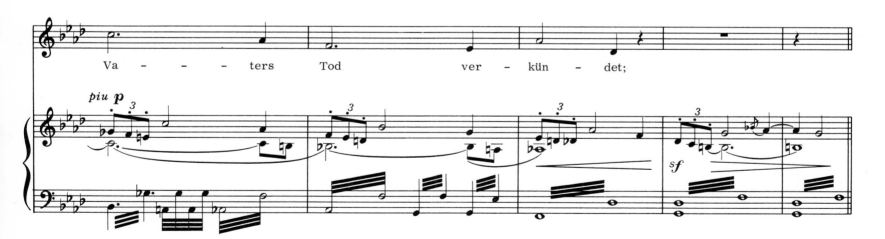

EXAMPLE 10-16 (continued)

a)

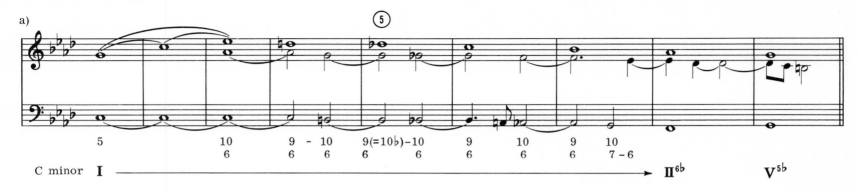

b)

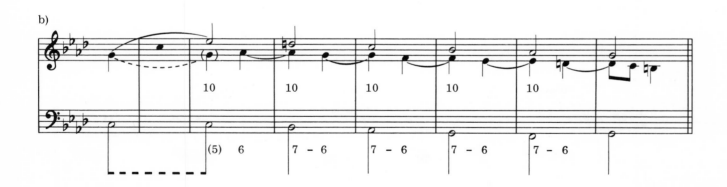

WAGNER: TRISTAN, ACT II, SCENE II

Our final excerpt from *Tristan* (see Example 10-17) is drawn from the great love duet of the second act. Like the other two Wagner examples this one is based on a chromatically manipulated suspension series. For purposes of orientation, concentrate first on graph *b*. The reader will note that this example, like the Chopin Waltz, is based on a 5-6 progression. Unlike the Chopin excerpt, the Wagner builds a 5-6 succession on every tone of the chromatic ascent up to measure 17. Chromaticism, therefore, is more deeply embedded in the compositional fabric than is the case in the Chopin excerpt. Note that the 5-6 progression, initiated in the vocal and orchestral top voice, finds its continuation beginning in measure 13 in the middle-voice region (violas, second group

of *divisi*). Note the indications of superposition in graph *b*, upper staff, measure 13ff. These result from voice crossings within the divided violas.

Graph *a* indicates more of the complex contrapuntal detail. In this excerpt almost all the sonorities stem from voice-leading; the only harmonic implications arise from the applied dominants derived from the sixths of the 5-6 progression. Note the rhythmic acceleration of the passage as a whole. The first two 5-6 successions are embodied in two phrases of six measures each. With measure 13 the 5-6's are compressed into three two-measure groups. Viewed as a whole the bass motion should be heard and understood as an ascent to E flat as a middle-voice tone of a vastly prolonged A flat tonic sonority.

EXAMPLE 10-17 Wagner, Tristan und Isolde, Act II, Scene 2

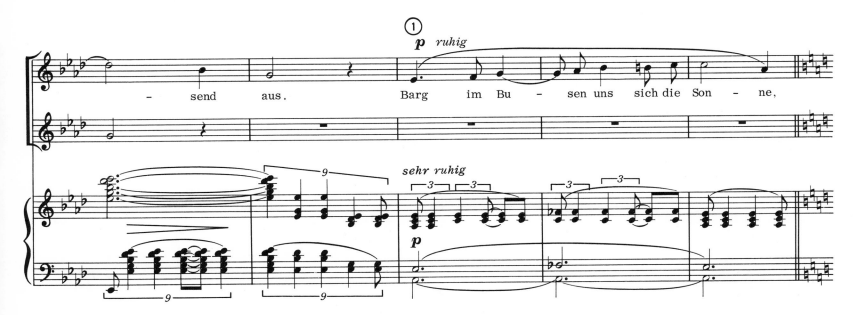

EXAMPLE 10-17 (continued)

leuch-ten la - chend Ster-ne der Won - ne.

Von dei - nem Zau - ber sanft um-spon - nen, vor

immer p

dei - nen Au - gen süss zer-ron - nen,

Herz an Herz dir, Mund an

EXAMPLE 10-17   (continued)

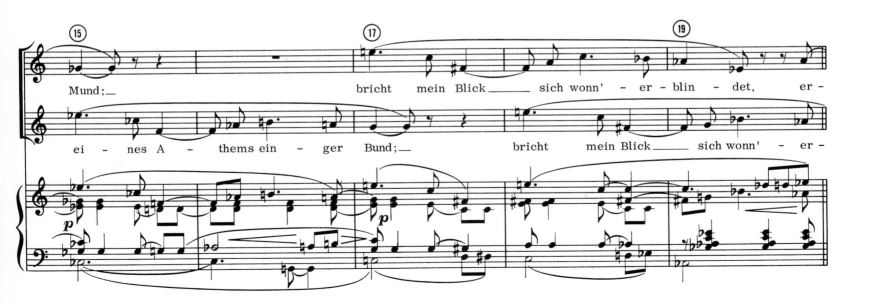

EXAMPLE 10-17   **(continued)**

a)

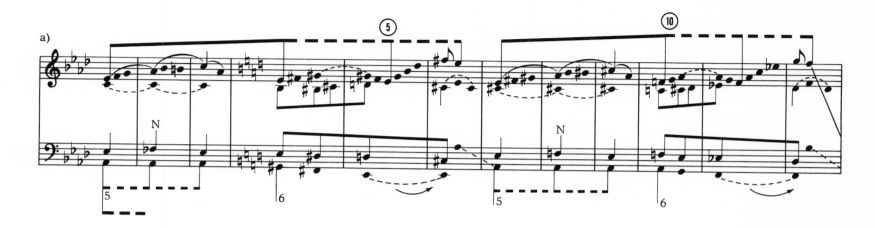

b)

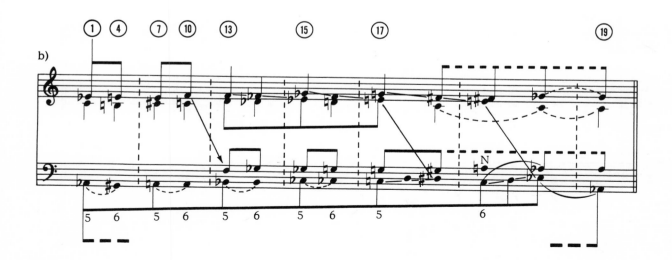

EXAMPLE 10-17 **(continued)**

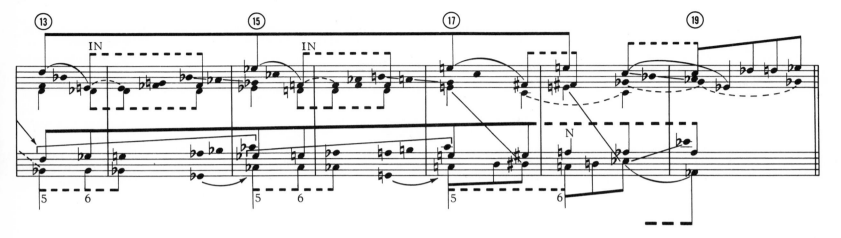

BRAHMS: INTERMEZZO, OP. 76, NO. 4

Unlike most compositions, which begin with a tonic or a short harmonic prolongation leading to a I, this intermezzo opens with a most extended prolongation of V (Example 10–18). The tonic chord appears only in the last 11 measures. The basic harmonic framework, therefore, is an incomplete progression V–I; the greater part of the piece is taken up with the contrapuntal prolongation of the V. The V is prolonged by a neighboring G minor chord (end of the first section), moving through a chromatic passing chord (just before the double bar), on G flat, This G flat supports a $\frac{6}{3}$ with E flat as top-voice tone. In measure 21 the E flat (inner voice) is displaced by its upper neighbor, F flat. However, E flat returns (measure 31) to prepare the seventh over the V of measure 32.

Pedal points in the inner voice play an important role in this piece. Note the extended pedals on E flat (measures 1-11), F flat (measures 21-28), and E flat (measures 31-42).

The end of the piece shows a descent of the top-voice seventh, E flat, to D; superimposed above this is a second neighboring note motion G flat–F as an echo and summary in the soprano of the significant bass motion G flat–F.

The V^7 at the beginning clearly tends toward B flat. The expected tonic, however, is delayed by means of the masterful contrapuntal progressions within the V; by these means Brahms achieves a fascinating suspense. The basic framework, of course, is harmonic, and there is a brief harmonic prolongation of the G-minor chord. However, the entire compositional fabric with its neighbors, passing motions, and suspensions is overwhelmingly contrapuntal. Even the progression from V to I is filled in by a chromatic passing motion.

EXAMPLE 10-18

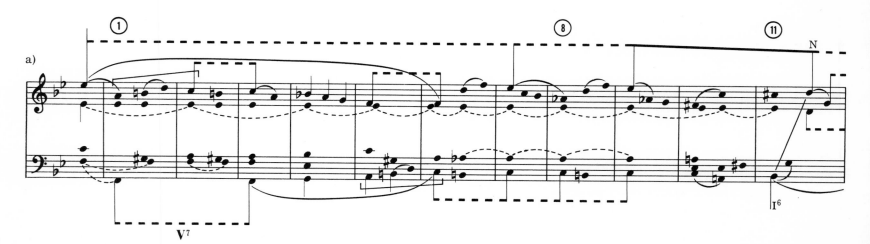

EXAMPLE 10-18 (continued)

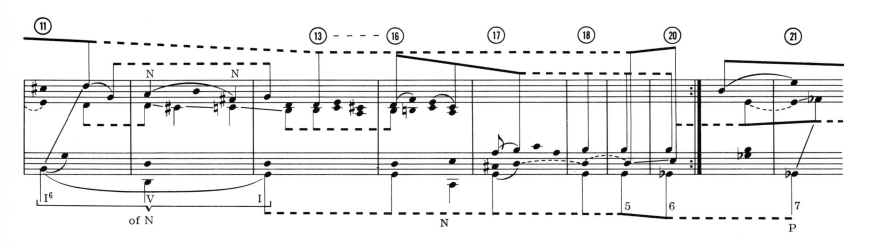

EXAMPLE 10-18   (continued)

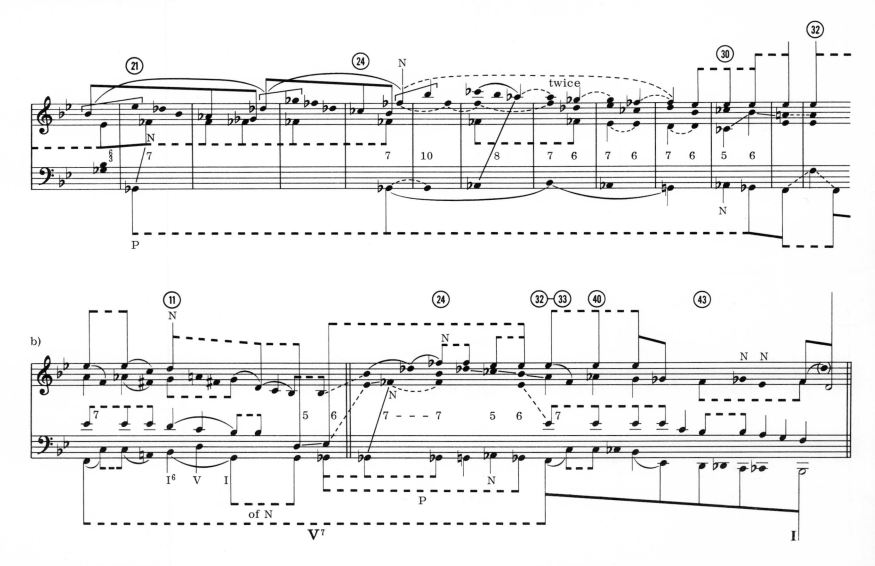

EXAMPLE 10-18   (continued)

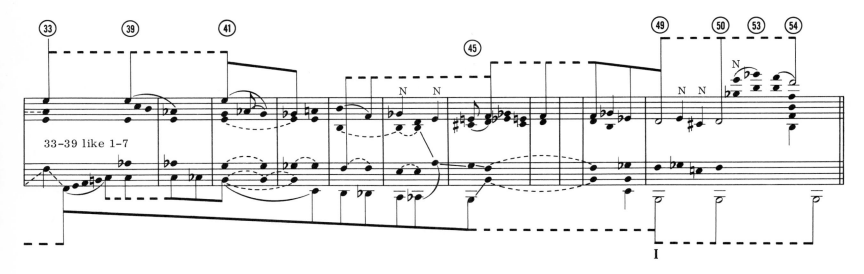

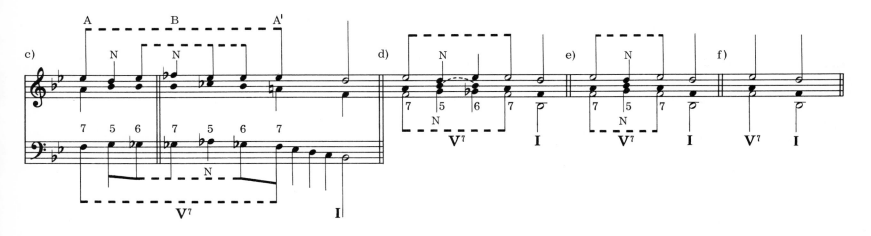

FAURÉ: APRÈS UN RÊVE

Unlike most other citations in this book, the Fauré excerpt (see Example 10-19) is presented from the voice-leading background to the compositional foreground. Graph a indicates the basic setting in tenths between the outer voices. This series is enriched (graph b) through suspensions in the middle voice. The contrapuntal suspension chain is prolonged through the activity of descending fifths in the bass (graph c) which add momentary harmonic impetus to this basically contrapuntal progression. The use of descending fifths in connection with 7-6 suspensions is characteristic of compositions in many styles from the seventeenth century on. The melodic structural tone D, from which the top voice takes its point of departure, is postponed so that D coincides not with its "original" bass, B, but with E, the prolonging fifth. This is shown in graph d together with the chromatic decoration of the soprano and alto lines. Graph e indicates the motivic descending fourths of the melody, and graph f completes the inner-voice detail that adds to the richness of sonority and disguises but does not fundamentally change the guiding 7-6 suspension series.

EXAMPLE 10-19

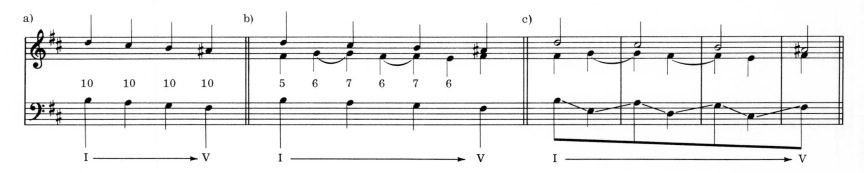

EXAMPLE 10-19 **(continued)**

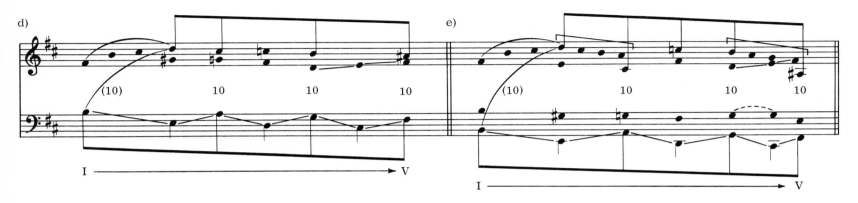

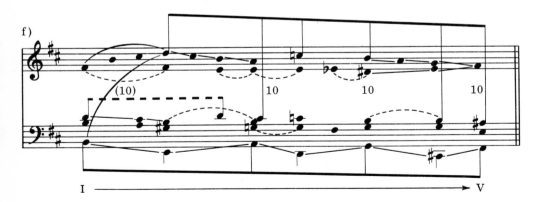

SCRIABIN: PRELUDE, OP. 39, NO. 2

This piece by Scriabin (Example 10-20) has been chosen to illustrate techniques of voice leading much utilized by twentieth-century composers but dating back at least as far as the Baroque period (see Example 7-44 by Heinichen). The piece unfolds within the framework of an incomplete progression IV–V–I of D major. The V is immediately preceded by a Phrygian II, a chord of harmonic emphasis. The progression of measures 2-3, with its bass motion G–E flat–A, foreshadows the

structural path of the bass up to the final tonic. The main prolongational events take place between the IV and the Phrygian II. This motion, in essence, consists of a series of chromatic parallel tenths between outer voices. Scriabin transfers the chromatic lines between soprano and bass so that the large continuities must be heard across the voices and through the apparent interruptions of the half-note chords. The use of leading-tone chords and of enharmonic exchange requires no comment.

EXAMPLE 10-20   Scriabin, Prelude, Op. 39, No. 2

EXAMPLE 10-20   (continued)

EXAMPLE 10-20   (continued)

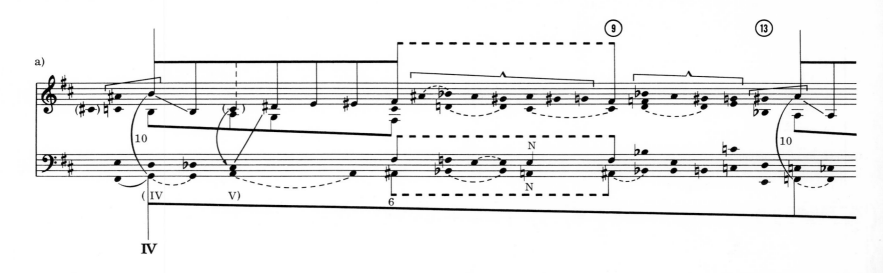

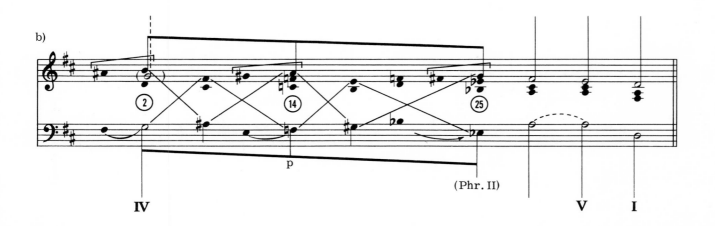

EXAMPLE 10-20 (continued)

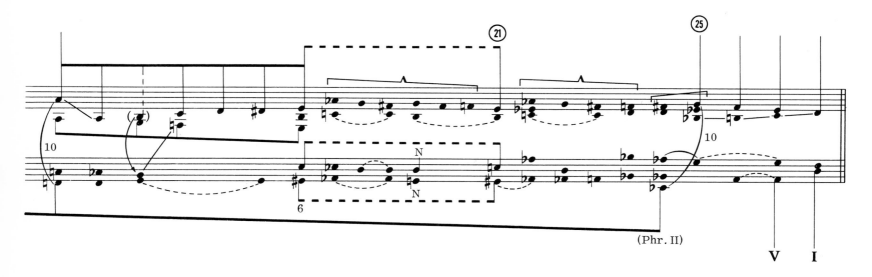

(Phr. II)

V   I

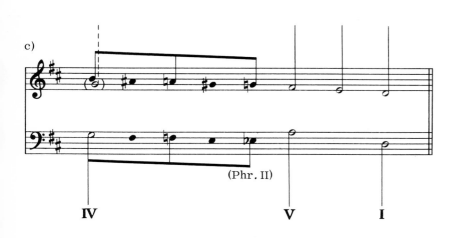

c)

(Phr. II)

IV   **V**   **I**

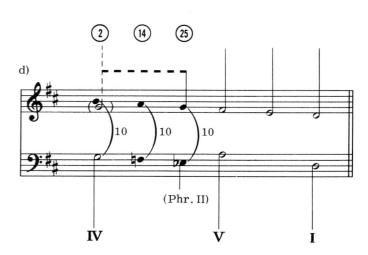

d)

(Phr. II)

IV   **V**   **I**

INDEX OF MUSICAL EXAMPLES

SUBJECT INDEX

This book was set in Optima, printed on permanent paper by Halliday Lithograph Corporation, and bound by The Maple Press Company. The designer was Tom Moreck. The editors were James Mirrielees and Carole Mahoney. Adam Jacobs supervised the production.